Annual Review of Information Science and Technology

Volume 29 1994

ISBN: 0-938734-91-1
ISSN: 0066-4200
CODEN:ARISBC
LC No. 66-25096

ANNUAL REVIEW OF INFORMATION SCIENCE AND TECHNOLOGY

Volume 29, 1994

Edited by

Martha E. Williams
University of Illinois
Urbana, Illinois, USA

asis

Published on behalf of the
American Society for Information Science
by Learned Information, Inc.

1994

Learned Information, Inc.
Medford, New Jersey

ISBN: 0-938734-91-1
ISSN: 0066-4200
CODEN: ARISBC
LC No. 66-25096

Published and distributed by:
Learned Information, Inc.,
143 Old Marlton Pike
Medford, NJ 08055-8750

for the
American Society for Information Science
8720 Georgia Avenue, Suite 501
Silver Spring, MD 20910-3602, U.S. A.

Distributed in Europe by:
Learned Information Ltd.
Woodside, Hinksey Hill
Oxford OX1 5AU
England

ARIST Production staff, for ASIS:
Charles & Linda Holder, Graphic Compositors
Cover design by Sandy Skalkowski
Printed in the U.S.A.

Contents

Preface

PUBLISHING HISTORY

This is the 29th volume of the *Annual Review of Information Science and Technology* (*ARIST*). It was produced for the American Society for Information Science (ASIS) and published by Learned Information, Inc. ASIS initiated the series in 1966 with the publication of Volume 1 under the editorship of Carlos A. Cuadra, who continued as Editor through Volume 10. Martha E. Williams has served as Editor starting with Volume 11. ASIS is the owner of *ARIST*, maintains the editorial control, and has the sole rights to the series in all forms.

Through the years several organizations have been responsible for publishing and marketing *ARIST*. Volumes 1 and 2 were published by Interscience Publishers, a division of John Wiley & Sons. Volumes 3 through 6 were published by Encyclopaedia Britannica, Inc. Volumes 7 through 11 were published by ASIS itself. Volumes 12 through 21 were published by Knowledge Industry Publications, Inc. Volumes 22 through 25 were published by Elsevier Science Publishers B.V., Amsterdam, The Netherlands. With Volume 26 Learned Information, Inc., assumed the role of publisher of *ARIST* for ASIS.

POLICY

ARIST is an annual publication that reviews numerous topics within the broad field of information science and technology. The contents vary from year to year; no single topic is treated on an annual basis. Inasmuch as the field is dynamic, the contents (chapters) of the various *ARIST* volumes must change to reflect this dynamism. *ARIST* chapters are scholarly reviews of specific topics as substantiated by the published literature. Some material may be included, even though not backed up by literature, if it is needed to provide a balanced and complete picture of the state of the art for the subject of the chapter. The time period covered varies from chapter to chapter, depending on whether the topic has been treated previously by *ARIST* and, if so, on the length of the interval from the last treatment to the current one. Thus, reviews may cover a one-year or a multiyear period. The reviews aim to be critical in that they provide the author's expert opinion regarding developments and activities within the chapter's subject area. The review guides the reader to or from specific publications. Chapters aim to be scholarly, thorough within the scope defined by the chapter author, up to date, well written, and readable by an audience that goes beyond the author's immediate peer group to researchers and practitioners in information science and technology, in general, and ASIS members, in particular.

PURPOSE

The purpose of *ARIST* is to describe and to appraise activities and trends in the field of information science and technology. Material presented should be substantiated by references to the literature. *ARIST* provides an annual review of topics in the field. One volume is provided each year. A master plan for the series encompasses the entire field in all its aspects, and topics for each volume are selected from the plan on the basis of timeliness and an assessment of reader interest.

REFERENCES CITED IN TEXT AND BIBLIOGRAPHY

The format for referring to bibliographic citations within the text involves use of the cited author's name instead of reference numbers. The cited author's surname is printed in upper case letters. The reader, wishing to find the bibliographic references, can readily locate the appropriate reference in the bibliography (alphabetically arranged by first author's last name). A single author appears as SMITH; coauthors as SMITH & JONES; and multiple authors as SMITH ET AL. If multiple papers by the same author are cited, the distinction is made by indicating the year of publication after the last name (e.g., SMITH, 1986), and if a further distinction is required for multiple papers within the same year, a lower case alpha character follows the year (e.g., SMITH, 1986a). Except for the fact that all authors in multi-authored papers are included bibliographic references, the same basic conventions are used in the chapter bibliographies. Thus, the reader can easily locate in the bibliography any references discussed in the text.

Because of the emphasis placed on the requirement for chapter authors to discuss the key papers and significant developments reported in the literature, and because *ARIST* readers have expressed their liking for comprehensive bibliographies associated with the chapters, more references may be listed in the bibliographies than are discussed and/or cited in the text.

The format used for references in the bibliographies is based on the *American National Standard for Bibliographic References*, ANS Z39.29. We have followed the ANSI guidelines with respect to the sequence of bibliographic data elements and the punctuation used to separate the elements. Adoption of this convention should facilitate conversion of the references to machine-readable form as need arises. Journal article references follow the ANSI guide as closely as possible. Conference papers and microform publications follow an *ARIST* adaptation of the format.

STRUCTURE OF THE VOLUME

In accordance with the *ARIST* master plan, this volume's nine chapters fit within a basic framework: I. Planning Information Systems and Services; II. Basic Techniques and Technologies; III. Applications; and IV. The Profession. Chapter titles are provided in the Table of Contents, and an Introduction to each section highlights the events, trends, and evaluations given by the chapter authors. An Index to the entire volume is provided to help the user locate material relevant to the subject content, authors, and organizations cited in the book. An explanation of the guidelines employed in the Index is provided in the Introduction to the Index. A Keyword and Author Index to this and all prior volumes follows the Index.

DATABASES AND ABSTRACTING AND INDEXING SERVICES COVERING *ARIST*

ARIST as a whole and/or individual chapters are included in a number of abstracting and indexing (A&I) journals both within the United States and internationally. Databases that both cover *ARIST* and are available through major online services in the United States are:

INSPEC (Computer and Control Abstracts)
Social SciSearch (Social Sciences Citation Index)
LISA (Library and Information Science Abstracts)
Information Science Abstracts
BIOSIS (Biological Abstracts)
Library Literature
Current Contents

Publishers of other A&I journals and databases who would like to include *ARIST* in their coverage are encouraged to contact the publisher for a review copy and notify the editor who will add the database name(s) to this list when appropriate.

Appreciation

Appreciation is expressed to many individuals and organizations for their roles in creating this volume. First and foremost are the authors of the individual chapters who have generously contributed their time and efforts in searching, reviewing, and evaluating the large body of literature on which their chapters are based. The *ARIST* Advisory Committee Members and *ARIST* Reviewers provided valuable feedback and constructive criticism of the content. DIALOG Information Services generously provided the authors with online access to databases. Appreciation is expressed to all of the members of the editorial staff and *ARIST* technical support staff who are listed on the Acknowledgments page.

Martha E. Williams

Acknowledgments

The American Society for Information Science and the Editor wish to acknowledge the contributions of the three principals on the editorial staff and the technical support staff.

Mary W. Rakow, Copy Editor

Debora Shaw, Index Editor

Linda C. Smith, Bibliographic Editor

Technical Support Staff

Laurence Lannom, Technical Advisor

Scott E. Preece, Technical Advisor

Linda C. Smith, Technical Advisor

Ann Knackstedt, Word Processing

Linda Holder, Compositor

Advisory Committee for *ARIST*

Contributors

J. Michael Brittain
School of Communication and Information Studies
University of South Australia
Adelaide SA 5000, Australia

Prudence W. Dalrymple
American Library Association
50 E. Huron St.
Chicago, IL 60611

Julie Dow
School of Communication and Information Studies
University of South Australia
Magill SA 5072, Australia

Patricia D. Fletcher
The Department of Information Systems
University of Maryland, Baltimore County
Baltimore, MD 21228-5378

Deborah Otis Foy
The Department of Information Systems
University of Maryland, Baltimore County
Baltimore, MD 21228-5378

Paul B. Kantor
School of Communication, Information, and Library Studies
Rutgers, The State University of New Jersey
4 Huntington St.
New Brunswick, NJ 08903

Jennifer MacDougall
Researcher and Information Consultant
6, Ullardmor
Ardeevin Rd.
Dalkey, County Dublin
Republic of Ireland

Anne Morris
Department of Information and Library Studies
Loughborough University
Ashby Rd.,
Loughborough, Leicestershire
LE11 3TU, England

Javed Mostafa
School of Library and Information Science
Indiana University
Indianapolis, IN 46202-5195

Ann O'Brien
Department of Information and Library Studies
Loughborough University
Ashby Rd.,
Loughborough, Leicestershire
LE11 3TU, England

Alan Poulter
Department of Information and Library Studies
Loughborough University
Ashby Rd.,
Loughborough, Leicestershire
LE11 3TU, England

Nancy K. Roderer
Cushing Whitney Medical Library
Yale University
333 Cedar St.
New Haven, CT 06510-8014

Dianne Rothenberg
ERIC Clearinghouse on Elementary and Early Childhood Education
University of Illinois
805 W. Pennsylvania Ave.
Urbana, IL 61801-4897

Linda Schamber
School of Library and Information Sciences
University of North Texas
P.O. Box 13796
Denton, TX 76203-3796

Chapter Reviewers

Marcia Bates
David Becker
Nicholas J. Belkin
Walter M. Carlson
Pauline Cochrane
Margaret Fischer
José-Marie Griffiths
Glynn Harmon
Peter Hernon
Mary Ellen Jacob
Michael Koenig
Taissa Kusma
Jessica L. Milstead
Edward T. O'Neill
Peter B. Schipma
Linda C. Smith
Fran Spigai
Carol Tenopir
Mickie Voges-Piatt

I

Planning Information Systems and Services

Section I of this *ARIST* volume contains one chapter; it is entitled "Relevance and Information Behavior" and is by Linda Schamber of the University of North Texas. "Relevance and Information Behavior" is the first *ARIST* chapter devoted specifically to relevance. However, as Schamber points out, many earlier chapters have devoted some attention to relevance as a necessary part of other topics, and she has cited them in hers.

The term relevance is used in many different ways both within information science and in other related disciplines, such as, cognitive science and management science. Schamber's treatment of relevance is restricted to relevance as it relates to the behavior of humans in seeking and using information rather than in evaluating retrieval systems' performance. The author views relevance "as a manifestation of human information behavior and excludes work that views relevance only as matching or computational functions of IR systems."

Schamber's chapter is divided into five major sections plus an introduction and conclusion. In the "Background" section she provides an IR interaction model and discusses the terminology of relevance from three viewpoints—the system view, the information view, and the situation view. There is an ongoing controversy about relevance, whether it be semantic or substantive. The term is frequently confused with "topicality" or "satisfaction." As Schamber reviews the work of others, she clarifies their uses of the term for the reader.

To put the chapter in context she discusses the early research on relevance, starting with the Cranfield Conference in 1964 and the studies it spawned, and then discusses major research projects from the 1970s through the 1990s with concentration on the period from 1983-1994. As evidence of the terminological problem of relevance and its many facets she provides a table (Table 1), which consists of a nonexhaustive list of 80 relevance factors mentioned in the literature.

She notes that Cranfield was especially important because it suggested many factors that affect relevance judgments, raised questions regarding the nature and effects of relevance factors, and addressed problems of measurement bias.

In the second section, "Evaluation and Measurement," she describes the role of relevance in IR systems evaluation, and looks at IR effectiveness in terms of four relevance-based measures: recall, precision, utility, and satisfaction. In the third section, "Factors and Effects," she covers the range of factors involved, judges and judgment conditions, and requests and documents. The fourth section, "User Criteria," covers recent research involving the users' perceptions of criteria or values underlying their relevance judgments and deals with the user criteria approach, related studies and results of the studies. The fifth section, "Models and Contexts," provides interdisciplinary models and theoretical approaches to relevance and relevance-related research.

At the end of each of the five major sections Schamber elucidates the research concerns for the area. In her conclusion she summarizes some basic questions. The questions about behavior are: "What factors contribute to human relevance judgments, and what processes does relevance judgment entail?" The measurement questions are: "What is the role of relevence in IR system evaluation," and "how should relevance judgments be measured?" The terminology question is: "What should relevance, or various kinds of relevance, be called?"

1 Relevance and Information Behavior

LINDA SCHAMBER
University of North Texas

INTRODUCTION

The meanings and uses of relevance have been examined by information scientists throughout the history of the field. Relevance is the field's central concept insofar as it serves, explicitly or implicitly, as the fundamental criterion for evaluating the effectiveness of information retrieval (IR) and use. It affects the practical design and evaluation of IR systems as well as theoretical and empirical understandings of human behavior in seeking and using information.

Relevance is also a confusing and much debated concept. The generally accepted theoretical conceptualization of relevance involves the relationship between a user's information problem or need and the information that could solve the problem. The generally accepted operational conceptualization involves a user's decision to accept or reject information retrieved from an information system. Beyond these shared understandings, however, information scientists have failed to reach a consensus in answering these questions:

- Behavior: What factors contribute to human relevance judgments? What processes does relevance assessment entail?
- Measurement: What is the role of relevance in IR system evaluation? How should relevance judgments be measured?
- Terminology: What should relevance, or various kinds of relevance, be called?

Annual Review of Information Science and Technology (*ARIST*), Volume 29, 1994
Martha E. Williams, Editor
Published for the American Society for Information Science (ASIS)
By Learned Information, Inc., Medford, N.J.

This chapter summarizes the literature on these issues, particularly problems, and findings of user-oriented research in the past decade, but with some historical background.

Scope

This is the first *ARIST* chapter devoted entirely to relevance. It focuses primarily on work that views relevance as a manifestation of human information behavior and excludes work that views relevance only as matching or computational functions of IR systems. The literature falls, roughly, into two categories.

First is the literature of IR system evaluation. Relevance and relevance-based measures are used throughout the applied research on IR system performance. Although applied studies comprise a major portion of work in the field, they are of little interest here because they tend not to add to our understanding of relevance. Of more interest is a complementary body of literature that questions evaluation research design in general and applications of relevance-based measures in particular. In critical essays and empirical tests of various measures, this work addresses issues of practical importance for IR system design. Excellent reviews of the evaluation literature can be found in BAWDEN, LANCASTER & WARNER (or the previous edition (LANCASTER)), and SPARCK JONES (1981a).

The second category is literature that theorizes about and explores the meanings or dimensions of relevance and human information behavior. This includes critical, theoretical, and philosophical essays that are of great interest here because they question assumptions about the concept of relevance and provide behavioral and cognitive models. This category also includes empirical studies that examine processes and phenomena of relevance evaluation, including recent and ongoing exploratory studies of users' relevance criteria that are discussed here in one place for the first time. All of this work comprises a minor, but rich, portion of the field's literature, best summarized to date in comprehensive reviews by SARACEVIC (1970; 1975) and SCHAMBER ET AL.

The remainder of the chapter is divided into five sections. The section on Background discusses the typical IR interaction model and relevance concepts, addresses the question of terminology, and presents a brief historical review. Subsequent sections refer to the older literature but focus primarily on work from 1983 to 1994. The section on Evaluation and Measurement describes the role of relevance in IR system evaluation, discusses four common relevance-based measures, and addresses user-oriented measurement issues. The section on Factors and Effects compares findings on factors or variables affecting relevance judgments in the old and new literature. The section on User Criteria reports on recent research involving users' own perceptions of criteria or values underlying their relevance judgments and discusses results. The section on Models and Contexts presents interdisciplinary models and theoretical approaches to relevance and relevance-related research. Methodological and other research concerns are addressed throughout.

BACKGROUND

IR Model and Assumptions

It is difficult to discuss relevance without first defining the context in which information scientists understand and apply the concept. Traditionally, they view relevance as evaluating a relationship between two or more components in the human–system IR interaction process. The typical model of this process (Figure 1), drawn essentially from communication theory, begins with a user in an information problem situation. The user perceives the problem and makes a request, interacting with an intermediary or directly with the system. The intermediary or the user inputs a formal search query, which is processed by the system, and receives and evaluates system output. The user pursues items that seem likely to contain information to solve the problem.

The model illustrates points at which relationships can be evaluated between tangible representations of the user's problem (request, query, query terms) and representations of the information (documents, abstracts, citations, index terms). In empirical studies, human relevance judgments are collected at points 8 and 9, when system output is

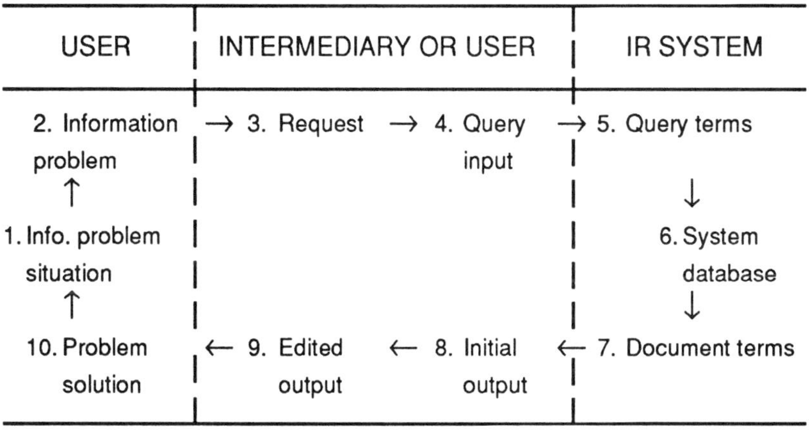

Figure 1. IR interaction model

examined and edited. In this chapter, the term *human* includes both user (end user of information; requester) and nonuser. *Nonuser* refers to a secondary judge, such as a professional intermediary or searcher, librarian, researcher, subject expert, or indexer. Although intermediaries are often considered to be part of the IR system, here they are discussed separately, with regard to human information behavior. The model is admittedly simplistic in that it fails to account for nondocument or nontext retrieval, iterative processes of query reformulation and relevance feedback, and so forth; these are discussed in subsequent sections. Generally, from a human judgment perspective, relevance is assumed to be:

- Subjective, depending on human (user or nonuser) judgment and thus not an inherent characteristic of information or a document;
- Cognitive, depending ultimately on human knowledge and perceptions;
- Situational, relating to individual users' information problems;
- Multidimensional, influenced by many factors;
- Dynamic, constantly changing over time; and
- Measurable, observable at a single point in time (see HARTER; SARACEVIC, 1970, 1975; SCHAMBER ET AL.).

The most striking assumption is the inescapable subjectivity of relevance evaluations as manifestations of human cognitive behavior. Further assumptions concern the degree of subjectivity (or objectivity) involved. Differing views on these matters have led to ongoing states of controversy and confusion.

Views and Terminology

Much of the controversy and confusion surrounding relevance stems from diverse conceptualizations, compounded by loose and inconsistent terminology. The three broad views presented below are intended to serve both as a brief summary of relevance concepts and as a means for clarifying the usage of relevance terms in the literature. The system view and two user views, one pertaining to information and the other to the user's situation, are considered to be objective, subjective, and very subjective, respectively.

System view. Information scientists first made—and debated—the distinction between system and user views of relevance in the 1950s in the field's seminal literature on IR system design (see SARACEVIC,

1970, 1975; SCHAMBER ET AL.). The system view refers to a direct match between query terms and document terms within a system. In the IR interaction model (Figure 1), this view focuses on system concerns from query input to initial output (points 4 to 8). The system view relies on phenomena such as document terms and exact or partial term-matching logics (see BELKIN & CROFT) that can be objectively observed, manipulated, and tested. Studies that center on technical input/output functions (e.g., indexing, retrieval) and internal matching or similarity functions (e.g., document weighting, clustering) of systems, particularly without relying on human judgments, can be said to adhere to a system view of relevance. Common terms for the system view of relevance, and a few authors who use them, include *matching, similarity* (BELKIN & CROFT; SALTON), *system relevance response* (KING & BRYANT), and *topicality* (BARRY, 1994; BOYCE; SCHAMBER ET AL.). The system view assumes that topic-relatedness is inherent in a document, or that terms represent content or meaning accurately and consistently. The fundamental difficulty, of course, is that no request or document representation represents content the same way to all people all the time.

Information view. The information view refers to a human judgment of conceptual relatedness between a request and a document. Judgments from this view are subjective: although they apparently are based on relationships between external representations of information problems and information (points 3-4 and 8-9 in Figure 1), they actually depend on the internal knowledge of the judge. Common terms include *aboutness* (INGWERSEN, 1992), *relevance* (KEMP; LANCASTER & WARNER; SARACEVIC ET AL., 1988), and *topicality* (COOL ET AL.; WANG). COOPER (1971) is often cited for proposing the concept of *logical relevance,* referring to relationships between sentences in queries and sentences in documents as determined by deductive logic. The information view assumes that nonusers can adequately predict whether certain information will solve users' information problems. In practice, professional search intermediaries assess the relevance of documents on behalf of actual users, indexers assess the "aboutness" of documents on behalf of potential users, and subject experts or researchers assess matches between queries and documents in testing IR systems. Ingwersen describes four kinds of aboutness: (1) author aboutness, determined by the author's language as matched by the system in natural language retrieval; (2) indexer aboutness, determined by the indexer's transformation of the author's natural language into controlled vocabulary; (3) request aboutness, determined by the user's or intermediary's processing of request into query; and (4) user (or user-related) aboutness, determined by the indexer's attempt to represent documents according to presuppositions about what users know or want. LANCASTER & WARNER distinguish between document-oriented judgments on which a group of judges (e.g., indexers, intermediaries) can reach a consensus and problem-oriented judgments that can be made only by the user. The distinction stems in part from the notion that both users and nonusers have access to public knowledge, which is shared among people and is somewhat objective, but only users have access to private knowledge, which relates to their personal situations and is highly subjective (see FOSKETT; KEMP). The difficulty with the information view is that all kinds of knowledge, and therefore judgments, vary considerably from one individual to the next (see SARACEVIC, 1991).

Situation view. The situation view refers to a relationship between information and the user's information problem situation. This view assumes that only users can make valid judgments concerning the potential ability of information to solve their problems. LANCASTER & WARNER provide a detailed comparison of information and situation views, calling them *relevance* and *pertinence,* respectively. Others have used *relevance* and *usefulness* (REES & SCHULTZ), *relevance* and *utility* (SARACEVIC ET AL., 1988), *relevance* and *satisfaction* (TESSIER ET AL.), and *topicality* and *relevance* (COOL ET AL.). COOPER (1973) contrasts his concept of logical relevance with the concept of *utility,* which he deems "a cover term for whatever the user finds to be of value about the system output, whether its usefulness, its entertainment or aesthetic value, or anything else" (p. 89). Following Cooper's concept of logical relevance, WILSON introduces the concept of *situational relevance* as the relationship between an item of information and an individual's situation as determined by probabilistic inductive logic. This is essentially a practical concept involving notions of the individual's personal concerns, preferences, and stock of knowledge. A number of writers, such as HARTER and SCHAMBER ET AL., use *relevance* in a broad sense, as depending on users' internal perceptions or on highly personal, dynamic psychological states. Harter has also called this an everyday use of the term; SARACEVIC (1975) called it an intuitive use. It is from the situation view, more than from the system or information view, that the multidimensional concept of relevance appears to be the most difficult and unmanageable because the situation view involves the most—and the most subjective—possible influences.

The system, information, and situation views are by no means intended to cover all definitions and terms in the literature for relevance. It is impossible, in a limited space, to explore conceptual gray areas such as the difference between system and information views in highly interactive and intelligent systems, or among the many interpretations of aboutness in the information view, or between information and situation views with regard to various types and levels of knowledge.

All of these views have been debated vigorously, and far more refined and philosophical distinctions have been made. SARACEVIC (1975), for example, summarizes other writers' views in terms of nine interrelated views of his own. BELKIN (1981), KING & BRYANT, LANCASTER & WARNER, REES & SCHULTZ, SARACEVIC (1970), SCHAMBER ET AL., and D.R. SWANSON (1986) also provide extensive explanations of relevance concepts.

Often it is not entirely clear whether the problems behind the ongoing controversy and confusion about relevance are semantic or substantive. Inconsistent usage of the term relevance and related terms such as topicality occurs in all kinds of information science literature, theoretical and empirical. In general, authors tend to use different terms to describe different kinds of relevance or to use one umbrella term, usually relevance or satisfaction, to describe a single global or generic concept. A distressing number of writers do not define their terms at all.

SARACEVIC (1970) says that substituting terms for relevance does not avoid the problem of defining the substantive meaning of the concept. On the other hand, FROEHLICH (1994) says the pursuit of any kind of definition of relevance is "wrongheaded"; that information scientists are unlikely ever to reach a consensus; and that the concept of relevance, like the concept of information, nevertheless functions usefully in a variety of situations. In this chapter, problems of "definition" are considered substantive if they pertain to matters such as operationalizing relevance concepts for testing IR effectiveness, identifying factors or criteria contributing to people's relevance judgments, or modeling situational contexts in which people make evaluations. Otherwise, the unavoidable semantic problem of definition is addressed by clarifying the terminology of individual authors with parenthetical references to the views above, as in "relevance (information view)" and "relevance (situation view)."

Early Research

The foundations for the use of relevance as a criterion for IR effectiveness can be traced to the beginnings of information science in the 1950s and 1960s. Researchers at that time were exploring the potential of computerized information retrieval, even before actual computerized systems were available. The National Science Foundation (NSF) boosted interest and action by sponsoring a conference on IR evaluation in 1964 and at least seven studies (see LANCASTER), including the two Cranfield studies and two relevance studies discussed here.

The Aslib Cranfield Project involved two major efforts, Cranfield I, which began in 1957 (CLEVERDON, 1962; LANCASTER & MILLS) and Cranfield II, which began in 1963 (CLEVERDON, 1967; CLEVERDON ET AL.). Both tested the effects of various types of controlled vocabulary and natural-language indexing on IR. In Cranfield I, the researchers essentially took a system view of relevance: questions were prepared by experts based on the titles of source documents, and relevance judgments were made by project staff searchers, who did not read the documents retrieved but checked document numbers against the questions. In Cranfield II, however, actual questions were put to the system by experts and relevance assessments were made by the questioners reading abstracts (see CLEVERDON, 1990; ROBERTSON, 1981; SPARCK JONES, 1981b).

The Cranfield tests are significant for at least three major reasons. (1) They identified various factors that influence IR performance and provided test data that were used for comparison in many subsequent studies. Of particular interest for later discussions about relevance were results showing the influence of human (indexer) error on retrieval performance. (2) They set a standard for experimental design in IR performance evaluation. Among other things, they were the first to use the relevance-based measures recall ratio and precision ratio (then called the relevance ratio). Recall is the ability of a system to retrieve all its relevant items, and precision is the ability of the system to retrieve only items that are relevant. They also demonstrated an inverse relationship between the measures: when one retrieves a large percentage of the relevant items from a database (high recall), one also may retrieve a large percentage of nonrelevant items (low precision). (3) Most important, the Cranfield tests stirred up controversy that continues to this day. Seemingly every aspect of the project was criticized and defended; SPARCK JONES (1981b) provides an excellent review of this literature. The improved methodology in Cranfield II responded in part to criticism centering on the use of small test collections and on the use of artificial queries and relevance judgments in controlled laboratory experiments. The questions led to more rigorous attention to research design generally, as well as a gradual shift away from the laboratory into operational or field settings.

Information scientists have long been troubled by the plethora of factors that apparently affect human relevance judgments. Two large-scale experimental studies, both begun in 1965, set out to identify and test the factors responsible for the most variation in relevance evaluations. CUADRA & KATTER (1967a) defined relevance as involving both the request and the use orientation. They named variables in five categories pertaining to judges, requests, documents, judgment conditions, and choice of scale (Table 1) and developed a model of relevance assessment that revolved around judges. Relevance judgments in their study were made by nonusers on the basis of document representations

Table 1. Eighty Relevance Factors Suggested in the Literature[a]

JUDGES

Biases (1)
Cognitive style (1)
Concept of relevance (1,2)
Error preference (1)
Expectations regarding distribution (1)
Formal education (2)
Intelligence (1)
Judging experience (1)
Judgment attitude (1)
Knowledge/experience (1,2)
Professional involvement (2)
Research stage (2)
Use orientation (1,2)
Vigilance level (1)

REQUESTS

Diversity of content (1)
Difficulty level (1)
Functional ambiguity (1)
Specificity/amount of information (1,2)
Subject matter (1)
Textual attributes (1)
Weighting of components (3)

DOCUMENTS

Aboutness (3)
Accuracy (truth) (3)
Aesthetic value (3)
Authorship (3)
Credibility (3)
Difficulty level (1)
Diversity of content (1)
Importance (3)
Informativeness (3)
Interesting content (3)
Level of condensation (1,2)
Logical relevance (3)
Novelty (3)
Pertinence (3)
Publication source (3)
Recency (3)
Scientific "hardness" (1,2)
Specificity/amount of information (1,2)
Style (1,3)
Subject matter (1)
Textual attributes (1)
Usefulness (2,3)

INFORMATION SYSTEM

Access (item identification) (4)
Access (subject description) (4)
Access (subject summary) (4)
Accuracy (data transfer) (4)
Browsability (4)
Comprehensiveness (coverage) (4)
Convenience of location (3)
Convenience of hours (3)
Cost saving (4)
Currency (updating) (4)
Ease of detection of relevance (3)
Effort expended (3)
Flexibility (dynamic interaction) (4)
Formatting (scannability) (4)
Interfacing (help, orientation) (4)
Links to external sources (4)
Ordering (subject matter) (4)
Physical accessibility (4)
Precision of subject output (4)
Reliability (consistency) (4)
Response speed (4)
Selectivity (input choices) (4)
Simplicity (clarity) (4)
Time spent (3)

JUDGMENT CONDITIONS

Breadth of document set (1)
Definition of relevance (1,2)
Order of presentation (1)
Size of document set (1)
Social pressure toward convergence (1)
Specification of the task (1,2)
Time for judging (1)
Use of control judgments (1)

CHOICE OF SCALE

Availability of anchors (1)
Ease of use (1,2)
Kind of response required (1,2)
Number of rating categories (1)
Type of scale (1,2)

[a]Based on (1) CUADRA & KATTER (1967a), (2) REES & SCHULTZ, (3) COOPER (1971; 1973), and (4) TAYLOR. Includes all factors suggested by Cuadra and Katter and selected factors suggested by others.

containing abstracts. The results showed that instructions to judges and choice of scale strongly affected relevance judgments. The researchers concluded that single measures should not be used nor should cross-study comparisons be made without controls on the many variables.

REES & SCHULTZ defined relevance as the relationship of information retrieved to an information need and usefulness as relating, additionally, to individual characteristics of the user. Many of their variables were similar to those of Cuadra and Katter, with the addition of an emphasis on research stage (see Table 1). Relevance judgments were made by nonusers on the basis of titles and citations. The results showed that documents contributed most significantly to variations in relevance ratings, followed by judgmental group and research stage. The researchers concluded that dichotomous relevance judgments are insensitive to the complex factors influencing them, that the role of the search intermediary needs clarification, and that stable, meaningful relevance judgments will result only within relatively homogeneous groups of judges.

SARACEVIC (1975) presents a particularly cogent summary of the results of these two studies and others; see also CUADRA & KATTER (1967b) and SCHAMBER ET AL. Like the Cranfield tests, the two relevance studies are significant for at least three reasons. (1) They suggested a wide range of factors that affect human relevance judgments, factors that are still important in current research. Although they tested fewer than half these factors, many of their conclusions still hold. Most important is the significance of characteristics of judges, especially individual cognitive characteristics. (2) Although the researchers did not examine real users and their problems, they raised important questions about the nature and effects of relevance factors and relationships among factors. (3) They addressed specific problems of measurement bias that have implications both for understanding relevance and for designing relevance-based research studies. Problems concerned operationalizations of measures, biases in laboratory settings, the influence of instructions to judges, and choice of rating scale. Neither study has been replicated. Both underscore the complexity of the IR process and the fact that the field cannot afford to investigate isolated components but must account for all contributing factors.

Interest in the concept of relevance waxed and waned in succeeding years. The 1970s were marked by essays on dimensions and definitions of relevance. These are best summarized by SARACEVIC (1975) and SCHAMBER ET AL., who attempted to establish theoretical frameworks for the concept of relevance. The 1980s and 1990s brought a new wave of empirical work on users' perceptions of relevance, part of a trend to user-oriented qualitative research across the field (see BAWDEN; BRADLEY & SUTTON; FIDEL; INGWERSEN, 1992). The rest of the chapter focuses primarily on work in the past decade, while noting the remarkable continuity of concerns about relevance and measurement from the earliest studies in the 1960s.

EVALUATION AND MEASUREMENT

IR Effectiveness

Relevance plays a relatively small but important role in the large and complex body of literature on IR system evaluation and testing. Several sources provide helpful overviews of the many types and levels of evaluation for various information systems and services, notably BAWDEN, KING & BRYANT, GRIFFITHS & KING, LANCASTER & WARNER, and SPARCK JONES (1981a). Of interest here are studies evaluating the effectiveness of system performance, or how well system performance satisfies users. The number and kinds of criteria[1] for evaluating effectiveness vary widely depending on the objectives of a particular study. Lancaster and Warner, for instance, describe three general categories of criteria related to cost, time, and quality of output. Quality of output includes coverage of the database, completeness of output, relevance of output, novelty (items new to the user), completeness of data, and accuracy of data. Relevance judgments are especially important for assessing completeness of output, used in calculating the ratio measure recall, and relevance of output, used in calculating the ratio measure precision. Recall and precision are among the most common relevance-based measures used in IR testing. Two others are the more qualitative measures utility and satisfaction, both of which represent users' overall assessments of system performance. This section looks first at recall and precision, then at utility and satisfaction, and finally at research concerns about the relevance judgments underlying such measures.

Recall and Precision

Recall ratio (the proportion of relevant items retrieved out of all relevant items in a system) and precision ratio (the proportion of relevant items retrieved out of all items retrieved) have been favored measures for at least 30 years, but not without having raised their share of questions. Recall is problematic, of course, because the absolute number of relevant documents in a system cannot be known except by examining every document. Instead, researchers estimate the number

[1]Criteria for system evaluation are not the same as criteria for relevance judgments: the latter are reasons underlying human assessments (discussed later).

of relevant documents (i.e., establish a recall base) by comparing the overlap in retrieval results from different searchers or searches in one or more databases. Less common techniques include sampling a database or referring to a bibliography of known relevant items (see KING & BRYANT; LANCASTER & WARNER). Clear explanations of overlap techniques can be found in MCKININ ET AL. (comprehensiveness) and PAO (relative recall ratio). Recall, precision, and overlap were among 21 measures tested for reliability and construct validity in a study by WILDEMUTH ET AL., who concluded that just 14 of the measures could be combined into three reliable scales.

LANCASTER & WARNER list alternative measures for recall and precision that are calculated with essentially the same data, including hit rate, sensitivity, pertinency factor, noise factor, fallout ratio, and specificity. They note that most users require only a minimum level of recall and suggest that a measure involving desired volume of output may be more appropriate. They also note that precision is actually an indirect measure of user time and effort (i.e., when precision is high, users exert less effort in assessing output) and that measures of time may be more appropriate. In fact, effectiveness criteria in general tend to be interrelated and to trade off in relative importance depending on the type of retrieval environment. In addition to time, for instance, measures for coverage of the database, novelty, or accuracy of data may complement or substitute for recall and precision. Generally, recall, precision, and similar measures concern the ability of the system to identify relevant documents without error, or what KING & BRYANT call system accuracy: the degree to which system relevance response predicts user relevance judgment. King and Bryant (see also GRIFFITHS & KING; KING), KEEN, and others describe a variety of computational approaches to measures involving both user and system data and discuss the ability of certain measures to represent users' judgments and accommodate their preferences (e.g., for high or low recall).

Interestingly, two notions about recall and precision that have persisted since the 1960s are still the source of some confusion. One is the observation, based on Cranfield results and generally accepted as a given, of an inverse relationship between recall and precision; that is, as recall increases, precision decreases, and vice versa (LANCASTER & MILLS). This does not appear to be universally true: one study found that both measures may increase or decrease at the same time, although not necessarily to the same extent (BELLARDO & SARACEVIC; SARACEVIC & KANTOR); and another study found that the tradeoff is usually unavoidable but can be mitigated under certain circumstances (BUCKLAND & GEY). The other observation has been that measures such as recall and precision based on binary judgments of "relevant" and "nonrelevant" should be avoided because they ignore the variability and complexity of relevance judgments (CUADRA & KATTER, 1967a) and because they distort the continuous nature of relevance judgments (REES & SCHULTZ). Instead it has been found that the ratio measures are remarkably stable or relatively unaffected by individual variances in relevance judgments (BURGIN; CLEVERDON, 1990; LESK & SALTON; SALTON).

Utility and Satisfaction

An ongoing quest has been to determine the most appropriate global measure of overall user satisfaction with IR performance. A common approach has been to collect judgments of relevance for relationships between documents and requests and judgments of pertinence or utility for relationships between documents and information problems. Examples can be found in studies by JANES (1994) and REGAZZI, among others. Quite a different approach was taken by SARACEVIC ET AL. (1988), who defined relevance as the aboutness of individual items in the retrieval set and utility as the usefulness of the entire retrieval set. Relevance was based on a single user response and utility was based on five responses, regarding whether the user: (1) said the results were worth more than the time it took to evaluate them; (2) took less time than average to evaluate the results; (3) assigned a high dollar value to the usefulness of results; (4) said the information made a substantial contribution to solving the problem; and (5) indicated a high level of overall satisfaction with the search. The researchers also employed a powerful technique, logarithmic cross product ratio analysis, that predicts the odds of high relevance, recall, or precision with regard to independent variables at an individual document level. The results showed that higher ratings on most utility measures could be linked more often to increases in relevance odds and precision odds than to increases in recall odds (SARACEVIC & KANTOR).

Other researchers have used relevance for the relationship of a document to a query and satisfaction for overall evaluation of an IR system or service. For example, SANDORE asked users to rate seven aspects of a library IR service, including the relevance of materials retrieved, and to rate satisfaction with the service as a whole. She found that low precision did not necessarily affect users' satisfaction with the service. TESSIER and TURNER each compared two satisfaction measures, one based on users' judgments of overall satisfaction and the other on the researcher's calculated summary measure of users' ratings of selected attributes, and found the two measures to correlate as reliable indicators of users' satisfaction.

SU (1991; 1992; 1994) compared 20 system performance measures in an attempt to identify the best measure(s) of IR effectiveness for users in an operational setting. The measures represented four criteria: (1) relevance (used to calculate precision), (2) efficiency (three time and cost measures), (3) utility (five user judgments of worth of search results), and (4) user satisfaction (11 user judgments of satisfaction with search interview, completeness of search results, precision, and so forth). She created a fifth criterion—success—a single user assessment of overall system success, to use in correlations with the first 20. The results showed seven measures to be significant correlates of success, with value of search results as a whole to be the best single performance measure. This measure correlated strongly with user's satisfaction with completeness of search results and user's satisfaction with search precision. She also found that precision itself was not significantly correlated with success and concluded that recall (as represented in users' estimates of completeness of search results) is more important to users. Su was further able to identify two factors underlying the seven significant correlates of success, related to interaction and effectiveness, which together accounted for 72.4% of the total variance. Interestingly, interaction was considerably more important to users than effectiveness, and effectiveness did not include actual precision ratio (the only relevance-based measure), but did include users' satisfaction with precision of the search.

Two conclusions emerge from these studies. First, researchers agree that document relevance plays a leading role—but not the only role—in users' satisfaction with retrieval effectiveness. Many writers have warned of the dangers of using relevance measures alone (COOPER, 1973; HERSH; LANCASTER & WARNER; SALTON) as well as the dangers of trusting a single summary measure of satisfaction (APPLEGATE; TAGLIACOZZO). Second, there is a lack of agreement on the relative importance of specific relevance measures. Notably, the results of studies by KINNUCAN, SARACEVIC ET AL. (1988), TESSIER, and TURNER generally indicate that precision or relevance of output played a greater role in global evaluations than recall or volume of output, whereas studies by SU (1992; 1993) and SANDORE did not.

Research Concerns

Some of the most troubling criticisms of IR system testing do not concern the choice of measures, but rather the methods for obtaining the relevance judgments underlying the measures. ROBERTSON (1981) says the questions that need to be asked include who is doing the judging, how judgments are made, and what is being judged. These are not new questions: they were important enough in the 1960s for the Cranfield II researchers to greatly improve their choice of relevance judges over Cranfield I, and for CUADRA & KATTER (1967a) to identify judgmental conditions and choice of scale as distinct categories of variables for testing (Table 1). To this day, the most pressing methodological considerations for relevance-based research seem to be the test setting, definition of relevance, presentation order of items judged, and choice of scale.

Test setting. An enduring debate concerns whether IR system tests should be conducted in laboratory or operational settings. The trend has been toward operational settings, particularly for relevance-based evaluations, on the supposition that only under natural conditions can valid judgments be collected from real users in real situations. Such settings allow researchers to explore certain factors, often human factors, that previously may not have been identified or understood. User-oriented evaluations tend to be investigative, eclectic and pragmatic, holistic in concerns, small, and qualitative (BAWDEN). Laboratory tests have been criticized as unrealistic, usually because of their small test collections and artificial queries and relevance judgments (BAWDEN; ELLIS, 1984a, 1984b).

At the same time, proponents of laboratory research simply do not see users' assessments as being absolutely necessary or feasible in the big picture of evaluation, particularly tests of isolated subsystems or purely computational retrieval techniques (KEEN; ROBERTSON & HANCOCK-BEAULIEU; WILLETT). Further, as SALTON points out, studies such as those of the Smart system over 20 years have developed several large test collections covering different subject areas and have obtained relevance assessments from a variety of users. SPARCK JONES (1988) emphasizes that it will become more important to study real users in the future in light of the increasing complexity, interactivity, and intelligence of systems that individualize the IR process more than ever. She compares strategies involving pseudo-users and real users and makes a strong case for using large samples of real users in real situations. ROBERTSON & HANCOCK-BEAULIEU propose a compromise in the form of an evaluation facility: an experimental but fully functional IR system with data-collection capabilities in an operational environment.

Definition of relevance. It would seem to be important, in light of the many meanings ascribed to relevance, to define the concept carefully for relevance judges. Exactly how important it is, however, is not entirely clear. The results of a study by CUADRA & KATTER (1967b) are the most detailed and conclusive. They found that judges who were given 14 sets of instructions simulating users' implicit use orientations (e.g., selective review task, methodological interest) produced different relevance judgments under all 14 sets of instructions than they did under initial instructions without use orientations. The researchers concluded that it is possible to raise or lower relevance scores simply by telling judges how documents are to be used. Other researchers have been reluctant to attribute observed differences in relevance results to changes in instructions, usually because of doubts as to how judges actually interpreted the definitions. REES & SCHULTZ noted that different definitions of relevance and usefulness did not necessarily affect judges' ratings. Later researchers also made tentative observations regarding *usefulness* and *helpfulness* (TAGLIACOZZO), *relevance* and *utility* (REGAZZI), and *relevance, topicality* and *utility* (JANES, 1994).

Order of presentation. Several studies have focused on presentation or stimulus order bias, which holds implications for the sequential IR judging process in general and the evaluation of highly interactive (e.g., relevance feedback) systems in particular. EISENBERG & BARRY observed that this bias affected both ratings and rankings of relevance. PURGAILIS PARKER & JOHNSON further identified a threshold of 15 documents at which order effects become evident. TIAMIYU & AJIFERUKE propose a "total relevance function" to counter what they call document interaction effects, that is, the tendency of the relevance judgment of each document to be affected by judgments of previous documents in the retrieval set. In experimental design, the suggestion has been to randomize the presentation order of documents.

Choice of scale. The relative merits of ranking, category rating scales, and continuous scales for assessing relevance were tested in the 1960s by CUADRA & KATTER (1967a), KATTER, and REES & SCHULTZ (see SARACEVIC, 1975). They found that type of scale may make a difference in relevance results. Since then, category scales are most commonly administered in IR testing, with category-scale results (e.g., relevant/partially relevant/nonrelevant) being collapsed into binary (relevant/nonrelevant) results for calculating measures such as precision ratio. In recent years, continuous-scale methods such as magnitude estimation have gained favor with some researchers who say they are more reliable than category scales and easier to administer and analyze (EISENBERG; RORVIG). The collapsing of continuous- or category-scale results into binary results, despite fears of losing information, has generally been supported. JANES (1993) compared distributions of scaled relevance judgments in his own studies with those of the 1960s studies, confirmed earlier observations of heavy use of end points by judges, and concluded that relevance seems to be essentially bipolar. EISENBERG & HU and JANES (1991a) demonstrated that when relevance judges themselves collapse scaled judgments into binary judgments, they tend to make the break well below the middle. This supports the practice by researchers of collapsing judgments of "partially relevant" on a three-point scale into the "relevant" category on a binary scale as in studies by, e.g., PAO, SARACEVIC ET AL. (1988), and SU (1992).

FACTORS AND EFFECTS

Range of Factors

The statement made earlier—that relevance is a multidimensional phenomenon—is, of course, a gross understatement. In fact, so many factors have been suggested as affecting relevance judgments that it is not possible to list them all here. The 80 factors[2] in Table 1, however, represent a reasonable sample. They are drawn from the experimental studies of CUADRA & KATTER (1967a) and REES & SCHULTZ in the 1960s and from later essays by COOPER (1971; 1973) and by TAYLOR. The categories of factors, with the exception of information system, and the 38 factors marked "(1)" are the full range suggested by Cuadra and Katter; Rees and Schultz suggested a similar range. Fewer than half of these factors were actually tested in the two studies, but all subsequent IR studies have involved at least some of them. Cooper takes a cost-benefit approach in which the broad concept of utility encompasses whatever qualities the user finds to be of value. He suggests subjective factors such as aesthetic value, credibility, and importance. Taylor developed a cost-benefit model in which aspects of users' information problem situations and of IR systems are seen as adding value to their perceptions of information quality. He suggests that users employ six criteria in choosing information (i.e., making accept-or-reject relevance decisions): (1) ease of use, (2) noise reduction (ability to exclude, include, or focus on specific information), (3) quality (of database content), (4) adaptability (ability to respond to user's problem), (5) time saving, and (6) cost saving. The criteria relate to certain interface values added by the system (listed as factors in Table 1), including dynamic and interactive characteristics such as browsability, flexibility, and response speed.

Beyond this list are refinements in concepts and terminology from many perspectives. LANCASTER & WARNER describe 21 system and human factors in seven categories as studied in evaluating IR systems. FIDEL & SOERGEL list more than 200 factors in eight categories affecting online retrieval. SARACEVIC ET AL. (1988) tested a complex set of variables (including relevance and utility as dependent variables) in 14 categories linked to their general model of information seeking and retrieving. TURNER identifies 160 information attributes and adjectives from 21 sources in the information/library science and business/management literature. She says that "accuracy" appears in 65% of the

[2]Although the items in Table 1 are labeled *factors*, they are called *attributes*, *characteristics*, *criteria*, *dimensions*, *standards*, *qualities*, *values*, or *variables* by various authors. In this section, the terms *factors* and *variables* are used. In the next section, the term *user criteria* is used for similar items elicited directly from users (i.e., not a priori variables).

sources, and "relevance," "reliability," and "timeliness" appear in 50%. In management, for example, BAILEY & PEARSON list 39 factors as contributing to computer users' satisfaction. In the remainder of this section, the term *relevance* usually refers to the information view.

Judges and Judgment Conditions

The research to date has established several major conclusions about the effects of certain factors on relevance judgments. The following are from CUADRA & KATTER (1967a), REES & SCHULTZ, and others, as summarized by SARACEVIC (1975). This first set involves factors of the judge and judgment conditions, including choice of scale:

- The most important characteristic of judges is degree of subject knowledge or related professional education.
- The more judges know about a given subject area, the more their judgments tend to agree.
- The more judges know about the subject area, the fewer documents of a retrieval set they tend to judge relevant.
- Judges who are most involved with the problem tend to agree in their judgments.
- Judges tend to agree on relevance rankings of documents in a set regardless of their relevance ratings of individual documents.
- Judges tend to agree more on judgments of "nonrelevant" than on judgments of "relevant."
- The type of scale used may affect relevance results.

Generally these conclusions have gained unquestioning acceptance, with knowledge or expertise of the judge playing the strongest role. The results of a study by JANES (1994) comparing nonusers' and users' judgments largely confirmed several conclusions above, with one exception: Janes found that agreement was not universally higher on judgments of "nonrelevant" than on judgments of "relevant." Janes and other researchers, including REGAZZI and GLUCK, have demonstrated that education and experience of several kinds make a difference in relevance judgments of both users and nonusers.

It is likely that the results of innumerable other studies—studies that relied on relevance judgments but were not primarily intended to address questions about relevance—have supported and added to the early conclusions. Perhaps the best example is the large-scale study of information seeking and retrieving by SARACEVIC & KANTOR. The study involved users, who provided questions and judged search results, and professional searchers. Some of the factors the researchers said increased the odds that retrieved items would be judged relevant include:

- A user with a well-defined problem;
- A user with a high estimate that information can be found;
- A searcher who is good with word association;
- A searcher who prefers learning in abstract terms; and
- A search that does not take a lot of time.

Requests and Documents

SARACEVIC (1975) also summarized conclusions about the effects of factors related to requests, documents, and their representations:

- The more judges know about a query, the more their judgments tend to agree.
- The more judges know about a query, the fewer documents they tend to judge relevant.
- A closer similarity tends to exist between texts of queries and texts of relevant documents than between texts of queries and texts of nonrelevant documents.
- The most important characteristic of documents affecting relevance judgments is subject content.
- Highly specific subject content in a document appears to stimulate more agreement in relevance judgments.
- Relevance judgments for the same document tend to differ depending on the length of the representation, from title to full text.
- Aspects of style may affect relevance judgments.

Here too, SARACEVIC & KANTOR contributed additional conclusions. Among factors they found increased the odds that retrieved items would be judged relevant are:

- A request that is low in clarity or specificity;
- A question that is high in complexity or presuppositions (i.e., implications of existence or identity as in "What is . . . ?");
- A search with a higher number of cycles (i.e., input-to-output sequences), allowing more opportunities to assess intermediate results;
- A search with a lower number of search terms;
- A document that is retrieved multiple times by different searchers or searches; and

- Items in an entire retrieval set judged by users to be of greatest overall value, including time or money saved, contribution to problem solution, and so forth.

Although the effects of factors related to requests and searches are well supported, the effects of factors related to documents seem to have been studied most frequently. In IR evaluation, researchers have been interested since the Cranfield tests in the relative effectiveness of retrieving documents represented by index terms, bibliographic citations, full text, and so forth. For example, in a study of searching by terms and citations in two health sciences databases, PAO found the odds of overlap items being relevant or partially relevant to be eight times greater. MCKININ ET AL., in a comparison of searching in indexed and full-text medical databases, found that full-text files yielded more relevant articles than indexed files, but that the output lacked precision.

In research focusing more directly on relevance, a number of studies have yielded detailed results concerning document representations and the complexity of the document judging process. REGAZZI found many significant interaction effects among multiple factors involving characteristics of judges and of documents when he asked judges to rate the importance of certain information and document attributes in making judgments. Some of the highest importance ratings were linked to the information attributes completeness, suggestiveness (ability to generate new ideas) and timeliness and the document attributes author, title, and publication source. In another study using different groups of judges, JANES & MCKINNEY observed user and nonuser judges as they made judgments first on the basis of document titles, then again after citation information was added from bibliographic, indexing or abstract fields. They concluded that secondary judges use citation fields differently from users.

Several researchers, including BARRY (1993b), PARK (1993), and WANG, were more interested in how and why certain document factors are employed in making relevance judgments. All conducted qualitative studies aimed at identifying and describing users' perceptions of information, documents and almost anything else users consider when making judgments. Wang pursued the role of documents the furthest in observing users' sequential patterns of processing some 21 document elements during document assessment and incorporating her findings in a model of the document selection process. These studies are described more fully in subsequent sections.

Research Concerns

The bulk of the empirical evidence seems to indicate that characteristics of judges, document contents (information) and document representations affect relevance judgments, in that order. But much remains unknown. Often the difficulty of predicting relevance outcomes is attributed to subjectivity, or the fact that meanings are not fixed in users' minds and thus cannot be adequately represented in systems (D.R. SWANSON, 1988). Put another way, subjectivity is reflected in the remarkably low agreement among human decisions of all kinds, as in judging relevance, indexing documents, or searching (SARACEVIC, 1991; SARACEVIC & KANTOR). On the other hand, ROBERTSON (1993) does not see subjectivity as the problem, but rather the practice of evaluating just one kind of system output (reference to a specific document) at one level of aggregation (whole document, not part) at one point in time (soon after the search). Also, as discussed earlier, relevance outcomes may be affected by biases in obtaining judgments. But it should be noted that "biases" may involve factors of major interest to relevance research. For instance, REGAZZI interprets presentation order effects as learning effects.

Finally, many researchers make (or tacitly accept) certain assumptions about what users need or want that may be incorrect. BELKIN (1981) points out a number of pitfalls related to assumptions in IR research. An often-noted assumption is that a user wants all the relevant documents, not just one useful document; but as COOPER (1973) says, "it is really documents with high utility, and not merely relevant documents, that the user wants to see" (p. 92). Various writers have speculated about what users really want or expect with regard to recall or precision (BAWDEN; LANCASTER & WARNER; SALTON; SANDORE), size of retrieval set (KINNUCAN), and satisfaction (APPLEGATE; O'BRIEN). Several studies reported earlier yielded conflicting results on the importance to users of recall and precision. SU (1992; 1994) found that users seemed to value interactivity over relevance-based precision, while GRIFFITHS & KING found that users will pay more for higher levels of relevance than for considerations such as speed of delivery. TENOPIR observes that users who conduct their own searches are often quite satisfied with what are horrible results (i.e., enormous retrieval sets) by librarians' standards and asks wryly whether it is "any of our business," so long as users are satisfied.

USER CRITERIA

User Criteria Approach

The eight studies summarized in this section, by BARRY (1993a), COOL ET AL., HOWARD, NILAN ET AL., PARK (1992), SCHAMBER (1991b), SU (1991), and THOMAS, cover only seven years, from 1988 to work in progress; they are reported here together for the first time. All of the studies were inspired, generally, by the idea that relevance judgments alone cannot convey the multiple meanings underlying users' decisions on whether to pursue or use information. All were able to identify numerous criteria applied by users making decisions in their own information problem situations. The studies were qualitative, exploratory, and descriptive; criteria were derived directly from users' explanations of their situations and decisions. The researchers elicited users' explanations through some form of open-ended questioning, then analyzed users' responses in order to identify criteria. The criteria they identified are too numerous to list individually, so they are presented as categorized by the researchers. Most of the criteria had been suggested in the previous literature (Table 1); a few that had not been suggested are described. Although the researchers differed considerably in their use of *relevance* and other terms, all took a situation view of the relevance assessment process.

User Criteria Studies

Five studies identified criteria of academic users (faculty and students) in several disciplines who assessed the results of searches for their own requests. The first of these is an extension of the project by SU (1991; 1993), described earlier, in which she tested 20 existing IR performance measures. Su ended her post-search interview by asking users to explain their ratings of overall success of the search. The analysis of their explanations yielded 26 success dimensions (criteria). When Su compared the users' success dimensions with the 20 performance measures, she determined that 17 dimensions were new or had no counterparts among the existing measures. Of these, users mentioned system capabilities most frequently. Su concludes that users evaluate not only product (retrieval output) but also the IR process (interaction) in information retrieval.

The study by BARRY (1993a; 1993b; 1994) yielded 23 criteria in seven categories pertaining to: (1) information content of documents, (2) the user's previous knowledge, (3) the user's beliefs and preferences, (4) other information and sources within the information environment, (5) sources of documents, (6) document as physical entity, and (7) the user's situation. Criteria that had not been suggested previously are presentation of an effective or successful technique, consensus within the field, and the user's relationship with the author.

PARK (1992; 1993) describes 22 factors (criteria) contributing to users' selection of citations. These involve interpretations based on citation characteristics (title, author, and so forth) and on users' own experiences, perceptions of the search, and knowledge about the information problem. A factor related to perceptions of the search, for instance, may concern whether the search appears to be addressing the search goal.

Park builds a relevance model around the contexts in which users make assessments. She concludes that although most of her factors have been discussed in the literature, some, such as the user's search goal, have not been connected to relevance evaluation.

The aim of HOWARD was not to identify user criteria per se but to identify users' personal constructs (see KELLY) or abstract structures underlying their concepts of relevance or pertinence. The constructs were based on users' explanations of similarities and differences among documents they had chosen for a particular task, including detail, scope, and illustrations (much like other researchers' user criteria). She found that nearly all the constructs could be sorted into two categories: topicality (subject matter and document characteristics) and informativeness (related to user's problem situation, as in usefulness).

The preliminary results of a study by COOL ET AL. identified at least 60 factors (criteria) underlying users' judgments of document usefulness grouped in six categories: (1) topic (on the topic); (2) content/information (concepts, facts contained in document); (3) format; (4) presentation; (5) values (used in judging, e.g., specificity); and (6) oneself (personal need or use for document). Respondents in this study were about 300 freshmen who had been assigned a single information task; a second, complementary study took an in-depth look at the multiple information activities of 11 senior scholars with the intent of identifying patterns in their interactions with texts. In the second study, the researchers say the scholars relied on multiple attributes of texts in relation to more than one information goal.

In the next three studies, users obtained information from multiple, often human, sources in environments distinctly different from the academic library. NILAN ET AL. asked users to describe their own serious life- and health-related situations and their information sources, primarily other people. The analysis yielded 36 criteria, which were notable for their emphasis on internal subjective responses (confidentiality, friendly/approachable) as well as on more external objective responses (ease of use). Six criteria concerned users themselves (experience, emotional), and six concerned source authority (credentials, reputation). At least one highly affective criterion, love, has yet to be suggested elsewhere in the relevance literature.

SCHAMBER (1991a; 1991b) interviewed professional users of weather information employed in aviation, electric power utilities, and construction. Their sources were themselves (personal experience), other people, weather information systems, and mass media. The analysis yielded ten criteria in three categories: (1) information (accuracy, currency, specificity, geographic proximity), (2) source (reliability, accessibility, verifiability), and (3) presentation (dynamism, presentation quality, clarity). The criterion geographic proximity had not been suggested previously, nor had several narrower definitions of criteria, including (weather map) zooming capability under dynamism and (weathercaster) personality under presentation quality.

In a pilot study, THOMAS investigated situational factors (criteria) contributing to new doctoral students' assessments of information as they interacted in an unfamiliar environment. She identified about 18 factors in four categories: (1) information and knowledge sources, (2) feelings of uncertainty, (3) endurance and coordination (responding to demands of the program), and (4) establishing professional relationships. She describes uncertainty factors as affective (needing self-confirmation and status), pragmatic and cultural (understanding procedures and expectations), and academic (understanding requirements).

Discussion of Results

Each study yielded criteria that were remarkably similar to criteria in the other user criteria studies as well as to factors suggested in the literature (Table 1). Considering the vast differences in research approaches and information environments represented in all the lists of criteria and factors, it can be said that the user criteria studies strongly support the notion that a finite range of criteria exists at some level for users in all types of information problem situations. The results can be summarized briefly in terms of information- and document-related criteria and criteria related to other aspects of the problem situation.

One finding was that the top priority of users regardless of type of situation, based on frequency of mentions of criteria in users' open-ended responses, seems to be information content. Further, the numerous content-related criteria identified, particularly in studies by BARRY (1993a; 1994), COOL ET AL., HOWARD, and PARK (1993), seem to confirm and illustrate the multidimensionality of an information view of relevance. The studies by Barry and Park were also able to discern, to some extent, ways in which certain features of document representations (e.g., author, index term, format) serve as clues to content for users. Several studies identified other criteria, beyond information and documents, that validated or expanded upon factors that had been suggested but not empirically tested by COOPER (1973) and TAYLOR. Where Cooper suggested affective factors, the studies involving critical personal situations yielded criteria relating to feelings of uncertainty and discomfort and to oneself (NILAN ET AL.; THOMAS). Where Taylor suggested system interface factors, some studies identified criteria relating to user–system interaction (SU, 1993), dynamic visual displays (SCHAMBER, 1991a), and interpersonal communication (NILAN ET AL.; THOMAS).

The categorization schemes for user criteria developed for these studies are also important because they shed light on relationships that previously may not have been considered. Generally, the schemes contribute to a holistic situation view of relevance, a view shared by researchers in other areas who have also conducted qualitative studies that yielded user criteria. One example is a study in the area of natural classification behavior by KWAŚNIK, who asked faculty members to describe the organization of documents in their offices and the process of sorting a day's mail. Her results yielded 33 dimensions of classificatory decisions in seven groups, including situation attributes (use/purpose) and document attributes (form). Another example is a series of studies on the natural searching behavior of students by KUHLTHAU (1991; 1993) that yielded insights into thoughts and feelings as well as decision criteria related to various stages of information seeking. The criteria are: (1) personal interest, (2) assignment requirements, (3) information available, and (4) time allotted. Kuhlthau incorporated her findings in a multilevel model of the information search process. Several relevance models have been proposed in addition to the model by Park mentioned above; these and other models are discussed in the next section.

Research Concerns

The user-criteria studies represent a trend toward qualitative methods in IR research (see BRADLEY & SUTTON; FIDEL). Most of the researchers are new to the field, having begun these projects as doctoral students. They employed a wide variety of techniques for eliciting and identifying users' criteria, such as structured interviews and content analyses of transcribed interview texts, some of which are described in detail in the dissertations. These techniques brought their own set of potential biases involving users' ability to recall and articulate perceptions, effects of interviewers and instructions on users' responses, and effects of coders and coding procedures in content analysis. Operationalization of concepts presented a challenge in that researchers who wanted to elicit open-ended responses from users in their own language could not use the usual relevance terms in their instructions. For example, users were asked: (1) what it was about a document representation that helped them decide whether to pursue the full-text document (BARRY, 1994); (2) what their reasons were for assigning a particular rating of overall success of the system in providing help (SU, 1993); and (3) what it was about the information source that made a difference in how they felt about the information (SCHAMBER, 1991a).

The methods did, however, produce extremely rich data; for example, in the study by BARRY (1994), 18 users generated 989 responses that contained 444 mentions of criteria. The data were also comprehensive; the fact that as few as nine users (taken in any order) mentioned all the criteria in a study was taken as an indication that the full range of criteria had been identified (BARRY, 1994).

MODELS AND CONTEXTS

Disciplinary Perspectives

Because relevance is a relative concept, entirely dependent on the context in which a judgment is made, the possible approaches to models and theories involving relevance are extraordinarily diverse. The typical IR interaction model (Figure 1) has been presented here only as a concrete point of departure for discussion. It describes a text-based retrieval process that produces output that is assessed by users and intermediaries. However, relevance researchers (and others) working in the context of information seeking and use explore human perceptions not just at the point of output but at all points in the IR process. Beyond IR, interest in relevance extends into seemingly disparate areas such as bibliometrics. SARACEVIC (1970) describes bibliometric literature distribution patterns as relevance-related, connecting source and destination in the communication process. HARTER points out that relevance is the connection between IR research and bibliometrics. Where IR emphasizes information retrieval and use, he says, bibliometrics emphasizes information production, particularly in citation behavior. When authors cite other authors' work, they are making relevance judgments, linking ideas for future readers. In IR, then, some research suggests that searching on authors' citations can improve relevance results.

The disciplinary implications clearly extend beyond research subfields in information science. The recent research on relevance assessment behavior represents a trend toward understanding all information behaviors as cognitive, situational, and dynamic. This trend supports a much-hailed paradigm shift throughout the discipline. ELLIS (1992) traces physical and cognitive paradigms in information science back to the Cranfield tests and argues that neither paradigm provides a strong explanatory framework. INGWERSEN (1987) describes the paradigm shift as a move toward cognitive approaches, merging system-driven and user-modeling approaches into a unified concern with interactive, intelligent IR processes and systems. ITOGA suggests an alternative paradigm that bridges the gap between cognitive and phenomenological views in that it seeks not to describe human information-seeking behavior but rather how to understand another person's information needs in a holistic contextual sense. DERVIN & NILAN characterize the paradigm shift as moving from "traditional" to "alternative" views, the alternative view being holistic and cognitive in nature, placing users in the role of active constructors of information. This is the same role in which HARTER, SCHAMBER ET AL. and others place relevance judges: as users whose relevance assessments are part of their ongoing internal construction of meaning.

The role of relevance in the holistic cognitive paradigm has been interpreted several ways. From the perspective of hermeneutics, according to FROEHLICH (1994), context shapes and makes interpretation. He sees relevance as evolving naturally from cultural experience, from the socialization of the user. Froehlich (1991) also suggests that relevance judgments are the result of natural categorization behavior (see MERVIS & ROSCH; ROSCH & LLOYD). HARTER writes about the interaction of citation and context during evaluation, about how reading a citation can create a new context for cognitive change. MANGRUM, drawing from the phenomenological views of SCHUTZ, makes a case for three forms of relevance: topical, interpretive, and motivational. For the purposes of relevance research, PARK (1994) advocates a naturalistic paradigm of inquiry (see BRADLEY & SUTTON; GUBA & LINCOLN). Unlike rationalistic inquiry, which views reality as objectively observable, predictable, and controllable, naturalistic inquiry views reality as subjective, full of multiple and value-laden perspectives that are to be understood, not controlled, by the investigator.

The disciplinary connections for relevance research extend to interests of user-oriented research across fields. There has been a persistent call in the literature, expressed by DERVIN & NILAN, HEWINS, ROUSE & ROUSE, and others, for attention to concepts of information and information value in user-oriented research. Rouse and Rouse describe central issues in research on human information seeking and information system design as interdisciplinary, concerning cognition, decision making, the value of information, and the dynamic modeling of human behavior. The relevance research described here addresses the same issues. Many relevance researchers have ventured into other disciplines, including management, marketing, economics, psychology, and communication. This section looks at some of the models they have adopted and developed, all representing some decision-making, cognitive, or dynamic approach to understanding the role of relevance in human information behavior, or relevance from a situation view.

Decision-Making Approaches

Generally the decision-making approaches to relevance are oriented toward goals, problems, or tasks, with the user playing a key role in valuing and using information and information systems. Most models encompass a range of variables involving attributes of users, information, and information sources in some rule-based relationship. The literature on decision making encompasses many fields, including business, management, marketing, consumer behavior, organizational communication, economics, and computer science. GRIFFITHS and KATZER & FLETCHER summarize economic and management perspectives, respectively, on issues related to values and uses of information. REPO elaborates on multidimensional and cognitive approaches to the value of information that fit well with interests in relevance. Where multiple information sources are important in decision making, models of channel selection, as discussed by O'REILLY and E. B. SWANSON, are helpful. Multiattribute models are often applied in evaluating computer user satisfaction in business and computer science, as in studies by BAROUDI ET AL., CHOE & LEE, and NATH. Management information scientists including BAILEY & PEARSON, DOLL & TORKZADEH, and IVES ET AL. have developed and validated specific multiattribute satisfaction measurement techniques.

Relevance-oriented decision-making approaches in information science have taken several avenues. WANG presents a model of the document selection process with components drawn from the relevance literature in information science and from decision making and consumer choice literature. In this model, the user: (1) processes information from document elements (title, author), (2) arrives at values of a number of criteria (subject area, novelty), (3) combines criterion values to assess a document value (functional, emotional), and (4) weighs document values to make a decision (accept, uncertain, reject). The final decision is based on decision rules or tradeoff principles such as elimination (finding reasons to reject) and multicriteria (accepting based on more than one criterion). Wang supports the model with qualitative data from academic library users and points out its flexibility: criteria can be added or subtracted, for instance, to suit a particular user group.

ATKINSON developed a model for librarians' decisions in book selection based on contexts involving citations, book reviews, and the librarian's own experience and knowledge. APPLEGATE proposes models of user satisfaction that can be applied to library services: (1) a material model concerning whether the user's stated question is answered; (2) an emotional simple-path model concerning whether users are emotionally satisfied when their questions are answered; and (3) an emotional multiple-path model concerning additional factors such as setting and expectations. TESSIER and TURNER each tested extensive multiattribute models involving relevance assessments throughout the user's problem situation, from initiation of information seeking to use of information. Both found that document relevance was quite important to users, but that it was sometimes overridden in importance by other factors such as source characteristics.

Cognitive Approaches

The literature provides many overviews of cognitive approaches in information science including: ALLEN; BELKIN (1984); BORGMAN (1984); BURT & KINNUCAN; DANIELS; and INGWERSEN (1992). Of particular interest to user-oriented IR research are individual differences (BORGMAN, 1989; EGAN), cognitive abilities and styles (ALLEN), mental models, user modeling, and information value (HEWINS), and information seeking and information value (ROUSE & ROUSE).

Virtually all the current relevance literature draws on at least one of four major approaches. Anomalous states of knowledge (ASK) (BELKIN, 1980a; BELKIN ET AL.) refers to ambiguities in the minds of users. In order to resolve users' ASKs, it is suggested that systems be designed to accept descriptions of goals, problems, and so forth in terms users can articulate. Sense making (DERVIN, 1983a, 1983b, 1992; see also MORRIS; SAVOLAINEN) concerns cognitive gaps or uncertainties that users must bridge to make sense of their information problem situations under constantly changing conditions. Sense-making research often involves methods to help users recall their cognitive states at certain times during their situations. The user-values or values-added processes model (TAYLOR) assumes that users add value to information according to their perceptions of information, the information system, and their own problems. Dimensions of problems are viewed in relation to information traits during the IR process. Psychological relevance (HARTER; based on SPERBER & WILSON) assumes that users are actively seeking information that will change their internal context or store of knowledge, and that if an information item does this, users will perceive it to be relevant.

Taken from a holistic cognitive perspective, relevance presumably can be fit into any information behavior model, or into users' perceptions at any point in the IR interaction process. Often relevance is modeled in the context of users' perceptions of the problem situations or tasks for which they make decisions. An excellent example is the relevance model proposed by PARK (1993). In this model, users' relevance assessments are seen as involving multiple layers of interpretations within three contexts: (1) the internal context, which includes the user's previous subject area and searching experience, (2) the external context, which includes the stage of research, search goal, and perceptions about search quality, and (3) the problem context, which includes the existence in document content of the same or different problems that are useful for definitions, methodology, framework, and so forth.

In addition to Park's model, the clustering of criteria into categories in other user criteria studies can also be seen as the beginnings of taxonomic or contextual models.

Dynamic Approaches

The dynamic nature of human information behavior has always been recognized; dynamics are implicit if not explicit in the decision-making and cognitive approaches above. Dynamic models, however, further describe distinct stages in a process of information seeking and use, including stages that involve relevance assessments.

The model of the information search process by KUHLTHAU (1991; 1993), mentioned earlier, takes several of the previous approaches into account. This model, based on observations of students with real information problems, has six stages: (1) initiation (recognizing a need for information), (2) selection (selecting the general topic), (3) exploration (investigating the general topic for understanding), (4) formulation (focusing on the topic), (5) collection (gathering information on the focused topic), and (6) presentation (completing the search and preparing to use the findings). All stages take place at affective, cognitive and physical levels. Kuhlthau sees relevance as a dynamic, personal, constructive, affective phenomenon, a perspective drawn in part from personal construct theory of KELLY. Generally, as users progress through the stages and become more focused on their topics, their judgments change from relevance (information view) to pertinence (situation view).

Also well worth noting is a framework developed by ELLIS (1989) for a flexible model of information seeking behavior based on interviews with social scientists about their information-related activities. From analysis of interview transcripts, he derived six dynamic behaviors: (1) starting (initial orientation), (2) chaining (via citations and footnotes), (3) browsing (of documents, references, index terms), (4) differentiating (filtering based on information features), (5) monitoring (of developments in a field), and (6) extracting (of relevant material). Three behaviors in Ellis's model—starting, chaining, and differentiating—are incorporated in a model proposed by SUTTON that addresses dynamic changes in the mental models of attorneys as they search for past legal cases relevant to their current clients' situations. Sutton's three stages of change are: (1) base-level modeling or maps, (2) context-sensitive exploration, and (3) disambiguating the event space. Sutton sees relevance judgments as shifting along a knowledge continuum depending on the status of the attorney's mental model.

A major area of interest is the iterative aspect of searching that makes evaluation of output and query reformulation almost simultaneous activities and raises questions about constant change in the internal state of the searcher. ROBERTSON & HANCOCK-BEAULIEU speculate on whether query reformulations in online searching are due to genuine changes in the searcher's state of knowledge or the searcher's expressing a previously unexpressed information need. They also wonder whether reformulations are due to positive effects of the interaction or just the searcher's adapting to the system or whether all of these are due to a combination of such factors. KATZER & SNYDER found that subsequent versions of users' questions were more clearly articulated and speculated as to whether it was really the information need or the articulation of need that improved with interaction.

Often these activities are discussed in terms of feedback. A distinction should be made between *relevance feedback,* which is a system mechanism that automatically reformulates searchers' queries in response to their relevance judgments (see MEADOW; SALTON & BUCKLEY) and *system feedback,* which is some output or display from the system that the searcher uses in reformulating the query or modifying the search strategy (see INGWERSEN, 1992; MEADOW). Here the interest is in searchers' responses to feedback of either sort. Research by SARACEVIC ET AL. (1991) suggests that for intermediaries the concept of feedback extends beyond relevance to include magnitude feedback, based on retrieval output size. SPINK (1993a; 1993b) extends the concept further to include three strategic aspects of output leading to query reformulation: (1) term relevance feedback, pulling a term from output to modify search strategy; (2) tactical review feedback, displaying the history of search strategy sets; and (3) technological review feedback, displaying available terms in an inverted file.

Some insights have also been gained from searchers' responses to relevance feedback. ROBERTSON (1993) reports on user interactions with Okapi, a highly interactive system that includes relevance feedback and query expansion capabilities. As part of an ongoing operational test of the system, users answer a relevance question whenever they view a full record. Robertson observed that rather than using relevance feedback to narrow their searches to relevant items, they use it more for navigating within the system; that is, they may repeat an identical query on subsequent searches to position themselves in the database, then continue to navigate using the interactive capabilities. He also found that searchers use relevance feedback about one-third of the time, and that they use it experimentally and constructively, not naively (see also ROBERTSON & HANCOCK-BEAULIEU).

Research Concerns

Much of the cognitive research reported in this chapter is naturalistic in philosophy and qualitative in specific techniques, as advocated by PARK (1994). Park points out that the user criteria studies have adopted one approach within the naturalistic paradigm, the grounded theory method, which derives theory from data rather than verifies existing theory. GUBA & LINCOLN (see also LINCOLN & GUBA) describe the approach to methodology for naturalistic research, which can be qualitative or quantitative. MELLON explains uses of naturalistic research in libraries; and FIDEL provides an overview of qualitative research in information science. The methodologies in the empirical studies represent a wide variety of specific techniques (see BRADLEY & SUTTON). Two researchers who used a remarkable diversity of approaches are KUHLTHAU (1991; 1993) and SU (1991; 1992; 1993).

Obviously, relevance researchers have had to deal with many methodological problems in their research. Those interested in investigating changes in relevance judgments over time must add to the usual problems the conceptual challenge of partitioning time for the purpose of a particular study and the methodological challenge of observing information behavior over time or at multiple points in time. At least two useful techniques have been developed in recent relevance research. One is time-line interviewing, a flexible approach described by DERVIN (1983b; 1992) and modified by NILAN ET AL. and SCHAMBER (1991b) for their user criteria studies. It involves personal interviews in which researchers work with users to map out the events in their information problem situations on index cards. The other technique is a motion index, a calculation based on psychometric magnitude scaling devised by JANES (1991b), which he used to record changes in relevance judgments as more information was added. BRUCE used the motion index to measure subtle changes in users' estimates of the importance of specific document and information attributes at various stages of search and retrieval.

CONCLUSIONS

At the beginning of the chapter, three kinds of questions are raised, pertaining to behavior, measurement, and terminology. Since the earliest IR research in the 1960s, all of these questions have been addressed. To this day, none of these questions has been answered completely or satisfactorily.

The two questions about behavior are: What factors contribute to human relevance judgments, and what processes does relevance assessment entail? Since the 1960s, the field has gained more consistent knowledge about relevance factors and their effects in 30 years than it has about the complex relationships among factors or the process of relevance assessment. The emerging view of relevance is that it is a cognitive, situational, dynamic phenomenon that is integral to a wide range of information-seeking and -use behaviors. In other words, relevance relates to people and their constantly changing perceptions. Unfortunately, it is likely that, as ELLIS (1992) indicates, the field will continue to be saddled with an "irreducible duality" of people and things. Essentially, the research is geared toward trying to reconcile people and things, and of trying to develop models and theories that will benefit both. Currently any research focusing on searching and retrieving behaviors, dynamic interactions, and feedback offers a great deal of promise. Certainly relevance fits into this picture. In the past decade, researchers have been able to offer several user-based models of relevance assessment processes and contexts, a large body of user criteria that beg to be consolidated, and early insights on relevance judgment behaviors in highly dynamic iterative searching.

The measurement questions are: What is the role of relevance in IR system evaluation, and how should relevance judgments be measured? It has been clear from the outset that relevance plays a relatively small—albeit contentious—role in the big picture of IR system evaluation. It is also clear that there is no agreement on the best relevance-based system performance measures or the best way to collect relevance judgments. The work on testing various existing measures has made helpful contributions; unfortunately, the field still lacks a set of standard measures that can be applied across information settings. Further, as ROBERTSON & HANCOCK-BEAULIEU point out, IR evaluation has become increasingly difficult as systems become more open, complex and interactive. The field's views of the boundaries of the system are changing, they say, due in part to the "relevance revolution": the notion that IR interaction processes (including relevance assessment) should not be bounded at points of requests and documents, but rather should extend into the realm of mental states of the user. One concern that has been implicit throughout the discussion of relevance is IR system design. Various authors have indicated that a surprising number of subjective user criteria can be implemented in IR systems and services (see ELLIS, 1989; MORRIS; and TAYLOR). This includes tangible document elements that users have said are important or that provide users with clues to relevance (see BARRY, 1993b; REGAZZI; SCHAMBER ET AL.; WANG). It remains to be seen what less tangible phenomena are implementable in systems, or even whether users can agree on what clues are important (see FROEHLICH, 1994; HARTER; SWANSON, 1988). Overriding all these concerns is perhaps the most crucial: the fact that information scientists lack a full, or fully reasoned, understanding of what users want or expect, and thus run the risk of predicating research on false assumptions.

Finally, there is the terminology question: What should relevance, or various kinds of relevance, be called? Despite endless haggling, and aside from all the really important questions the field has about relevance, the irritating, niggling issue of terminology persists. Information science has no consistent term for its central concept and no standard operational definition to use in empirical work. Neither researchers nor relevance judges seem to be able to distinguish among various relevance concepts. Perhaps as the field becomes more holistic and situational in its perspective, the everyday, intuitive meaning of the concept may become more common. That is an optimistic view; in the meantime, information scientists need to clarify how they are using the term *relevance.*

In the course of endless debates, relevance has not only been called many terms, it has also been called many names. Some of the kinder names are "ineffable," "elusive," and "ubiquitous" (BELKIN, 1981). Less complimentary are: "slippery, treacherous," and something "emanating from a 'black box'" (CUADRA & KATTER, 1967b); "nebulous" and "a can of worms" (BAWDEN); the "dark matter problem in IR" (INGWERSEN, 1992); the "big black question mark" (JANES, 1994); and, for this author and colleagues, the "R word." Nevertheless, regardless of what information scientists (or users) think about it, relevance is a necessary part of understanding human information behavior. The field should be encouraged by commonalities across perspectives, not discouraged by disagreements. Relevance presents a frustrating, provocative, rich, and—undeniably—relevant area of inquiry.

BIBLIOGRAPHY

ALLEN, BRYCE L. 1991. Cognitive Research in Information Science: Implications for Design. In: Williams, Martha E., ed. Annual Review of Information Science and Technology: Volume 26. Medford, NJ: Learned Information, Inc. for the American Society for Information Science; 1991. 3-37. ISSN: 0066-4200; ISBN: 0-938734-55-5; LC: 66-25096.

APPLEGATE, RACHEL. 1993. Models of User Satisfaction: Understanding False Positives. RQ. 1993 Summer; 32(4): 525-539. ISSN: 0033-7072.

ATKINSON, ROSS. 1984. The Citation as Intertext: Toward a Theory of the Selection Process. Library Resources and Technical Services. 1984 April/June; 28(2): 109-119. ISSN: 0024-2527.

BAILEY, J.E.; PEARSON, S.W. 1983. Development of a Tool for Measuring and Analyzing Computer User Satisfaction. Management Science. 1983; 29(6): 530-545. ISSN: 0025-1909.

BAROUDI, JACK J.; OLSON, MARGRETHE H.; IVES, BLAKE. 1986. An Empirical Study of the Impact of User Involvement on System Usage and Information Satisfaction. Communications of the ACM. 1986 March; 29(3): 233-238. ISSN: 0001-0782.

BARRY, CAROL L. 1993a. The Identification of User Criteria and Document Characteristics: Beyond the Topical Approach to Information Retrieval. Syracuse, NY: Syracuse University, School of Information Studies; 1993.

236p. (Ph.D. dissertation). Available from: University Microfilms, Ann Arbor, MI.

BARRY, CAROL L. 1993b. A Preliminary Examination of Clues to Relevance Criteria within Document Representations. See reference: BONZI, SUSAN, ed. 81-86.

BARRY, CAROL L. 1994. User-Defined Relevance Criteria: An Exploratory Study. Journal of the American Society for Information Science. 1994 April; 45(3): 149-159. ISSN: 0002-8231.

BAWDEN, DAVID. 1990. User-Oriented Evaluation of Information Systems and Services. Brookfield, VT: Gower; 1990. 209p. ISBN: 0-566-05209-1.

BELKIN, NICHOLAS J. 1980a. Anomalous States of Knowledge as a Basis for Information Retrieval. Canadian Journal of Information Science. 1980 May; 5: 133-143. ISSN: 0380-9218.

BELKIN, NICHOLAS J. 1980b. The Problem of "Matching" in Information Retrieval. In: Harbo, O.; Kajberg, L., eds. Theory and Application of Information Research: Proceedings of the 2nd International Research Forum on Information Science; 1977 August 3-6; Copenhagen, Denmark. London, England: Mansell; 1980. 187-197. ISBN: 0-7201-1513-2.

BELKIN, NICHOLAS J. 1981. Ineffable Concepts in Information Retrieval. In: Sparck Jones, Karen, ed. Information Retrieval Experiment. London, England: Butterworths; 1981. 44-58. ISBN: 0-408-10648-4; LC: 80-42222.

BELKIN, NICHOLAS J. 1984. Cognitive Models and Information Transfer. Social Science Information Studies. 1984 April-July; 4(2-3): 111-129. ISSN: 0143-6236.

BELKIN, NICHOLAS J.; CROFT, W. BRUCE. 1987. Retrieval Techniques. In: Williams, Martha E., ed. Annual Review of Information Science and Technology: Volume 22. Amsterdam, The Netherlands: Elsevier Science Publishers for the American Society for Information Science; 1987. 109-145. ISSN: 0066-4200; ISBN: 0-444-70302-0.

BELKIN, NICHOLAS J.; ODDY, ROBERT N.; BROOKS, HELEN M. 1982. ASK for Information Retrieval. Part I: Background and Theory. Journal of Documentation. 1982 June; 38(2): 61-71. Part II: Results of a Design Study. Journal of Documentation. 1982 September; 38(3): 145-164. ISSN: 0022-0418.

BELLARDO, TRUDI; SARACEVIC, TEFKO. 1987. Online Searching and Search Output: Relationships between Overlap, Relevance, Recall and Precision. In: Chen, Ching-chih, ed. ASIS '87: Proceedings of the American Society for Information Science (ASIS) 50th Annual Meeting: Volume 24; 1987 October 4-8; Boston, MA. Medford, NJ: Learned Information, Inc. for the American Society for Information Science; 1987. 11-13. ISSN: 0044-7870; ISBN: 0-938734-19-9.

BONZI, SUSAN, ed. 1993. ASIS '93: Proceedings of the American Society for Information Science (ASIS) 56th Annual Meeting: Volume 30; 1993 October 24-28; Columbus, OH. Medford, NJ: Learned Information, Inc. for the American Society for Information Science; 1993. 334p. ISSN: 0044-7870; ISBN: 0-938734-78-4.

BORGMAN, CHRISTINE L. 1984. Psychological Research in Human-Computer Interaction. In: Williams, Martha E., ed. Annual Review of Information Science and Technology: Volume 19. White Plains, NY: Knowledge

Industry Publications, Inc. for the American Society for Information Science; 1984. 33-64. ISSN: 0066-4200; ISBN: 0-86729-093-5.

BORGMAN, CHRISTINE L. 1989. All Users of Information Retrieval Systems Are Not Created Equal: An Exploration into Individual Differences. Information Processing & Management. 1989; 25(3): 237-252. ISSN: 0306-4573.

BOYCE, BERT. 1982. Beyond Topicality: A Two Stage View of Relevance and the Retrieval Process. Information Processing & Management. 1982; 18(3): 105-109. ISSN: 0306-4573.

BRADLEY, JANA; SUTTON, BRETT. 1993. Reframing the Paradigm Debate. Library Quarterly. 1993 October; 63(4): 405-410. ISSN: 0024-2519.

BRUCE, HARRY W. 1994. A Cognitive View of the Situational Dynamism of User-Centered Relevance Estimation. Journal of the American Society for Information Science. 1994 April; 45(3): 142-148. ISSN: 0002-8231.

BUCKLAND, MICHAEL K.; GEY, FREDRIC. 1994. The Relationship between Recall and Precision. Journal of the American Society for Information Science. 1994 January; 45(1): 12-19. ISSN: 0002-8231.

BURGIN, ROBERT. 1992. Variations in Relevance Judgments and the Evaluation of Retrieval Performance. Information Processing & Management. 1992 September/October; 28(5): 619-627. ISSN: 0306-4573.

BURT, PATRICIA V.; KINNUCAN, MARK T. 1990. Information Models and Modeling Techniques for Information Systems. In: Williams, Martha E., ed. Annual Review of Information Science and Technology: Volume 25. Amsterdam, The Netherlands: Elsevier Science Publishers B.V. for the American Society for Information Science; 1990. 175-208. ISSN: 0066-4200; ISBN: 0-444-88531-5; LC: 66-25096.

CHOE, JONG-MIN; LEE, JINJOO. 1993. Factors Affecting Relationships between the Contextual Variables and the Information Characteristics of Accounting Information Systems. Information Processing & Management. 1993 July/August; 29(4): 471-486. ISSN: 0306-4573.

CLEVERDON, CYRIL WILLIAM. 1962. Report on the Testing and Analysis of an Investigation into the Comparative Efficiency of Indexing Systems. Cranfield, England: College of Aeronautics; 1962. 305p. LC: 63-60414.

CLEVERDON, CYRIL WILLIAM. 1967. The Cranfield Tests on Index Language Devices. Aslib Proceedings. 1967 June; 19(6): 173-194. ISSN: 0001-253X.

CLEVERDON, CYRIL WILLIAM. 1990. Questions of Relevance. In: Bawden, David. User-Oriented Evaluation of Information Systems and Services. Brookfield, VT: Gower; 1990. 165-171. ISBN: 0-566-05209-1.

CLEVERDON, CYRIL WILLIAM; MILLS, JACK; KEEN, E. MICHAEL. 1966. Factors Determining the Performance of Indexing Systems. Cranfield, England: ASLIB; 1966. 2 volumes (Volume 1: Design; Volume 2: Test Results). LC: 67-81732; OCLC: 3911240.

COOL, COLLEEN; BELKIN, NICHOLAS J.; KANTOR, PAUL B. 1993. Characteristics of Texts Affecting Relevance Judgments. In: Williams, Martha E., ed. Proceedings of the 14th National Online Meeting; 1993 May 4-6: New York, NY. Medford, NJ: Learned Information, Inc.; 1993. 77-84. ISBN: 0-938734-73-3.

COOPER, WILLIAM S. 1971. A Definition of Relevance for Information Retrieval. Information Storage and Retrieval. 1971 June; 7(1): 19-37. ISSN: 0020-0271.

COOPER, WILLIAM S. 1973. On Selecting a Measure of Retrieval Effectiveness. Journal of the American Society for Information Science. 1973 March/April; 24(2): 87-100. ISSN: 0002-8231.

CUADRA, CARLOS A.; KATTER, ROBERT V. 1967a. Experimental Studies of Relevance Judgments Final Report. Volume I: Project Summary. Santa Monica, CA: System Development Corp.; 1967. 129p. (TM-3520/001/00). NTIS: PB 175518.

CUADRA, CARLOS A.; KATTER, ROBERT V. 1967b. Opening the Black Box of "Relevance." Journal of Documentation. 1967 December; 23(4): 291-303. ISSN: 0022-0418.

DANIELS, P.J. 1986. Cognitive Models in Information Retrieval: An Evaluative Review. Journal of Documentation. 1986 December; 42(4): 272-304. ISSN: 0022-0418.

DERVIN, BRENDA. 1983a. Information as a User Construct: The Relevance of Perceived Information Needs to Synthesis and Interpretation. In: Ward, Spencer A.; Reed, Linda J., eds. Knowledge Structures and Use: Implications for Synthesis and Interpretation. Philadelphia, PA: Temple University Press; 1983. 153-184. ISBN: 0-87722-331-9.

DERVIN, BRENDA. 1983b. An Overview of Sense-Making Research: Concepts, Methods, and Results to Date. Paper presented at: International Communication Association Annual Meeting; 1983 May 26-30; Dallas, TX. 68p. Available from: the author, Department of Communication, Ohio State University, Columbus, OH 43210.

DERVIN, BRENDA. 1992. From the Mind's Eye of the User: The Sense-Making Qualitative-Quantitative Methodology. In: Glazier, Jack D.; Powell, Ronald R., eds. Qualitative Research in Information Management. Englewood, CO: Libraries Unlimited; 1992. 61-84. ISBN: 0-87287-806-6.

DERVIN, BRENDA; NILAN, MICHAEL S. 1986. Information Needs and Uses. In: Williams, Martha E., ed. Annual Review of Information Science and Technology: Volume 21. White Plains, NY: Knowledge Industry Publications, Inc. for the American Society for Information Science; 1986. 3-33. ISSN: 0066-4200; ISBN: 0-87815-035-8; LC: 66-25096.

DOLL, WILLIAM J.; TORKZADEH, GOLAMREZA. 1988. The Measurement of End-User Computing Satisfaction. MIS Quarterly. 1988 June; 23(2): 259-274. ISSN: 0276-7783.

EGAN, D.E. 1988. Individual Differences in Human-Computer Interaction. In: Helander, M., ed. Handbook of Human-Computer Interaction. New York, NY: Elsevier; 1988. 543-579. ISBN: 0-444-070536-8.

EISENBERG, MICHAEL B. 1988. Measuring Relevance Judgments. Information Processing & Management. 1988; 24(4): 373-389. ISSN: 0306-4573.

EISENBERG, MICHAEL B.; BARRY, CAROL L. 1986. Order Effects: A Preliminary Study of the Possible Influence of Presentation Order on User Judgments of Document Relevance. In: Hurd, Julie M., ed. ASIS '86: Proceedings of the American Society for Information Science (ASIS) 49th Annual

Meeting: Volume 23; 1986 September 28-October 2; Chicago, IL. Medford, NJ: Learned Information, Inc. for the American Society for Information Science; 1986. 80-86. ISSN: 0044-7870; ISBN: 0-938734-14-8.

EISENBERG, MICHAEL B.; HU, XIULAN. 1987. Dichotomous Relevance Judgments and the Evaluation of Information Systems. In: Chen, Ching-chih, ed. ASIS '87: Proceedings of the American Society for Information Science (ASIS) 50th Annual Meeting: Volume 24; 1987 October 4-8; Boston, MA. Medford, NJ: Learned Information, Inc. for the American Society for Information Science; 1987. 66-70. ISSN: 0044-7870; ISBN: 0-938734-19-9.

ELLIS, DAVID. 1984a. The Effectiveness of Information Retrieval Systems: The Need for Improved Explanatory Frameworks. Social Science Information Studies. 1984; 4: 261-272. ISSN: 0143-6236.

ELLIS, DAVID. 1984b. Theory and Explanation in Information Retrieval Research. Journal of Information Science. 1984 February; 8(1): 25-28. ISSN: 0165-5515.

ELLIS, DAVID. 1989. A Behavioural Approach to Information Retrieval System Design. Journal of Documentation. 1989 September; 45(3): 171-212. ISSN: 0022-0418.

ELLIS, DAVID. 1992. The Physical and Cognitive Paradigms in Information Retrieval Research. Journal of Documentation. 1992 March; 48(1): 45-64. ISSN: 0022-0418.

FIDEL, RAYA. 1993. Qualitative Methods in Information Retrieval Research. Library & Information Science Research. 1993 Summer; 15(3): 219-247. ISSN: 0740-8188.

FIDEL, RAYA; SOERGEL, DAGOBERT. 1983. Factors Affecting Online Bibliographic Retrieval: A Conceptual Framework for Research. Journal of the American Society for Information Science. 1983 May; 34(3): 163-180. ISSN: 0002-8231.

FOSKETT, D.J. 1972. A Note on the Concept of "Relevance." Information Storage and Retrieval. 1972 April; 8(2): 77-78. ISSN: 0020-0271.

FROEHLICH, THOMAS J. 1991. Towards a Better Conceptual Framework for Understanding Relevance for Information Science Research. In: Griffiths, José-Marie, ed. ASIS '91: Proceedings of the American Society for Information Science (ASIS) 54th Annual Meeting: Volume 28; 1991 October 27-31; Washington, DC. Medford, NJ: Learned Information, Inc. for the American Society for Information Science; 1991. 118-125. ISSN: 0044-7870; ISBN: 0-938734-56-3.

FROEHLICH, THOMAS J. 1994. Relevance Reconsidered—Towards an Agenda for the 21st Century: Introduction to Special Topic Issue on Relevance Research. Journal of the American Society for Information Science. 1994 April; 45(3): 124-134. ISSN: 0002-8231.

GLUCK, MYKE. 1994. Understanding Performance in Information Systems: Blending Relevance and Competence. 35p. (Unpublished paper). Available from: the author, School of Library and Information Studies, 244 Louis Shores Building, Florida State University, Tallahassee, FL 32306-2048.

GRIFFITHS, JOSÉ-MARIE. 1982. The Value of Information and Related Systems, Products and Services. In: Williams, Martha E., ed. Annual Review of Information Science and Technology: Volume 17. White Plains, NY:

Knowledge Industry Publications, Inc. for the American Society for Information Science; 1982. 269-283. ISSN: 0066-4200; ISBN: 0-86729-032-3.

GRIFFITHS, JOSÉ-MARIE; KING, DONALD W. 1993. Special Libraries: Increasing the Information Edge. Washington, DC: Special Libraries Association; 1993. 197p. ISBN: 0-87111-414-3.

GUBA, EGON G.; LINCOLN, YVONNA S. 1982. Epistemological and Methodological Bases of Naturalistic Inquiry. Educational Communication and Technology. 1982 Winter; 30(4): 233-252. ISSN: 0148-5806.

HARTER, STEPHEN P. 1992. Psychological Relevance and Information Science. Journal of the American Society for Information Science. 1992 October; 43(9): 602-615. ISSN: 0002-8231.

HERSH, WILLIAM. 1994. Relevance and Retrieval Evaluation: Perspectives from Medicine. Journal of the American Society for Information Science. 1994 April; 45(3): 201-206. ISSN: 0002-8231.

HEWINS, ELIZABETH T. 1990. Information Need and Use Studies. In: Williams, Martha E., ed. Annual Review of Information Science and Technology: Volume 25. Amsterdam, The Netherlands: Elsevier Science Publishers for the American Society for Information Science; 1990. 145-172. ISSN: 0066-4200; ISBN: 0-444-88531-5.

HOWARD, DARA LEE. 1994. Pertinence as Reflected in Personal Constructs. Journal of the American Society for Information Science. 1994 April; 45(3): 172-185. ISSN: 0002-8231.

INGWERSEN, PETER. 1984. Psychological Aspects of Information Retrieval. Social Science Information Studies. 1984 April-July; 4(2-3): 83-95. ISSN: 0143-6236.

INGWERSEN, PETER. 1987. Towards a New Research Paradigm in Information Retrieval. In: Wormell, Irene, ed. Knowledge Engineering: Expert Systems and Information Retrieval. London, England: Taylor Graham; 1987. 150-168. ISBN: 0-947568-30-1.

INGWERSEN, PETER. 1992. Information Retrieval Interaction. London, England: Taylor Graham; 1992. 246p. ISBN: 0-947568-54-9; LC: 92-49311.

ITOGA, MASARU. 1992. Seeking Understanding beneath the Unspecifiable: An Alternative Framework for Mapping Information Needs in Communication. Libri. 1992 October-December; 42(4): 330-344. ISSN: 0024-2667.

IVES, BLAKE; OLSON, MARGRETHE H.; BAROUDI, JACK J. 1983. The Measurement of User Information Satisfaction. Communications of the ACM. 1983 October; 26(10): 785-793. ISSN: 0001-0782.

JANES, JOSEPH W. 1991a. The Binary Nature of Continuous Relevance Judgments: A Study of Users' Perceptions. Journal of the American Society for Information Science. 1991 December; 42(10): 754-756. ISSN: 0002-8231.

JANES, JOSEPH W. 1991b. Relevance Judgments and the Incremental Presentation of Document Representations. Information Processing & Management. 1991; 27(6): 629-646. ISSN: 0306-4573.

JANES, JOSEPH W. 1993. On the Distribution of Relevance Judgments. See reference: BONZI, SUSAN, ed. 104-114.

JANES, JOSEPH W. 1994. Other People's Judgments: A Comparison of Users' and Others' Judgments of Document Relevance, Topicality, and Utility.

Journal of the American Society for Information Science. 1994 April; 45(3): 160-171. ISSN: 0002-8231.

JANES, JOSEPH W.; MCKINNEY, RENEE. 1992. Relevance Judgments of Actual Users and Secondary Judges: A Comparative Study. Library Quarterly. 1992 April; 62(2): 150-168. ISSN: 0024-2519.

KATTER, ROBERT V. 1968. The Influence of Scale Form on Relevance Judgments. Information Storage and Retrieval. 1968; 4: 1-11. ISSN: 0020-0271.

KATZER, JEFFREY; FLETCHER, PATRICIA T. 1992. The Information Environment of Managers. In: Williams, Martha E., ed. Annual Review of Information Science and Technology: Volume 27. Medford, NJ: Learned Information, Inc. for the American Society for Information Science; 1992. 227-263. ISSN: 0066-4200; ISBN: 0-938734-66-0; LC: 66-25096.

KATZER, JEFFREY; SNYDER, HERBERT W. 1990. Toward a More Realistic Assessment of Information Retrieval Performance. In: Henderson, Diane, ed. ASIS '90: Proceedings of the American Society for Information Science (ASIS) 53rd Annual Meeting: Volume 27; 1990 November 4-8; Toronto, Ontario. Medford, NJ: Learned Information, Inc. for the American Society for Information Science; 1990. 80-85. ISSN: 0044-7870; ISBN: 0-938734-43-2; LC: 64-8303.

KEEN, E. MICHAEL. 1992. Presenting Results of Experimental Retrieval Comparisons. Information Processing & Management. 1992 July/August; 28(4): 491-502. ISSN: 0306-4573.

KELLY, GEORGE ALEXANDER. 1963. A Theory of Personality: The Psychology of Personal Constructs. New York, NY: Norton; 1963. 190p. LC: 63-4737.

KEMP, D. A. 1974. Relevance, Pertinence and Information System Development. Information Storage and Retrieval. 1974 February; 10(2): 37-47. ISSN: 0020-0271.

KING, DONALD W. 1968. Design and Evaluation of Information Systems. In: Cuadra, Carlos A., ed. Annual Review of Information Science and Technology: Volume 3. Chicago, IL: Encyclopaedia Britannica, Inc. for the American Society for Information Science; 1968. 61-103. ISSN: 0066-4200; LC: 66-25096.

KING, DONALD W.; BRYANT, EDWARD C. 1971. The Evaluation of Information Services and Products. Washington, DC: Information Resources Press; 1971. 306p. ISBN: 0-87815-003-X.

KINNUCAN, MARK T. 1992. The Size of Retrieval Sets. Journal of the American Society for Information Science. 1992 January; 43(1): 72-79. ISSN: 0002-8231.

KUHLTHAU, CAROL COLLIER. 1991. Inside the Search Process: Information Seeking from the User's Perspective. Journal of the American Society for Information Science. 1991 June; 42(5): 361-371. ISSN: 0002-8231.

KUHLTHAU, CAROL COLLIER. 1993. Seeking Meaning: A Process Approach to Library and Information Services. Norwood, NJ: Ablex Publishing Corp.; 1993. 199p. ISBN: 0-89391-968-3.

KWAŚNIK, BARBARA H. 1991. The Importance of Factors That Are Not Document Attributes in the Organisation of Personal Documents. Journal of Documentation. 1991 December; 47(4): 389-398. ISSN: 0022-0418.

LANCASTER, F. WILFRID. 1979. Information Retrieval Systems: Characteristics, Testing, and Evaluation. 2nd ed. New York, NY: John Wiley & Sons; 1979. 222p. ISBN: 0-471-04673-6.

LANCASTER, F. WILFRID; MILLS, JACK. 1964. Testing Indexes and Index Language Devices: The Aslib Cranfield Project. American Documentation. 1964 January; 15(1): 4-13. ISSN: 0002-8231.

LANCASTER, F. WILFRID; WARNER, AMY J. 1993. Information Retrieval Today. Arlington, VA: Information Resources Press; 1993. 341p. ISBN: 0-87815-064-1.

LESK, MICHAEL E.; SALTON, GERARD. 1968. Relevance Assessments and Retrieval System Evaluation. Information Storage and Retrieval. 1968 December; 4(4): 343-359. ISSN: 0020-0271.

LINCOLN, YVONNA S.; GUBA, EGON G. 1985. Naturalistic Inquiry. Beverly Hills, CA: Sage Publications; 1985. 416p. ISBN: 0-8039-2431-3.

MANGRUM, ELAINE WARD. 1988. Relevance in Information Retrieval: A Critical Review. Chapel Hill, NC: University of North Carolina; 1988. 37p. (M.S.L.S. thesis).

MCKININ, EMMA JEAN; SIEVERT, MARYELLEN; JOHNSON, E. DIANE; MITCHELL, JOYCE A. 1991. The Medline/Full-Text Research Project. Journal of the American Society for Information Science. 1991 May; 42(4): 297-307. ISSN: 0002-8231.

MEADOW, CHARLES T. 1992. Text Information Retrieval Systems. San Diego, CA: Academic Press; 1992. 302p. ISBN: 0-12-487410-X.

MELLON, CONSTANCE A. 1990. Naturalistic Inquiry for Library Science: Methods and Applications for Research, Evaluation and Teaching. New York, NY: Greenwood; 1990. 201p. ISSN: 0084-9243; ISBN: 0-313-25653-5.

MERVIS, C.B.; ROSCH, E. 1981. Categorization of Natural Objects. In: Rosenzweig, Mark R.; Porter, Lyman W., eds. Annual Review of Psychology: Volume 32. Palo Alto, CA: Annual Reviews, Inc.; 1981. 89-115. ISSN: 0066-4308; ISBN: 0-8243-0232-X; LC: 50-13143.

MORRIS, RUTH C.T. 1994. Toward a User-Centered Information Service. Journal of the American Society for Information Science. 1994 January; 45(1): 20-30. ISSN: 0002-8231.

NATH, RAVINDER. 1989. Are Frequent Computer Users More Satisfied? Information Processing & Management. 1989; 25(5): 557-562. ISSN: 0306-4573.

NILAN, MICHAEL S.; PEEK, ROBIN P.; SNYDER, HERBERT W. 1988. A Methodology for Tapping User Evaluation Behaviors: An Exploration of Users' Strategy, Source and Information Evaluating. In: Borgman, Christine L.; Pai, Edward Y.H., eds. ASIS '88: Proceedings of the American Society for Information Science (ASIS) 51st Annual Meeting: Volume 25; 1988 October 23-27; Atlanta, GA. Medford, NJ: Learned Information, Inc. for the American Society for Information Science; 1988. 152-159. ISSN: 0044-7870; ISBN: 0-938734-29-6.

O'BRIEN, ANN. 1990. Relevance as an Aid to Evaluation in OPACs. Journal of Information Science. 1990 Winter; 16(4): 265-271. ISSN: 0165-5515.

O'REILLY, CHARLES A., III. 1980. Variations in Decision Makers' Use of Information Sources: The Impact of Quality and Accessibility of Information. In: Huseman, Richard C., ed. Proceedings of the 40th Annual Meeting of the Academy of Management; 1980 August 9-13; Detroit, MI. [Ada, OH]: Academy of Management; 1980. 183-187. ISSN: 0065-0668; ISBN: 0-915350-19-X.

PAO, MIRANDA LEE. 1993. Term and Citation Retrieval: A Field Study. Information Processing & Management. 1993 January/February; 29(1): 95-112. ISSN: 0306-4573.

PARK, TAEMIN KIM. 1992. The Nature of Relevance in Information Retrieval: An Empirical Study. Bloomington, IN: Indiana University; 1992. 209p. (Ph.D. dissertation). Available from: University Microfilms, Ann Arbor, MI. (UMI order no. 9231644).

PARK, TAEMIN KIM. 1993. The Nature of Relevance in Information Retrieval: An Empirical Study. Library Quarterly. 1993 July; 63(3): 318-351. ISSN: 0024-2519.

PARK, TAEMIN KIM. 1994. Toward a Theory of User-Based Relevance: A Call for a New Paradigm of Inquiry. Journal of the American Society for Information Science. 1994 April; 45(3): 135-141. ISSN: 0002-8231.

PURGAILIS PARKER, LORRAINE M.; JOHNSON, ROBERT E. 1990. Does Order of Presentation Affect Users' Judgment of Documents? Journal of the American Society for Information Science. 1990 October; 41(7): 493-494. ISSN: 0002-8231.

REES, ALAN M. 1966. The Relevance of Relevance to the Testing and Evaluation of Document Retrieval Systems. Aslib Proceedings. 1966 November; 18(11): 316-324. ISSN: 0001-253X.

REES, ALAN M.; SCHULTZ, DOUGLAS G. 1967. A Field Experimental Approach to the Study of Relevance Assessments in Relation to Document Searching: Final Report: Volume I. Cleveland, OH: Case Western Reserve University, School of Library Science, Center for Documentation and Communication Research; 1967. 305p. NTIS: PB 176 080.

REGAZZI, JOHN J. 1988. Performance Measures for Information Retrieval Systems—An Experimental Approach. Journal of the American Society for Information Science. 1988 July; 39(4): 235-251. ISSN: 0002-8231.

REPO, AATTO J. 1989. The Value of Information: Approaches in Economics, Accounting, and Management Science. Journal of the American Society for Information Science. 1989 March; 40(2): 68-85. ISSN: 0002-8231.

ROBERTSON, STEPHEN E. 1981. The Methodology of Information Retrieval Experiment. In: Sparck Jones, Karen, ed. Information Retrieval Experiment. London, England: Butterworths; 1981. 9-31. ISBN: 0-408-10648-4; LC: 80-42222.

ROBERTSON, STEPHEN E. 1993. Retrieval and Relevance: On the Evaluation of IR Systems. Paper presented at: The ISI Lazerow Lecture; 1993 November 11; University of California, Los Angeles. 14p. Available from: the author, Centre for Interactive Systems Research, Department of Information Science, City University, Northampton Square, London EC1V 0HB UK.

ROBERTSON, STEPHEN E.; HANCOCK-BEAULIEU, MICHELINE. 1992. On the Evaluation of IR Systems. Information Processing & Management. 1992 July/August; 28(4): 457-466. ISSN: 0306-4573.

RORVIG, MARK E. 1988. Psychometric Measurement and Information Retrieval. In: Williams, Martha E., ed. Annual Review of Information Science and Technology: Volume 23. Amsterdam, The Netherlands: Elsevier Science Publishers for the American Society for Information Science; 1988. 157-189. ISSN: 0066-4200; ISBN: 0-444-70543-0.

ROSCH, E.; LLOYD, B.B., eds. 1978. Cognition and Categorization. Hillsdale, NJ: Lawrence Erlbaum Associates; 1978. 328p. ISBN: 0-470-26377-6.

ROUSE, WILLIAM B.; ROUSE, SANDRA H. 1984. Human Information Seeking and Design of Information Systems. Information Processing & Management. 1984; 20(1-2): 129-138. ISSN: 0306-4573.

SALTON, GERARD. 1992. The State of Retrieval System Evaluation. Information Processing & Management. 1992; 28(4): 441-449. ISSN: 0306-4573.

SALTON, GERARD; BUCKLEY, CHRIS. 1990. Improving Retrieval Performance by Relevance Feedback. Journal of the American Society for Information Science. 1990 June; 41(4): 288-297. ISSN: 0002-8231.

SANDORE, BETH. 1990. Online Searching: What Measure Satisfaction? Library & Information Science Research. 1990 January-March; 12(1): 33-54. ISSN: 0740-8188.

SARACEVIC, TEFKO. 1970. The Concept of "Relevance" in Information Science: A Historical Review. In: Saracevic, Tefko, ed. Introduction to Information Science. New York, NY: R.R. Bowker; 1970. 111-151. ISBN: 0-8352-0313-1.

SARACEVIC, TEFKO. 1975. Relevance: A Review of and a Framework for the Thinking on the Notion in Information Science. Journal of the American Society for Information Science. 1975 November/December; 26(6): 321-343. ISSN: 0002-8231.

SARACEVIC, TEFKO. 1991. Individual Differences in Organizing, Searching and Retrieving Information. In: Griffiths, José-Marie, ed. ASIS '91: Proceedings of the American Society for Information Science (ASIS) 54th Annual Meeting; Volume 28; 1991 October 27-31; Washington, DC. Medford, NJ: Learned Information, Inc. for the American Society for Information Science; 1991. 82-86. ISSN: 0044-7870; ISBN: 0-938734-56-3.

SARACEVIC, TEFKO; KANTOR, PAUL B. 1988. A Study of Information Seeking and Retrieving. Part II: Users, Questions, and Effectiveness. Journal of the American Society for Information Science. 1988 May; 39(3): 177-196. Part III: Searchers, Searches, and Overlap. Journal of the American Society for Information Science. 1988 May; 39(3): 197-216. ISSN: 0002-8231.

SARACEVIC, TEFKO; KANTOR, PAUL B.; CHAMIS, ALICE Y.; TRIVISON, DONNA. 1988. A Study of Information Seeking and Retrieving. Part I: Background and Methodology. Journal of the American Society for Information Science. 1988 May; 39(3): 161-176. ISSN: 0002-8231.

SARACEVIC, TEFKO; MOKROS, HARTMUT; SU, LOUISE T.; SPINK, AMANDA. 1991. Interaction between Users and Intermediaries in Online Searching. In: Williams, Martha E., ed. Proceedings of the 12th National Online Meeting; 1991 May 7-9: New York, NY. Medford, NJ: Learned Information, Inc.; 1991. 329-341. ISBN: 0-938734-51-2.

SAVOLAINEN, REIJO. 1993. The Sense-Making Theory: Reviewing the Interests of a User-Centered Approach to Information Seeking and Use. Information Processing & Management. 1993; 29(1): 13-28. ISSN: 0306-4573.

SCHAMBER, LINDA. 1991a. Users' Criteria for Evaluation in a Multimedia Environment. In: Griffiths, José-Marie, ed. ASIS '91: Proceedings of the American Society for Information Science (ASIS) 54th Annual Meeting: Volume 28; 1991 October 27-31; Washington, DC. Medford, NJ: Learned Information, Inc. for the American Society for Information Science; 1991. 126-133. ISSN: 0044-7870; ISBN: 0-938734-56-3.

SCHAMBER, LINDA. 1991b. Users' Criteria for Evaluation in Multimedia Information Seeking and Use Situations. Syracuse, NY: Syracuse University; 1991. 327p. (Ph.D. dissertation). Available from: University Microfilms, Ann Arbor, MI. (UMI order no. 9214390).

SCHAMBER, LINDA; EISENBERG, MICHAEL B.; NILAN, MICHAEL S. 1990. A Re-examination of Relevance: Toward a Dynamic, Situational Definition. Information Processing & Management. 1990; 26(6): 755-776. ISSN: 0306-4573.

SCHUTZ, ALFRED. 1970. Reflections on the Problem of Relevance. New Haven, CT: Yale University Press; 1970. 186p. ISBN: 0-300-01221-7; LC: 78-99840.

SPARCK JONES, KAREN. 1981a. Information Retrieval Experiment. London, England: Butterworths; 1981. 352p. ISBN: 0-408-10648-4; LC: 80-42222.

SPARCK JONES, KAREN. 1981b. Retrieval System Tests 1958-1978. [and] The Cranfield Tests. In: Sparck Jones, Karen, ed. Information Retrieval Experiment. London, England: Butterworths; 1981. 213-284. ISBN: 0-408-10648-4; LC: 80-42222.

SPARCK JONES, KAREN. 1988. Fashionable Trends and Feasible Strategies in Information Management. Information Processing & Management. 1988 November/December; 24(6): 703-711. ISSN: 0306-4573.

SPERBER, DAN; WILSON, DEIRDRE. 1986. Relevance: Communication and Cognition. Cambridge, MA: Harvard University Press; 1986. 279p. ISBN: 0-674-75475-1.

SPINK, AMANDA. 1993a. Feedback in Information Retrieval. New Brunswick, NJ: Rutgers, The State University of New Jersey, School of Communication, Information and Library Studies; 1993. 311p. (Ph.D. dissertation). Available from: University Microfilms, Ann Arbor, MI. (UMI order no. 9401925).

SPINK, AMANDA. 1993b. Interaction with Information Retrieval Systems: Reflections on Feedback. See reference: BONZI, SUSAN, ed. 115-121.

SU, LOUISE T. 1991. An Investigation to Find Appropriate Measures for Evaluating Interactive Information Retrieval. New Brunswick, NJ: Rutgers, the State University of New Jersey; 1991. 307p. (Ph.D. dissertation). Available from: University Microfilms, Ann Arbor, MI. (UMI order no. 9125400).

SU, LOUISE T. 1992. Evaluation Measures for Interactive Information Retrieval. Information Processing & Management. 1992 July/August; 28(4): 503-516. ISSN: 0306-4573.

SU, LOUISE T. 1993. Is Relevance an Adequate Criterion for Retrieval System Evaluation: An Empirical Inquiry into the User's Evaluation. See reference: BONZI, SUSAN, ed. 93-103.

SU, LOUISE T. 1994. The Relevance of Recall and Precision in User Evaluation. Journal of the American Society for Information Science. 1994 April; 45(3): 207-217. ISSN: 0002-8231.

SUTTON, STUART A. 1994. The Role of Attorney Mental Models of Law in Case Relevance Determinations: An Exploratory Analysis. Journal of the American Society for Information Science. 1994 April; 45(3): 186-200. ISSN: 0002-8231.

SWANSON, DON RICHARD. 1986. Subjective Versus Objective Relevance in Bibliographic Retrieval Systems. Library Quarterly. 1986 October; 56(4): 389-398. ISSN: 0024-2519.

SWANSON, DON RICHARD. 1988. Historical Note: Information Retrieval and the Future of an Illusion. Journal of the American Society for Information Science. 1988 March; 39(2): 92-98. ISSN: 0002-8231.

SWANSON, E. BURTON. 1987. Information Channel Disposition and Use. Decision Sciences. 1987; 18: 131-145. ISSN: 0011-7315.

TAGLIACOZZO, RENATA. 1977. Estimating the Satisfaction of Information Users. Bulletin of the Medical Library Association. 1977 April; 65(2): 243-248. ISSN: 0025-7338.

TAYLOR, ROBERT S. 1986. Value-Added Processes in Information Systems. Norwood, NJ: Ablex Publishing Corp.; 1986. 257p. ISBN: 0-89391-273-5.

TENOPIR, CAROL. 1992. Is It Any of Our Business? Library Journal. 1992 April 1; 117(6): 96, 98. ISSN: 0363-0277.

TESSIER, JUDITH ANNE. 1981. Toward the Understanding of User Satisfaction: A Multiattribute Study of User Evaluations of Computer-Based Literature Searches in Medical Libraries. Syracuse, NY: Syracuse University, School of Information Studies; 1981. 318p. (Ph.D. dissertation). Available from: University Microfilms, Ann Arbor, MI. (UMI order no. 8212935).

TESSIER, JUDITH ANNE; CROUCH, WAYNE W.; ATHERTON, PAULINE. 1977. New Measures of User Satisfaction with Computer-Based Literature Searches. Special Libraries. 1977 November; 68(11): 383-389. ISSN: 0038-6723.

THOMAS, NANCY P. 1993. Information-Seeking and the Nature of Relevance: Ph.D. Student Orientation as an Exercise in Information Retrieval. See reference: BONZI, SUSAN, ed. 126-130.

TIAMIYU, MUTAWAKILA A.; AJIFERUKE, ISOLA Y. 1988. A Total Relevance and Document Interaction Effects Model for the Evaluation of Information Retrieval Processes. Information Processing & Management. 1988; 24(4): 391-404. ISSN: 0306-4573.

TURNER, MARSHA KAY. 1992. A Study Regarding Information-Seeking Behavior, Valuation of Information Including Perceptions of Information Attributes, and Associated Correlates Pertaining to Information Usage. Tallahassee, FL: Florida State University; 1992. 357p. (Ph.D. dissertation). Available from: University Microfilms, Ann Arbor, MI. (UMI order no. 9222427).

WANG, PEILING. 1994. A Cognitive Model of Document Selection of Real Users of IR Systems. College Park, MD: University of Maryland, College of Library and Information Services; 1994. 232p. (Ph.D. dissertation). Available from: University Microfilms, Ann Arbor, MI.

WILDEMUTH, BARBARA M.; DE BLIEK, RUTH; FRIEDMAN, CHARLES P. 1993. Measures of Searcher Performance: A Psychometric Evaluation. Information Processing & Management. 1993 September/October; 29(5): 533-550. ISSN: 0306-4573.

WILLETT, PETER. 1990. Laboratory Experimentation: An Experimentalist's Viewpoint. In: Bawden, David. User-Oriented Evaluation of Information Systems and Services. Brookfield, VT: Gower; 1990. 180-187. ISBN: 0-566-05209-1.

WILSON, PATRICK. 1973. Situational Relevance. Information Storage and Retrieval. 1973; 9(8): 457-471. ISSN: 0020-0271.

II

Basic Techniques and Technologies

Section II includes three chapters: "Information Retrieval Techniques" by Paul B. Kantor of Rutgers, The State University of New Jersey, "Digital Image Representation and Access" by Javed Mostafa of Indiana University, and "Database Access Systems" by Prudence W. Dalrymple of the American Library Association and Nancy K. Roderer of the Cushing Whitney Medical Library of Yale University.

In his chapter Kantor tells us that information retrieval techniques "reflect a growing effort to implement concept-based retrieval in the automatable regime of content-based algorithms." He traces the appearance of this effort in indexing, retrieval, and interface design and considers briefly the changes in evaluation of IR systems that will be needed to cope with very large dataspaces. He notes that IR has expanded from librarianship into fields such as office automation and multimedia management and that with the current effort toward the development of digital libraries IR has become the key issue of modern librarianship, challenging research in areas as diverse as artificial intelligence, natural-language processing, and the statistical theory of inference.

Kantor identifies the current trends in the automation of indexing, retrieval, and the interaction between systems and users. He identifies three central issues: (1) What does the system do to describe the documents for purposes of retrieval? (2) How does the system compute the degree of match between a given document and the current state of the query? (3) What does the system do with the information that it obtains from the users?

Kantor looks at IR techniques in terms of: location, navigation, and indexing; documents, queries, structures, and concepts; matching documents to queries; restoring query structure; algorithms and content vs. concepts; formulation of concepts in terms of contents; formulation of concepts with the assistance of the users; complex system codes vs. underlying principles; and evaluation of systems.

The first *ARIST* chapter on "Digital Image Representation and Access" by Javed Mostafa begins by presenting data on imaging literature that demonstrate the diversity of the field. He then explains basic terms and concepts related to image representation and describes the differences between bilevel, grayscale, and color images. He introduces the reader to additional image related data, specifically color standards, correction values, resolution parameters, and look-up tables. He illustrates how compression can aid in better image representation and covers the widely applied compression techniques, both lossless and lossy. He covers the numerous image data formats that have been devised for different hardware and software platforms and summarizes the basic differences in formats regarding encoding, compression, resolution, supporting platforms, and standards. More in-depth treatment is given to the formats: TIFF, JPEG, HDF, PostScript, and QuickTime "MooV".

Mostafa identifies four branches of imaging research related to data indexing and modeling: verbal indexing, visual surrogates, image indexing, and data structures. Because user interfaces directly determine the means and the effectiveness of IR, he discusses these with special attention to both general design techniques and image retrieval techniques and treats query language design in this context. He concludes by discussing the state of the art in networking technology with consideration of image distribution, local system requirements and data integrity.

Prudence W. Dalrymple and Nancy K. Roderer review the status of "Database Access Systems," putting emphasis on end-user access to databases. Their review covers largely the period from 1987, when CD-ROM systems were beginning to make an impact on libraries, through 1993, as locally mounted database systems and Internet access to databases came into play. While they use the terms "end user" and "intermediary," they note that the distinction is coming to have less meaning. In their chapter they explore recent developments in databases, access channels, and interfaces to the systems in order to demonstrate the magnitude of the changes that have taken place and show the effect of the changes on database selection, library management, economics, and use and users.

Recent developments in databases have seen an increase in databases targeted toward the end user and those with software features making them easy to use for the application intended. With respect to access channels the biggest change has been an increase in telecommunications capabilities and options and especially the increased use and availability of the Internet. Advances in interface design include improvements in screen design, retrieval engines together with the command structures, and the search features.

Database selection has been the subject of numerous studies as discussed by Dalrymple and Roderer, and they note that as the use of the Internet grows and the resources made available on the net grow, the problems regarding database selection will become much larger and less tractable. Library management continues to face the problem of bibliographic access, but the options are far more numerous because databases are available in many different forms and on different media. Choices cannot be made solely on the basis of need or economics; many more variables are relevant, and the new products involve librarians in training users to conduct their own searches. The economic issues involve database service pricing by vendors and costing and cost comparisons by the users. As Dalrymple and Roderer discuss use and users, they look at who uses databases and when, how the users conduct their searches, and the question of evaluating the outcome of the search process.

While the chapter reviews many research activities dealing with database access, the authors note that most of the research has dealt with bibliographic databases and much more work is needed to learn about the search process as it relates to full-text, numeric, image, and multimedia databases.

2 Information Retrieval Techniques

PAUL B. KANTOR
Rutgers, The State University of
New Jersey

INTRODUCTION

Information retrieval (IR) technique stands today at a crossroads. Originally an outgrowth of librarianship, it has expanded into fields such as office automation, genome databases, fingerprint identification, medical image management, knowledge finding in databases, and multimedia management. Now with the national emphasis on digital libraries, it stands as the key issue of modern librarianship and challenges research in areas as diverse as artificial intelligence (AI), natural-language processing, and the statistical theory of inference. By "digital library" we mean the ensemble consisting of (1) a collection of texts, images, or data in digitized form; (2) a set of systems for indexing and navigating or retrieving in that collection; and (3) one or more defined communities of users. I propose that the global internetworked set of such libraries be thought of as "The Digital Library." This review aims to identify the current trends in the automation of indexing, of retrieval, and of the interaction between the systems and the users. The central issues are: (1) what the system does to describe the documents for purposes of retrieval; (2) how the system computes the degree of

---

This paper has been influenced by almost everyone with whom I have discussed information retrieval over many years, in particular Richard Blankenbecler, Abraham Bookstein, and William Cooper, and, at Rutgers, Nicholas Belkin and Tefko Saracevic. One cannot review this literature without being struck by the prescience of Hans Peter Luhn and by the enormous impact of Gerry Salton and, more recently, Bruce Croft. Parts of this work were done during a visit at the University of Michigan School of Information and Library Studies, during fall 1993.

Annual Review of Information Science and Technology (*ARIST*), Volume 29, 1994
Martha E. Williams, Editor
Published for the American Society for Information Science (ASIS)
By Learned Information, Inc., Medford, N.J.

match between a given document and the current state of the query; and (3) what the system does with the information it obtains from the users.

There are a number of general sources. BELKIN & CROFT have last reviewed information retrieval in *ARIST*. FRAKES & BAEZA-YATES cover a range of issues, several more technical than those covered here. HARMAN (1992; 1993a) reports on the TRECs (Text REtrieval Conferences), which present the state of the art for some two dozen systems that all undertook retrieval from some 750,000 documents for a set of 100 preassigned topics or problems. HEAPS addresses some computational aspects of IRT. The INTERNATIONAL ORGANIZATION FOR STANDARDIZATION (ISO) presents the important Standard Generalized Markup Language (SGML), which serves to let an algorithm identify conceptual slots for concepts, such as title, author, personal name, etc., in a machine-readable document. PEARL is an important source on the general question of probabilistic reasoning, which is having a strong impact on the interpretation of current algorithms.

In this review I describe matching algorithms in terms of what they calculate, avoiding a discussion of why the designers have chosen to calculate in this way. This reflects my view that the proof of a theoretical formulation can be found only in the performance of the algorithms that are realizing that formulation and not in the formulation's self-evidence or rhetorical strength. ROBERTSON ET AL. (1982) have integrated several probabilistic approaches. An excellent source for the basic concepts of probability theory itself is FELLER. The classic source for Bayesian analysis and inference remains LINDLEY. A more recent source on the same issues is VAN DER GAAG.

SALTON remains a classic which deserves study by anyone new to the field. Some additional material is added in SALTON & MCGILL, reflecting the advance of the field during that period. SPARCK JONES is an important source for understanding how the conventions of this field have arisen. More recently, STANFILL & WALTZ surveyed a number of approaches. TAGUE ET AL. offer a formal model of an IR system. Other models, either explicit or implicit, can be found in the works of most of the authors cited here. VAN RIJSBERGEN (1979) remains an important source for some of the probabilistic and Bayesian arguments.

In preparing this review the most recent conference proceedings proved to be the richest sources. In addition to the TREC conferences already mentioned, the annual conferences of the Association for Computing Machinery Special Interest Group on Information Retrieval (ACM SIGIR) are excellent sources; the most recent is the 1993 meeting (KORFHAGE ET AL.). The *JOURNAL OF THE AMERICAN SOCIETY FOR INFORMATION SCIENCE* and the independent journal *INFORMATION PROCESSING AND MANAGEMENT* are the leading current resources. Other relevant work is widely scattered, as reflected in the bibliography. In selecting articles I have tried to represent the major themes currently important in the development of information retrieval technique at the expense of omitting many interesting papers.

LOCATION, NAVIGATION, AND INDEXING

Libraries, Catalogs, and Databases

In a classical library a book is in one place, collocated by author and subject, insofar as the book can be assigned a primary subject and a single author. To compensate for this loss of accessibility, libraries maintain a set of catalogs (author, title, subject, shelf list, authority files) to increase the chance of a user's being able to locate a needed book without having to examine (even superficially) every book in the library. It is well known in librarianship that this application of mixed controlled (subject headings) and free (title words) access both aids and confounds the readers. Controlled vocabulary, with all its power, relies on the user's ability to speak the same language as the indexers. The IR technique problem is to create in cyberspace the benefits that location and examination of documents provide in physical space.

The first contribution of the computer is that all of the contents of all of the several catalogs can be read by the computer and can be indexed both by their tagged fields and as free text. This permits a user to find all records that have "history" as a controlled descriptor or as a term in the title or in a note field. A full inverted file, in which each posting for a term is accompanied by a "document ID," and field or other tag information as well as position information, supports complex Boolean searches and proximity searches. In the final analysis, the results are pointers to the true information-bearing materials. The materials still must be "physically fetched." However, there is some work on OPACs (online public access catalogs) that is conceptually relevant for IR in general, and it is mentioned below as needed.

The next level of development is the bibliographic database, which typically contains citation information, descriptor and keyword fields, and the full text of an abstract. If we regard these abstracts as the documents of the database, we see that they are not located in one particular place as far as the user is concerned. In a sense the abstract is "located" in a cyberspace, at *all* the points through which it can be accessed.

We are accustomed to thinking of the bibliographic database as an access tool, but it is in fact the prototype of the digital library. It has been treated that way ever since the experiments by CLEVERDON, in which the performance of a retrieval system was judged on the basis of the abstracts retrieved, without reference to the real documents (see also CLEVERDON ET AL.).

Digital Libraries and Ideal Retrieval

Whatever is meant by a digital library (LUNIN & FOX; as this chapter is being prepared, numerous conferences on digital libraries are being scheduled for 1994), it is clear that its contents, like the abstracts in a database, are located anywhere in cyberspace that the user can find them. Further, just as users cannot look at every book in a conventional library, so they cannot look at every retrievable document in a digital library.

The central role of IR techniques is to bring this potentially suffocating quantity of information under control and make it available to the immediate users and to the world at large. To do this, IRT should ideally produce results similar to those that would be achieved if the users could scan all retrievable documents and rank them in order of usefulness. The possible results of such an (impossible) scanning may have a very complicated structure. For example, there might be nonoverlapping heaps, each labeled "if I can have this, I don't need anything more;" there would be an enormous heap labeled "not interesting"; and there might be overlapping heaps, ranked lists, and so on. Information retrieval as practiced today simplifies this problem by assuming that every retrievable item is either "relevant" or "not relevant" (for further information on relevance see SCHAMBER). This consists of the weak assertion that relevance is binary and the strong assertion that relevance is a property of documents in isolation, unaffected by the other documents that have been retrieved. The weak assertion is easily corrected using a fractional indicator of relevance. The strong assertion is not easily corrected in present systems.

Thus, of the whole complex structure that the (impossible) scan of a complex dataspace might reveal, current IRT concentrates on reproducing the ranked lists of documents, with the more relevant ones ranked closer to the top. We note that a Boolean (set) retrieval is a very weak form of ranked list, in which all the retrieved documents are given one rank (call it "1") and all the other documents are given another rank (call it "2"). With these restrictions, IRT seeks to make this ranked list perform as well as possible.

DOCUMENTS, QUERIES, STRUCTURES, AND CONCEPTS

The evolution of IRT, from the classical library to present research, may be viewed as an effort to first move away from concept-based indexing and then to move back toward it with content-based algorithms. In a sense the issue is whether knowledge of the contents of a document takes the place of knowledge of its concepts.

A document (in its entirety rather than as represented by its abstract) has in it both concepts and a conceptual structure. There are relationships among the concepts present in the document, and often those relationships are the essential meaning of the document. The relationships are what must be preserved under paraphrase in order for us to believe that the document has been "understood." Representation of the conceptual structures is being pursued under the general title of "fact retrieval" or "message understanding." The most widely used method is a frame-based approach. In this approach the set of conceptual relations is schematized, and the instances of concepts (actors, objects) for the present document are labeled by the slot in the frame which they seem to fill. This topic is outside of the scope of this review.

When we set aside the structure, a document may be thought of as a "sack of concepts" or set of concepts. These concepts no longer have specific roles to play or specific relationships to each other. They have become in fact a set of "labels." Historically, indexers translate these labels into the language of some controlled vocabulary. The words of that vocabulary are in turn assigned as indicators of the content. This could be expressed numerically as:

$$Ind(d, c) = \begin{cases} 1 \text{ if concept } c \text{ describes document } d \\ 0 \text{ otherwise} \end{cases}$$

The index file contains entries labeled by the various values of *c* (the concept), and the postings for that entry are precisely the pointers to the documents for which the relationship *Ind* has the value 1.

The relationship *Ind* can be thought of as defining a table or matrix, and each entry in that table can be anything at all so long as it is determined only by the document and the concept. Typically we think of entering some numerical indication of the degree to which the concept describes the document. We ought not at this point enter anything that is dependent on the entire corpus of documents or on the entire universe of concepts. To do so would destroy the locality of the definition. Such nonlocal concepts (the so-called inverse document frequency is a prime example) can be introduced at retrieval time without loss of generality. Related discussions are given by FUHR (1992). PAICE & JONES offer a different view, in which structure is maintained. A formal model for IR systems is given by TAGUE ET AL.

The basic event for analyzing the workings of an IR system is the retrieval instance. An instance is characterized by the presence at the system of a user with a single coherent (possibly complex) need or problem of some kind such that the user (at least) is able to decide whether a retrieved item helps to solve that problem. Our knowledge of this situation, and in particular the inputs governing the behavior of the system, are limited to the utterances of the user. However, the user draws on a rich understanding of the situation to form such utterances as "document A is not relevant" or "I'm interested in rocket science."

In any specific retrieval instance, the information need will at first be represented by a query statement. When such a statement is "processed" by a human interpreter, it yields a structure and a (very small) set of concepts. When the structure is removed, each query may be represented as a set of numbers, which can be thought of as the degree to which each of several concepts is present in or implied by that query.

MATCHING DOCUMENTS TO QUERIES

When two sets of numbers refer to the same index set, the set of concepts, they can be treated as the components of an abstract vector. In particular, an inner product can be calculated. This inner product can be taken as an indicator of the match between a specific document and a specific query.

$$\text{Match } (d, q) = \sum_{\text{concepts } c} d(c)q(c)$$

We have switched from the more complex notation $Ind(d,c)$ to the more compact $d(c)$. In this notation c labels a specific concept, and d is somewhat overworked since it stands for the document whose label is d. It can be called a "document vector in concept space." In the same way, $q(c)$ represents the degree to which the concept c is "called for" by the query q.

In practice, the vectors d, q may have to be normalized to correct for the difference between documents with many concepts and those with few. In fact, as discussed below, most systems label the components of the vectors by terms, but they intend to label concepts, and we continue to use the character c in this part of the discussion. For another perspective on the representation of concepts, see HEARST (1993a; 1993b). For more detail on vector space modeling see WONG ET AL. (1987). For a description in the language of probabilistic indexing (which seeks to assess the probability that assigning concept c to document d would be effective), see FUHR (1989b).

Weight of Concepts

In principle, finding matches with regard to some concepts may be more important than finding matches with regard to others. This can be represented mathematically by introducing a weight into the sum. The weight can also be thought of as a table whose nonzero elements lie only on the diagonal.

$$\text{Match}\ (d, q) = \Sigma_{\text{concepts}\ c}\ d(c)W(c)q(c)$$

or

$$\text{Match}\ (d, q) = \Sigma_{\text{concepts}\ c,c'}\ d(c)W(c,c')q(c')$$

with

$$W(c, c') = 0 \text{ if } c \neq c'.$$

The problem of choosing weights for terms so that retrieval works well is discussed by SALTON & BUCKLEY (1988). The problem of choosing those weights so that documents are ranked in the best order and at the same time the relevant fraction is predicted is considered by COOPER ET AL. See also FUHR (1989a; 1990), FUHR & BUCKLEY, and FUHR ET AL. For an application of the probabilistic indexing ideas, in the context of selecting an optimal indexing and weighting, see FUHR & BUCKLEY.

Relations between Concepts

In principle concepts may be related to each other, either in general, in a specific domain, or perhaps only in the case of a specific query. Such relations can be set out in a thesaurus and can be represented by tables of numbers $T(c, c')$ whose entries indicate the degree to which the concepts are related to each other. In principle a standard thesaurus gives rise to several different tables, which can be labeled by the type of relation ("see also"; "related concept"; the pair of relations: "broader/narrower concept" can be represented together in a single table).

The entries of this table can be inserted into the sum defining the match:

$$\text{Match}\ (d, q) = \sum_{\text{concepts}\ c,c',\ c''} d(c)W(c, c')T(c,c'')q(c'').$$

In short, the idea of matching a query to a document, when both are thought of as sets of concepts, can be well represented by linear expressions which can be thought of as operations on (suitably normalized) vectors in some abstract space. We may say that the vector q is transformed through a matrix multiplication to:

$$q \rightarrow q' = WTq.$$

When training data are available (i.e., documents of known relevance), the problem of designing an IR system may be restated as:

what choice of *WT* works best for a specific query q at discriminating the documents whose relevance is known? This may be thought of as finding the best q' for each specific q or as the more general problem of handling all q at once (see discussions in WONG ET AL. (1987) and WONG & YAO). The general discrimination problem can be treated by linear programming (along the lines discussed by MANGASARIAN). When it is cast in quadratic form, the method of YANG & CHUTE results. For a theoretical framing in terms of a general probabilistic model, see BOOKSTEIN. For an extension to nonlinear (polynomial) functions involving the *tf* and *idf* measures, see FUHR (1989b). Another perspective is found in ROBERTSON ET AL. (1994) who use an intractable formal model to suggest specific term weighting formulae.

RESTORING QUERY STRUCTURE

Under the influence of Boolean-based online retrieval systems, users of retrieval systems have learned to formulate queries with a modest logical structure. Typically this takes the form of the conjunction (or intersection, or logical *AND*) of several parts, each of which is a disjunction (union, logical *OR*) of its own components. Each of these components could be a concept. Similar concepts (really, substitutable concepts) are banded together in the parts, and some representative of each must be present in the whole. This may be represented as

$$\text{Structure}\,(q \mid c_1, \ldots c_m) = \bigcap_{\text{subparts of } q} \left[\bigcup_{c_i\, \varepsilon\, \text{subpart}} c_i \right].$$

When the relation of a document to a concept takes only the values 1 and 0, these logical operations are easily represented mathematically. There are several ways to extend those representations to relations that take values between 0 and 1. Without going into the rationale for developing each of them, we summarize them below.

All of these methods respect DeMorgan's rules relating unions and intersections, that the complement of the intersection is the union of the complements. One retains the other key properties of Boolean algebra, while the other two do not (see also BOOKSTEIN; KANTOR (1981)). For a different approach, based on object-oriented query languages, see BERTINO ET AL. CHIARAMELLA & NIE consider an alternative approach based on modal logics. JACOBS ET AL. (1993) consider a Boolean approximation method. LEE ET AL. discuss evaluation of Boolean operators and structural relations. PRADE & TESTEMALE consider generalizing database algebra to deal with vagueness in query representation. SCHÄUBLE (1993) considers dynamic variation in the data structures and its impact on query formulation.

Fuzzy-Set Representations

Fuzzy subset theory (ZADEH) replaces the Boolean notion that an object either does or does not belong to a set with the notion of a generalized membership function, which can assume any value between 0 and 1. A fuzzy subset S of a set of elements $\{x \varepsilon X\}$ is defined by a membership function:

$$0 \leq f_S(x) \leq 1.$$

If $f_s(x) = 1$, we say that x is definitely in S, and if $f_s(x) = 0$, we say that it is definitely not in S. The operations of union and intersection have been defined for fuzzy sets by the rules:

$$f_{S \cap T}(x) = \min_{x \varepsilon X} \{f_S(x), f_T(x)\}$$
$$f_{S \cup T}(x) = \max_{x \varepsilon X} \{f_S(x), f_T(x)\}.$$

A structured query can then be interpreted by transforming each term of the query to the corresponding one-component vector in concept space, calculating all of the similarity measures using W and T and computing the score overall according to the rules of fuzzy logic.

For example (neglecting for the moment the possibility of off-diagonal effects), we can calculate the fuzzy logic value of the similarity of the query:

$$q = fish \cap (oil \cup scales)$$

and a document d as:

$$Sim\ (q, d{:}\ FL) = \min\{d\ (fish), \max\{d(oil), d(scales)\}\}$$

BUCKLES & PETRY discuss the use of fuzzy concepts in databases. NEGOITA is a source on fuzzy sets and expert systems generally. OGAWA ET AL. (1991) apply fuzzy concepts to document retrieval, and H.-J. ZIMMERMAN is a general source on fuzzy-set theory.

Product-Based Representations

These combine two measures of relatedness according to the rules (here f_z represents the match of some specific document to the concept z):

$$f_{x\ AND\ y} = f_x f_y$$
$$f_{x\ OR\ y} = 1 - (1 - f_x)(1 - f_y)$$

This really calculates the *OR* function from the *AND* function by DeMorgan's rules. In practice (CROFT ET AL., 1991; TURTLE) the strict product penalizes absent terms too heavily. This can be prevented by adjusting the definition of f_x so that it ranges from, say 0.3 to 1. For more on the development of this inference scheme in information retrieval see TURTLE & CROFT (1991; 1992) and CROFT ET AL. (1991).

Sum-Based Representations: *p*-Norms

The *p*-Norm rules combine two measures of the match between a document and a concept according to the rules:

$$f_{x\,OR\,y} = \frac{1}{2^{1/p}} (f_x^p + f_y^p)^{1/p}$$

$$f_x = 1 - f_x$$

$$f_{x\,AND\,y} = 1 - f_{\bar{x}\,OR\,\bar{y}}$$

When $p = 1$, the rule for *OR* is the same as a linear combination. In a typical application, values of p are between 1 and 2. If p becomes very large, this rule approaches the fuzzy-set rule. Again the DeMorgan relation is respected, but this time *OR* is taken as fundamental, and *AND* is computed. As for the product form, it is found (FOX & SHAW) that better performance is obtained when f is restricted, typically to the range 0.5–1.0. This approach to modeling structure was developed by FOX.

Numerical Methods, Structured Queries, and Sets of Concepts

Using any of these three approaches, one may convert a query in, for example, the form:

$$\text{query} = \bigcap_{\text{parts}} \Big(\bigcup_{concepts\ \varepsilon\ part} \text{concepts} \Big)$$

into a numerical expression of the match between a given document, described by the numbers $d(c)$, and the query as shown here. The indicated operations are simply applied to the numbers representing the importance of each of the concepts in the document. In this fashion, numerically based methods can encompass the fundamental Boolean operations.

In sum, we see that by admitting a fairly complex linear structure and then embellishing it with selected extensions to represent the residual structure of a query, the representation of documents as vectors labeled by the concepts, and of queries as structures of concepts, can support a rich program of retrieval. We note that this kind of matching scheme, which we have expressed in terms of linear algebra and slight nonlinear generalizations, can be arrived at from a variety of theoretical perspectives, such as natural-language concepts, probabilistic or statistical retrieval, and frame-based reasoning. In fact, most of the methods have been applied directly to terms rather than to concepts. We now consider what happens when the concepts are no longer assumed to be known.

ALGORITHMS AND CONTENT VS. CONCEPTS

The algorithms that process a text for retrieval can be said to "know" the terms in that text with near certainty. In English (or European languages generally), for example, a term corresponds at first to a word. That is, a term is anything delimited by white space or punctuation. In some approaches (recently, CAVNAR) terms are defined arbitrarily as *n–grams* of characters. This approach sacrifices all prior knowledge of the meaning of terms. FUJII & CROFT report that 1–*grams*, i.e., character-based retrieval, works nearly as well as word-based retrieval for Japanese texts and is computationally easier. On the other hand, phrases such as "health care" could be seen as terms in a more general sense. Such noun phrases are difficult to incorporate in indexes because there are so many of them.

Whether terms are identified with words, with *n–grams*, or with phrases, the processing of both the query and the retrievable documents follows the same lines as those described in our discussion of concepts, but instead of indexing the weights and relations by *c*, representing "concepts," we are forced to index them by *t*, representing *terms that actually appear in the text of the document or the query*. Because they are present in the text, we call them the "contents" of the text as opposed to the concepts which are intended or perceived by a human agent.

Preprocessing is a step in extracting concepts from contents. Older methods of preprocessing a document replace all words by their uppercase forms and replace many words by their stems. Finally, a list of common words (the stop words) are often not indexed, although they may be counted as place holders in determining the position of words. All of this helps to focus on the concepts that the words represent without regard to the specific morphological variants (i.e., forms) in which they appear. We mention that the indexing of a text in this way can consume an enormous amount of space as phrases and word combinations are added to the inverted file. A compression scheme to alleviate this problem is suggested by LINOFF & STANFILL.

FORMULATING CONCEPTS IN TERMS OF CONTENTS

The linear formulation discussed above is the famous vector method incorporated in the SMART system and its descendants. Documents are represented by vectors whose elements are related to the frequency with which terms appear in them, and queries are expressed on the same basis. Certain basic principles had already been proposed by LUHN (1959) prior to the development of the SMART system. The most important are: (1) the degree to which the document and the term are related should increase as the frequency of the term in the document increases (the term frequency or *tf* principle); and (2) the usefulness of a term in discriminating among documents should decrease as the number of documents in which it appears increases (the inverse document frequency, or *idf* principle). While *tf* is a strictly local concept, *idf* is a corpus-based concept. In the simplest interpretations, the sum defining the match contains terms corresponding to the terms in a query, and each term involves the product $d(t)W(t)$ for some t which appears in the query. Hence such methods are generically referred to as *tf.idf* methods.

Some recent work (COOPER ET AL.; FUHR, 1989b) asks whether systematic search in a space of alternate formulas for *tf*, for *idf*, and for the product leads to improved retrieval performance. Of course, expanding the range of alternatives can improve performance, and the results are not yet definitive. (As noted, COOPER ET AL. ask whether some combinations of the variables can predict the fraction of a document, in a given range of the ranking, that will be judged relevant to the problem at hand. This does not bear on the ranking problem per se but is of interest in the development of theoretical models (ROBERTSON ET AL., 1982) regarding that fraction). TONG & APPELBAUM seek to define term weights based on the classificatory power of specific query terms, as determined from a training set of documents. The definition of power is based on the concept of Classification Analysis with Regression Trees (CART). It is somewhat like the development of optimal strategies for a sequential binary choice game such as Twenty Questions.

Term Refinement

In addition to this work, which seeks to fine tune the general *tf.idf* concept, there is much work on restoring the conceptual dimension to a system that processes text strictly in terms of its content. The problem of disambiguation is important. The same character string, for example, "bank" has quite a different meaning in a discussion of flight vs. a discussion of finance. In effect, a single term is resolved into several different terms which have different weights and different relations to other terms. There is a consensus that human readers disambiguate these cases by using the surrounding text to establish a context (see VORHEES ET AL. for further discussion). A discussion in the context of inference-based retrieval is given by KROVETZ & CROFT.

Stemming as a Relation between Terms

Stemming can be represented by direct conflation in the postings (that is, all trace of the morphology is destroyed in building the table of document–term relations), or it can be represented by off-diagonal weights $W(t, t') = 1$. The latter has the same effect as far as computation of the match between documents and queries, but the issue of weighting terms must be considered in more detail. For example, consider the popular "inverse document frequency" weighting scheme,

$$W(t, t') = \ln \left(\frac{|\,Document\ Set\,|}{|\,Set\ (t\ is\ in\ the\ document)\,|} \right).$$

If stemming is done first, this will include all variant forms of the term. (In this equation $|\,Set\,|$ represents the number of elements in the set.) To accomplish the same effect if stemming is implemented through the off-diagonal weight matrix, the calculation must include a count of all of the documents in which the related terms appear, and to preserve the same meaning, this must refer to the union of the several sets. This is a more complex calculation, although there is no difficulty in principle.

Terms, Proximity, and Concepts

Even systems that are Boolean, in the sense that they retrieve sets without ranking them, admit more than just Boolean operations on the set of terms. First, they admit and use predefined conceptual entities by permitting the user to specify that a search be confined to the title, keywords, and so on. The rapid development of markup languages, which identify the parts of a text in a machine-readable way, greatly facilitates the automation of text processing for retrieval (see, for example, GOLDFARB). Second, for the reconstruction of concepts from free text, they admit proximity operators. Typical are the DIALOG operators $t(nW)\ t'$ and $t(nN)\ t'$.

The first operator specifies that there be no more than n terms between t and t' and that they be in the specified order; the second does not require the specified order. Given the linguistic conventions of English, this tool lets the system move a long way toward the representation of concepts by terms. In particular, it brings together essential ingredients of a phrase (the open-class words) while the remaining parts of the phrase may be an array of closed-class words or "boiler plate" unique to the author's style and point of view.

These are relations among terms that are expressed only at search time and calculated explicitly during retrieval. Insofar as I know, no system indexes text by such proximity relationships. M. ZIMMERMAN discusses proximity correlation. In all the cases considered here the relations among terms are defined by the user at retrieval time.

More Complex Relations among Terms: Corpus-Independent Case

The corpus-independent approach to developing term–term relationships requires study of the lexicon of the underlying language in which the documents are written. The approaches range from thesaurus construction to natural-language processing. Efforts in this direction (VOORHEES) have used the WordNet (MILLER ET AL., 1990a, 1990b) semantic network structure as a basis. Results to date have not been as successful as hoped, and it has been suggested that the specificity of relationships required cannot be found in a universal network of term–term relations. If so, further improvement along these lines will require the development of domain-specific networks of term–term relations corresponding to the underlying concepts of the domains. This is akin to the widespread finding in AI that the solution to a specific problem requires development of domain-specific intelligence. Other papers that address the issue of domain-independent term–term relations include those by EVANS & LEFFERTS, JACOBS ET AL. (1991), KROVETZ (1992), and LESK.

Formulating Term–Term Relations with the Aid of the Corpus

If universal term–term nets (or semantic nets) approach the issue of extracting concepts from one side, we may say that corpus-specific methods approach it from the other. These methods suppose that the corpus already represents only one domain. They seek to build relations among terms from the co-occurrence of terms within documents. Returning to the fundamental matrix *Ind(d,t)*, note that while the rows of this matrix or table represent "document vectors," the columns are vectors representing the terms. Thus, various metric schemes similar to those for expressing the relations between documents and queries may be used to express relations between terms and terms. One natural form for the term–term matrix is:

$$T(t, t') = \sum_{d \,\varepsilon\, corpus} Ind(d, t) Ind(d, t')$$

More complex formulations might give documents different weights, based on, for example, the number of terms occurring in them. In general, one would expect documents containing many terms to yield more spurious relations among terms, and might wish to assign them a lower weight. In addition to some works cited earlier, VAN RIJSBERGEN (1977) discusses a theoretical basis for some of this work (see also CAN & OZKARAHAN (1987; 1990) and PEAT & WILLETT). For a natural-language perspective, see STRZALKOWSKI & PEREZ CARBALLO. WONG ET AL. (1993) consider the computation of term associations by neural network methods.

Reducing the Dimension of the Concept Space

Since the dimension of the term space is very large, the term–term relations can also be used to reduce the dimensionality of this space. This is conceptually similar to principal component analysis or factor analysis in statistics. Such approaches are best illustrated by the Latent Semantic Analysis of DEERWESTER ET AL. and DUMAIS. Essentially a matrix such as $T(t, t')$ is analyzed to find a space of lower dimension that contains most of the significant parts of the matrix. The corresponding axes in the original term space deserve to be called concepts even if we cannot name or label those concepts in natural language alone.

Another way to reduce the dimension of the concept space is to use adaptive classification techniques that do not rely on linear operations. The Kohonen feature map (GALLANT ET AL.) is a technique to develop a few vectors that describe a much larger number of objects. The vectors are constrained to lie on some surface in the original space and are adjusted so that they are near the original entities (e.g., the concepts) and also are not too close to each other. This latter condition is met by imposing a so-called "conscience" mechanism which effectively causes the vectors to repel each other if they get too close. The resulting concept vectors can then be used to support a classification of documents and queries, as suggested in the first part of this chapter. For another perspective, see TZERAS & HARTMANN and YANG & CHUTE.

Reducing the Cardinality of the Document Space: Clustering

Rather than use the $Ind(d, t)$ table to define a relation among the terms, one could use it to define a relation among the documents:

$$U(d, d') = \sum_{t\ \varepsilon\ \textit{inverted file}} Ind(d, t)\, Ind(d', t).$$

Any relation of this kind may be used to group the documents into so-called document clusters. The most intellectually satisfying but computationally intensive approach is to define clusters, all of whose members have a specified level of similarity to one another. In this regard, WILLETT remains an important source. For an introduction to clustering, see KAUFMAN & ROUSSEEUW. These clusters may then be represented by either a selected specific document vector or by the average of all of the vectors corresponding to documents in the cluster. The issues of how to build clusters, which vectors to include, and when to draw the boundary have been with IR from the beginning (ROCCHIO).

Clusters of documents, like clusters of terms, represent concepts. While each document no doubt contains many concepts, the cluster will rank some concepts more highly (e.g., because they appear in more of the documents). Thus, although a cluster may not represent a specific concept, it is more specific in concept space than is an individual document. Recent discussions of issues related to clustering are given by BOTAFOGO and by FULLER ET AL.

FORMULATING CONCEPTS WITH THE ASSISTANCE OF THE USERS

In concert with the development of algorithms to find concepts in texts, there is a major thrust to enlist the user in the real-time definition of concepts. This draws on the (often unstated) realization that the user possesses a more powerful mechanism for scanning, reasoning, and evaluating than any mechanism the program could provide.

Hence, the best system, at least for now, will have a Person in The Loop (PiTL). The issue is to find the best ways to extract useful information from the person and to find the best ways to use that information in iterated retrieval. Methods under investigation include: (1) iconic and graphic metaphors for collections of items (ROSE ET AL.); (2) efforts to represent the links among concepts or documents that are stored within the machine; (3) thumbnail representation of the graphics within a document; and (4) representation of title page layout to ease the user's scanning process (HOFFMAN ET AL.).

The twofold challenge of the PiTL idea is: (1) to tell the user what the system has found so that the user's feedback is really helpful, and (2) to incorporate the user's feedback in a way that improves performance. General papers dealing with these issues include those by AGOSTI ET AL., ANICK, FURNAS ET AL., and HARMAN (1988). A review of gateway devices is given by EFTHIMIADIS (1990).

Automatic Summarization and Theme Sentence Extraction

Automatic summarization by extraction of key sentences (LUHN, 1958, 1959; SALTON & BUCKLEY, 1991a, 1991b; SALTON ET AL., 1993) and by explicit formulation of sentences (MCKEOWN; MCKEOWN ET AL.) provides a way for the system to describe the dataspace to the user. This helps the PiTL to navigate and to clarify the information need. The scatter/gather approach (CUTTING ET AL., 1992, 1993) tries to move the user through successive layers of query refinement by offering titles or phrases typical of a subset of the documents and following the user's selections. All of these can be seen as different ways to make the user a more effective component of the retrieval system and help the user to refine and express the concepts of the query in paths that the system can use. FOX ET AL. trace the evolution of the interactive approach in the setting of an online catalog.

Relevance Feedback and Query Expansion

Research on putting the user in the loop includes study of the weights to attach to terms in the documents that a user finds relevant. This is a difficult area since the value of a single term may not be a definable concept. That is, the effects of terms are generally seen in combination, and we cannot say that each of the components of the combination has a value of its own unless we know how those values combine to achieve retrieval. Pursuing this issue takes us deep into probabilistic retrieval. Roughly, it is known that under term-independence assumptions or maximum-entropy assumptions, there will be (in a specific logistic sense) a value attributable to each term appearing in the collection (KANTOR, 1984), but the assumptions of these models are not yet verified. There are not yet satisfactory studies of the joint distribution of terms in the subsets *G* (good or relevant) and *B* (bad or not relevant) of documents for a set of queries. However, the large TREC collections could support an ambitious study of these issues. The essential issues of relevance feedback today are: (1) given that a document is judged relevant, how should the weights, the query vector, or both be changed in a vectorial formulation; and (2) if the system admits structured queries originally, can the feedback information be incorporated into the structure, or must it be treated in a different way from the original information?

Note that end-user retrieval and mediated retrieval often incorporate new information into a semi-Boolean structure by adding synonyms as they are found in early retrievals or by introducing negation to block unwanted documents including unwanted terms. An early study of the effect of query expansion is found in SMEATON & VAN RIJSBERGEN. Recent papers dealing with the issues of query revision, in technical terms, include those by EFTHIMIADIS (1993), PEDERSEN, ROBERTSON, and ROBERTSON ET AL. (1986). The relation of the query expansion to a concept space is discussed by QIU & FREI. HAINES & CROFT explore relevance feedback in the inference network framework (discussed earlier).

COMPLEX SYSTEM CODES VS. UNDERLYING PRINCIPLES

Like computer codes in other areas of science and engineering, the cutting-edge retrieval codes have been built up over years of modification by large teams of scientists and programmers. The result is that a program is not adequately characterized by an enumeration of its design principles. Another system, adhering to the same principles, may perform quite differently.

Examples of the areas in which undocumented program differences arise are: (1) choice of the dimension to which some space is to be reduced; (2) selection of the conscience parameters for a Kohonen algorithm; (3) selection of the interval within which "document frequency parameters" are allowed to vary; (4) specific choice of stemming rules and stop lists; and (5) hand built sets of terms to represent concepts.

Each of these choices has an effect on the performance of the system, but systems are so complex and the space of options so large that there is little chance of isolating the effect of any one choice. In practice, systems are run, bugs are tracked down and eliminated, and features are improved until time or resources run out.

Thus, information retrieval method has become a mature technology with both a science and a practice. This makes it possible for the science to develop more rapidly as it learns which practices are most effective. At the same time, because the practices are realized in enormously complex programs, it is difficult to design experiments that will determine which principles most contribute to the success of those practices. Because human users are more intelligent than the systems they use, perhaps several quite different systems are equally effective for users who have adapted to them.

EVALUATION OF SYSTEMS: BEYOND PRECISION AND RECALL

Precision and Recall

The classic concepts of precision and recall (CLEVERDON) are still used today. Briefly, all calculations are based on the assumption that for each query every retrievable document is either good or bad ("relevant" or "not relevant"). It is assumed that the total number good, G is known in advance. It is assumed that every retrieved document (up to some point of exhaustion) is judged as to its relevance. When the documents are ranked according to some parameter, with ranks 1,2,. . ., we can define $g(r)$ to be the number of good documents among the first r documents. The precision at this point is g/r, and the recall is $g(r)/G$. These two functions of r can be summarized by a graph showing precision as a function of recall. There is a remarkably large literature on how to draw this graph.

In real-world retrieval, the value of *G* is estimated typically by pooling the retrieved documents for several systems. In the TREC-2 (HARMAN, 1994) experiments, for example, the top 100 documents retrieved by each of more than 30 participating systems were actually reviewed and the systems were judged using this definition of recall. For the better systems, the performance was slightly above 40% precision at 40% recall. When the systems were trained on one body of full texts and then applied to another (the so-called "routing" task), system performance rose to over 50% precision at 40% recall. This measure is the average over all the queries of the precision for that query at 40% recall (see HARMAN, 1993a; 1993b; 1994).

Characterizing the Power of Systems

All previous efforts to reduce the performance of systems to a single number have proved unsatisfactory. Even for a simple-set retrieval system, the performance is essentially two dimensional. For ranking systems the performance is characterized by a curve. Recent new work which suggests ways to deal with this problem includes that of FREI & SCHÄUBLE, who introduce the notion of "usefulness," and HULL, who summarizes ways to deal with the nonparametric nature of the scores as currently calculated. A typical score is the average precision averaged over several levels of recall and averaged over all of the queries to which the system has been applied.

The search for ways to summarize a system's performance may proceed along either of two paths. One is to develop a theory of precision–recall curves that reveals a single parameter at work. There is no published work on this issue, and it presents interesting possibilities for evaluation research.

The other path is to find a nonparametric characterization of the relation between two systems. Such an approach might determine whether system A performs better than system B while ignoring the question of how much better. This could provide a new path to the selection and evaluation of systems. However, in the final analysis it will be necessary to say "how good" a system is in order to justify its cost of development and operation.

As the world of information becomes a single linked entity, the notion of recall (or even the "relative recall" defined in terms of the number of retrieved good documents) will have to fall out of use. Rather, much in the spirit of combination of information and of data fusion, we will be led to ask: given the results of retrieval using algorithms *A*, *B*, *C*, suitably combined, should we do any more work? This question is best answered in principle, by reporting, for each possible increment of value (v) the probability $Pr(v \mid \text{adding } S \text{ to } A, B, C)$ that we can realize that added value by using algorithm S in addition to A, B, and C. Of course, answering this question depends on knowing how to use several systems together, which we consider below. The concept of decision rules for stopping has been applied to the single search by KANTOR (1987).

For any given bi-corpus, the first choice system will be the one that maximizes expected value. An alternative rule would be to choose the system that maximizes the probability of getting the amount of value that we need. Each of these would be calculated for the case of no prior search. However, an IR technique or system might remain important because it is the right second choice for many problems where the performance of the first algorithm is not good enough. In general then, evaluation of systems will enter the work-a-day world in which the cost of using the system is balanced against the expected value to be derived from using it, and precision–recall measures appear, if at all, as intermediary steps in the estimation of value.

FUTURE: COMBINATION OF INFORMATION AND USE OF EXOGENOUS INFORMATION

Combination of Evidence, Data Fusion, and Combination of Information

It has long been known that human indexers and searchers do not agree in their assignment of index terms, retrieval of relevant documents, or even in judgments of relevance (KATZER ET AL.). Initially this was viewed as a flaw in the performance of rules or of humans, but more recently it has been situated in the general problem of detection and decision or inference. The fact that an indicator of relevance (such as a human judge) is imperfect opens the possibility that combinations of several indicators will yield a better performance than any of them alone (see SARACEVIC & KANTOR and KANTOR (1992) for an implementation of this idea when the indicators are distinct trained searchers). In what follows we refer to each indicator as a "scheme," which might be either a particular searcher, a particular automated system, or even a particular combination of several systems. To simplify the example, suppose that retrieval is set-wise, and that scheme 1 retrieves good documents with probability d_1, while scheme 2 does so with probability d_2. That is, each good document has a probability d_1 to be retrieved by scheme 1. The expected number of good documents retrieved by scheme 1 is d_1G.

Let the corresponding probabilities for retrieving bad documents be f_1 and f_2. The a priori odds that a document is relevant are $G : B$. As before, G represents the number of good documents, and B represents the number of bad documents in the dataspace. The corresponding odds for documents retrieved by scheme 1 are: $dG : fB$. Thus, as long as $d > f$, the odds of finding a good document in the retrieved set are better than the a priori odds. If the two retrieval systems are stochastically independent with respect to "goodness," the odds for documents retrieved by both schemes are $d_1d_2G : f_1f_2B$. Thus, if both schemes are effective, the intersection of the retrieved sets is even more effective. Hence, the intersection of the retrieved sets should be ranked above the remainder of their union. Available data (KANTOR, 1992) indicate that this independence assumption is too strong because it predicts too strong an improvement in the odds.

The Inquery system is built explicitly on combination of evidence (PEARL; TURTLE & CROFT, 1991) as the logical foundation for its numerical algorithms. The idea of data fusion appears in the work of FOX & SHAW, BELKIN ET AL. (1994), and KANTOR (1994). All of these are examples of what is now called in statistics the "combination of information." In a nutshell, these methods propose that several imperfect indicators of the relevance of a document to a query instance can be combined to provide a more reliable indicator. A presentation in Bayesian language is given by THOMPSON (1994).

In the Inquery system the fundamental indicators are the presence or absence of terms in the document, together with constructed concepts, and some attempt to add phrase-finding capabilities. In the data-fusion approaches, the indicators are the ranked outputs of several separate systems, each working the same dataspace for the same query.

In general, expanding a parameter space always opens the possibility for improving performance. So it is not surprising that these methods do yield a posteriori better performance than those methods of the systems or indicators that they combine. To be specific, we might combine a vector space method with a p-norm method, with relative weights α and $1 - \alpha$. The original system, whose parameters characterize the rule for forming term frequencies and inverse document frequency, had some parameter space P. The new one has parameters in $P \times \{(\alpha, p)\}$. This new space is larger and contains the original subspace as the special case $\alpha = 1$ (p doesn't matter). So every performance that could be achieved before can still be achieved, and so can other values of the performance. If even one of these value is better than the original, then a combination of systems has improved system performance.

Thus, it is not surprising that in each instance such combinations can often yield a performance that is better than the best achieved by the original systems (KANTOR, 1994). An important research issue is to find rules of combination that are stable and effective across a full range of queries and/or documents.

Feedback of Exogenous Information: Relations among Documents

As described above, developments in interfaces and feedback are permitting users to play a role in the definition of concepts at retrieval time, either explicitly or implicitly. These concepts can be captured in two ways. One is to permit users to annotate the descriptions of documents. This information then becomes internal to the system (part of the contents) and can be processed in the same way as all other contents. Users can also provide information in the form of direct links among documents. This type of link can reflect a conceptual relationship without making it explicit. In particular, the link is supplied exogenously (from outside the system), and its specific nature (or the name of the concept which it reflects) is never available to the system per se. This idea has been proposed for library catalogs by KOENIG (see also CROFT & TURTLE). This type of link is realized for catalogs in the Adaptive Network Library Interface System (KANTOR, 1993; ZHAO & KANTOR). It represents a way to include concepts in the system without naming them, by simply storing direct links among the retrievable documents.

This concept is related to the hypercatalog concept discussed by HJERPPE, with the specific proviso that the links cannot be found algorithmically from the contents alone—i.e., they are available only because there are human users of the system.

HUMAN SCANNING: A NEW SOURCE OF IDEAS?

In all studies of system performance, human judgment is the final standard of effectiveness. The implication is that we strive to make systems as good as people, but people are extremely variable in their judgment of the match between concepts and documents and in all other decision tasks related to IR. It may be argued that this is due to an essential imprecision in the expression of ideas in language or to an essential imprecision in the ideas themselves. In any case, we can follow this insight in two complementary directions. One affects the evaluation process; the other suggests a new source for development of algorithms.

Fractional Relevance Judgments and Inconsistency of Human Evaluations

Evaluation is performed against a "golden rule" in which the items deemed relevant are to be recovered before those deemed not relevant. When the system is serving the real user in a real retrieval instance, this seems the best possible approach. However, when the system is being judged offline, as in the TREC conferences, there should be some way to improve on this by using several judges for each query–document pair. The relevance score will then be a fraction (the number of judges asserting relevance divided by the total number of judges). This is a direct operational "fuzzification" of the notion of relevance. With this information the notion of precision–recall, or of cumulated relevance, can be suitably generalized. Rather than the total number of relevant documents *G*, one would speak of the total relevance scores of all the documents and so forth. This will move us toward a more "impersonal" characterization of what the system wants to achieve.

Human Scanning and Recognition Primitives

We have asserted that the user is being put back into the loop for query reformulation and the interactive refinement of concepts from content because the human outperforms any existing computer. This suggests that we might use the study of human scanning (of text, images, data) for new insights into the identification of concepts.

Although beyond the scope of this article, there are important and puzzling results from image processing (JULESZ), which suggest that the human eye responds instantly to characteristics that are, from the point of view of algorithm development, very high order indeed. This suggests that the rational path for algorithm development that has been followed so far (see MYLER & WEEKS) may lack crucial recognition primitives (basic elements to which the human mind responds) that would facilitate the retrieval of relevant images.

By a modest leap, I propose that there are also recognition primitives at work when a reader with suitable training apprehends that "a concept is present" in a text. The research necessary to identify these primitives is likely to involve studies of psychology and language and may need to develop very slowly, beginning with the study of how children acquire language. There is already work under way on "reverse-engineering" the human process of language acquisition to understand what kinds of computations are being performed. These efforts aim to develop computer algorithms which exhibit the same successes and failures as human language learners. In this connection it is suggestive to note that a text that has been preprocessed (stop words removed and stemmed) looks a great deal like the utterances of an infant who has not yet mastered the role of function words in language. The development of concept recognition in algorithmic form will have to progress, with great effort, from matching the abilities of infants, through progressive improvements, to matching or exceeding the abilities of the author and readers of an article such as this one.

A PHASE CHANGE IN THE WORLD OF INFORMATION

Physicists speak of "phase changes" when, for example, a gas condenses into a liquid or a liquid suddenly becomes a rigid crystalline structure. The development of machine-readable records and of the worldwide network creates the potential for a phase transition in the state of human knowledge.

With no increase in the amount of what is "known and recorded" (as opposed to simply known by one person privately) there could be a dramatic phase transition in what is "known to the world." With worldwide access to virtually all publicly available electronic information, mutually relevant and synergistic atoms of information could be instantly brought together. In the hands (minds?) of the right users this information could solve problems and improve conditions for people anywhere in the world. Of course, the ultimate limiting factor is the capacity of the human mind to absorb and transform information. The effect of this global change will be to sharply reduce the latency or cycle time between the creation and application of relevant information.

As a practical matter, the path to this global phase transition will be built by work on problems less grandiose than improving the human condition. For example, the phase transition might occur first in surveillance activities. It would be excellent, on the other hand, to have such progress in the health sciences. The enormous engineering files of the Department of Energy or the Strategic Defense Initiative are also ripe for conversion to digital form and for the phase change to take place.

However, this is a chicken or egg proposition. Our IR technologies will only flourish as enormous, potentially coherent dataspaces become available, but the motivation for putting them into machine-readable form will not be strong until the IR technologies are mature. So the impulse may come from agencies that have a less public mission—e.g., those charged with monitoring the flow of electronic messages for indications of terrorism and conspiracy. At the same time, we must be wary of the potential for superficiality that is encouraged by the possibility of "surfing" the Internet or wandering through some virtual reality. The systems that give us the incredible computational power and the sophisticated retrieval algorithms needed to wander in this way were created by people schooled in rigorous thought. I hope that the acquisition and organization of information will not come to be seen as an adequate substitute for such rigor. (For a brief polemic on this issue, see FLORMAN.) The transformative power of this potential phase change is beyond my powers of speculation. The possibility of making it a reality turns what could be a dry academic pursuit into an exciting quest.

BIBLIOGRAPHY

AGOSTI, MARISTELLA; COLOTTI, ROBERTO; GRADENIGO, GIROLAMO. 1991. A Two-Level Hypertext Retrieval Model for Legal Data. In: Bookstein, A.; Chiaramella, Y.; Salton, G.; Raghavan, V.V., eds. SIGIR '91: Proceedings of the Association for Computing Machinery Special Interest Group on Information Retrieval (ACM/SIGIR) 14th Annual International Conference on Research and Development in Information Retrieval; 1991 October 13-16; Chicago, IL. New York, NY: ACM; 1991. 316-325. ISBN: 0-89791-448-1.

ANICK, P.G. 1992. Lexicon Assisted Information Retrieval for the Help-Desk. In: Proceedings of IEEE CAIA-92 Workshop on Artificial Intelligence for Customer Service and Support; Monterey, CA.

ANWYL, P.; KANAYA, M.; MORITA, T. 1990. Automatic Keyword Assignment in English Documents. In: Proceedings of the 41st Conference of the Information Processing Society of Japan. 3-87-88.

BADECKER, W.; CARAMAZZA, A. 1989. A Lexical Distinction between Inflection and Derivation. Linguistic Inquiry. 1989 Winter; 20(1): 108-116. ISSN: 0024-3892.

BELKIN, NICHOLAS J.; COOL, COLLEEN; CROFT, W. BRUCE; CALLAN, JAMES P. 1993. The Effect of Multiple Query Representations on Information Retrieval System Performance. See reference: KORFHAGE ET AL., eds. 339-346.

BELKIN, NICHOLAS J.; CROFT, W. BRUCE. 1987. Retrieval Techniques. In: Williams, Martha E., ed. Annual Review of Information Science and Technology: Volume 22. Amsterdam, The Netherlands: Elsevier Science Publishers for the American Society for Information Science; 1987. 109-145. ISSN: 0066-4200; ISBN: 0-444-70302-0.

BELKIN, NICHOLAS J.; INGWERSEN, PETER; PEJTERSEN, ANNELISE MARK, eds. 1992. SIGIR '92: Proceedings of the Association for Computing Machinery Special Interest Group on Information Retrieval (ACM/SIGIR) 15th Annual International Conference on Research and Development in Information Retrieval; 1992 June 21-24; Copenhagen, Denmark. New York, NY: ACM; 1992. 353p. ISBN: 0-89791-523-2.

BELKIN, NICHOLAS J.; KANTOR, PAUL B.; COOL, COLLEEN; QUATRAIN, R. 1994. Combining Evidence for Information Retrieval. See reference: HARMAN, ed., 1994. 35-44.

BERTINO, ELISA; NEGRI, MAURO; PELAGATTI, GIUSEPPE; SBATTELLA, LICIA. 1992. Object-Oriented Query Languages: The Notion and the Issues. IEEE Transactions on Knowledge and Data Engineering. 1992 June; 4(3): 223-237. ISSN: 1041-4347.

BOOKSTEIN, ABRAHAM. 1983. Outline of a General Probabilistic Retrieval Model. Journal of Documentation. 1983; 39(2): 63-72. ISSN: 0022-0418.

BOTAFOGO, RODRIGO A. 1993. Cluster Analysis for Hypertext Systems. See reference: KORFHAGE ET AL., eds. 116-125.

BOTAFOGO, RODRIGO A.; SHNEIDERMAN, BEN. 1991. Identifying Aggregates in Hypertext Structures. In: Hypertext '91: Proceedings of the Association for Computing Machinery (ACM) 3rd Conference on Hypertext; 1991 December 15-18; San Antonio, TX. New York, NY: ACM; 1991. 63-74. ISBN: 0-89791-461-9.

BRUZA, P.D.; VAN DER GAAG, L.C. 1993. Efficient Context-Sensitive Plausible Inference for Information Disclosure. See reference: KORFHAGE ET AL., eds. 12-21.

BUCKLAND, MICHAEL K.; BUTLER, MARK H.; NORGARD, BARBARA A.; PLAUNT, CHRISTIAN J. 1993. OASIS: Prototyping Graphical Interfaces to Networked Information. In: Bonzi, Susan, ed. ASIS '93: Proceedings of the American Society for Information Science (ASIS) 56th Annual Meeting: Volume 30; 1993 October 24-28; Columbus, OH. Medford, NJ: Learned Information, Inc. for ASIS; 1993. 204-210. ISSN: 0044-7870; ISBN: 0-938734-78-4.

BUCKLES, BILLY P.; PETRY, FREDERICK E. 1982. A Fuzzy Representation of Data for Relational Databases. Fuzzy Sets and Systems. 1982 May; 7(3): 213-226. ISSN: 0165-0114.

BUCKLEY, CHRIS; SALTON, GERARD; ALLAN, J. 1993. Automatic Retrieval with Locality Information Using SMART. See reference: HARMAN, ed., 1993a. 59-72.

BURKOWSKI, FORBES J. 1992. Retrieval Activities in a Database Consisting of Heterogeneous Collections of Structured Text. See reference: BELKIN ET AL., eds., 1992. 112-125.

CALLAN, JAMES P.; CROFT, W. BRUCE. 1993. An Evaluation of Query Processing Strategies Using the TIPSTER Collection. See reference: KORFHAGE ET AL., eds. 347-355.

CAN, FAZLI; OZKARAHAN, ESEN A. 1987. Computation of Term/Document Discrimination Values by Use of the Cover Coefficient Concept. Journal of the American Society for Information Science. 1987; 38(3): 171-183. ISSN: 0002-8231.

CAN, FAZLI; OZKARAHAN, ESEN A. 1990. Concepts and Effectiveness of the Cover-Coefficient-Based Clustering Methodology for Text Databases. ACM Transactions on Database Systems. 1990 December; 15(4): 483-517. ISSN: 0362-5915.

CAVNAR, WILLIAM B. 1994. N-Gram-Based Text Filtering for TREC-2. See reference: HARMAN, ed., 1994. 171-180.

CHANG, S.-C.; DEDIU, H.; AZZAM, H.; DU, M.-W. 1993. Multilevel Ranking in Large Text Collections Using FAIRS. See reference: HARMAN, ed., 1993. 329-336.

CHERIKH, MOULA. 1989. Optimal Decision and Detection in the Decentralized Case. Cleveland, OH: Case Western Reserve University; 1989. 211p. (Ph.D. dissertation). Available from: University Microfilms, Ann Arbor, MI. (UMI order no. 90-04501).

CHIARAMELLA, YVES; NIE, JIANYUN. 1990. A Retrieval Model Based on an Extended Modal Logic and Its Application to the RIME Experimental Approach. In: Vidick, Jean-Luc, ed. Proceedings of the Association for Computing Machinery Special Interest Group on Information Retrieval (ACM/SIGIR) 13th International Conference on Research and Development in Information Retrieval; 1990 September 5-7; Brussels, Belgium. New York, NY: ACM; 1990. 25-43. ISBN: 0-89791-408-2.

CLEVERDON, CYRIL WILLIAM. 1962. Report on the Testing and Analysis of an Investigation into the Comparative Efficiency of Indexing Systems. Cranfield, England: College of Aeronautics; 1962. 305p. LC: 63-60414.

CLEVERDON, CYRIL WILLIAM; MILLS, JACK; KEEN, E. MICHAEL. 1966. Factors Determining the Performance of Indexing Systems. Cranfield, England: ASLIB; 1966. 2 volumes. (Volume 1: Design; Volume 2: Test Results). LC: 67-81732; OCLC: 3911240.

COOPER, WILLIAM S.; CHEN, AITAO; GEY, FREDRIC C. 1994. Full Text Retrieval Based on Probabilistic Equations with Coefficients Fitted by Logistic Regression. See reference: HARMAN, ed., 1994. 57-66.

CROFT, W. BRUCE; KROVETZ, ROBERT; TURTLE, HOWARD R. 1990. Interactive Retrieval of Complex Documents. Information Processing and Management. 1990; 26(5): 593-613. ISSN: 0306-4573.

CROFT, W. BRUCE; SMITH, LISA A.; TURTLE, HOWARD R. 1992. A Loosely-Coupled Integration of a Text Retrieval System and an Object-Oriented Database System. See reference: BELKIN ET AL., eds., 1992. 223-232.

CROFT, W. BRUCE; TURTLE, HOWARD R. 1989. A Retrieval Model for Incorporating Hypertext Links. In: Hypertext '89: Proceedings of the Association for Computing Machinery (ACM) 2nd Conference on Hypertext; 1989 November 5-8; Pittsburgh, PA. New York, NY: ACM; 1989. 213-224. ISBN: 0-89791-339-6.

CROFT, W. BRUCE; TURTLE, HOWARD R.; LEWIS, DAVID D. 1991. The Use of Phrases and Structured Queries in Information Retrieval. In: Bookstein, A.; Chiaramella, Y.; Salton, G.; Raghavan, V.V., eds. SIGIR '91: Proceedings of the Association for Computing Machinery Special Interest Group on Information Retrieval (ACM/SIGIR) 14th Annual International Conference on Research and Development in Information Retrieval; 1991 October 13-16; Chicago, IL. New York, NY: ACM; 1991. 32-45. ISBN: 0-89791-448-1.

CROUCH, CAROLYN J.; YANG, BOKYUNG. 1992. Experiments in Automatic Statistical Thesaurus Construction. See reference: BELKIN ET AL., eds., 1992. 77-88.

CUTTING, DOUGLASS R.; KARGER, DAVID R.; PEDERSEN, JAN O. 1993. Constant Interaction-Time Scatter/Gather Browsing of Very Large Document Collections. See reference: KORFHAGE ET AL., eds. 126-134.

CUTTING, DOUGLASS R.; KARGER, DAVID R.; PEDERSEN, JAN O.; TUKEY, JOHN W. 1992. Scatter/Gather: A Cluster-Based Approach to Browsing Large Document Collections. See reference: BELKIN ET AL., eds., 1992. 318-329.

CUTTING, DOUGLASS R.; PEDERSEN, JAN O. 1990. Optimizations for Dynamic Inverted Index Maintenance. In: Vidick, Jean-Luc, ed. SIGIR '90: Proceedings of the Association for Computing Machinery Special Interest Group on Information Retrieval (ACM/SIGIR) 13th International Conference on Research and Development in Information Retrieval; 1990 September 5-7; Brussels, Belgium. New York, NY: ACM; 1990. 405-411. ISBN: 0-89791-408-2.

DEERWESTER, SCOTT; DUMAIS, SUSAN T.; FURNAS, GEORGE W.; LANDAUER, THOMAS K.; HARSHMAN, RICHARD. 1990. Indexing by Latent Semantic Analysis. Journal of the American Society for Information Science. 1990; 41(6): 391-407. ISSN: 0002-8231.

DRABENSTOTT, KAREN MARKEY; VIZINE-GOETZ, DIANE. 1990. Search Trees for Subject Searching in Online Catalogs. Library Hi Tech. 1990; 8(3): 7-20. ISSN: 0737-8831.

DUMAIS, SUSAN T. 1994. Latent Semantic Indexing and TREC-2. See reference: HARMAN, ed., 1994. 105-116.

EFTHIMIADIS, EFTHIMIS N. 1990. Online Searching Aids: A Review of Front Ends, Gateways and Other Interfaces. Journal of Documentation. 1990 September; 46(3): 218-262. ISSN: 0022-0418.

EFTHIMIADIS, EFTHIMIS N. 1993. A User-Centred Evaluation of Ranking Algorithms for Interactive Query Expansion. See reference: KORFHAGE ET AL., eds. 146-159.

EVANS, DAVID A.; LEFFERTS, ROBERT G. 1994. Design and Evaluation of the CLARIT-TREC-2 System. See reference: HARMAN, ed., 1994. 137-150.

FELLER, WILLIAM. 1968. An Introduction to Probability Theory and Its Applications. 3rd edition. New York, NY: John Wiley & Sons; 1968. 2 volumes. LC: 68-11708.

FLORMAN, SAMUEL C. 1994. Odysseus in Cyberspace. Technology Review. 1994 April; 97(3): 65. ISSN: 0040-1692.

FOX, EDWARD A. 1983. Extending the Boolean and Vector Space Models of Information Retrieval with P-norm Queries and Multiple Concept Types. Ithaca, NY: Cornell University; 1983. 386p. (Ph.D. dissertation). Available from: University Microfilms, Ann Arbor, MI. (UMI order no. 83-28584).

FOX, EDWARD A.; FRANCE, ROBERT K.; SAHLE, ESKINDER; DAOUD, AMJAD; CLINE, BEN E. 1993. Development of a Modern OPAC: From REVTOLC to MARIAN. See reference: KORFHAGE ET AL., eds. 248-259.

FOX, EDWARD A.; SHAW, JOSEPH A. 1994. Combination of Multiple Searches. See reference: HARMAN, ed., 1994. 243-252.

FRAKES, WILLIAM B.; BAEZA-YATES, RICARDO. 1992. Information Retrieval: Data Structures and Algorithms. Englewood Cliffs, NJ: Prentice Hall; 1992. 504p. ISBN: 0-13-463837-9.

FREI, H.P.; SCHÄUBLE, PETER. 1991. Determining the Effectiveness of Retrieval Algorithms. Information Processing and Management. 1991; 27(2/3): 153-164. ISSN: 0306-4573.

FUHR, NORBERT. 1989a. Models for Retrieval with Probabilistic Indexing. Information Processing and Management. 1989; 25(1): 55-72. ISSN: 0306-4573.

FUHR, NORBERT. 1989b. Optimum Polynomial Retrieval Functions Based on the Probability Ranking Principle. ACM Transactions on Information Systems. 1989 July; 7(3): 183-204. ISSN: 0734-2047.

FUHR, NORBERT. 1990. A Probabilistic Framework for Vague Queries and Imprecise Information in Databases. In: McLeod, D.; Sacks-Davis, R.; Schek, H., eds. Proceedings of the 16th International Conference on Very Large Databases; 1990 August 13-16; Brisbane, Australia. Palo Alto, CA: Morgan Kaufmann; 1990. 696-707. ISBN: 0-55860-149-X.

FUHR, NORBERT. 1992. Integration of Probabilistic Fact and Text Retrieval. See reference: BELKIN ET AL., eds., 1992. 211-222.

FUHR, NORBERT. 1993. A Probabilistic Relational Model for the Integration of IR and Databases. See reference: KORFHAGE ET AL., eds. 309-317.

FUHR, NORBERT; BUCKLEY, CHRIS. 1993. Optimizing Document Indexing and Search Term Weighting Based on Probabilistic Models. See reference: HARMAN, ed., 1993. 89-99.

FUHR, NORBERT; PFEIFER, ULRICH; BREMKAMP, CHRISTOPHER; POLLMANN, MICHAEL. 1994. Probabilistic Learning Approaches for Indexing and Retrieval with the TREC-2 Collection. See reference: HARMAN, ed., 1994. 67-74.

FUJII, HIDEO; CROFT, W. BRUCE. 1993. A Comparison of Indexing Techniques for Japanese Text Retrieval. See reference: KORFHAGE ET AL., eds. 237-246.

FULLER, MICHAEL; MACKIE, ERIC; SACKS-DAVIS, RON; WILKINSON, ROSS. 1993. Structured Answers for a Large Structured Document Collection. See reference: KORFHAGE ET AL., eds. 204-213.

FURNAS, GEORGE W.; LANDAUER, THOMAS K.; GOMEZ, LOUIS M.; DUMAIS, SUSAN T. 1987. The Vocabulary Problem in Human-System Commmunication. Communications of the ACM. 1987; 30(11): 964-971. ISSN: 0001-0782.

GALLANT, STEPHEN I.; CAID, WILLIAM R.; CARLETON, JOEL; GUTSCHOW, TODD W.; HECHT-NIELSEN, ROBERT; QING, KENT PU; SUDBECK, DAVID. 1994. Feedback and Mixing Experiments with MatchPlus. See reference: HARMAN, ed., 1994. 101-104.

GOLDFARB, CHARLES F. 1990. The SGML Handbook. New York, NY: Oxford University Press; 1990. 664p. ISBN: 0-19-853737-9.

HAINES, DAVID; CROFT, W. BRUCE. 1993. Relevance Feedback and Inference Networks. See reference: KORFHAGE ET AL., eds. 2-11.

HARADA, T.; HOSONO, K.; TAMURA, S. 1989. Developing an Automatic Construction Method of the BT-NT Relations from Japanese Compound Nouns. SIGNL Record of the Information Processing Society of Japan. 1989; 70(5): 1-8. (In Japanese).

HARMAN, DONNA. 1988. Towards Interactive Query Expansion. In: Chiaramella, Yves, ed. Proceedings of the Association for Computing Machinery Special Interest Group on Information Retrieval (ACM/SIGIR) 11th International Conference on Research and Development in Information Retrieval; 1988 June 13-15; Grenoble, France. New York, NY: ACM; 1988. 321-331. ISBN: 2-7061-0309-4.

HARMAN, DONNA. 1992. The DARPA TIPSTER Project. SIGIR Forum. 1992 Fall; 26(2): 26-28. Available from: Association for Computing Machinery, 1515 Broadway, New York, NY 10036.

HARMAN, DONNA, ed. 1993a. The 1st Text REtrieval Conference (TREC-1); 1992 November 4-6; Gaithersburg, MD. Gaithersburg, MD: National Institute of Standards and Technology; 1993. 518p. (NIST Special Publication 500-207). ISBN: 0-16-042265-5; NTIS: PB 93-191641.

HARMAN, DONNA. 1993b. Overview of the First TREC Conference. See reference: KORFHAGE ET AL., eds. 36-47.

HARMAN, DONNA, ed. 1994. The 2nd Text REtrieval Conference (TREC-2); 1993 August 31-September 2; Gaithersburg, MD. Gaithersburg, MD: National Institute of Standards and Technology; 1994. 497p. (NIST Special Publication 500-215). CODEN: NSPUE2; NTIS: PB94-178407.

HARNEY, ROBERT C., ed. 1990. Sensor Fusion III: Sponsored by SPIE—the International Society for Optical Engineering; 1990 April 19-20; Orlando, FL. Bellingham, WA: SPIE; 1990. 230p. (Proceedings/SPIE volume 1306). ISSN: 0277-786X; ISBN: 0-8194-0357-1.

HEAPS, H.S. 1978. Information Retrieval, Computational and Theoretical Aspects. New York, NY: Academic Press; 1978. 344p. ISBN: 0-12-335750-0.

HEARST, MARTI A. 1992. Automatic Acquisition of Hyponyms from Large Text Corpora. In: COLING-92: Proceedings of the 15th International Conference on Computational Linguistics; 1992 August 23-28; Nantes, France. Grenoble, France: ICCL; 1992. 539-545. OCLC: 27857672.

HEARST, MARTI A. 1993a. Cases as Structured Indexes for Full-Length Documents. In: Proceedings of the American Association for Artificial Intelligence 1993 Spring Symposium on Case-Based Reasoning and Information Retrieval; Stanford, CA.

HEARST, MARTI A. 1993b. TextTiling. Berkeley, CA: University of California at Berkeley; 1993. (Sequoia 2000 Technical Report 93/24).

HEARST, MARTI A.; PLAUNT, CHRISTIAN. 1993. Subtopic Structuring for Full-Length Document Access. See reference: KORFHAGE ET AL., eds. 59-68.

HJERPPE, ROLAND. 1986. HYPERCATalog and Three Meta-Schemata for Database Views: Knowledge Organising, Collection Derived and User Established Structures. In: Kinsella, Janet, ed. Online Public Access to Library Files. Oxford, England: Elsevier International Bulletins; 1986. 101-110. ISBN: 0-946395-25-X.

HOFFMAN, MELIA M.; O'GORMAN, LAWRENCE; STORY, GUY A.; ARNOLD, JAMES Q.; MACDONALD, NINA H. 1993. The RightPages Service: An Image-Based Electronic Library. Journal of the American Society for Information Science. 1993 September; 44(8): 446-452. ISSN: 0002-8231.

HULL, DAVID. 1993. Using Statistical Testing in the Evaluation of Retrieval Experiments. See reference: KORFHAGE ET AL., eds. 329-338.

INFORMATION PROCESSING AND MANAGEMENT. 1963-. Saracevic, Tefko, ed. Oxford, England: Pergamon Press. (Formerly titled Information Storage and Retrieval). ISSN: 0306-4573.

INTERNATIONAL ORGANIZATION FOR STANDARDIZATION. 1986. Information Processing Systems—Text and Office Systems—Standard Generalized Markup Language (SGML). Geneva, Switzerland: International Organization for Standardization; 1986 October. (International Standard 8879).

JACOBS, PAUL S.; KRUPKA, G.R.; RAU, LISA F. 1991. Lexico-Semantic Pattern Matching as a Companion to Parsing in Text Understanding. In: Proceedings of the 4th DARPA Speech and Natural Language Workshop;

1991 February. San Mateo, CA: Morgan Kaufmann; 1991. 337-342. ISBN: 1-55860-207-0.

JACOBS, PAUL S.; KRUPKA, G.R.; RAU, LISA F. 1993. A Boolean Approximation Method for Query Construction and Topic Assignment in TREC. See reference: HARMAN, ed., 1993a. 297-308.

JANES, JOSEPH W. 1993. On the Distribution of Relevance Judgments. In: Bonzi, Susan, ed. ASIS '93: Proceedings of the American Society for Information Science (ASIS) 56th Annual Meeting: Volume 30; 1993 October 24-28; Columbus, OH. Medford, NJ: Learned Information, Inc. for ASIS; 1993. 104-114. ISSN: 0044-7870; ISBN: 0-938734-78-4.

JOURNAL OF THE AMERICAN SOCIETY FOR INFORMATION SCIENCE. 1950-. Kraft, Donald, ed. New York, NY: John Wiley & Sons. (Formerly titled American Documentation). ISSN: 0002-8231.

JULESZ, BELA. 1991. Early Vision and Focal Attention. Reviews of Modern Physics. 1991 July; 63(3): 735-772. ISSN: 0034-6861.

KANTOR, PAUL B. 1981. The Logic of Weighted Queries. IEEE Transactions on Systems, Man and Cybernetics. 1981; 11(12): 816-821. ISSN: 0018-9472.

KANTOR, PAUL B. 1984. Maximum Entropy Principle and the Optimal Design of Automated Information Retrieval Systems. Information Technology: Research and Development. 1984; 3(2): 88-94. ISSN: 0144-817X.

KANTOR, PAUL B. 1987. A Model for the Stopping Behavior of Users of Online Systems. Journal of the American Society for Information Science. 1987; 38(3): 211-214. ISSN: 0002-8231.

KANTOR, PAUL B. 1992. Two Heads Are Better Than One: The Potential of Data Fusion Concepts for Improvement of Online Searching. In: Williams, Martha E., comp. Proceedings of the 13th National Online Meeting; 1992 May 5-7; New York, NY. Medford, NJ: Learned Information, Inc.; 1992. 147-151. ISBN: 0-938734-63-6.

KANTOR, PAUL B. 1993. The Adaptive Network Library Interface: A Historical Overview and Interim Report. Library Hi Tech. 1993; 11(3): 81-92. ISSN: 0737-8831.

KANTOR, PAUL B. 1994. Data Fusion in Information Retrieval: Issues of Justification, Simulation and Evaluation. New Brunswick, NJ: Rutgers University; 1994. (Alexandria Project Laboratory Technical Report APLab/TR-94/1). Available from: APLab/SCILS, Rutgers University, 4 Huntington St., New Brunswick, NJ 08903.

KANTOR, PAUL B.; BLANKENBECLER, RICHARD; CHERIKH, MOULA. 1988. Sensor Calculus. Cleveland, OH: Tantalus Inc.; 1988 June. 88p. (Report TANTALUS/CT-88/3). NTIS: AD-197250. Also available from: Tantalus Inc., 362 N. 4th Ave., Highland Park, NJ 08904.

KANTOR, PAUL B.; LEE, JUNG JIN. 1986. The Maximum Entropy Principle in Information Retrieval. In: Rabitti, Fausto, ed. Proceedings of the Association for Computing Machinery Special Interest Group on Information Retrieval (ACM/SIGIR) 9th Conference on Research and Development in Information Retrieval; 1986 September 8-10; Pisa, Italy. New York, NY: ACM; 1986. 269-274. ISBN: 0-89791-187-3.

KATZER, JEFFREY; MCGILL, MICHAEL J.; TESSIER, JUDITH A.; FRAKES, WILLIAM; DASGUPTA, PADMINI. 1982. A Study of the Overlap among

Document Representations. Information Technology: Research and Development. 1982 October; 1(4): 261-274. ISSN: 0144-817X.

KAUFMAN, LEONARD; ROUSSEEUW, PETER J. 1990. Finding Groups in Data: An Introduction to Cluster Analysis. New York, NY: Wiley; 1990. 342p. ISBN: 0-471-87876-6.

KILPELAINEN, P.; LINDEN, G.; MANNILA, H.; NIKUNEN, E. 1990. A Structured Document Database System. In: Furuta, R., ed. EP90: Proceedings of the International Conference on Electronic Publishing, Document Manipulation and Typography; 1990 September 18-20; Gaithersburg, MD. Cambridge, England: Cambridge University Press; 1990. 139-151. ISBN: 0-521-40246- 8.

KOENIG, MICHAEL E.D. 1990. Linking Library Users: A Culture Change in Librarianship. American Libraries. 1990 October; 21(9): 844-845, 847, 849. ISSN: 0002-9769.

KORFHAGE, ROBERT; RASMUSSEN, EDIE; WILLETT, PETER, eds. 1993. SIGIR '93: Proceedings of the Association for Computing Machinery Special Interest Group on Information Retrieval (ACM/SIGIR) 16th Annual International Conference on Research and Development in Information Retrieval; 1993 June 27-July 1; Pittsburgh, PA. New York, NY: ACM; 1993. 361p. ISBN: 0-89791-605-0.

KROVETZ, ROBERT. 1992. Sense-Linking in a Machine Readable Dictionary. In: Proceedings of the Association for Computational Linguistics 30th Annual Meeting; 1992 June 28-July 2; Newark, DE. Morristown, NJ: Association for Computational Linguistics; 1992. 330-332.

KROVETZ, ROBERT. 1993. Viewing Morphology as an Inference Process. See reference: KORFHAGE ET AL., eds. 191-202.

KROVETZ, ROBERT; CROFT, W. BRUCE. 1992. Lexical Ambiguity and Information Retrieval. ACM Transactions on Information Systems. 1992 April; 10(2): 115-141. ISSN: 1046-8188.

KUPIEC, JULIAN M. 1992a. Hidden Markov Estimation for Unrestricted Stochastic Context-Free Grammars. In: ICASSP-92: Proceedings of the 1992 IEEE International Conference on Acoustics, Speech and Signal Processing; 1992 March 23-26; San Francisco, CA. New York, NY: IEEE; 1992. Volume 1: 177-180. ISBN: 0-7803-0532-9.

KUPIEC, JULIAN M. 1992b. Robust Part-of-Speech Tagging Using a Hidden Markov Model. Computer Speech and Language. 1992 July; 6(3): 225-242. ISSN: 0885-2308.

KUPIEC, JULIAN M. 1993. MURAX: A Robust Linguistic Approach for Question Answering Using an On-line Encyclopedia. See reference: KORFHAGE ET AL., eds. 181-190.

LEE, JOON HO; KIM, WON YONG; KIM, MYOUNG HO; LEE, YOON JOON. 1993. On the Evaluation of Boolean Operators in the Extended Boolean Retrieval Framework. See reference: KORFHAGE ET AL., eds. 291-297.

LEE, JUNG JIN; KANTOR, PAUL B. 1991. A Study of Probabilistic Information Retrieval Systems in the Case of Inconsistent Expert Judgments. Journal of the American Society for Information Science. 1991; 42(3): 166-172. ISSN: 0002-8231.

LESK, MICHAEL E. 1986. Automatic Sense Disambiguation Using Machine Readable Dictionaries: How to Tell a Pine Cone from an Ice Cream Cone. In: Proceedings of SIGDOC. 1986. 24-26.

LINDLEY, D.V. 1965. Introduction to Probability and Statistics from a Bayesian Viewpoint. Cambridge, England: Cambridge University Press; 1965. 2 volumes. LC: 64-24313.

LINOFF, GORDON; STANFILL, CRAIG. 1993. Compression of Indexes with Full Positional Information in Very Large Text Databases. See reference: KORFHAGE ET AL., eds. 88-95.

LOVINS, JULIE BETH. 1968. Development of a Stemming Algorithm. Mechanical Translation and Computational Linguistics. 1968 March; 11: 22-31. ISSN: 0543-2073.

LUHN, H.P. 1958. The Automatic Creation of Literature Abstracts. IBM Journal of Research and Development. 1958 April; 2(2): 159-165. ISSN: 0018-8646.

LUHN, H.P. 1959. Auto-Encoding of Documents for Information Retrieval Systems. In: Boaz, M., ed. Modern Trends in Documentation. London, England: Pergamon Press; 1959. 45-58. LC: 59-10081.

LUNIN, LOIS; FOX, EDWARD A., eds. 1993. Perspectives on Digital Libraries. Journal of the American Society for Information Science. 1993 September; 44(8): 440-491. ISSN: 0002-8231.

MANGASARIAN, OLVI L. 1965. Linear and Non-Linear Separation of Patterns by Linear Programming. Operations Research. 1965; 13: 444-452. ISSN: 0030-364X.

MARUYAMA, HIROSHI; WATANABE, HIDEO; OGINO, SHIHO. 1990. An Interactive Japanese Parser for Machine Translation. In: Karlgren, Hans, ed. Proceedings of the 13th International Conference on Computational Linguistics. Helsinki, Finland: University of Helsinki; 1990. Volume 2: 257-262. ISBN: 952-90-2028-7.

MCKEOWN, KATHLEEN R. 1985. Text Generation: Using Discourse Strategies and Focus Constraints to Generate Natural Language Text. Cambridge, England: Cambridge University Press; 1985. 246p. ISBN: 0-521-30116-5.

MCKEOWN, KATHLEEN R.; FEINER, STEVEN K.; ROBIN, JACQUES; SELIGMANN, DOREE D.; TANENBLATT, MICHAEL. 1992. Generating Cross-References for Multimedia Explanation. In: Proceedings of the 10th National Conference on Artificial Intelligence; 1992 July 12-16; San Jose, CA. Menlo Park, CA: AAAI Press; 1992. 9-16. ISBN: 0-262-51063-4.

MILLER, GEORGE A.; BECKWITH, RICHARD; FELLBAUM, CHRISTINE; GROSS, DEREK; MILLER, KATHERINE J. 1990a. Five Papers on WordNet. Princeton, NJ: Princeton University Computer Science Laboratory; 1990 July.

MILLER, GEORGE A.; BECKWITH, RICHARD; FELLBAUM, CHRISTINE; GROSS, DEREK; MILLER, KATHERINE J. 1990b. Introduction to WordNet: An On-line Lexical Database. International Journal of Lexicography. 1990; 3(4): 235-244. ISSN: 0950-3846.

MYLER, HARLEY R.; WEEKS, ARTHUR R. 1993. The Pocket Handbook of Image Processing Algorithms in C. Englewood Cliffs, NJ: Prentice-Hall; 1993. ISBN: 0-13-642240-3.

NEGOITA, C.V. 1985. Expert Systems and Fuzzy Systems. Menlo Park, CA: Benjamin/Cummings; 1985. 190p. ISBN: 0-8053-6840-X.

O'CONNOR, JOHN. 1975. Retrieval of Answer-Sentences and Answer-Figures from Papers by Text Searching. Information Processing and Management. 1975; 11(5/7): 155-164. ISSN: 0306-4573.

ODDY, ROBERT N.; BALAKRISHNAN, BHASKARAN. 1991. PThomas: An Adaptive Information Retrieval System on the Connection Machine. Information Processing and Management. 1991; 27(4): 317-335. ISSN: 0306-4573.

OGAWA, YASUSHI; BESSHO, AYAKO; HIROSE, MASAKO. 1993. Simple Word Strings as Compound Keywords: An Indexing and Ranking Method for Japanese Texts. See reference: KORFHAGE ET AL., eds. 227-236.

OGAWA, YASUSHI; MORITA, T.; KOBAYASHI, K. 1991. A Fuzzy Document Retrieval System Using the Keyword Connection Matrix and Its Learning Method. Fuzzy Sets and Systems. 1991; 39(2): 163-179. ISSN: 0165-0114.

OZKARAHAN, ESEN A.; CAN, FAZLI. 1986. An Automatic and Tunable Document Indexing System. In: Rabitti, Fausto, ed. Proceedings of the Association for Computing Machinery Special Interest Group on Information Retrieval (ACM/SIGIR) 9th Conference on Research and Development in Information Retrieval; 1986 September 8-10; Pisa, Italy. New York, NY: ACM; 1986. 234-243. ISBN: 0-89791-187-3.

PAICE, CHRIS D. 1990. Constructing Literature Abstracts by Computer: Techniques and Prospects. Information Processing and Management. 1990; 26(1): 171-186. ISSN: 0306-4573.

PAICE, CHRIS D.; JONES, PAUL A. 1993. The Identification of Important Concepts in Highly Structured Technical Papers. See reference: KORFHAGE ET AL., eds. 69-78.

PEARL, JUDEA. 1988. Probabilistic Reasoning in Intelligent Systems: Networks of Plausible Inference. San Mateo, CA: Morgan Kaufmann; 1988. 552p. ISBN: 0-934613-73-7.

PEAT, HELEN J.; WILLETT, PETER. 1991. The Limitations of Term Co-Occurrence Data for Query Expansion in Document Retrieval Systems. Journal of the American Society for Information Science. 1991; 42(5): 378-383. ISSN: 0002-8231.

PEDERSEN, GERT SCHMELTZ. 1993. A Browser for Bibliographic Information Retrieval Based on an Application of Lattice Theory. See reference: KORFHAGE ET AL., eds. 270-279.

POPOVIČ, MIRKO; WILLETT, PETER. 1992. The Effectiveness of Stemming for Natural-Language Access to Slovene Textual Data. Journal of the American Society for Information Science. 1992; 43(5): 384-390. ISSN: 0002-8231.

PORTER, M.F. 1980. An Algorithm for Suffix Stripping. Program. 1980 July; 14(3): 130-137. ISSN: 0033-0337.

PRADE, HENRI; TESTEMALE, CLAUDETTE. 1984. Generalizing Database Relational Algebra for the Treatment of Incomplete or Uncertain Information and Vague Queries. Information Sciences. 1984 November; 34(2): 115-143.ISSN: 0020-0255.

QIU, YONGGANG; FREI, H. P. 1993. Concept Based Query Expansion. See reference: KORFHAGE ET AL., eds. 160-169.

RAYMOND, D.R. 1990. LECTOR—An Interactive Formatter for Tagged Text. Waterloo, Ontario: University of Waterloo; 1990. (Technical Report OED-90-02). Available from: Centre for the New Oxford Dictionary and Text Research, University of Waterloo.

RO, JUNG SOON. 1988. An Evaluation of the Applicability of Ranking Algorithms to Improve the Effectiveness of Full-Text Retrieval. Part I. On the Effectiveness of Full-Text Retrieval. Journal of the American Society for Information Science. 1988; 39(2): 73-78. Part II. On the Effectiveness of Ranking Algorithms on Full-Text Retrieval. Journal of the American Society for Information Science. 1988; 39(3): 147-160. ISSN: 0002-8231.

ROBERTSON, STEPHEN E. 1990. On Term Selection for Query Expansion. Journal of Documentation. 1990 December; 46(4): 359-364. ISSN: 0022-0418.

ROBERTSON, STEPHEN E.; BOVEY, J.D.; THOMPSON, C.L.; MACASKILL, M.J. 1986. Weighting, Ranking and Relevance Feedback in a Front-End System. Journal of Information Science. 1986; 12: 71-75. ISSN: 0165-5515.

ROBERTSON, STEPHEN E.; MARON, M.E.; COOPER, WILLIAM S. 1982. Probability of Relevance: A Unification of Two Competing Models for Document Retrieval. Information Technology: Research and Development. 1982 January; 1(1): 1-21. ISSN: 0144-817X.

ROBERTSON, STEPHEN E.; WALKER, STEPHEN; HANCOCK-BEAULIEU, MICHELINE; GULL, A.; LAU, M. 1993. Okapi at TREC. See reference: HARMAN, ed., 1993a. 21-30.

ROBERTSON, STEPHEN E.; WALKER, STEPHEN; JONES, S.; HANCOCK-BEAULIEU, MICHELINE; GATFORD, M. 1994. Okapi at TREC-2. See reference: HARMAN, ed., 1994. 21-34.

ROCCHIO, J.J., JR. 1971. Relevance Feedback in Information Retrieval. In: Salton, Gerard, ed. The SMART Retrieval System: Experiments in Automatic Document Processing. Englewood Cliffs, NJ: Prentice-Hall; 1971. 313-323. LC: 70-159122.

ROSE, DANIEL E.; MANDER, RICHARD; OREN, TIM; PONCELEÓN, DULCE B.; SALOMON, GITTA; WONG, YIN YIN. 1993. Content Awareness in a File System Interface: Implementing the "Pile" Metaphor for Organizing Information. See reference: KORFHAGE ET AL., eds. 260-269.

SALTON, GERARD, ed. 1971. The SMART Retrieval System: Experiments in Automatic Document Processing. Englewood Cliffs, NJ: Prentice-Hall; 1971. 556p. LC: 70-159122.

SALTON, GERARD; ALLAN, J.; BUCKLEY, CHRIS. 1993. Approaches to Passage Retrieval in Full Text Information Systems. See reference: KORFHAGE ET AL., eds. 49-58.

SALTON, GERARD; BUCKLEY, CHRIS. 1988. Term-Weighting Approaches in Automatic Text Retrieval. Information Processing and Management. 1988; 24(5): 513-523. ISSN: 0306-4573.

SALTON, GERARD; BUCKLEY, CHRIS. 1990. Improving Retrieval Performance by Relevance Feedback. Journal of the American Society for Information Science. 1990; 41(4): 288-297. ISSN: 0002-8231.

SALTON, GERARD; BUCKLEY, CHRIS. 1991a. Automatic Text Structuring and Retrieval: Experiments in Automatic Encyclopedia Searching. In: Bookstein, A.; Chiaramella, Y.; Salton, G.; Raghavan, V.V., eds. SIGIR '91: Proceedings of the Association for Computing Machinery Special Interest Group on Information Retrieval (ACM/SIGIR) 14th Annual International Conference on Research and Development in Information Retrieval; 1991 October 13-16; Chicago, IL. New York, NY: ACM; 1991. 21-30. ISBN: 0-89791-448-1.

SALTON, GERARD; BUCKLEY, CHRIS. 1991b. Global Text Matching for Information Retrieval. Science. 1991 August 30; 253(5023): 1012-1015. ISSN: 0036- 8075.

SALTON, GERARD; BUCKLEY, CHRIS; FOX, EDWARD A. 1983. Automatic Query Formulations in Information Retrieval. Journal of the American Society for Information Science. 1983; 34(4): 262-280. ISSN: 0002-8231.

SALTON, GERARD; MCGILL, MICHAEL J. 1983. Introduction to Modern Information Retrieval. New York, NY: McGraw-Hill; 1983. 448p. ISBN: 0-07-054484-0.

SARACEVIC, TEFKO; KANTOR, PAUL B. 1988. A Study of Information Seeking and Retrieving. III. Searchers, Searches, and Overlap. Journal of the American Society for Information Science. 1988; 39(3): 197-216. ISSN: 0002-8231.

SCHAMBER, LINDA. 1994. Relevance and Information Behavior. In: Williams, Martha E., ed. Annual Review of Information Science and Technology: Volume 29. Medford, NJ: Learned Information, Inc. for the American Society for Information Science; 1994. 3-48. ISSN: 0066-4200; ISBN: 0-938734-91-1.

SCHÄUBLE, PETER. 1989. The Compatibility of Retrieval Functions, Preference Relations, and Document Descriptions. Zurich, Switzerland: Department Informatik; 1989. (Technical Report no. 113).

SCHÄUBLE, PETER. 1993. SPIDER: A Multiuser Information Retrieval System for Semistructured and Dynamic Data. See reference: KORFHAGE ET AL., eds. 318-327.

SMEATON, A.F.; VAN RIJSBERGEN, C.J. 1983. The Retrieval Effects of Query Expansion on a Feedback Document Retrieval System. Computer Journal. 1983; 26(3): 239-246. ISSN: 0010-4620.

SPARCK JONES, KAREN, ed. 1981. Information Retrieval Experiment. London, England: Butterworths; 1981. 352p. ISBN: 0-408-10648-4.

STANFILL, CRAIG; WALTZ, DAVID L. 1992. Statistical Methods, Artificial Intelligence, and Information Retrieval. In: Jacobs, Paul S., ed. Text-Based Intelligent Systems: Current Research and Practice in Information Extraction and Retrieval. Hillsdale, NJ: Lawrence Erlbaum Associates; 1992. 215-225. ISBN: 0-8058-1188-5.

STRZALKOWSKI, TOMEK. 1993. Natural Language Processing in Large-Scale Text Retrieval Tasks. See reference: HARMAN, ed., 1993a. 173-188.

STRZALKOWSKI, TOMEK; PEREZ CARBALLO, JOSE. 1994. Recent Developments in Natural Language Text Retrieval. See reference: HARMAN, ed., 1994. 123-136.

TAGUE, JEAN; SALMINEN, AIRI; MCCLELLAN, CHARLES. 1991. Complete Formal Model for Information Retrieval Systems. In: Bookstein, A.; Chiaramella, Y.; Salton, G.; Raghavan, V.V., eds. SIGIR '91: Proceedings of the Association for Computing Machinery Special Interest Group on Information Retrieval (ACM/SIGIR) 14th Annual International Conference on Research and Development in Information Retrieval; 1991 October 13-16; Chicago, IL. New York, NY: ACM; 1991. 14-20. ISBN: 0-89791-448-1.

THOMPSON, PAUL. 1990. A Combination of Expert Opinion Approach to Probabilistic Information Retrieval. Part I: The Conceptual Model. Information Processing and Management. 1990; 26(3): 371-382. Part II. Mathematical Treatment of CEO Model 3. Information Processing and Management. 1990; 26(3): 383-394. ISSN: 0306-4573.

THOMPSON, PAUL. 1994. Description of the PRC CEO Algorithm for TREC-2. See reference: HARMAN, ed., 1994. 271-274.

TONG, RICHARD M.; APPELBAUM, LEE A. 1994. Machine Learning for Knowledge-Based Document Routing. See reference: HARMAN, ed., 1994. 253-264.

TURTLE, HOWARD R. 1991. Inference Networks for Document Retrieval. Amherst, MA: University of Massachusetts; 1991. 211p. (Ph.D. dissertation). Available from: University Microfilms, Ann Arbor, MI. (UMI order no. 91-20950).

TURTLE, HOWARD R.; CROFT, W. BRUCE. 1991. Evaluation of an Inference Network-Based Retrieval Model. ACM Transactions on Information Systems. 1991 July; 9(3): 187-222. ISSN: 0734-2047.

TURTLE, HOWARD R.; CROFT, W. BRUCE. 1992. A Comparison of Text Retrieval Models. Computer Journal. 1992 June; 35(3): 279-290. ISSN: 0010-4620.

TZERAS, KOSTAS; HARTMANN, STEPHAN. 1993. Automatic Indexing Based on Bayesian Inference Networks. See reference: KORFHAGE ET AL., eds. 22-34.

VAN DER GAAG, L.C. 1990. Probability-Based Models for Plausible Reasoning. Amsterdam, The Netherlands: University of Amsterdam; 1990. (Ph.D. dissertation).

VAN RIJSBERGEN, C.J. 1977. A Theoretical Basis for the Use of Co-Occurrence Data in Information Retrieval. Journal of Documentation. 1977 June; 33(2): 106-119. ISSN: 0022-0418.

VAN RIJSBERGEN, C.J. 1979. Information Retrieval. 2nd edition. London, England: Butterworths; 1979. 208p. ISBN: 0-408-70929-4.

VAN RIJSBERGEN, C.J.; HARPER, D.J.; PORTER, M.F. 1981. The Selection of Good Search Terms. Information Processing and Management. 1981; 17(2): 77-91. ISSN: 0306-4573.

VOORHEES, ELLEN M. 1993. Using WordNet to Disambiguate Word Senses for Text Retrieval. See reference: KORFHAGE ET AL., eds. 171-180.

VOORHEES, ELLEN M.; HOU, YUAN-WANG. 1993. Vector Expansion in a Large Collection. See reference: HARMAN, ed., 1993. 343-351.

VOORHEES, ELLEN M.; LEACOCK, CLAUDIA; TOWELL, GEOFFREY. 1992. Learning Context to Disambiguate Word Senses. In: Proceedings of the

3rd Computational Learning Theory and Natural Learning Systems Conference.

WANG, PEILING; SOERGEL, DAGOBERT. 1993. Beyond Topical Relevance: Document Selection Behavior of Real Users of IR Systems. In: Bonzi, Susan, ed. ASIS '93: Proceedings of the American Society for Information Science (ASIS) 56th Annual Meeting: Volume 30; 1993 October 24-28; Columbus, OH. Medford, NJ: Learned Information, Inc. for ASIS; 1993. 87-92. ISSN: 0044-7870; ISBN: 0-938734-78-4.

WILLETT, PETER. 1980. Document Clustering Using an Inverted File Approach. Journal of Information Science. 1980; 2(5): 223-231. ISSN: 0165-5515.

WITTGENSTEIN, LUDWIG. 1953. Philosophical Investigations. Oxford, England: Basil Blackwell; 1953. 232p.

WONG, S.K.M.; CAI, Y.J.; YAO, Y.Y. 1993. Computation of Term Associations by a Neural Network. See reference: KORFHAGE ET AL., ed. 107-115.

WONG, S.K.M.; YAO, Y.Y. 1990. Query Formulation in Linear Retrieval Models. Journal of the American Society for Information Science. 1990; 41(5): 334-341. ISSN: 0002-8231.

WONG, S.K.M.; ZIARKO, W.; RAGHAVAN, V.V.; WONG, P.C.N. 1987. On Modeling of Information Retrieval Concepts in Vector Spaces. ACM Transactions on Database Systems. 1987 June; 12(2): 299-321. ISSN: 0362-5915.

YANG, YIMING; CHUTE, CHRISTOPHER G. 1993. An Application of Least Squares Fit Mapping to Text Information Retrieval. See reference: KORFHAGE ET AL., eds. 281-290.

ZADEH, LOTFI A. 1994. Fuzzy Logic, Neural Networks and Soft Computing. Communications of the ACM. 1994 March; 37(3): 77-84. ISSN: 0001-0782.

ZHAO, SHUYUAN; KANTOR, PAUL B. 1993. Development of an Adaptive Network Library Interface: Progress Report and System Design Issues. In: Bonzi, Susan, ed. ASIS '93: Proceedings of the American Society for Information Science (ASIS) 56th Annual Meeting: Volume 30; 1993 October 24-28; Columbus, OH. Medford, NJ: Learned Information, Inc. for ASIS; 1993. 211-216. ISSN: 0044-7870; ISBN: 0-938734-78-4.

ZIMMERMAN, H.-J. 1991. Fuzzy Set Theory and Its Applications. 2nd edition. Boston, MA: Academic Publishers; 1991. 399p. ISBN: 0-7923-9075-X.

ZIMMERMAN, M. 1993. Proximity-Correlation for Document Ranking: The PARA Group's TREC Experiment. See reference: HARMAN, ed., 1993a. 353-364.

3 Digital Image Representation and Access

JAVED MOSTAFA
Indiana University, Indianapolis[1]

INTRODUCTION

The development and application of modern imaging technology can be traced back to the 1960s, when NASA's Mariner 4 mission to Mars transmitted several digital images back to earth (GREEN). Since then the area of digital imaging has experienced tremendous growth and the volume of literature that exists on the topic reflects that growth. The last *ARIST* chapter on this topic was published in 1987 (LUNIN). Hence, this chapter focuses on the literature published in the years 1987–1993. The chapter also includes some pre-1987 literature, but only what adds significantly to the topic and does not overlap previous coverage.

Searches performed on DIALOG Information Services's LCMARC database revealed 180 monographs on digital imaging published in our time frame (1987–1993). The highest frequency of publication was observed during 1991–1993 (80). Searches performed on DIALOG's Ulrich's International Periodicals Directory revealed that 81 serials (English and other languages) are presently being published that have major emphasis on digital imaging. This topic is studied and applied in a wide variety of disciplines. Nine of the serials are concerned with medical imaging, four cover imaging in geographic information systems (GISs) and geology, two are from astronomy, and three originate from physics. Fourteen serials focus on image processing, pattern recognition,

[1]The chapter was completed while the author was affiliated with the University of Texas at Austin.

Annual Review of Information Science and Technology (*ARIST*), Volume 29, 1994
Martha E. Williams, Editor
Published for the American Society for Information Science (ASIS)
By Learned Information, Inc., Medford, N.J.

and vision. The largest number of serials (48) are of a general nature, covering both theoretical and applied issues in imaging technology (information science, digital photography, mass media, education, and business).

Scope

Digital images originate from various sources, including flat-bed scanners, charge-coupled devices such as digital cameras, and x-ray instruments capable of computer assisted tomography. Digital images are also produced as output of numerical simulations and by tools used for image editing and production. Digital images, however, cannot simply be equated with all computer-generated graphical representations. A particular type of graphical representation is produced from geometric primitives such as lines, triangles, and polygons. These representations, containing information about size, shape, and location of objects depicted in them, are called vector graphics. Digital images are not produced from geometrical primitives, and they do not contain information about particular objects depicted in them. They are produced from a set of points and additional data that express where on the display raster particular points should appear. This is why digital images are sometimes referred to as "raster graphics." Instead of the term raster graphics, we use the more modern term "digital images" in this chapter. There are also other terms for digital images, including bit-mapped graphics, pictures, and scans. In certain scientific fields, especially in remote sensing and astronomy, digital images are sometimes referred to simply as "data." In the arts, they are often categorized under the broad term visual resources. All these variations were considered when the literature was searched for this chapter.

Digital image output from devices and software needs to be stored in some format for subsequent reference, processing, or transfer. The form used for digital image storage is highly important because it determines, among other things, storage space required, time necessary to transfer the data, quality of the data, and hardware platforms that can process the data. Many data formats have been devised for storing images (KAY & LEVINE; RIMMER), creating what amounts to a patchwork of image formats. Image formats vary according to their developers' (industry, government labs, academia, and standardization bodies) biases and needs. The situation can be quite confusing for imaging professionals or other interested parties because hidden in the various image formats are structural choices, some of them quite subtle, that affect how images are stored. The literature on image formats is quite diverse and "scattered" due to the origin of the formats. An attempt is made here to bring together important sources that can shed some light on structural and functional components of image formats in use today.

Image data can be stored piece by piece, as individual files, when output volume is small. When many image files are generated, however, efficient access to image information becomes a problem. A substantial amount of literature deals with the problem of image access (ARNDT; CHANG; JAMBERDINO & NIBLACK). One area of research has closely examined the nature of visual data to develop effective data models for indexing and storing image data; another has concentrated on developing effective user interfaces, focusing mainly on issues surrounding query languages. Some recent work attempts to integrate research on data modeling, user interfaces, and pattern recognition into a single system called an image information system (CHANG & HSU). With significant studies in networking technologies, the area of distributed access to image data has also become highly active. Problems associated with the transfer of digital imagery from centralized repositories through networks have been studied for the scientific community in general (CATLETT & TERSTRIEP; PERDUE) and for the medical community specifically (JOST). Important branches of research on user interface design, data modeling, and networking receive strong emphasis in this chapter.

Literature on copyright, optical character recognition (OCR), input/output (I/O) devices, secondary storage media, and computer vision is not considered here. Literature on image analysis, image enhancement, and pattern recognition is not emphasized in this chapter. Coverage of data-compression literature is restricted to those items that deal with techniques or algorithms applied in common image formats.

IMAGE REPRESENTATION

Image Data

Before the literature on image representation can be discussed, it is necessary to define a few basic terms and concepts. Image data in a computer are usually stored in a primary memory area known as the frame buffer (ROBINSON, 1989; SALMON & SLATER). Here information is logically separated into two-dimensional (2-D) matrices of single bits called bit planes. The bit plane data structure provides a certain amount of independence to an image application. The application does not have to be "aware" of the low level details of how the computer displays the image on the screen. If a new image needs to be displayed or an old one modified, the application simply updates the bit map data in the frame buffer.

A bit plane containing variants of one bit, either 0 or 1, is sufficient to represent a black-and-white image. A video controller transforms each bit to a point, either black or white, on the screen. These points are called pixels, short for picture elements. Images represented by single bits are called bilevel images. There are many different applications for bilevel images (GREEN), including facsimile transmission (fax), OCR, and edge detection. The bit plane data are the most important data necessary to generate an image. Along with other data that contain information about the image (discussed below), they make up the image file.

Single bits can be used to simulate shades of gray by a technique called halftoning (GREEN; RIMMER). Halftoning involves transforming the gray image into a set of small uniformly shaped segments. The segments are subsequently filled with black and white pixels in proportion to the grayness in that area. Halftoning is common in newspaper printing. It is also used in some computer displays—e.g., in NEXT's NEXTSTEP and Silicon Graphic's Indigo—to represent gray levels (KAY & LEVINE). Most computers, however, do not use the halftoning technique to display shades of gray. More commonly, multiple bit planes, between 2 and 16, are used. A bit plane is used to store only one bit; hence, the video controller needs to group bits in the same relative position together. This grouping of bits per position collectively produces a numerical value that determines a specific gray intensity level for each pixel. The numerical value attained depends on the number of bit planes used; for example, in a 2-bit image (an image with two bit planes), $2^2 = 4$ variations of gray levels are possible, while in a 16-bit image, $2^{16} = 65{,}536$ gray levels can be represented. Black-and-white images based on multiple bit planes are commonly referred to as grayscale images. These are preferred over color images in many scientific applications, especially where small-shape recognition is important (WOLFF & YAEGER).

Representation of color images follows the same principle used for grayscale images. Multiple bit planes are necessary, usually between 8 bit planes and 24 bit planes to store color information. Computer displays use the additive color model known as red-green-blue or RGB for short (FRIEDHOFF & BENZON). Bits stored in all the bit planes are grouped into three sets, producing three separate intensities. Each group of three intensity values is transformed into three nearly contiguous red, green, and blue dots on the screen. The combination of three color dots together make up a pixel, and to the eyes they appear as a single colored dot. A 24-bit color image is commonly referred to as a true color image. If used properly, color images can be very useful in analyzing complex phenomena such as tornadoes or heat distribution in sea surfaces. Differentiating attributes of the phenomena can be achieved by cueing a particular color to a specific attribute (WOLFF & YAEGER).

When images are represented using multiple bit planes, the range of shades of grays or colors is called the dynamic range of the image. Not all devices represent values for the dynamic range in the same way.

Due to the difference in handling dynamic range values between the capture equipment (input) and display equipment (output), inaccuracies are introduced in the image data (KAY & LEVINE). For grayscale images the effects of these inaccuracies are minimized by storing a correction factor with each image file. It is left up to the application program that displays the image to apply the following equation on images to remove inaccuracies:

$$\text{Image}(x, y) = \text{Image}(x, y)^{\Gamma}$$

where image(x, y) represents the 2-D array of pixel intensities, and Γ is the correction factor. For color images, the data are usually corrected in two steps. In the first step, the correction factor Γ is applied per bit plane; in the second step, interplane intensity values are adjusted against a standard table of color values. Several international standards have been established to consistently represent color intensity values across devices. The most famous and popular standard was established by the CIE (Commission Internationale de l'Eclairage) (MURCH). The standard intensity values and name of the particular standard used are stored in the image file.

The concept of image resolution is often presented ambiguously in the literature (KERLOW & ROSEBUSH). A particular image can have two types of resolution parameters associated with it: spatial and intensity. Spatial resolution is the total pixel area of an image, calculated by multiplying the vertical pixel frequency by the horizontal pixel frequency. Intensity resolution is the pixel depth of an image expressed as the total number of bit planes used to represent an image; this value also determines the dynamic range of each pixel in the image. The higher the intensity resolution, the sharper the image. Aspect ratio is a parameter that is related to resolution; it refers to the value attained by dividing the number of horizontal pixels by the number of vertical pixels. The spatial resolution, intensity resolution, and, in some cases, the aspect ratio are stored in the image file.

The display system has its own resolution parameters. Although they are similarly derived as an image resolution, they can be different from it. Display resolution is expressed in terms of the pixel area of the screen (horizontal pixels × vertical pixels) and the bit-depth displayable. Another value sometimes used to express screen resolution, although somewhat indirectly, is dots (pixels) that can be represented per inch (DPI). The DPI unit is also commonly used in scanners to express image-capture resolution. Today, a 640 × 480 pixel area with 8- to 16-bit depth is quite common on most display systems.

If the pixel area of the screen is smaller than the pixel area of the image, then an image area equal only to the size of the screen area will be visible—i.e., parts of the image will not be visible. Differences in bit depth of the screen and bit depth of an image are handled in a special way. For example, if the image bit depth is 4 bits and the screen bit depth is 24 bits, then a data structure called a look-up table (LUT) is used to map the $2^4 = 16$ image intensity values to 16 colors out of a possible $2^{24} = 16,777,216$ colors. One would say, 16 colors were displayed out of a palette of 16,777,216 colors to describe this mapping. Conversely, using a LUT, it is possible to map a high-resolution image to a low-resolution screen. A LUT used for a particular image is usually stored in the image file. If a LUT is not stored with the image file, then the display software may use a default LUT to reproduce the image.

In certain applications, image data stored in three-dimensional (3-D) formats are necessary. RUSS and FRIEDHOFF & BENZON describe how 3-D images are generated and represented. The Friedhoff and Benzon book is introductory, whereas Russ's handbook provides in-depth treatment. Computed tomography (CT), positron emission tomography (PET), and magnetic resonance imaging (MRI) are 3-D imaging techniques extensively used in medicine, biology, and industry. Commonly, 3-D image data are stored as a series of 2-D images, each representing a serial section of the volumetric object. For computing purposes, however, it is more effective to store spatial depth information for each object point. A 3-D matrix is used to store the location and intensity of all the points of a 3-D imaged object. Each point in the 3-D matrix is called a voxel to signify that it is a volumetric pixel. Imaged 3-D objects represented as voxels permit highly realistic simulations of natural objects with the capability to zoom, rotate, disassemble, move, and steer the simulation process.

Graphical representations produced as output of the computer-aided design (CAD) process or numerical simulations can be transformed to more realistic "image-like" representations by applying rendering algorithms. FRIEDHOFF & BENZON provide a lucid description of various rendering techniques. FOLEY ET AL. explain how various rendering techniques are algorithmically implemented. Common rendering techniques used today include Lambert shading. Gouraud shading, Phong shading, texture mapping, and ray tracing. With the increasing popularity of imaging technology, certain techniques used in traditional computer graphics are merging with those used in digital imaging. This is resulting in the development of techniques that transform geometrically based graphical representations to image data. For example, various algorithms generally termed "scan conversion routines" have been developed that accept graphical representations of objects as input and produce their pixelized counterparts (FOLEY ET AL.). KAUFMAN reports that an algorithm called 3-D scan conversion routine has been developed that can generate the voxelized 3-D image from a geometrically represented 3-D object.

Compression

Digital image data are voluminous. We reproduce in Table 1 data by CATLETT & TERSTRIEP that compare the approximate storage requirements of a typical journal article (five pages long) represented as text, formatted text, and image.

Obviously the image representation of the article demands the most storage space. It should be apparent from the earlier discussion that the size of an image increases with higher image resolution because more information needs to be maintained per image (more pixels or more bit planes). According to another estimate by BAXTER, if pages are scanned in 400 DPI instead of 300 DPI, the total size of the article file will be approximately 9.3 Mbytes (nearly 374 times the size of the text version). The voluminous nature of image documents hinders development of image repositories because of the high cost of storage and increases in access time.

To generate more compact and parsimonious image representations, many compression techniques have been developed. An excellent theoretical treatment of these is in a recent monograph (CHELLAPPA). Practical accounts of compression algorithms applied in image storage today are offered by ANSON, MORRISON, BELL ET AL., WALLACE (1990; 1991), RIMMER, and STORER. Image compression algorithms can be roughly divided into two types: lossless and lossy. Lossless algorithms are applied when it is critical to maintain completeness in the data—e.g., in medical images or images that are to be subjected to pattern recognition processes. Lossless algorithms are also applied in text compression where perfect regeneration is necessary. BELL ET AL. provide a lucid description of major compression techniques applied to textual documents, including run-length encoding (RLE), Huffman en-

Table 1
Storage Requirements of Typical Journal Articles[a]

Article As:	Calculation	Storage (Bytes)
Plain text	5 kbytes/page × 5	25 kbytes
Formatted text	5.5 kbytes (10% overhead)/page × 5	28 kbytes
Scanned page image (not compressed)	1 Mbyte (a page 7.5 inches × 10 inches scanned in 300 DPI)/page × 5	5,000 kbytes

[a]From CATLETT & TERSTRIEP. Table data reproduced by permission of the University of Illinois.

coding, and Lempel-Ziv-Welch encoding (LZW). All of the latter compression techniques have been also applied in lossless image compression (MORRISON).

CCITT's (Consultative Committee on International Telegraphy and Telephony) Group 3 algorithm for image compression is commonly used for fax transmission of documents (COURTOT). It uses the RLE technique to compress documents. In Group 3 implementation, RLE makes assumptions about certain features of the document. Most significantly, it assumes that the document is a bilevel (black-and-white) image with the black and white areas uniformly distributed. In RLE, long runs of repeatedly occurring patterns are replaced with more economically represented codes. So, for example, a Group 3 implementation would first divide an image into thinly spaced lines, then each black or white run of patterns occurring in a line would be encoded according to an internal table. LYNCH (1991) and PENNEBAKER & MITCHELL report another CCITT algorithm, Group 4, that improves on Group 3 in compression ratio but at the cost of error recovery. Group 4 compression assumes that the environment of data communication is totally digital and therefore error free, whereas Group 3 encoding, designed to work over telephone networks, can tolerate some minor errors in communication.

The Group 3 implementation of the RLE algorithm works quite well for applications such as facsimile transmission because its assumption about the uniformity of black-and-white patterns in the images matches the structure and representation of most office documents. To accommodate images of varied structures and representations, more general lossless algorithms have been developed. The closest to RLE, by design, are various implementations of Huffman encoding. Huffman encoding is commonly applied as a general-purpose image compression algorithm on both black-and-white and color images. KAY & LEVINE point out how a particular version of Huffman encoding improves on RLE. In this implementation, Huffman encoding does not use a fixed code table. Using two passes over the data set, the Huffman algorithm generates code tables based on the distribution of pixels in individual images and then uses these code tables for compressing the images. After applying Huffman encoding, code tables must be stored with the compressed images for decompression.

The LZW algorithm is another lossless image compression technique commonly applied to both color and black-and-white images. LZW also uses a code substitution method for compression. LZW achieves more efficient results than Huffman encoding because it reduces the number of times the image needs to be parsed for compression. Beginning with a simple code table, LZW, in one pass, builds a more effective code table (adaptive to the distribution of pixel values in the image) and uses those codes to compress the image. Due to the adaptive nature of the LZW code table, it needs to be stored with the compressed image. BELL ET AL., RIMMER, and KAY & LEVINE provide more details on how LZW is applied in image compression. LZW is currently the most popular lossless image compression algorithm.

Lossless compression algorithms have an upper bound of a 3:1 compression ratio in typical applications (BESSER, 1991a). This is too small a margin to make storing a large volume of image data economically viable. LO ET AL. provide an overview of several lossy compression techniques that can produce much higher compression ratios but at the cost of sacrificing some data. These include: block discrete cosine transformation (DCT), adaptive block DCT, and prune tree structure vector quantization (VQ). CHELLAPPA provides an in-depth treatment of several DCT and VQ compression algorithms. ANSON and BARNSLEY & HURD describe a more recently developed lossy image compression technique based on fractal transform compression. Depending on the image characteristics, DCT-based lossy algorithms can produce compression ratios of 40:1 whereas fractal transform-based algorithms can produce compression ratios as high as 100:1.

Until recently, lossy algorithms were not in common use due to concerns about image quality. However, recent algorithms based on DCT and fractal transform take into account attributes of the human visual system and take advantage of redundancies in natural scenes in an attempt to sacrifice only those data that are not visually significant or discernible. In June 1988 such a "visually-sensitive" DCT-based compression algorithm was selected by the Joint Photographic Experts Group (JPEG). JPEG is a standardization body created by the ISO (International Organization for Standardization) and CCITT. The candidate algorithm, also known as JPEG, will be the first international compression standard for color images. PENNEBAKER & MITCHELL and WALLACE (1990; 1991) provide the most authoritative sources on the JPEG initiative. ANSON and BARNSLEY & HURD also offer detailed treatment of the JPEG compression technique, especially how it compares with fractal transform compression. The JPEG algorithm uses an extension of DCT known as baseline sequential DCT compression, which comprises three main steps: (1) DCT encoding, (2) coefficient quantization, and (3) entropy encoding. In the first step, the input image is divided into 8 × 8 pixel blocks and a coefficient value is calculated for each pixel by DCT, producing 64 values per block. In the second step, the 64 coefficient values for each block are subjected to quantization (a process in which continuous input data are converted to a limited number of discrete integer values). This is the step that is principally responsible for the amount of difference between the input image and the compressed output image (loss). In the final step, the mean DCT coefficient value for each block is subtracted from the next block, producing 63 coefficient mean difference values. This approach works because in most natural scenes block-to-block changes are usually minimal. The mean differences are sorted such that low-frequency coefficients appear before high-frequency coefficients and then Huffman encoding is applied on the ordered sequence.

One important feature built into the JPEG algorithm is that the user can select a tradeoff factor between compression ratio and the decompressed image quality. JPEG compression is also symmetric, which means that about the same amount of time is necessary for compression and decompression. JPEG compression has been selected by Apple Computer, Inc. for compression of QuickTime-based still images (HOFFERT ET AL.), and other large computer organizations are working on implementing JPEG in their systems (PENNEBAKER & MITCHELL). According to Anson, fractal-based techniques can produce higher levels of compression than JPEG and other DCT-based techniques. Because substantial information redundancy exists in most images, it is possible to rotate, contract, move, or even skew large portions of an image to reproduce smaller portions. Affine mapping is a technique based on fractal mathematics that takes advantage of the latter situation to compress images. The fractal transform algorithm described by BARNSLEY & HURD is an excellent example of a compression technique that applies affine mapping. Fractal compression is nonsymmetrical—i.e., it takes longer to compress than decompress an image. This is actually an advantage because access and display time is reduced. Recently, Microsoft Corp. has selected fractal transform compression for its multimedia products.

Compression standards activities. PENNEBAKER & MITCHELL reported that work is in progress toward a new ISO-sponsored algorithm (ISO DIS 11544) for lossless compression of bilevel and limited bits/pixel images. A joint committee, consisting of members from ISO and CCITT called JBIG (Joint Bilevel Image Group), is overseeing this activity. The JBIG algorithm is likely to supersede the Group 3 and Group 4 algorithms because it achieves higher compression ratios (about 30% more) on typical bilevel images and it can also compress halftone images. Work is also in progress on an algorithm that can compress moving images or multiple frame images. This activity is sponsored by ISO alone and is being done by the Moving Picture Experts Group (MPEG). The most authoriative source on MPEG compression is LE GALL. The MPEG effort is divided into two groups, one responsible for image compression (MPEG-Video) and the other for audio compression (MPEG-Audio). MPEG uses interpolation as a key technique to reduce redundancy among frames and achieve compression. For individual frame compression MPEG uses DCT and Huffman compression.

Image Formats

This section begins with general coverage of the literature on image formats. It is beyond the chapter's scope to offer a detailed description of all the major image formats in use today. Instead the major formats using the dimensions of efficiency, quality, and portability are compared in Table 2. Following that a subset of the major formats that deserve more attention from the user and the developer community are reviewed. We discuss why the formats in the subset deserve more attention and point to the literature that contains additional information on them.

Unfortunately, not much research has been conducted on the development and improvement of image formats. The JPEG initiative, although founded on image compression objectives, has been the most sensitive to quality, efficiency, and portability in image representation. The JPEG algorithm is described particularly well by WALLACE (1991) and PENNEBAKER & MITCHELL. EARNSHAW & WISEMAN cover a few important image formats in use today by the scientific community. SHAFFER, in a recent *ARIST* chapter, surveys data representations used in GISs, which includes a discussion of image formats. BESSER (1991a) provides an excellent overview, from the perspective of visual arts, of the trade-offs among factors that determine digital image quality. D'ALLEYRAND offers good treatment of the diverse needs associated with image management in office environments. UDUPA ET AL. report on the development of a new image format for handling multidimensional image data generated by the medical community. Most of the data formats for image representation in use today originated from the computer industry to serve the needs of specific image-generating or -processing tools. RIMMER and KAY & LEVINE are the most comprehensive sources found that cover image formats used in a wide variety of software and hardware platforms. Rimmer also includes customized algorithms for image decompression and display.

Developing effective image formats involves careful consideration of efficiency, quality, and portability factors (see Table 2). Provision for storing image-related information, such as resolution, multiple color LUTs, color models, and correction data, determines how faithfully and accurately the original image can be reproduced—in other words, the quality of the representation. Features related to compression and network transmission, if built into the format, can make the representation more efficient. Factors such as the encoding scheme chosen to store the data, the level of support from the user and developer community, and consideration of established standards related to imaging technology, can make a particular image representation more portable than others.

Important subset. Of all the formats mentioned above, TIFF (Tagged Image File Format) is the most popular in terms of the number of

Table 2
Comparison of Image Formats

	Efficiency		Quality (Resolution)		Portability		
Format	Encoding[a]	Compression	Intensity	Spatial	Platform	Standard[b]	Origin-Use
MacPaint	Binary	PackBits	1 bit	720 × 576 pixels	Mac	No	Apple (for general use)
PICT2	Binary	PackBits	24 bits	No limit	Mac	No	Apple (for general use)
BMP	Binary	RLE	24 bits	Undetermined	PC	No	Microsoft (for general use)
PCX	Binary	RLE	24 bits	64K × 64K pixels	PC	No	Zsoft (for general use)
SunRaster	Binary	RLE	32 bits	Undetermined	UNIX	No	Sun (for general use)
XWD (X Window Dump)	Binary	None	32 bits	Undetermined	UNIX	No	MIT (for screen dump)
TGA (Targa)	Binary	RLE	32 bits	Undetermined	Mac and PC	No	Truevision (for general use)
GIF (Graphics Interchange Format)	Binary	LZW	8 bits	64K × 64K pixels	Mac, PC and UNIX	No, but widely used	CompuServe (for general use)
TIFF (Tagged Image File Format)	Binary; Supports inclusion of some ASCII data	CCITT Group 3 and 4, LZW, RLE or JPEG	24 bits	2^{32}bytes Maximum file size	Mac, PC and UNIX	No, but widely supported and used	Aldus and Microsoft (for general use)

Table 2
Comparison of Image Formats (Continued)

	Efficiency		Quality (Resolution)		Portability		
Format	Encoding[a]	Compression	Intensity	Spatial	Platform	Standard[b]	Origin-Use
JFIF (JPEG File Interchange Format)	Binary	JPEG	24 bits	No limit	Mac, PC and UNIX	No, but JPEG is soon to be a ISO/CCITT standard	C-Cube Micro-systems (for general use)
HDF (Hierarchical Data Format)	Binary	RLE and JPEG	24 bits	No limit	Platform independent	No	National Center for Super-computing Applications (for scientific use)
PostScript	ASCII and binary	Usually none, recently added JPEG	32 bits	No limit	Platform independent	No	Adobe Systems (mainly for printing)
QuickTime "MooV"	Binary	Apple's proprietary compression and JPEG	32 bits	160 × 120 pixels at 30 frames per second	Mac and PC	No	Apple (for time-based information)

[a]Encoding: the symbol system or codes used to store image and image-related information. Binary is a lower level form than ASCII, thus more efficient.
[b]Standard: used in the formal sense, as in national or international standard, not de facto standard.

applications that support it. The authoritative source to learn more about TIFF is the official TIFF documentation published by ALDUS CORPORATION. TIFF is also well covered by RIMMER and KAY & LEVINE. POOR, POYNTON, and WARNER provide brief but more readable coverage of the TIFF format. TIFF can be used to store bilevel, grayscale, and color images using five different compression schemes. What sets TIFF apart from the other formats is the wide range of image-related information that it can store; some of it is devoted exclusively to image accuracy, including correction values for grayscale and color, CIE standard values for color, color LUTs, name and model number of the device that generated the image and the software that produced the image. Other information that can be stored in TIFF can be used to facilitate indexing and retrieval—e.g., the name of the person who generated the image, the date and time of generation, and objects depicted in the image. A very useful feature offered by TIFF is the possibility of creating a linked list of multiple images maintained in a single file. One can imagine using this feature to store multipart documents (multiple pages), such as a journal article. Perhaps in anticipation of such applications, TIFF designers included facilities to store a document name and page numbers in a TIFF file.

A structural feature that makes TIFF superior to many other image formats is the use of tags to store image-related information. Tags are brief identifiers that precede each unique data segment in a TIFF file; they add flexibility to the format. Individual data segments can appear in any order in the file since the tag preceding each data segment uniquely identifies it. Also the format can be easily extended to include new information by creating additional tags. Aldus and Microsoft publish these tags, describing how they should be used in a file. The current TIFF 6.0 specification contains reference to 36 tags recommended for baseline TIFF.

Presently there is no international standard for digital image formats. JFIF (JPEG File Interchange Format) comes closest because it was the first image format created to store image information using JPEG compression. This format was devised by C-Cube Microsystems, a principal private sponsor of JPEG activities. More information on this format can be found in KAY & LEVINE and HAMILTON. JFIF does not add much to the core JPEG compressed image information except a version number, resolution information, and an optional thumbnail version of the image. As noted earlier, JPEG compression was developed under the collaboration of ISO and CCITT. In September 1992 the initial JPEG recommendation officially became a CCITT "Recommendation", Rec. T.81. It is expected that the JPEG recommendation will become an international standard. The JPEG effort did not result in a full-fledged international image format standard due to internal disagreements. However, a close reading of any of the authoritative materials on JPEG (mentioned elsewhere in this chapter) will show that the JPEG effort has produced much more than an internationally approved image compression scheme. WALLACE (1991) and HUDSON ET AL. are two particularly good sources for reviewing the wide variety of image-related problems the JPEG committee focused on and some of their solutions.

Three specific areas tackled by the JPEG committee make JFIF, or any other formats based on JPEG, important formats to consider. One of these areas is the use of a quantization table during DCT quantization (which is responsible for maximum compression during application of JPEG). The JPEG recommendation states that the 64-element quantization table can be specified by the application or the user as an input to the encoder. This open approach to quantization ensures that the visual quality of the image and the quantity of information lost is controllable by the user. The second important area in JPEG is the way it achieves resolution independence (or device independence). This aspect is called hierarchical mode of operation in the JPEG recommendation. This mode allows storage of compressed images in gradations of multiple resolutions such that particular image resolutions can be matched with the resolutions of the device for optimal display and printing. The third area in JPEG, known as progressive DCT encoding, can be extremely important to users accessing images over a network. This mode performs multiple compression cycles through the image data. In each compression cycle a set of pixels (covering the full image) is transmitted to the receiving screen. In this way the compressed image is progressively built up in the receiving display, from lower resolution to higher resolution. Compared to the raster mode of transmission, which builds the image on the output device one line at a time, the progressive mode gives the user more control over the transmission session. The user who is receiving an image in the progressive mode will be able to tell quickly if the image being transmitted is the desired one and stop the transmission if it is not.

In certain disciplines, such as astronomy, biology, medicine, and engineering, digital images are now regularly produced and manipulated, and the trend is toward increased use of digital images in the sciences (TREINISH). An organization that has been at the forefront of new scientific visualization techniques, the National Center for Supercomputing Applications at the University of Illinois at Urbana-Champaign, conducted a search in 1987 for a digital image format that could adequately support the needs of scientists. It found none and decided to develop a new format that came to be called the Hierarchical

Data Format (HDF). Today, HDF is in its third version (3.3) and is well supported on various computer platforms (NATIONAL CENTER FOR SUPERCOMPUTING APPLICATIONS).

EARNSHAW & WISEMAN present a brief overview of the HDF format and discuss its use in current scientific visualization applications. TREINISH stated that a visualization application should not be required to have a detailed description of the data to be displayed. An important contributing factor to HDF's popularity is its unique design known as the metafile structure. Besides the image data, a metafile contains information that describes the data—e.g., data type, size, and location. This approach reduces the burden on the application to interpret the data. HDF uses TIFF-like tags to identify specific data segments, and it can be used to store numeric as well as image data. Figure 1 is an example of an image data object (containing two images) in HDF format.

Tag	Ref	Data
DFTAG-FD	1	FILE IDENTIFIER
DFTAG_FD	1	FILE DESCRIPTOR
DFTAG_LUT	1	LOOK UP TABLE
DFTAG_ID	1	X AND Y DIMENSIONS OF IMAGE ARRAYS
DFTAG_RI	1	FIRST 2-D IMAGE ARRAY
DFTAG_RI	2	SECOND 2-D IMAGE ARRAY

Figure 1. An image metafile containing two images in HDF format

Ref" refers to a counter that keeps track of the frequency of the same tags used in the file (e.g., see the Ref value for the last tag). Only one resolution tag is used in the file because the two image files are the same size. TREINISH had further stated that in an effective visualization environment, management of and access to data must be decoupled from the visualization software. Included with HDF are software routines that perform functions such as file I/O, error handling, memory management, and physical storage. Application software can call these routines as functions to access and manage HDF-based data.

Strictly speaking, PostScript is not an image format. It is a page-description language that can render images on a page or a computer screen. PostScript also accepts image pixel arrays from which it can generate images. It is widely used in high quality printers, but it has also been used in computer displays. The best source for learning more about PostScript is the documentation available from its developers (ADOBE SYSTEMS INCORPORATED). ROTH is also a good source for an overview of the basic programming techniques necessary to use

PostScript, and HOLZGANG offers a more in-depth treatment of PostScript programming. For understanding the structure of PostScript rather than developing PostScript programming skills, consult JONES, GOSWELL, and SCHONHUT. A PostScript representation of an image has some distinguishing attributes that are advantages not available to most of the other formats discussed in this chapter. For example, a PostScript image can be represented using ASCII (referred to as Level 1 syntax), ensuring its transportability across diverse hardware platforms because ASCII is a universally accepted symbol system. Since PostScript is an interpreted language, a driver is necessary to process and print a PostScript image. Such drivers are now widely available as part of image and graphics applications. The ASCII encoding scheme and the PostScript interpretation process make PostScript image generation somewhat slow. However, PostScript is not a static representation like the other image representations discussed so far. The PostScript language offers powerful image manipulation operations that can be used by someone who is knowledgeable to regenerate the image in a way that best matches the user's needs (only a word processor is necessary for editing). For those users more interested in preservation of space than flexibility of manipulation, a PostScript image can also be encoded in binary (Level 2 syntax) and compressed using the JPEG algorithm. Another feature that makes PostScript representation more portable than others is its separation of spatial reference into two spaces: user and device. The PostScript interpreter can automatically scale-up images drawn in the user's (virtual) space to the highest spatial resolution available on the user's screen or printer.

Computer-based representation of certain complex phenomena, such as storms or volcanic eruptions, can be presented more realistically by adding the dimension of time to the final output. Traditionally, scientists had to record a sequence of frames on an analog video unit and play back that recording to achieve animation, a burdensome effort that most scientists avoided. By introducing the QuickTime operating system extension, Apple brought digital video and animation to the desktop in late 1991. With QuickTime extension, animation or digital video output from a computer-based simulation can be directly recorded on a secondary storage medium. QuickTime-based scientific visualization examples from many fields, including medicine, astronomy, biology, and physics, are provided on a CD-ROM included with the excellent book on visualization by WOLFF & YAEGER. This book contains a short section on the generation of QuickTime-based visualization effects. For a more in-depth treatment of QuickTime architecture and its application, the APPLE COMPUTER, INCORPORATED guide on QuickTime is highly recommended. ROSEBUSH provides a highly readable description of QuickTime features and a good overview of current tools that make it possible to capture video sequences from analog video. WALSH discusses major components of QuickTime along with programming techniques in a concise and clear manner. HOFFERT ET AL. (QuickTime's development team) describe QuickTime as an architecture for manipulating time-based data. Generally, time-based data type refers to any data that can be stored and retrieved as a function of time.

QuickTime provides a data type called MooV that can be used to store a "movie." A movie file comprises multiple pointer lists called "tracks" that point to the raw data named "media." The "MooV" format allows image data to be stored in alternative-intensity resolutions using multiple tracks. Thus, for example, a frame sequence can be stored in alternative bit depths of 8, 16, and 24 in the same file, and QuickTime can automatically select the appropriate track to play depending on the resolution of the screen in use. Digitized sound can be synchronized and stored with image data using additional tracks. A track can also be used to store "poster frames" that act as a preview of the movie. The separation of tracks and media in the MooV format makes efficient searching and updating possible. Since image data stored in MooV format can take up a lot of space (a minute-long compressed 160 × 120 pixels, 24-bits/pixel movie is about 2 Mbytes), someone browsing movie files over a narrow bandwidth network can access the preview tracks (each about 100 Mbytes compressed) thus avoiding unnecessary monopolization of computing resources. When frames are deleted or moved about in a movie, the actual data (media) do not have to be accessed; only the pointers in the appropriate tracks need to be manipulated. An image compression tool is included with QuickTime that takes advantage of interframe redundancies to achieve compression ratios that range from 5:1 to as high as 50:1. Apple also provides a player with QuickTime that can be used to display movies. Many currently available popular applications, including word processors, databases, spreadsheets, and mathematical analysis tools, are designed to be "QuickTime aware," which means they can store and display QuickTime movies.

Interchange and standardization issues. The many formats presently available to store images reflect the intense interest and growth in digital imaging technology. The diversity of formats, however, makes exchange, display, and manipulation of digital images a challenging and sometimes frustrating task. As Table 2 shows, almost all the major formats in use today were developed in the computing industry, with little serious research behind them on specific applications and user needs. Few works were found that attempted an analysis of the state of the art in image data formats. BELLAMY ET AL. compared five image formats, primarily in the context of scientific visualization, and concluded that a format developed by the University of Utah, called UTAH-RLE, was superior to the rest. The study did not include any JPEG-based format, nor did it include HDF. GERSHON & DOZIER investigated the proliferation of image formats and the problems this raises for managing image data. They concluded that problems can be alleviated through the development of standard formats and flexible format conversion tools. The only literature identified that can be described as a serious effort toward the development of an international standard for digital images are the works by HOFMANN & BLUM and BLUM & HOFMANN. They describe a proposal that has been accepted as a work item by the "information processing and computer graphics" committee (ISO/IEC/JTC1/SC24). This project aims to achieve international agreement in three areas: (1) formal definition of an image data model, (2) an image interchange format, and (3) application programming interface. According to the approved schedule, this proposal should reach DIS stage (draft international standard) by July 1994.

For those readers interested in international information technology standards (any serious researcher or developer of information technology should be), a number of sources describe the principal organizations and the procedures involved. PENNEBAKER & MITCHELL dedicate a chapter to a description of ISO, CCITT, and IEC (International Electrotechnical Commission). They explain how, in 1987, ISO and IEC decided to collaborate formally on issues of mutual interest, resulting in the creation of JTC1 (Joint Technical Committee 1) for overseeing standardization in information technology. Presently, other collaborative projects exist among ISO, IEC, and CCITT in the areas of data networks and telematic services. CRAWFORD discusses information standards and related issues from the perspective of librarians. The book of ARNOLD & DUCE is dedicated to ISO vector graphics standards. The authors discuss the structure of ISO in relation to national and international information technology standards organizations. They also describe the history and process behind the standardization of all the international graphics standards established until 1990, including GKS, GKS 3-D, CGM, and PHIGS. The major vector graphics standards are explained in detail using a layered reference model comprising application, graphics system, device driver, operating system, and terminal. The content and scope of Arnold and Duce's work is sufficiently close to the area of digital imaging that it is highly recommended as an important information source on standards. COURTOT is a good source for a quick overview of imaging technology standards related to applications, storage devices, display devices, and information transfer, presented from the perspective of record/document managers. RESSLER also explains several ISO standards and the standardization process; the focus, however, is on text representation standards such as ODA

(Office Document Architecture), SGML (Standard Generalized Markup Language) and SDIF (SGML Document Interchange Format).

IMAGE ACCESS

A substantial amount of the literature reviewed in this section concerns research on image databases. For a system to qualify as an image database, it must include data management facilities (LUNIN). Many works describe highly innovative approaches for improving image access, but these do not reflect any concern for image management. Hence, we use the more general term "image access" to refer to a broader subset of the literature. We consider here three important research areas concerned with image access: (1) data indexing and modeling, (2) user interface design, and (3) distributed access. As background for user interface design and distributed access, we discuss literature that provides a foundation for these areas. Some research efforts were identified that have contributed to two or all three of the areas, taking an integrated approach to system design. A survey of the three main areas of image access, basic background literature, and integrated approaches is presented below.

Data Indexing and Modeling

Large-scale image database projects have been undertaken in chemistry (LESK, 1991), astronomy (CATLETT & TERSTRIEP), earth science (CROMP & DORFMAN), medicine (GITLIN; JOST), and arts (BESSER, 1990; FANTINI ET AL.; WENTZ). A few image database systems are now available that can store and retrieve images in popular formats in powerful desktop computers (STEUER). However, basic problems in image retrieval still remain. CHANG & HSU observe in a recent article, "With a growing list of new applications based on image information handling, little success has been achieved on the direct management of image information" (p. 433). They conclude that commercial image databases treat images as "black-boxes," meaning that they provide limited access to image content. According to HIBLER ET AL., one of the most formidable problems in developing image retrieval systems is devising an efficient means of indexing the images.

Verbal indexing. One branch of work on image access focuses on issues associated with verbal indexing of images (in the context of this chapter the term verbal means textual, not oral). In these efforts, the semantic or interpretive elements of images are emphasized, regardless of the medium of image representation. This general approach makes outcomes or conclusions from such efforts applicable to digital images as well. KRAUSE considers the intellectual problems one faces in indexing images—viz., how one interprets the subject matter represented in an image and how one chooses particular aspects of an image to index. He presents examples of various images and shows how different choices of index terms can lead to different meanings being associated with the same image. ORBACH investigated critical features to attend to during cataloging of images and evaluates manual cataloging tools that can facilitate image cataloging. She notes that images are not self-identifying—i.e., by merely looking at an image one cannot determine the purpose or situation under which the image was produced. Although cataloging tools can be helpful, they leave much to the judgment of the cataloger. According to Orbach, the most important tool in cataloging visual materials is the cataloger. With regard to images in the visual arts, MARKEY states that there can be two levels of interpretation: primary and secondary. Primary meanings are the most direct interpretations and are based on practical and common-sense experience; secondary interpretations, however, require familiarity with customs and cultures or additional background information. Based on the difference in interpretation levels, several implications for image indexing are identified, the most important of which is that indexing images at the secondary level requires highly skilled and trained indexers. BROOKS has conducted a comprehensive review of indexing systems (both computerized and manual) for visual materials and concludes that the main obstacle in indexing is the lack of standardized subject indexes.

To ease the task of indexing images at the secondary level and also to promote indexing consistency, several classification systems have been developed. One of the most significant is the ICONCLASS system, which is a classification system for visual resources in the arts. ICONCLASS suffers from its narrow emphasis (the arts), and it has certain intrinsic structural limitations. HIBLER ET AL. analyzed the utility of ICONCLASS in indexing images of general subject matter. Three significant limitations were discovered (which, they conclude, may also apply to other specialized classification systems): (1) too much knowledge of the underlying arrangement of subjects is assumed on the part of users, (2) different image collections may use the classification system differently, and (3) it is hard to specify relationships among individual objects depicted in an image. Yet, indexing manually, without the aid of controlled vocabulary, is costly. In the research of HIBLER ET AL., each image required, on the average, 30 minutes to index manually. Indexing images on the basis of purely descriptive features (e.g., creator, title, date) may, however, lead to poor use of collections. BARNETT, in a review of the storage and retrieval needs of art information systems, concluded that one needs both descriptive and interpretive information for efficient access.

Although there seems to be a lack of useful techniques and tools for verbal indexing of images, successful systems have been developed that provide access to images based on verbal terms. This area of work was found to be the second major trend in image access. MULLER offers an in-depth treatment of document imaging systems. JONES summarizes the components and operations required in document imaging systems, with examples of systems currently in operation. The input to a document imaging system usually involves scanning (typically at a resolution of 200–400 DPI), OCR, compression (usually RLE), and indexing. All documents are identified with a unique verbal key and other verbal terms that the user may know. For example, paperwork associated with a particular client is indexed by an account number, name, address, time of entry, and class of document (e.g., agreement, claim, letter). PAN ET AL. reviewed various approaches currently applied in generating indexes for document images. One interesting technology they discuss is ICR (intelligent character recognition). ICR, also known as omnifont recognition, aims to eliminate the limitation of OCR's dependence on a font library. ICR applies recent techniques developed in pattern recognition, morphological image processing, expert systems, and fuzzy logic. PAN ET AL. describe how ICR technology combined with various indexing tools (e.g., an online thesaurus) can be used to automate the indexing. LESK (1991) discusses design of a prototype chemistry database that will eventually contain both ASCII and imaged versions of 500,000 pages of journal articles. In a prototype implementation of the system, the ASCII version of articles was used for full-text indexing. Documents were also indexed based on words in spatially relevant locations in the text, including the title, author, institutional affiliation, captions, experimental design, conclusion, and reference sections.

One of the largest online information vendors in the world, DIALOG, has added images to its database (THOMPSON). The images are linked to a single file in the database of trademarks. Thompson reviews the various operations associated with DIALOG image searching and identifies the weak point in the system: poor indexing of images. The DIALOG images are not indexed with a controlled vocabulary, resulting in inconsistent and ambiguous terminology. BOVEY reports on the development of an image database containing 12,000 records of 20th-century British newspaper cartoons at the University of Kent. Each image was indexed by multiple attributes, including date, artist, size, periodical, and caption. Subject access was provided using additional subject headings, a text field, and a notes field. Instead of using a controlled vocabulary for indexing images, certain systems allow descriptive free-text information to be linked to images. This involves a trade-off between cost of indexing and lack of precision in search results. FANTINI ET AL. describe an automated image archive in which users can attach descriptive text and an abstract with each image. Free-text information is supplemented with system-generated information, such as image file name, size, and resolution.

Visual surrogates. There is a distinct difference between how people interpret words and images. O'CONNOR (1985) summarizes it nicely: "Broadly, words are general signs. . .made more specific by syntax, whereas pictures are specific and made general by their context" (p. 212). In other words, pictures refer to instances, whereas words refer to classes. Therefore, image indexing based on verbal terms alone may cause search difficulty for users.

A third dominant line of research attempts to use both verbal and visual cues to enhance access to images. A common approach is the use of scaled-down versions of images as visual surrogates. It is worth elaborating on the interesting way the visual information is associated with verbal information in these systems. The visual surrogates are linked to a verbal index in a manner that allows mutual referencing. A user can start a verbal search and retrieve a set of visual surrogates, or a user can refer to a visual surrogate and retrieve the verbal indexing information. Using either the verbal index terms or the visual surrogates, the user can retrieve the desired image from the database or retrieve information on how to access the desired image from a separate repository. The key idea here is to capitalize on semantic or descriptive qualities of both images and words to find a particular image.

SELOFF describes the development of a system that uses an online thesaurus to provide access to NASA's image archive. The thesaurus contains both verbal terms and visual surrogates that are linked to each other. The images from the archives are not included in the system. Verbal index terms are used from the thesaurus to generate records for images. To search for an image, users select one or more terms from the thesaurus, which are then matched against the index records. The user can also initiate a search based on a visual surrogate from the thesaurus, in which case the terms linked to the surrogate are used to search for matching index record(s). Results of initial search experiences showed that as users become more adroit in using the system, they tend to perform more searches using verbal terms. Seloff states that verbal searching occurs more frequently because there are relatively fewer visual surrogates than verbal terms in the online thesaurus.

Photo CD displays a sheet of tiny representations of each image with a slide, or image, number to provide its simple, visual surrogates for locating images quickly. ASSMANN ET AL. report on the development of an image database that also utilizes visual surrogates to assist searching. This system, named Image Structured Query Language (ISQL) was created as an extension of the relational language Structured Query

Language (SQL) to allow retrieval of radiological images. Patient records are indexed according to such data as name of patient, date of image creation, and modality of image creation (e.g., magnetic resonance). In ISQL, scaled-down visual surrogates of images can be retrieved using these data. Using any one of the current batch of surrogates, the user can retrieve other related items, both images and text.

In discussing the image database project at Berkeley, BESSER (1990) makes a convincing case for the utility of visual surrogates in providing access to collections of rare or hard-to-replace visual materials. He argues that visual surrogates in combination with verbal indexing not only leads to more efficient searching but may also lead to less wear and tear on the visual materials in the collection. In the IMAGEQUERY system (developed at Berkeley) users narrow a search by directing queries to progressively smaller sets of terms associated with the visual surrogates retrieved in each search cycle (BESSER, 1990). A similar search can also be performed in the ISQL system. GECSEI & MARTIN designed a system that allows users to narrow a search quickly by exploiting relationships among visual surrogates. This system retrieves related surrogates when a particular surrogate is selected for closer investigation. Relationships among surrogates are established by calculating the similarity distances among surrogates using the frequency of common index terms shared among surrogates. This system adapts to users' preferences by automatically applying a narrowing threshold based only on those index terms associated with the last *N* surrogates chosen by the user (where *N* determines the convergence speed and can be adjusted by the user).

Image indexing. In all the research efforts mentioned in the visual surrogates section, image-based access is implemented by linking an image to one or more similar images; no effort is made to extract shapes or patterns from images and to link these elements to images. A fourth research trend was observed that merges techniques of pattern recognition with those of indexing to enhance image access. This trend is sustained mainly by research in computer vision, pattern recognition, and GISs (BROLIO ET AL.; GARY & MEHOTRA; GROSKY & JIANG; KASTURI ET AL.; PIZANO ET AL.; RABITTI & SAVINO). According to CHANG & HSU, as well as other researchers, the association of meanings (index terms) to whole images severely limits the use of image information. Chang and Hsu believe that computer vision technology has not matured enough to provide automated mapping among individual image features and associated meanings. Regardless of the difficulty in mapping, they acknowledge that the latter approach will eventually lead to more robust and effective systems.

ISR (Intermediate Symbolic Representation) combines database management and knowledge representation methods to allow access to multiple representations of images generated by a computer vision system (BROLIO ET AL.). In vision research, features and relationships among features are extracted from images as a byproduct of image processing techniques applied at various levels. At the low level of image processing, features such as edges, lines, and homogeneous regions (collections of contiguous data points with similar properties) may be generated. At the intermediate level the image may be transformed into a 1-bit depiction of region segmentation. At the highest level the image may be changed into a wire-frame model. ISR uses the information output from each stage to generate indexing data. After low and intermediate levels of processing, a data object, called a token, is used to store attribute pair information—e.g., the color and texture of a region or the length and location of a line segment. These tokens are logically grouped (based on associations among tokens) and stored in frames. Frames are organized into higher level networked structures called schemas. A schema can contain information on an entire image. Using schemas, frames, and tokens, ISR can answer queries dealing with spatial characteristics of images. An example of such a query applied to a schema of a city scene is: Find and display the longest road in the scene.

Access to images based on spatial characteristics is also possible in an image database described by CHANG ET AL. (1988). However, this system uses a different technique to index spatial features in images. This system, called Intelligent Image Database (IID), performs orthogonal projections on images to generate two keys, one representing the vertical projection and the other representing the horizontal projection. Pairs of these keys (2-D strings) are used to index images. Users pose visual queries to IID by arranging icons on the screen, which are transformed to 2-D strings and matched against the index. The 2-D string indexing of images is claimed to be faster than other pattern matching techniques due to the simplicity of the matching procedure and the parsimonious storage requirement. CHANG ET AL. (1992) extends the original 2-D string indexing technique to support visual queries that refer to nested and composite objects.

KATO proposes techniques for image indexing based on graphical features, subjective features, and unified features. For each image in the database, a vector is generated, using statistical measures to calculate distribution of pixels per image. This vector is called the graphical feature (GF) vector. Kato's system can be "trained" to generate indexes based on attributes chosen by a user. The user is presented with a learning set of images that he or she classifies into subsets according to the perceived existence of common attributes present in the images. Then a linear mapping matrix is derived by performing discriminant analysis on the GF vectors of images in the classified sets. Using the transpose of the linear mapping matrix, subject feature (SF) vectors are calculated for each image. This transformation is shown below:

$$r_k = A'p_k$$

In the equation, r_k is a SF vector, A' is the transposed linear mapping matrix, p_k is a GF vector, and k represents a particular image. Kato comments that once a linear mapping matrix A is calculated based on a small image set classified by the user, it can be used to generate SF vectors for all images in the database, greatly reducing indexing costs.

A third indexing approach, described by Kato, extends the system to color images. GF vectors are calculated based on RGB intensity distribution in images. SF vectors are calculated by using weights of keywords assigned to images. Again statistical techniques are proposed—this time canonical correlation and regression—that can map GF vectors and SF vectors to unified feature space (containing vector representation of images called unified features). Kato also presents several algorithms demonstrating how results of each indexing method can be used to implement powerful search options. In one approach, the user can query the system by sketching a representation of the desired image. The user can also search for images by keywords that express subjective features (pleasant, comfortable, desirable). Of all the indexing approaches suggested, keyword indexing is the most labor intensive.

KOFAKIS ET AL. present an object-oriented approach to image indexing and retrieval. Images are subjected to operations that generate information on segments, relationships among segments, and points per segment. Information on individual segments is treated as an object. Like the ISR system, knowledge representation techniques are used to transform images into hierarchical data structures using classes of objects that contain other subclasses of objects related to lower levels of image representation. The object-oriented methodology may prove to be a superior environment to bring together diverse data and processing techniques to develop an image database. Inheritance and data abstraction principles of object-oriented data representation aid in data reduction and consistency. The modular architecture of object-oriented databases can easily accommodate multilevel image representations.

In all the literature reviewed on image indexing, few research efforts were found that aimed at the indexing of 3-D images. COSTAGLIOLA ET AL. extend the 2-D string indexing method described earlier to 3-D scenes. BENSON & ZICK recently proposed an innovative object-oriented solution to the indexing of 3-D medical images.

Image data structures. Access to images can be accommodated and even improved by using specialized data structures. This area of work somewhat overlaps image indexing (described above). However, a distinct difference was noticed in methods emphasized for facilitating image access. In some research, the methods of extracting information from images are emphasized, and conventional or existing data models are used to store the information. In another research trend data modeling is emphasized and new data structures are proposed to represent image information. This research trend is the fifth most dominant in image access.

One popular approach applied is the use of tree structures to represent image information. Tree structures for image data representation are efficient because logarithmic search time can be achieved, data can be conveniently reorganized, and storage space is used economically (ROUSSOPOULOS ET AL.). SAMET discusses the application of quadtrees and several of their variants in representing image information. In transforming an image into a quadtree representation the image is decomposed into four equally partitioned parts, at each iteration, until the total image area is accounted for. The nonleaf nodes contain spatial information describing the total area covered by their successor nodes. The leaf nodes usually contain atomic information on a predefined unit of image area. SHAFFER gives excellent coverage of the application of spatial image indexing techniques in a recent *ARIST* chapter on GISs. Here we present additional coverage of literature that originates from other areas or that does not overlap Shaffer's work.

PIZANO ET AL. extend the entity-relation model to develop a database capable of maintaining the spatial integrity of pictorial objects. In this database, image segments, at several levels of granularity (e.g., points, lines, regions, or even the whole image) can be represented as entities. Primitive pictorial attributes are used to store data that can determine the appearance of a pictorial object; for example, there are primitives for location, boundary, color, and size. Properties and values, such as the population of a city, the year a road was built, or the name of the mayor, are represented by nonpictorial attributes. Another attribute, "derived attribute," is used to store data that can be computed by applying filters and mathematical functions to the primitive attributes (e.g., length of a road). The relationships between entities (E) and associated attributes (A) were represented in the database using the following form: $R(E_1, \ldots, E_N, A_1, \ldots, A_M)$, where N is the degree of the relationship, and M is the total number of attributes that characterizes the relation R. For example, a simple relationship, such as the distance between a road and a landmark, would be represented as: Distance (road, landmark, distance).

JOSEPH & CARDENAS developed a 2-D gridded data structure for storing images. In this approach multiple image representations (raw RGB layers and derived structures) covering a particular physical area are stacked on top of each other and stored in variable-length records. New derivatives of images can be added to the record structure as additional attributes, not just as static data instances. Data can be accessed by running a window over pixels in raster scan order, which can pick up data values from any or all the image layers for each pixel stored in a record. For minimizing search time R^+ trees have been applied in an image database (ROUSSOPOULOS ET AL.). R^+ trees gain better search efficiency over R trees by eliminating overlaps. At the leaf level, if a node contains a rectangle that overlaps a rectangle covered by another node, the rectangle is decomposed into smaller rectangles until the overlapping area is removed. This splitting may propagate to nonleaf nodes, but no bounding rectangles at any level will be enlarged. Here search efficiency is gained at the expense of space.

User Interface Design

Many objects have been devised to facilitate human–computer communication. These include software objects such as Microsoft Windows for IBM and IBM-clone computers, System 7 for the Macintosh, and the X Window environment for UNIX-based workstations. Semimechanical objects, such as digitizing tablets, light pens, display units, keyboards, and mice, also facilitate human–computer communication. Each object requires specific actions (e.g., pressure on a mouse button or selection of the "print" option from the menu) to activate various functions. Techniques related to implementation of all such actions, covering all the functioning objects, comprise the domain of user interface design (MOSTAFA). A user interface is the top layer or the perceived part of an interactive computer system. In information retrieval systems, the user interface is the principal component responsible for supporting information retrieval.

User interface design evolved into an independent field relatively recently, reaching prominence in the 1980s (GRUDIN). It originated from a serious focus on human–computer interaction problems in systems developed by large software companies. SHAW has written a highly readable and informative *ARIST* chapter on this topic. Some seminal work has been conducted by SHNEIDERMAN, CARD ET AL., and NORMAN. Because this field is so new, few broadly applicable theories have been put forth for attaining effective design. Theoretical and empirical contributions toward user interface design in image retrieval systems are even rarer. The few relevant works that we identified are discussed below.

User modeling. NORMAN believes that the designer must understand the user's mental model of the system to attain good user interface design. Various factors can shape these models, but characteristics of the system (e.g., screen/image resolution and processing speed) and user attributes (e.g., visual perception and experience level) are usually the most important factors. Neuropsychological evidence shows that people process visual information differently from verbal information (PAIVIO). In research on cognitive processes associated with TV imagery SALOMON demonstrated that images tend to "short-circuit" the cognition process, allowing humans to process images more quickly than verbal information. This particular research may have direct implications for systems designed for accessing moving images. HABER & WILKINSON present an excellent overview of theories associated with human cognitive constructs and how they can be applied toward the design of computer displays. One conclusion they draw is that visual data, in the form of images, are frequently processed in visual terms alone, with no recoding into verbal representations.

A few studies have considered the current capabilities of display devices and their influence on image quality. Extensions to the CIE standard have been proposed since different devices tend to map CIE to RGB in different ways, producing inconsistent results (BESSER, 1991a). The CIE-LUV and CIE-LAB color space extensions produce highly precise results because they produce consistent mapping to RGB; the mapping process, however, is quite complex (PENNEBAKER & MITCHELL). ESTER performed a highly relevant experiment to assess the connection between human perception and image resolution. Fifty-six art historians had to accurately rate intensity and spatial resolutions of a set of images. Spatial resolution test results showed that observers rated grayscale images more accurately than color images; however, this difference eroded as resolution increased. Generally, low-resolution images (400 × 400 pixels or below) were accurately discerned and acknowledged to be of poor quality for both color and grayscale images. At the high end, for both color and grayscale, 1,500 × 1,500 pixels seemed to be a good breaking point at which the advantage of higher perceived quality remained intact. Results of the intensity resolution test showed that viewers were much more sensitive to changes in bit depths for color images than for grayscale images. There was a steady drop in participants' abilities to distinguish between successive grayscale bit-depth values, whereas discrimination remained quite high for intermediate bit-depth values for color. One important conclusion Ester drew was that spatial resolution may be more important to grayscale images while intensity resolution may be more relevant for color images.

Ester's results are supported by other studies on human perception, which show that the eye has less spatial sensitivity to color (chrominance) than to brightness (luminance). The JPEG compression algorithm was designed to take advantage of this difference to achieve greater compression with no perceived data loss (PENNEBAKER & MITCHELL). BEARD discusses perception studies conducted on users of radiological images. For this group a minimum intensity resolution of 12 bits/pixel and spatial resolution of 4,000 × 4,000 pixels may be necessary. More research on the link between perception and image quality needs to be done for different types of image collections and different user groups (BESSER, 1991a).

Interaction modes. Among the many interaction modes, the direct-manipulation window-based environment, collectively known as graphical user interface (GUI), is the most popular. HUANG compares various interaction modes in a comprehensive review of this area. Direct manipulation interaction takes advantage of two psychological factors: distance and engagement. In the user interface, distance is proportional to the amount of user effort needed to translate tasks to interface functions. The notion of engagement refers to the feeling of having direct control over system operations. The interface should be a seamless and predictable communication medium through which the user can quickly change system states. To achieve this effect, system components are represented as graphical objects (e.g., icons) with specific properties. In a system that attempts to facilitate access to images, the use of iconic or other visual cues would match the underlying information domain. This in turn would reduce the cognitive effort necessary for task translations, and it would also support direct engagement. Numerous GUI environments have been developed that cover all the major computer platforms (ORR), attesting to the popularity of this interaction modality. Recently, ROBERTSON ET AL. reported on some innovative techniques being developed at Xerox-PARC that extend the traditional GUI mode. The Xerox-PARC team is implementing a new interaction mode called the Information Visualizer. This mode combines techniques from information retrieval and computer graphics to support information-intensive interactions—e.g., retrieving and viewing file directories several levels deep.

Query languages. Query languages to support image retrieval range from those that are purely verbal (e.g., in DIALOG) to those that are purely pictorial (e.g., in the system devised by KATO as discussed previously). Some command-based visual query languages attempted to improve on conventional query languages by extending the Query-by-Example language. One good example of this type of effort is the PICQUERY language (JOSEPH & CARDENAS). A user can formulate a PICQUERY using a whole picture or individual objects represented in a picture. Figure 2 shows a PICQUERY based on a whole picture.

Picture	Region	Object
PIC	EGYPT	P.

Figure 2. A simple PICQUERY based on a whole picture

The PICQUERY above specifies that a region named EGYPT should be found in the picture PIC and printed out (PIC is a verbal identifier, EGYPT is a whole picture, and P. under a column indicates that the values of that column are to be printed out).

Figure 3 shows another PICQUERY formulation based on individual objects represented in two different pictures.

Picture 1	Object Name	Basis	Picture 2	Object Name
PIC1	C1	Shape	PIC2	P.

Figure 3. A PICQUERY based on individual objects in pictures

Here the PICQUERY specifies that objects similar in shape to C1 as depicted in picture PIC1 should be retrieved from the picture PIC2, and the names of the objects retrieved should be printed (PIC1, PIC2, and C1 are verbal identifiers). A few additional efforts in development of visual query languages were found that extended the highly flexible and popular SQL language for relational databases. Good examples of these languages are PSQL (ROUSSOPOULOS ET AL.) and ISQL (ASSMANN ET AL.).

CHANG ET AL. (1988) and KATO report on query languages that allow users to specify visual features in queries (both systems also allow keyword-based searching). In the system designed by Chang et al. the user can query the entire database of images or individual images. The user specifies a query incorporating visual features by arranging icons on the screen of elementary shapes or objects (circles, rectangles, and houses). The system then generates a 2-D query string based on horizontal and vertical projections performed on the icons. The query string is matched against an index of 2-D strings generated from images in the database. When a matching image is retrieved, the user can specify a query such as: surrounded by (*X*,*Y*), which retrieves the names of all objects *X* (e.g., islands) surrounded by object *Y* (e.g., sea). In the system designed by Kato, the user can specify a visual query by sketching a rough outline of the desired image. However, individual images cannot be queried for extracting additional information.

In systems that allow query by visual features the level of specificity expressible in queries does not usually match the complexity and richness of the information present in images. In a few systems (especially in GISs) strong emphasis on image data structures has produced some techniques that allow users to refer to relatively fine-grained features in images. However, this is achieved only at extremely high computational and labor cost in indexing. BESSER (1991b), in reporting on the development of selection systems for visual materials in the arts, architecture, and anthropology, stated that pattern recognition techniques have not matured enough to be useful in indexing such materials. An alternative visual querying approach based on visual surrogates is computationally less expensive. Good examples of systems based on visual surrogates are described by BESSER (1991a) and GECSEI & MARTIN. In the system developed by Gecsei and Martin, the user selects a particular visual surrogate from a "context" of visual surrogates represented on the screen; this tells the system that images similar to the selected surrogate should be retrieved. Similarity is determined based on frequency of keywords in common between the selected image and other images in the database. If the user continues to select surrogates, weights of keywords assigned to selected surrogates are increased, which results in a display of the contexts that more closely match the selected surrogates. The user can zoom on a surrogate to inspect the corresponding image in full scale. One of the primary drawbacks of systems based on visual surrogates is that they depend on selection of appropriate keywords/terms by a human indexer.

Limitations. For the uninitiated, the ability to represent millions of colors (e.g., in 24-bit resolution) sometimes leads to misuse of colors. TUFTE (1990) presents some examples of color misuse in computer displays and shows how, with a few shades of colors, effective interface components can be designed. In the experiments conducted by ESTER, the art historians stated that they work mostly with grayscale photographs because color can seduce the eye with a false sense of fidelity. In discussing image representation in scientific image analysis tasks, WOLFF & YAEGER report that grayscale images often provide better structural detail to the eye. Problems with image accuracy sometimes have roots in image conversion from one medium to another or in the representation techniques applied (SHAFFER; WOLFF & YAEGER). For example, a color LUT optimized to enhance small structures may pick up superfluous features or introduce spurious artifacts in the image. The power to distill output from hours' worth of numerical simulations (in scientific visualization applications) into a single image should be exercised cautiously. In a drive to add realism to the resulting data, misuse of visualization tools may produce "patterns" from the data set where none really exists (WEBER).

MITCHELL presents several examples of image manipulation to deceive the viewer. With advances in digital imaging technology such manipulations have become relatively simple to effect and hard to detect. Digital images are altered by manipulating pixel values in the memory rather than mechanically altering surfaces; thus, digital images may show fewer traces of the artist's hand. The fact that an image has a seamless surface may no longer provide strong evidence for concluding that it has not been manipulated. The viewer must look for other clues, such as internal consistency and consistency with existing knowledge to verify image authenticity.

Distributed Access

WORTHINGTON & ROBINSON categorize current network technologies into three classes based on their physical extent (local area networks (LANs), metropolitan area networks (MANs), and wide area network (WANs)) and summarize their strengths and weaknesses. Popular network technologies include Ethernet (used as LANs), Token Ring (used as LANs), Fiber Distributed Data Interface (used as MANs) and Integrated Services Digital Network (used for WANs). Standard protocols have been developed to allow communication among diverse network technologies. Prime examples of these are the Transmission Control Protocol/Internet Protocol (TCP/IP) suite (HUNT) and protocols for Open System Interconnect (OSI) Reference Model (DAVISON; DENENBERG). Internet, the world's largest network, uses the widely accepted TCP/IP protocols and powerful data routing computers distributed strategically in various geographic locations to link networks of different sizes and types (CERF; MOSTAFA ET AL.).

How fast and how much image data can be transferred are functions of network bandwidth. LYNCH (1988) presented a useful table comparing the time that would be necessary to transfer a bilevel image over networks of different bandwidth rates. Lynch assumed an image size of 800 kbytes and ideal conditions for transmission. We present the table in a slightly modified form as Table 3.

Bandwidth constraints should always be considered in terms of the context of the application(s) the network serves. LESK (1990), in a report presented to the Commission on Preservation and Access, estimated that six books (each 300 pages long) digitally represented in 300 DPI resolution would take up about 1 gigabyte or 1,000 Mbytes. Using the measures proposed by Lynch, we can predict that it would take slightly longer than thirteen minutes to transmit six books over an

Table 3
Comparison of Image Transfer Rates of Different Media[a]

Medium	Bandwidth (Bits/Second)	Image Transfer Time
Dial-up phone line	2.4 k	55 minutes
Leased line	9.6 k	14 minutes
Leased line (T1)	1.5 M	4 seconds
Token Ring	4 M	1 second
Ethernet	10 M	1 second

[a]From LYNCH (1988). Reproduced by permission of Learned Information, Inc.

Ethernet network. To support interactive browsing operations on a database of digital books, the Ethernet bandwidth would surely prove to be highly restrictive.

For downloading, display, or any other local manipulation of images, users' workstations may impose additional constraints on distributed image applications. LYNCH (1988) pointed out that if the images were to be compressed, each image would be reduced to 80 kbytes (assuming 10:1 compression ratio). However, this would require at least 1 Mbyte of memory per image (size of an image after decompression) in the user's workstation for manipulation. Further, the user's workstation must have access to appropriate algorithms to decompress the images locally. Recent advances in client-server based technologies (RENAUD), which aid in, among other things, sharing of processing burdens between a remote server and distributed clients, can resolve part of the problem. Client software packages are now available that can quickly decompress and display images locally without user intervention (e.g., TurboGopher or Mosaic on the Macintosh); however, the local memory requirement and requirements of client tools would still need to be satisfied.

CATLETT & TERSTRIEP had described the demands a multimedia digital library may place on the network. They discussed one data source, the Hat Creek radio telescope, whose output for a single pass may amount to 2,048 images, each having intensity resolution of 24 bits and spatial resolution of 2,048 × 2,048 pixels. This amounts to approximately 26 gigabytes of data. Assuming that a user wishes only to browse such a data set (no other local manipulation), even frame-by-frame retrieval of the data set may overtax a typical network's capacity. One solution has been discussed before, known as progressive DCT encoding used in the JPEG compression algorithm. Another possible solution is transmission of low-resolution visual surrogates, from which the user can decide to retrieve the full-resolution frames (BESSER, 1990). It is interesting that for images of textual records, LYNCH (1988) proposed automatically isolating features, such as the first and last line, headings, and captions, and sending these data in place of actual images to conserve network capacity.

Catlett and Terstriep raise another important point related to data integrity. When a large image data set is sent over a network in frame by frame sequence some isochronous protection measures are needed to order the frames correctly at the receiving end. In such a process it is better to skip faulty frames than try to recover all the frames because the delay in transmission necessary for image recovery may cause more disruption to the image stream than the original error might have caused. Distributed access to digital image archives is an important area of work in radiology (sometimes called teleradiology) that generates valuable research results (GITLIN; JOST). A major thrust in medical image networking is comparative evaluations that examine how available technologies influence transfer rate, volume, and display (JOST).

The information science community recently called for serious attention to the development of digital libraries (LUNIN & FOX). As justification for the creation of such libraries, recent advances in network infrastructure and the availability of network search and retrieval tools are cited. However, most of the network tools currently available are text oriented and the present bandwidth of the nationwide network infrastructure is hardly adequate to support useful distributed image-based applications. The vision of digital libraries is good, but significant advances in image access are required for this vision to be realized.

CONCLUSION

Digital imaging is studied and applied in diverse fields. At present the main thrust in imaging research, development, and literature is on application: developing and improving techniques to use image-based information effectively. The main focus of this chapter, however, is more basic in nature. Literature on image formats, data structures, modeling, indexing, user interface design, distribution, efficiency and quality is given primary emphasis. The treatment, though, is not purely theoretical—influences of specific applications, computer industry and standardizing bodies receive ample attention in the chapter.

One will achieve more fruitful results, in the short term, in the area of image representation and access through empirical research than through theoretical development. An example will illustrate this point. Upon discovery of a large volume of literature on query languages, one may be motivated to develop general principles of image query language design. Such a project, however, risks being quickly outdated as new modes of interactions (through voice, touch, eye-tracking, and body movements) become widely available in the near future. Developments in digital imaging technology and other related technologies are too dynamic for useful theoretical projects to be pursued at this time. If empirical research is not an option, one can provide a crucial service to the imaging community by conducting critical surveys of research in imaging applications. Certain applied imaging areas have attained substantive maturity and deserve serious attention. This author recommends that in the near future *ARIST* chapters be devoted to one or more of the following areas: applied imaging in entertainment and arts, scientific visualization, and medical imaging.

BIBLIOGRAPHY

ADOBE SYSTEMS INCORPORATED. 1985. PostScript Language Tutorial and Cookbook. Reading, MA: Addison-Wesley; 1985. 243p. ISBN: 0-201-10179-3.

ALDUS CORPORATION. 1992. TIFF: Revision 6.0. Available: Anonymous FTP to ftp.ncsa.uiuc.edu. Directory: /misc/file.formats/graphics.formats.

ANSON, LOUISA. 1993. Image Compression: Making Multimedia Publishing a Reality. CD-ROM Professional. 1993 September; 6(5): 16-29. ISSN: 1049-0833.

APPLE COMPUTER, INCORPORATED. 1993. Inside Macintosh: QuickTime Components. Reading, MA: Addison-Wesley Publishing Company; 1993. 1 volume. ISBN: 0-201-62202-5.

ARNDT, TIMOTHY. 1990. A Survey of Recent Research in Image Database Management. In: Chang, Shi-Kuo, ed. Proceedings of the 1990 IEEE Workshop on Visual Languages; 1990 October 4-6; Skokie, IL. Los Alamitos, CA: IEEE Computer Society Press; 1990. 92-97. ISSN: 1049-2615.

ARNOLD, DAVID B.; DUCE, D.A. 1990. ISO Standards for Computer Graphics. London, England: Butterworths; 1990. 264p. ISBN: 0-408-04017-3.

ASSMANN, K.; VENEMA, R.; HOHNE, K.H. 1986. The ISQL Language: A Software Tool for the Development of Pictorial Information Systems in Medicine. In: Chang, Shi-Kuo; Ichikawa, Tadao; Ligomenides, Panos A., eds. Visual Languages. New York, NY: Plenum Press; 1986. 261-283. ISBN: 0-306-42350-2.

BARNETT, PATRICIA J. 1988. An Art Information System: From Integration to Interpretation. Library Trends. 1988 Fall; 37(2): 194-205. ISSN: 0024-2594.

BARNSLEY, MICHAEL F.; HURD, LYMAN P. 1993. Fractal Image Compression. Wellesley, MA: AK Peters; 1993. 244p. ISBN: 1-56881-000-8.

BAXTER, GRAHAM C. 1992. Selecting a Mass Storage Device. In: D'Alleyrand, Marc R., ed. Handbook of Image Storage and Retrieval Systems. New York, NY: Van Nostrand Reinhold; 1992. 239-257. ISBN: 0-442-00846-5.

BEARD, DAVID VOLK. 1991. Computer Human Interactions for Image Information Systems. Journal of the American Society for Information Science. 1991 September; 42(8): 600-608. ISSN: 0002-8231.

BELL, TIMOTHY C.; CLEARY, JOHN G.; WITTEN, IAN H. 1990. Text Compression. Englewood Cliffs, NJ: Prentice Hall; 1990. 318p. ISBN: 0-13-911991-4.

BELLAMY, JEAN-CLAUDE; DELASALLE, CATHERINE; FERTEY, GILLES; SUIGNARD, PHILIPPE. 1992. Using Images Regardless of Their Format. In: Post, F.H.; Hin, A.J.S., eds. Advances in Scientific Visualization. Berlin, Germany: Springer-Verlag; 1992. 145-157. ISBN: 3-540-55203-0.

BENSON, DAN; ZICK, GREG. 1992. Spatial and Symbolic Queries for 3-D Image Data. See reference: JAMBERDINO, ALBERT A.; NIBLACK, WAYNE, eds. 134-145.

BESSER, HOWARD. 1990. Visual Access to Visual Images: The UC Berkeley Image Database Project. Library Trends. 1990 Spring; 38(4): 787-798. ISSN: 0024-2594.

BESSER, HOWARD. 1991a. Imaging: Fine Arts. Journal of the American Society for Information Science. 1991; 42(8): 589-596. ISSN: 0002-8231.

BESSER, HOWARD. 1991b. User Interface for Museums. Visual Resources. 1991; 7: 293-309. ISSN: 0197-3762.

BLUM, CHRISTOF; HOFMANN, GEORG RAINER. 1992. ISO/IEC'S Image Interchange Facility (IIF). In: Arps, Ronald B.; Pratt, William K., eds. Image Processing and Interchange: Implementation and Systems: Proceedings of the International Society for Optical Engineering; 1992 February 12-14; San Jose, CA. Bellingham, WA: SPIE-The International Society for Optical Engineering; 1992. 130-141. ISBN: 0-8194-0813-1.

BOVEY, J.D. 1993. A Graphical Retrieval System. Journal of Information Science. 1993; 19: 179-188. ISSN: 0165-5515.

BRESLOW, NORMAN. 1991. Basic Digital Photography. Boston, MA: Focal Press; 1991. 193p. ISBN: 0-240-80055-9.

BROLIO, JOHN; DRAPER, BRUCE A.; BEVERIDGE, R.J.; HANSON, ALLEN R. 1989. ISR: A Database for Symbolic Processing in Computer Vision. Computer. 1989 December; 22(12): 22-30. ISSN: 0018-9162.

BROOKS, DIANE. 1988. System-System Interaction in Computerized Indexing of Visual Materials: A Selected Review. Information Technology and Libraries. 1988 June; 7(2): 111-123. ISSN: 0730-9295.

CARD, STUART K.; MORAN, THOMAS P.; NEWELL, ALLEN. 1983. The Psychology of Human-Computer Interaction. Hillsdale, NJ: Lawrence Erlbaum Associates; 1983. 469p. ISBN: 0-89859-243-7.

CATLETT, CHARLES E.; TERSTRIEP, JEFFREY A. 1992. The Use and Effect of Multimedia Digital Libraries in a National Network. In: Sutton, Brett; Davis, Charles H., eds. Networks, Open Access, and Virtual Libraries: Implications for the Research Library: Papers Presented at the 1991 Clinic on Library Applications of Data Processing; 1991 April 7-9; Urbana, IL. Urbana, IL: Graduate School of Library and Information Science, University of Illinois at Urbana-Champaign; 1992. 84-98. ISSN: 0069-4789; ISBN: 0-87845-087-4.

CAVALLARO, UMBERTO; PAOLINI, PAOLO; CHRISTODOULAKIS, STAVROS; DALLAS, COSTIS; ENOTIADIS, ANDREAS; PROIA, SAVERIO; SCHIFF, JACK; SCHULER, WOLFGANG. 1993. HIFI: Hypertext Interface for Information: Multimedia and Relational Databases. The Electronic Library. 1993 April; 11(2): 65-71. ISSN: 0264-0473.

CERF, VINTON G. 1991. Networks. Scientific American. 1991 September; 265: 72-81. ISSN: 0036-8733.

CHAMPINE, GEORGE A. 1991. MIT Project Athena: A Model for Distributed Campus Computing. Bedford, MA: Digital Press; 1991. 282p. ISBN: 1-55558-072-6.

CHANG, SHI-KUO. 1989. Principles of Pictorial Information Systems Design. Englewood Cliffs, NJ: Prentice Hall; 1989. 369p. ISBN: 0-13-710195-3.

CHANG, SHI-KUO; HSU, ARDING. 1992. Image Information Systems: Where Do We Go from Here? IEEE Transactions on Knowledge and Data Engineering. 1992 October; 4(5): 431-442. ISSN: 1041-4347.

CHANG, SHI-KUO; JUNGERT, ERLAND. 1990. A Spatial Knowledge Structure for Visual Information Systems. In: Ichikawa, Tadeo; Jungert, Erland;

Korfhage, Robert R., eds. Visual Languages and Applications. New York, NY: Plenum Press; 1990. 277-304. ISBN: 0-306-43427-X.

CHANG, SHI-KUO; LEE, C.M.; DOW, C.R. 1992. A 2-D String Matching Algorithm for Conceptual Pictorial Queries. See reference: JAMBERDINO, ALBERT A.; NIBLACK, WAYNE, eds. 47-58.

CHANG, SHI-KUO; YAN, C.W.; DIMITROFF, DONALD C.; ARNDT, TIMOTHY. 1988. An Intelligent Image Database System. IEEE Transactions on Software Engineering. 1988 May; 14(5): 681-688. ISSN: 0098-5589.

CHELLAPPA, RAMA. 1992. Digital Image Processing. Los Alamitos, CA: IEEE Computer Society Press; 1992. 801p. ISBN: 0-8186-2362-4.

COSTAGLIOLA, GENNARO; TORTORA, GENOVEFFA; ARNDT, TIMOTHY. 1992. A Unifying Approach to Iconic Indexing for 2-D and 3-D Scenes. IEEE Transactions on Knowledge and Data Engineering. 1992 June; 4(3): 205-222. ISSN: 1041-4347.

COURTOT, MARILYN E. 1992. Standards for Electronic Document Imaging Systems. In: D'Alleyrand, Marc R., ed. Handbook of Image Storage and Retrieval Systems. New York, NY: Van Nostrand Reinhold; 1992. 31-61. ISBN: 0-442-00846-5.

CRAWFORD, WALT. 1991. Technical Standards: An Introduction for Librarians. Boston, MA: G.K. Hall; 1991. 333p. ISBN: 0-8161-1950-3.

CROMP, ROBERT F.; DORFMAN, ERIK. 1992. A Spatial Data Handling System for Retrieval of Images by Unrestricted Regions of User Interest. Telematics and Informatics. 1992; 9(3/4): 221-241. ISSN: 0736-5853.

D'ALLEYRAND, MARC R., ed. 1992. Handbook of Image Storage and Retrieval Systems. New York, NY: Van Nostrand Reinhold; 1992. 370p. ISBN: 0-442-00846-5.

DAVISON, WAYNE. 1990. OSI Upper Layers Support for Applications. Library Hi Tech. 1990; 32(4): 33-42. ISSN: 0737-8831.

DENENBERG, RAY. 1990. Data Communications and OSI. Library Hi Tech. 1990; 32(4): 15-32. ISSN: 0737-8831.

EARNSHAW, RAE A.; WISEMAN, N. 1992. An Introductory Guide to Scientific Visualization. Berlin, Germany: Springer-Verlag; 1992. 156p. ISBN: 3-540-54664-2.

ESTER, MICHAEL. 1991. Image Quality and Viewer Perception. Visual Resources. 1991; 7: 327-351. ISSN: 0197-3762.

FANTINI, M.; PRAMPOLINI, F.; TURTUR, A. 1990. An Archive of Digital Images. Microcomputers for Information Management. 1990 March; 7(1): 25-40. ISSN: 0742-2343.

FOLEY, JAMES D.; VAN DAM, ANDRIES; FEINER, STEVEN K.; HUGHES, JOHN F. 1990. Computer Graphics: Principles and Practice. 2nd edition. Reading, MA: Addison-Wesley; 1990. 1,174p. ISBN: 0-201-12110-7.

FRIEDHOFF, RICHARD; BENZON, WILLIAM. 1989. Visualization: The Second Computer Revolution. New York, NY: Abrams; 1989. 215p. ISBN: 0-8109-1709-2.

GARY, JAMES E.; MEHOTRA, RAJIV. 1992. Shape Similarity-Based Retrieval in Image Database Systems. See reference: JAMBERDINO, ALBERT A.; NIBLACK, WAYNE, eds. 2-8.

GECSEI, JAN; MARTIN, DANIEL. 1989. Browsing Access to Visual Information. Optical Information Systems. 1989 September-October; 9(5): 237-241. ISSN: 0886-5809.

GERSHON, NAHUM; DOZIER, JEFF. 1993. The Difficulty with Data. Byte. 1993 April; 18: 143-148. ISSN: 0360-5280.

GITLIN, JOSEPH N. 1992. Application of the Management of Digital Images to the Medical Field. In: D'Alleyrand, Marc R., ed. Handbook of Image Storage and Retrieval Systems. New York, NY: Van Nostrand Reinhold; 1992. 311-323. ISBN: 0-442-00846-5.

GOSWELL, CRISPIN A.A. 1987. An Implementation of PostScript. In: Earnshaw, Rae E., ed. Workstations and Publication Systems. New York, NY: Springer-Verlag; 1987. 40-53. ISBN: 0-387-96527-0.

GREEN, WILLIAM. 1989. Digital Image Processing. New York, NY: Van Nostrand Reinhold; 1989. 249p. ISBN: 0-442-23052-4.

GROSKY, WILLIAM I.; JIANG, ZHAOWEI. 1992. A Hierarchical Approach to Feature Indexing. See reference: JAMBERDINO, ALBERT A.; NIBLACK, WAYNE, eds. 9-20.

GRUDIN, JONATHAN. 1993. Interface: An Evolving Concept. Communications of the ACM. 1993 April; 36(4): 110-119. ISSN: 0001-0782.

HABER, RALPH NORMAN; WILKINSON, LELAND. 1982. Perceptual Components of Computer Displays. IEEE Computer Graphics and Applications. 1982 May; 2(3): 23-35. ISSN: 0272-1716.

HAMILTON, ERIC. 1992. JPEG File Interchange Format. Available: Anonymous FTP to ftp.ncsa.uiuc.edu. Directory: /misc/file.formats/graphics.formats.

HIBLER, DAVID J.N.; LEUNG, CLEMENT H.C.; MANNOCK, KEITH L.; MWARA, NJAGI K. 1992. A System for Content-Based Storage and Retrieval in an Image Database. See reference: JAMBERDINO, ALBERT A.; NIBLACK, WAYNE, eds. 80-92.

HOFFERT, ERIC; KRUEGER, MARK; MIGHDOLL, LEE; MILLS, MICHAEL; COHEN, JOHNATHAN; CAMPLEJOHN, DOUG; LEAK, BRUCE; BATSON, JIM; VAN BRINK, DAVID; BLACKKETTER, DEAN; ARENT, MICHAEL; WILLIAMS, RICH; THORMAN, CHRIS; YAWITZ, MITCH; DOYLE, KEN; CALLAHAN, SEAN. 1992. QuickTime: An Extensible Standard for Digital Multimedia. In: Werner, Robert, ed. Digest of Papers: COMPCON; 1992 February 24-28; San Francisco, CA. Los Alamitos, CA: IEEE Computer Society Press; 1992. 15-20. ISBN: 0-8186-2655-0.

HOFMANN, GEORG RAINER; BLUM, CHRISTOF. 1991. The Image Model and the Image Interchange Format. In: Arnold, D.B.; Day, R.A.; Duce, D.A.; Fuhrhop, C.; Gallop, J.R.; Maybury, R.; Sutcliffe, D.C., eds. Graphics and Communications: Proceedings of an International Workshop; 1990 October 15-17; Breuberg, Germany. Berlin, Germany: Springer-Verlag; 1991. 238-253. ISBN: 3-540-54001-6.

HOLZGANG, DAVID A. 1987. Understanding PostScript Programming. San Francisco, CA: Sybex; 1987. 459p. ISBN: 0-89588-396-1.

HUANG, KUAN-TSAE. 1990. Visual Interface Design Systems. In: Chang, Shi-Kuo, ed. Principles of Visual Programming Systems. Englewood, NJ: Prentice Hall; 1990. 60-143. ISBN: 0-13-710765-X.

HUDSON, GRAHAM P.; YASUDA, HIROSHI; SEBESTYEN, ISTVAN. 1988. The International Standardisation of a Still Picture Compression Technique. In: GLOBECOM '88: IEEE Global Telecommunications Conference and Exhibition: Communications for the Information Age: Conference Record: Volume 2; 1988 November 28-December 1; Hollywood, FL. New York, NY: Institute of Electrical and Electronics Engineers; 1988. 1016-1021. Available from: IEEE, 445 Hoes Lane, Piscataway, NJ 08854.

HUNT, CRAIG. 1992. TCP/IP: Network Administration. Sebastopol, CA: O'Reilly & Associates, Inc.; 1992. 472p. ISBN: 0-937175-82-X.

JAMBERDINO, ALBERT A.; NIBLACK, WAYNE, eds. 1992. Image Storage and Retrieval Systems: Proceedings of the International Society for Optical Engineering: 1992 February 13-14; San Jose, CA. Bellingham, WA: SPIE-The International Society for Optical Engineering; 1992. 310p. ISBN: 0-8194-0816-5.

JERN, MIKAEL. 1989. Visualization of Scientific Data. In: Purgathofer, W.; Schonhut, J., eds. Advances in Computer Graphics V. Berlin, Germany: Springer-Verlag; 1989. 1-17. ISBN: 3-540-51420-1.

JONES, SUSAN. 1991. Text and Context: Document Storage and Processing. London, England: Springer-Verlag; 1991. 298p. ISBN: 3-540-19604-8.

JOSEPH, THOMAS; CARDENAS, ALFONSO F. 1988. PICQUERY: A High Level Query Language for Pictorial Database Management. IEEE Transactions on Software Engineering. 1988 May; 14(5): 630-638. ISSN: 0098-5589.

JOST, GILBERT R., ed. 1992. Medical Imaging VI: PACS Design and Evaluation: Proceedings of the International Society for Optical Engineering; 1992 February 24-27; Newport Beach, CA. Bellingham, WA: SPIE-The International Society for Optical Engineering; 1992. 604p. ISBN: 0-8194-0806-9.

KASTURI, RANGACHAR; FERNANDEZ, RODNEY; AMLANI, MUKESH L.; FENG, WU-CHUN. 1989. Map Data Processing in Geographic Information Systems. Computer. 1989 December; 22(12): 10-21. ISSN: 0018-9162.

KATO, TOSHIKAZU. 1992. Database Architecture for Content-Based Image Retrieval. See reference: JAMBERDINO, ALBERT A.; NIBLACK, WAYNE, eds. 112-123.

KAUFMAN, ARIE E. 1993. Volume Synthesis Principles. In: Hagen, H.; Muller, H.; Nielson, G.M., eds. Focus on Scientific Visualization. Berlin, Germany: Springer-Verlag; 1993. 122-137. ISBN: 3-540-54940-4.

KAY, DAVID C.; LEVINE, JOHN R. 1992. Graphics File Formats. New York, NY: McGraw-Hill; 1992. 278p. ISBN: 0-8306-3060-0.

KERLOW, ISAAC V.; ROSEBUSH, JUDSON. 1986. Computer Graphics for Designers and Artists. New York, NY: Van Nostrand Reinhold Company; 1986. 298p. ISBN: 0-442-24712-5.

KOFAKIS, P.; KARMIRANTZOS, A.; KAVAKLIS, E.; PETRAKIS, E.; ORPHANOUDAKIS, S. 1990. Image Archiving by Content: An Object-Oriented Approach. In: Dwyer, Samuel J.; Jost, Gilbert R., eds. Medical Imaging IV: PACS System Design and Evaluation: Proceedings of the International Society for Optical Engineering; 1990 February 6-9; Newport Beach, CA. Bellingham, WA: SPIE-The International Society for Optical Engineering; 1990. 275-286. ISBN: 0-8194-0278-8.

KRAUSE, MICHAEL G. 1988. Intellectual Problems in Indexing Picture Collections. Audiovisual Librarian. 1988 May; 14(2): 73-81. ISSN: 0302-3451.

LANG, U.; LANG, R.; RUHLE, R. 1992. Visualization in a Software System for Scientific Computing. In: Post, F.H.; Hin, A.J.S., eds. Advances in Scientific Visualization. Berlin, Germany: Springer-Verlag; 1992. 37-52. ISBN: 3-540-55203-0.

LE GALL, DIDIER. 1991. MPEG: A Video Compression Standard for Multimedia Applications. Communications of the ACM. 1991 April; 34(4): 47-58. ISSN: 0001-0782.

LEGER, ALAIN; MITCHELL, JOAN L.; YAMAZAKI, YASUHIRO. 1988. Still Picture Compression Algorithms Evaluated for International Standardisation. In: GLOBECOM '88: IEEE Global Telecommunications Conference and Exhibition: Communications for the Information Age: Conference Record: Volume 2; 1988 November 28-December 1; Hollywood, FL. New York, NY: Institute of Electrical and Electronics Engineers; 1988. 1028-1032. Available from: IEEE, 445 Hoes Lane, Piscataway, NJ 08854.

LESK, MICHAEL. 1990. Image Formats for Preservation and Access. Information Technology and Libraries. 1990 December; 9(4): 300-308. ISSN: 0730-9295.

LESK, MICHAEL. 1991. The CORE Electronic Chemistry Library. In: Bookstein, Abraham; Chiaramella, Y.; Salton, Gerard; Raghavan, V.V., eds. Proceedings of the Association for Computing Machinery Special Interest Group on Information Retrieval (ACM/SIGIR) 14th Annual International Conference on Research and Development in Information Retrieval; 1991 October 13-16; Chicago, IL. New York, NY: ACM; 1991. 93-112. ISBN: 0-89791-448-1.

LO, SHIH-CHUNG B.; KRASNER, BRIAN H.; MUN, SEONG K.; HORII, STEVEN C. 1992. A Hybrid Coding for Split Gray Values in Radiological Image Compression. In: Kim, Yongmin, ed. Medical Imaging VI: Image Capture, Formatting, and Display: Proceedings of the International Society for Optical Engineering; 1992 February 23-24; Newport Beach, CA. Bellingham, WA: SPIE-The International Society for Optical Engineering; 1992. 194-202. ISBN: 0-8194-0805-0.

LUNIN, LOIS F. 1987. Electronic Image Information. In: Williams, Martha E., ed. Annual Review of Information Science and Technology: Volume 22. Amsterdam, The Netherlands: Elsevier Science Publishers for the American Society for Information Science; 1987. 179-224. ISSN: 0066-4200; ISBN: 0-444-70302-0.

LUNIN, LOIS F.; FOX, EDWARD. 1993. Perspectives on. . .Digital Libraries: Introduction and Overview. Journal of the American Society for Information Science. 1993 September; 44(8): 441-445. ISSN: 0002-8231.

LYNCH, CLIFFORD A. 1988. Image Retrieval, Display, and Reproduction. In: Williams, Martha E.; Hogan, Thomas H., eds. Proceedings of the 9th National Online Meeting; 1988 May 10-12; New York, NY. Medford, NJ: Learned Information, Inc.; 1988. 227-232. ISBN: 0-938734-26-1.

LYNCH, CLIFFORD A. 1991. The Technologies of Electronic Imaging. Journal of the American Society for Information Science. 1991; 42(8): 578-585. ISSN: 0002-8231.

MARKEY, KAREN. 1986. Subject Access to Visual Resources Collections: A Model for Computer Construction of Thematic Catalogs. New York, NY: Greenwood Press; 1986. 189p. ISBN: 0-312-24031-0.

MCCORMICK, BRUCE H. 1990. Advanced Visualization Environments: Knowledge Based Image Modeling. In: Mendez, Raul H., ed. Visualization in Supercomputing. New York, NY: Springer-Verlag; 1990. 135-150. ISBN: 0-387-97149-1.

MITCHELL, WILLIAM J. 1994. When Is Seeing Believing? Scientific American. 1994 February; 270: 68-73. ISSN: 0036-8733.

MITTELSTAEDT, MICHAEL; MUMFORD, ANNE M. 1989. Standards for Computer Graphics and Product Model Data Exchange. In: Purgathofer, W.; Schonhut, J., eds. Advances in Computer Graphics V. Berlin, Germany: Springer-Verlag; 1989. 181-221. ISBN: 3-540-51420-1.

MORRISON, MIKE. 1993. The Magic of Image Processing. Carmel, IN: Sams Publishing; 1993. 303p. ISBN: 0-672-30315-9.

MOSTAFA, JAVED. 1990. Interaction and Instruction: A Balanced Approach for User Interface Design. Columbus, OH: Ohio State University; 1990. 115p. (M.S. thesis). OCLC: 22331307.

MOSTAFA, JAVED; NEWELL, THOMAS; TRENTHEM, RICHARD. 1994. The Easy Internet Handbook. Englewood, CO: Libraries Unlimited; 1994. 140p. ISBN: 0-931510-50-3.

MULLER, NATHAN J. 1993. Computerized Document Imaging Systems: Technology and Applications. Norwood, MA: Artech House; 1993. 303p. ISBN: 0-89006-661-2.

MURCH, GERALD. 1987. Color Displays and Color Science. In: Durett, H.J., ed. Color and the Computer. Boston, MA: Academic Press; 1987. 1-25. ISBN: 0-12-225210-1.

NATIONAL CENTER FOR SUPERCOMPUTING APPLICATIONS. 1993. NCSA HDF: Specification and Developer's Guide. Available: Anonymous FTP to ftp.ncsa.uiuc.edu. Directory: /misc/file.formats/graphics.formats.

NORMAN, DONALD A. 1988. The Psychology of Everyday Things. New York, NY: Basic Books; 1988. 257p. ISBN: 0-465-06709-3.

NUGENT, WILLIAM R. 1991. Virtual Reality: Advanced Imaging Special Effects Let You Roam Cyberspace. Journal of the American Society for Information Science. 1991; 42(8): 609-617. ISSN: 0002-8231.

O'CONNOR, BRIAN C. 1985. Access to Moving Image Documents: Background Concepts and Proposals for Surrogates for Film and Video Works. Journal of Documentation. 1985 December; 41(4): 209-220. ISSN: 0022-0418.

O'CONNOR, BRIAN C. 1991. Selecting Key Frames of Moving Image Documents: A Digital Environment for Analysis and Navigation. Microcomputers for Information Management. 1991 June; 8(2): 119-133. ISSN: 0742-2343.

ORBACH, BARBARA. 1990. So That Others May See: Tools for Cataloging Still Images. Cataloging and Classification Quarterly. 1990; 11(3/4): 163-191. ISSN: 0163-9374.

ORR, JOEL N. 1990. Sorting through the GUIs. Computer Graphics World. 1990 June; 13(6): 83-84, 86, 89-90. ISSN: 0271-4159.

PAIVIO, ALLAN. 1989. A Dual Coding Perspective on Imagery and the Brain. In: Brown, Jason W., ed. Neuropsychology of Visual Perception. Hillsdale, NJ: Erlbaum Associates; 1989. 203-216. ISBN: 0-8058-0284-3.

PAN, ELIZABETH; DALE, TOM; BEVERLEY, KEVIN. 1992. Selecting Indexing and Document Conversion Methodologies. In: D'Alleyrand, Marc R., ed. Handbook of Image Storage and Retrieval Systems. New York, NY: Van Nostrand Reinhold; 1992. 193-214. ISBN: 0-442-00846-5.

PENNEBAKER, WILLIAM B.; MITCHELL, JOAN. 1993. JPEG: Still Image Data Compression Standard. New York, NY: Van Nostrand Reinhold; 1993. 638p. ISBN: 0-442-01272-1.

PERDUE, JAMES "NEWT". 1990. High Bandwidth Interactivity and Super Networks. In: Mendez, Raul H., ed. Visualization in Supercomputing. New York, NY: Springer-Verlag; 1990. 80-99. ISBN: 0-387-97149-1.

PIZANO, ARTURO; KLINGER, ALLEN; CARDENAS, ALFONSO. 1989. Specification of Spatial Integrity Constraints in Pictorial Databases. Computer. 1989 December; 22(12): 59-71. ISSN: 0018-9162.

POMMERT, ANDREAS; BOMANS, MICHAEL; RIEMAR, MARTIN. 1993. Volume Visualization in Medicine: Techniques and Applications. In: Hagen, H.; Muller, H.; Nielson, G.M., eds. Focus on Scientific Visualization. Berlin, Germany: Springer-Verlag; 1993. 41-71. ISBN: 3-540-54940-4.

POOR, ALFRED. 1991. Lab Notes: Looking at the TIFF Specification from the Inside. PC Magazine. 1991 December 17; 10(21): 371-376. ISSN: 0888-8507.

POYNTON, CHARLES A. 1992. Overview of TIFF 5.0. In: Arps, Ronald B.; Pratt, William K., eds. Image Processing and Interchange: Implementation and Systems: Proceedings of the International Society for Optical Engineering; 1992 February 12-14; San Jose, CA. Bellingham, WA: SPIE-The International Society for Optical Engineering; 1992. 152-158. ISBN: 0-8194-0813-1.

RABITTI, FAUSTO; SAVINO, PASQUALE. 1992. Querying Semantic Image Databases. See reference: JAMBERDINO, ALBERT A.; NIBLACK, WAYNE, eds. 69-78.

RENAUD, PAUL E. 1993. Introduction to Client/Server Systems: A Practical Guide for Systems Professionals. New York, NY: Wiley & Sons; 1993. 333p. ISBN: 0-471-57773-1.

RESSLER, SANFORD. 1993. Perspectives on Electronic Publishing: Standards, Solutions, and More. Englewood Cliffs, NJ: PRT Prentice Hall; 1993. 343p. ISBN: 0-13-287491-1.

RIMMER, STEVE. 1993. Bit-Mapped Graphics. Blue Ridge Summit, PA: Windcrest Books; 1993. 484p. ISBN: 0-8306-4209-9.

ROBERTSON, GEORGE G.; CARD, STUART K.; MACKINLAY, JOCK D. 1993. Information Visualization Using 3D Interactive Animation. Communications of the ACM. 1993 April; 36(4): 57-71. ISSN: 0001-0782.

ROBINSON, PETER J. 1991. Office Document Architecture (ODA). In: Arnold, D.B.; Day, R.A.; Duce, D.A.; Fuhrhop, C.; Gallop, J.R.; Maybury, R.; Sutcliffe, D.C., eds. Graphics and Communications: Proceedings of an International Workshop; 1990 October 15-17; Breuberg, Germany. Berlin, Germany: Springer-Verlag; 1991. 48-67. ISBN: 3-540-54001-6.

ROBINSON, PHILLIP. 1989. Variations on a Screen. Byte. 1989 April; 14(4); 251-264. ISSN: 0360-5280.

RORVIG, MARK E. 1993. A Method for Automatically Abstracting Visual Documents. Journal of the American Society for Information Science. 1993 January; 44(1): 40-56. ISSN: 0002-8231.

ROSEBUSH, JUDSON. 1992. Adventures in QuickTime, Simple Player and Digitizing QuickTime Movies. CD-ROM Professional. 1992 November; 5(6): 17-23. ISSN: 1049-0833.

ROTH, STEPHEN E., ed. 1988. Real World PostScript: Techniques from PostScript Professionals. Reading, MA: Addison-Wesley; 1988. 383p. ISBN: 0-201-06663-7.

ROUSSOPOULOS, NICK; FALOUTSOS, CHRISTOS; SELLIS, TIMOS. 1988. An Efficient Pictorial Database System for PSQL. IEEE Transactions on Software Engineering. 1988 May; 14(5): 639-650. ISSN: 0098-5589.

RUSS, JOHN C. 1992. The Image Processing Handbook. Boca Raton, FL: CRC Press; 1992. 445p. ISBN: 0-8493-4233-3.

SALMON, ROD; SLATER, MEL. 1987. Computer Graphics: Systems & Concepts. Reading, MA: Addison-Wesley; 1987. 702p. (p. 558). ISBN: 0-201-14656-8.

SALOMON, GAVRIEL. 1979. Interaction of Media, Cognition and Learning. San Francisco, CA: Jossey-Bass; 1979. 282p. ISBN: 0-87589-403-8.

SAMET, HANAN. 1990. Applications of Spatial Data Structures. Reading, MA: Addison-Wesley; 1990. 507p. ISBN: 0-201-50300-X.

SCHONHUT, JURGEN. 1989. Page Description Languages (PDLs). In: Purgathofer W.; Schonhut, J., eds. Advances in Computer Graphics V. Berlin, Germany: Springer-Verlag; 1989. 155-180. ISBN: 3-540-51420-1.

SELOFF, GARY A. 1990. Automated Access to NASA-JSC Image Archives. Library Trends. 1990 Spring; 38(4): 682-696. ISSN: 0024-2594.

SHAFFER, CLIFFORD A. 1992. Data Representations for Geographic Information Systems. In: Williams, Martha E., ed. Annual Review of Information Science and Technology: Volume 27. Medford, NJ: Learned Information, Inc. for the American Society for Information Science; 1992. 135-172. ISSN: 0066-4200; ISBN: 0-938734-66-0.

SHAW, DEBORA. 1991. The Human-Computer Interface for Information Retrieval. In: Williams, Martha E., ed. Annual Review of Information Science and Technology: Volume 26. Medford, NJ: Learned Information, Inc. for the American Society for Information Science; 1991. 155-195. ISSN: 0066-4200; ISBN: 0-938734-55-5.

SHNEIDERMAN, BEN. 1987. Designing the User Interface: Strategies for Effective Human-Computer Interaction. Reading, MA: Addison-Wesley; 1987. 448p. ISBN: 0-201-16505-8.

STEUER, SHARON. 1993. Image Databases for the Desktop. Computer Graphics World. 1993 February; 16(2): 55-58. ISSN: 0271-4159.

STORER, JAMES A. 1992. Image and Text Compression. Boston, MA: Kluwer Academic Publishers; 1992. 354p. ISBN: 0-7923-9243-4.

THOMPSON, N.J. 1989. DIALOGLINK and TRADEMARKSCAN—Federal: Pioneers in Online Images. Online. 1989 May; 13(3): 15-26. ISSN: 0146-5422.

TREINISH, LLOYD A. 1989. An Interactive, Discipline-Independent Data Visualization System. Computers in Physics. 1989 July/August; 3(4): 55-64. ISSN: 0894-1866.

TUFTE, EDWARD. 1989. Visual Design of the User Interface. Armonk, NY: International Business Machines Corporation; 1989. (unpaged). OCLC: 20425355.

TUFTE, EDWARD. 1990. Envisioning Information. Chesire, CT: Graphics Press; 1990. 126p. OCLC: 21270160.

UDUPA, JAYARAM K.; HUNG, HSIU-MEI; ODHNER, DEWEY; GONCLAVES, ROBERTO. 1992. A Multidimensional Data Format Specification: A Generalization of the ACR-NEMA Standards. In: Jost, Gilbert R., ed. Medical Imaging VI: PACS Design and Evaluation: Proceedings of the International Society for Optical Engineering; 1992 February 24-27; Newport Beach, CA. Bellingham, WA: SPIE-The International Society for Optical Engineering; 1992. 266-277. ISBN: 0-8194-0806-9.

WALLACE, GREGORY K. 1990. Overview of the JPEG (ISO/CCITT) Still Image Compression Standard. In: Pennington, Keith S.; Moorhead, Robert J., eds. Image Processing Algorithms and Techniques: Proceedings of the International Society for Optical Engineering; 1990 February 12-14; Santa Clara, CA. Bellingham, WA: SPIE-The International Society for Optical Engineering; 1990. 220-232. ISBN: 0-8194-0291-5.

WALLACE, GREGORY K. 1991. The JPEG Still Picture Compression Standard. Communications of the ACM. 1991 April; 34(4): 30-44. ISSN: 0001-0782.

WALSH, AARON E. 1992. Programming QuickTime: Multimedia to the Macs. Dr. Dobb's Journal. 1992 July; 17(7): 76, 78-80, 102, 104-105. ISSN: 0884-5395.

WARNER, WILL. 1991. An Introduction to TIFF. Inform. 1991 February; 5(2): 32-35. ISSN: 0892-3876.

WEBER, JACK. 1993. Visualization: Seeing Is Believing. Byte. 1993 April; 18(4): 120-128. ISSN: 0360-5280.

WENTZ, PNINA. 1989. Computerization in Museums: Databases to Image Bases. Online Information 89: Proceedings of the 13th International Online Information Meeting; 1989 December 12-14; London, England. Oxford, England: Learned Information; 1989. 337-348. ISBN: 0-904933-72-5.

WOLFF, ROBERT S.; YAEGER, LARRY. 1993. Visualization of Natural Phenomena. New York, NY: Springer-Verlag; 1993. 373p. ISBN: 0-387-97809-7.

WORTHINGTON, BILL; ROBINSON, BRIAN. 1991. The Medium Is Not the Message: Mixed Mode Document Technology. In: Feeney, Mary; Day, Shirley, eds. Multimedia Information: Proceedings of a Conference; 1991 July 15-18; Cambridge, England. London, England: Bowker-Saur; 1991. 13-66. ISBN: 1-85739-090-3.

4 Database Access Systems

PRUDENCE W. DALRYMPLE
American Library Association

NANCY K. RODERER
Yale University

INTRODUCTION

Over its history *ARIST* has reflected the development and evolution of online search or database access systems. In 1967 GECHMAN wrote the first *ARIST* chapter on the generation and use of machine-readable databases. In 1969 BERUL first mentioned DIALOG and ORBIT in *ARIST*. Several chapters devoted to the design, generation, evaluation, and use of databases appeared in 1974 (WILLIAMS, 1974), 1975 (SCHIPMA), 1976 (WILDE), and 1977 (STERN). By 1981 HAWKINS described more than ten years of dialup online retrieval activities, and in 1987, MISCHO & LEE focused on the "growing interest in end-user or direct patron access to online bibliographic databases" (p. 227).

Both the Hawkins and Mischo and Lee chapters addressed the online search world in a broad sense, covering not only the technology involved but also databases, access and retrieval, training and library management, and users and their patterns of use. Other chapters over the years have addressed specific components within this environment, such as the MCCARN chapter in 1978 on online techniques and services and the WANGER chapter a year later on education and training for online systems, or have restricted themselves to a particular type of database, such as numeric (LUEDKE ET AL.) or full text (TENOPIR, 1984), or have limited their scope by discussing online searching in a

The authors thank Janet Miller of Yale University for her generous and patient support in developing the bibliography for this chapter.

Annual Review of Information Science and Technology (*ARIST*), Volume 29, 1994
Martha E. Williams, Editor
Published for the American Society for Information Science (ASIS)
By Learned Information, Inc., Medford, N.J.

particular environment, such as law (VOGES), business (OJALA & BATES), or medicine (TILLEY).

Since 1987, there have continued to be considerable changes in online search systems, most notably increases in their access and use. Terminology has changed as well, so that we have chosen to label this field "database access systems" rather than "online search systems." This acknowledges the information sources, i.e., databases, that are involved and substitutes the broad concept of access for the narrower concept of searching. We retain the concept of this field as a system, and note with INGWERSEN the continuing need to consider how components of the system interact as we strive to achieve the goal of "harmony between information and user."

In 1994, database access systems seem near-ubiquitous, with new databases and systems commonly covered in the popular press and of interest to an ever-broadening group of information seekers. This chapter highlights the changes that have occurred over the past seven years to bring us to this new stage in the evolution of database access systems. The review starts in 1987, just as CD-ROM systems were beginning to make an impact in libraries. During the years covered (1987-1993), locally mounted database systems and Internet access to databases also came into play.

Some early studies of end-user performance were conducted in online catalogs (OPACs) because researchers could observe casual users' searching without the pressure of the connect-time charges typical of commercial databases. In a complementary fashion, some researchers drew on our understanding of end-user bibliographic searching in order to understand problems users were having with OPACs (BORGMAN, 1986). With the widespread availability of CD-ROMs and the introduction of new access methods alternative testbeds have opened for researchers interested in observing end-user search behavior. In the new CD-ROM testbeds subject coverage, size, and indexing policy are more similar to online bibliographic databases than were the OPACs used for similar purposes.

Not surprisingly, much research on users is done so that more effective information retrieval systems can be designed. Another large body of research uses information retrieval systems as a laboratory for gaining greater understanding of human–computer interaction. Given the broad scope and ill-defined boundaries of the field, tracking the literature has become both easier and more frustrating. The total body of literature is considerable, but the literature relevant to the problem of providing efficient and effective information retrieval to a diverse population of users in different settings continues to grow exponentially.

To identify materials for this review, we began with a mediated search of four databases: (1) ABI/INFORM, (2) ERIC, (3) ISA (Information Science Abstracts), and (4) LISA (Library and Information Science

Abstracts), using primarily variations on the terms "database" and "use." This yielded a very large set of references that we reviewed for items of interest and for developing our chapter organization. Later we became end users ourselves, accessing the library catalog, Expanded Academic Index and CINAHL (Cumulative Index to Nursing and Allied Health Literature) at Yale and other library catalogs and files that are available over the Internet. Based on the database sources that we used this chapter has only limited coverage of developments outside the United States.

The terms end user and intermediary are used frequently in this chapter. An intermediary stands between the consumer of the information and the medium (the database) itself. An end user is a person who searches online databases directly to satisfy his/her own information needs. A human intermediary is an individual specially trained to search online databases quickly and efficiently and has the knowledge and experience to conduct an interview to ascertain the precise information needed and to focus the scope of the request. More recently the term intermediary has been used to refer to software that performs search assistance functions that have traditionally been done by human intermediaries. In this chapter we use the term to refer to human intermediaries.

With new, easier-to-use and more readily available database access methods, the number of end users as well as searches is increasing. Librarians are actively involved in instruction and program development in support of searching, and in addressing how best to select and pay for database access systems. This chapter explores the developments over the past seven years in databases, access channels, and interfaces to demonstrate the magnitude of the changes that have occurred. It then considers the effect of these changes as reflected in issues of database selection, library management, economics, and use and users.

DATABASES

The definition of database used in this review is taken from the 1993 *Gale Directory of Databases* (MARCACCIO). A database contains a collection of data or a body of information that is organized for retrieval via a computer in any storage medium. It may be available online directly from a producer or through a third-party online service or in CD-ROM format. It can contain data in the form of words, numbers, images, or sounds (WILLIAMS, 1994). For this chapter it must be available publicly.

Databases can be further categorized into bibliographic databases, which point to information located elsewhere, and full-text databases, which contain the full body of information. Databases that contain music, numeric data, and images can be considered full text because their information is accessible directly.

The directories that list and categorize machine readable databases have undergone several transformations over the past several years. From the first printed directory, *Computer Readable Bibliographic Databases* (WILLIAMS & ROUSE, 1976), which provided comprehensive coverage of databases in a single volume, to a directory of online databases, *Directory of Online Databases* (CUADRA ASSOCIATES), accurate, consistent information about the availability, coverage, pricing, and scope of databases has been an important consideration. As the number of databases increased and the subject coverage and format expanded, a single volume directory was replaced with several separate directories. Recently, however, the *Gale Directory of Databases* (MARCACCIO, 1993) drew together once again three directories which had been separated by format to form a consolidated volume with comprehensive coverage. That is, in 1993, Gale's *Computer-Readable Databases* (formerly Williams's *Computer Readable Databases*) combined with Cuadra/Gale's *Directory of Online Databases* and *Directory of Portable Databases* (formerly Cuadra's) to form the *Gale Directory of Databases*. Although the directory continues to organize the sources by format, the listings are consistent and each volume includes an analysis of databases by Williams that pulls together a wide variety of statistics to illustrate the remarkable growth of the database industry since 1979. In the early 1980s the industry experienced major growth, and the number of databases, the number of records contained in the databases, and the number of searches run against the databases all increased substantially. In 1975 there were 300 databases; by 1994, there were 8,261 (WILLIAMS, 1994).

The distinction between end user searchers and intermediary searchers is decreasing in importance as more "end users" conduct searchers. We are coming to simply use the term searcher to mean both. Similarly, the concept of a database is becoming less relevant to the average information user and is on the verge of losing meaning for the information profession as well. BASCH (1993) relates this phenomenon to the growth of the Internet; vast amounts of information are available for search and retrieval, yet this information highway lacks the organizational characteristics of a database. Organized databases are available on the Internet along with a variety of other compilations of materials such as hot topic files, browsable tables of contents, and automatic updates. Some of these materials can be filtered by means of software programs established by the user, but by and large, the vast amount of material available on the Internet does not fit the definition of a database used in this chapter.

The growth of CD-ROM databases has been at least as rapid as that of online databases, although their history is shorter and there are only about one third as many CD-ROM databases as online databases. Only two databases were available on CD-ROM in 1985. There were 496 in 1990, 1,025 in 1991, and 1,951 in 1992 (NICHOLLS, 1991, 1992a; NICHOLLS & VAN DEN ELSHOUT). Three major sources emerged as directory listings for CD-ROMs: *Optical/Electronic Publishing Directory* (BOWERS), *CD-ROM Directory* (CORMACK), and *CD-ROMs in Print* (EMARD).

CD-ROM may have the most potential as a relatively inexpensive publishing and distribution medium for stable databases containing full-text source data. The Government Printing Office (GPO) has been distributing documents on CD-ROM since 1988, and CD-ROM use by depository libraries is widespread (KOVACS). Reference materials are also appropriate for CD-ROM because they are usually updated annually or less frequently, and the digital CD-ROM format offers easier search and retrieval than a printed product.

An area of significant growth in recent years, involving both CD-ROM and other formats, is the full-text database. In 1993 DIALOG Information Services produced and introduced U.S. Patents Fulltext; it covers 1.4 million patents issued since 1974, with partial coverage for 1971–1973 (BASCH, 1993). This database seems to be a precursor of other full-text patent files to follow, complementing an already strong array of bibliographic patent databases. UMI's ABI/INFORM management literature database continues to add full-text articles from about 250 publications (BASCH, 1993). In the legal and news fields, always rich in full-text files, more sources continue to be made available as databases. Finally, ADONIS, the long awaited outcome of a cooperative effort among publishers in the scientific, technical and medical arena, was introduced (RICHARDSON).

CD-ROM is well suited to multimedia as well as full-text applications and will become even more so as data-compression technology improves. Thus, a growth area for CD-ROM publication is likely to be in full-text sources with graphics, video, and sound (SCHWERIN). The first mixed mode CD-ROM ever produced appeared in 1987 and others continue to be introduced. As the products become more complex and include sound and images, the traditional access points of subject, title, and keyword are enhanced with a variety of other access points.

Product usage is different for multimedia than for strictly textual database products. Many multimedia items are used more for teaching than as information resources, while others are used almost purely for entertainment. Indeed, in early 1994 several rock bands distributed interactive, multimedia CD-ROMs. Although the end users may be more like the consumers of print and broadcast materials than information seekers, the contents of the CD-ROM can be used in either way.

While the distinction between databases and reference books is blurring, NICHOLLS & SUTHERLAND predict distinctly different patterns of growth for online and CD-ROM. While the most typical conversion is from a print to a CD-ROM product, many databases, such as Online Mendelian Inheritance in Man (OMIM), began as print publications, and were converted to online products. They have remained online rather than going to CD-ROM in order to facilitate a continuous update process (BRANDT). Other products, particularly those that are largely visual, originate in CD-ROM because of the medium's ability to store many visual images (e.g., the contents of London's National Gallery) (SHARRATT).

One factor slowing the growth of indexes on CD-ROM is the updating needed to keep them current. Online indexes can be updated daily at minimal cost, but updating a CD-ROM entails disc replacement. Many A & I services, however, do provide and regularly update their indexes on CD-ROM.

In 1990 NICHOLLS reviewed CD-ROM directories and reviews as sources for descriptive and evaluative information about optical publications. He found that reviewing mechanisms for optical media were similar to those for printed materials. For reviews of CD-ROM databases in a particular subject area, Nicholls found that journal articles were the most effective. Good analytic reviews of subject area databases are given by KUBLI and G. WALKER, who look at issues such as overlap of coverage, accuracy of data, and timeliness of publication. Some reviewers examine the user interface, screen design, help mechanisms, retrieval software, speed of search and retrieval, and command structure. An extensive evaluation of MEDLINE on CD-ROM was conducted by the National Library of Medicine (NLM) in 1988 in which seven CD-ROM systems were evaluated at 21 sites. The results were presented at an evaluation forum that included librarians from the test sites as well as CD-ROM publishers (RAPP ET AL.; WOODSMALL ET AL.).

In many fields, databases in both CD-ROM and online versions targeted to the end user are a compilation of different materials—textbooks, journals, reference sources, and bibliographic databases. While the convenience of having these materials in both formats is a definite advantage, the expense of purchasing them for use in a single location, such as an office, may be prohibitive unless the materials themselves are inexpensive for the publisher to obtain and convert. In scientific and technical fields the cost of acquiring the information is often very high.

In addition to bibliographic, full-text, multimedia, and combination databases, this review period has also seen the introduction of database products notable for their unique software features. Travelpilot IDS is a database product providing geographic information. It is designed to be mounted on an automobile dashboard, and it provides both continuous location information as well as maps and routing instructions (CUADRA, 1991). The personal newspaper prototyped by the Media Center at MIT some years ago has also recently become commercially available. Journalist, a software package from PEP Software, scans CompuServe wires for stories that fit an individual's profile and then displays them in a personally designed layout (BASCH, 1993). With its Mercury Center service, available through America Online, the San Jose Mercury News provides not only access to current and past articles but also to related background materials and transcripts, and allows readers to communicate with editors and other readers and to participate in bulletin boards on current affairs (VALAUSKAS, 1993a). Databases such as these hold promise for more personalized products in the future.

DATABASE ACCESS CHANNELS

While the number of formats in which databases are available has expanded significantly over the years covered by this review, the increased variety of access channels is more notable. In addition to online services, we now have stand-alone and networked CD-ROMs, locally mounted databases available over networks, and Internet access to a whole range of resources. The most important factor here has been the increase in telecommunications capabilities and options.

In the online services arena, vendors have increased their offerings and expanded their connections to other vendor systems, as is the case with the gateway service that provides Westlaw users access to DIALOG (HOGAN). Perhaps the greatest change in the online environment, however, has been the emergence of large commercial services that offer both database access and other information services, such as electronic mail (e-mail). In 1994, KANTOR reviewed five major commercial services that are aimed at the end user market using personal computers: America Online, CompuServe Information Service, Dow Jones News/Retrieval with MCI Mail, GEnie, and Prodigy Interactive Personal Services. He compared them on the basis of the number and type of databases and services, cost, service factors, and the suitability of the services' interfaces for various tasks. It is noteworthy that more than 3.5 million people were using these services at that time, reflecting a growing interest by end users.

The first major alternative to the online systems adopted by libraries was the local mounting of databases. With these, telecommunication problems can be minimized, costs can be controlled, and local systems can be linked. At first, individual institutions built local systems using full database-building and text-retrieval software (such as BASIS, BRS software and STAR). They used general database managers, and leased databases and loaded them on their local mainframes or minicomputers. This allowed considerable flexibility in the choice of a database interface, generally at the expense of more effort spent on development. The alternative approach is to use a vendor, such as NOTIS or CD Plus, who provides the software and preloaded databases as a package. NOTIS software uses a modification of the interface used in their library catalog system (MILLER), while the CD Plus system was originally designed to deal with the more complex record structure of the MEDLINE database (JACSÓ, 1994).

CD-ROMs were introduced only shortly before this review period and were rapidly adopted, especially by libraries. An early developer was SilverPlatter Information, Inc., which began to develop retrieval software in 1984 and shipped its first products in 1986 (RIETDYK). DUGGAN describes early experiences with DIALOG's OnDisc ERIC, which was used in 1986 to teach searching to library school students. By 1992, CD-ROMs were commonplace in libraries: DESMARAIS reported the results of a survey that showed very high use of CD-ROM products in academic and research libraries (69% and 99%, respectively), with somewhat lower rates in corporate and school libraries (51% and 20%, respectively).

CD-ROMs were first provided to users on individual workstations, but technological improvements coupled with user demand led to rapid adoption of networking. KITTLE, KOREN, and ONSI ET AL. describe the organizational and technical issues in CD-ROM networking, including the selection of network software and testing for speed and functionality. In 1993 DESMARAIS described CD-ROM networking as "poised to take off," with college, university, corporate, and public libraries all predicting much greater use of local and wide-area networks (LANs and WANs) over the next two years. While less than one-third of the member libraries of the Association of Research Libraries (ARL) had CD-ROM networks in place in 1991, almost all expected to by 1994.

Certainly the most significant telecommunications advance affecting online searching over the review period has been the Internet, nicely defined and described by LYNCH & PRESTON (1990) in the first *ARIST* chapter on this topic. The Internet provides a rapidly growing web of connection points to an equally rapidly growing number of resources, including databases in all formats, file archives, online journal article repositories, and information servers.

The size of the Internet requires methods for locating and tracking resources, generally known as resource discovery or navigation services (OBRACZKA ET AL.). These tools, such as WAIS (Wide Area Information Servers), World-Wide Web, Archie and Gopher, allow the user to browse and/or search for resources. Depending on the tool used, a search may be of file names, file descriptions, and/or file contents. As pointed out by Lynch and Preston, WAIS and Gopher are not only directory services but are part of broader access systems. Another access system is Mosaic, designed by the University of Illinois National Center for Supercomputing Applications to organize multimedia resources under menus within one framework (VALAUSKAS, 1993b). A number of libraries and institutions are using these tools to provide their constituents with tailored menus of databases and other resources.

THE END-USER INTERFACE

A critical component of providing access to databases to end users is the interface—i.e., the combination of the screen design, the retrieval engine including command structure, and the search features. SHAW gives a more vivid definition in her *ARIST* review of the human–computer interface for information retrieval. She defines the interface as what the user sees, hears, and touches in interacting with a computer system. As interfaces have become more sophisticated, more and more functions previously handled only by a human intermediary, particularly those supporting and guiding the user, have been assigned to the interface.

Along with the proliferation of CD-ROM databases has come a multiplicity of interfaces, making the need for standardization acute. A common command language (CCL) has been proposed by the National Information Standards Organization (NISO) as part of the ANSI/NISO Z39.58 standard for online systems. BEHESHTI suggests that CD-ROM producers also adopt the CCL but that they provide the user with the ability to select the CCL option for searching on the producer's customized interface. This would balance the advantages gained from standardization against the need to encourage innovation and continued product improvement. In the absence of a CCL, ALI published a quick reference guide to the command language of six major CD-ROM database producers, an attempt to complement the International Command Chart produced by Online, Inc., for online databases. KAHN also reviewed the interfaces of six major CD-ROM producers.

New client/server technologies could pave the way for a common interface to an array of databases. The client is a software package that includes the interface of choice, and the ANSI/NISO Z39.50 protocol is used to communicate with servers/host computers that contain the databases. Most of the library vendors are currently involved in the development of client and/or server software based on Z39.50 for use on the Internet (HINNEBUSCH).

Recently the professional literature has paid more attention to retrieval engines. Earlier, basic research on information retrieval methods and recognition of the retrieval features of operational systems were separate topics, but basic research results seem to be finding their way into systems as well as the professional literature with some frequency now. One example of this dissemination is Aries Systems' Knowledge Finder, which incorporates a number of features originally proposed in the experimental information retrieval literature such as "soft" or "fuzzy" Boolean searching and relevancy ranking (SCHWARTZ).

Coverage in the professional literature is important because librarians must be alert to the different retrieval performances of various products when selecting systems and advising users. In studies of multiple systems for MEDLINE access, HAYNES ET AL. (1994) and DALRYMPLE & COX found that different systems yielded different results.

One of the first innovations aimed at the end-user market was menu-driven searching, which was frequently provided as a convenience in online systems along with reduced connect-time charges. Recently, features such as search advice and feedback during the search were introduced. MEADOW reported on OAKDEC, an interface designed to assist searchers during a search; PaperChase (HOROWITZ & BLEICH) also provides this kind of support. As diagnostic tools, these interface features can be tapped for insights into a searcher's behavior and attitudes during the search.

INGWERSEN provides and analyzes recent theoretical developments and proposes several models through which to examine information retrieval interaction. We can anticipate that these models may be used to inform research and development of more advanced information retrieval systems and that such systems will guide and support the user in more flexible and diverse ways in the future.

Database structure and indexing also affect end-user retrieval. Librarians, particularly catalogers, have assisted searchers of catalogs by providing precoordinated subject headings. Database searching has relied primarily on post-coordinate indexing, which places a greater burden on the ability of the searcher to select and combine terms. The 1992 review by MILSTEAD of techniques for subject analysis in databases quickly reminds the reader of the complexity of achieving optimal results from a database search. Even the professional searcher is frequently unaware of all the ways to exploit the subject analysis available in a database, and end users are surely unaware of and unable to take advantage of this investment unless personal or machine assistance is available. Articles in the professional literature aimed at search intermediaries, such as that by BATES (1988), show how to use the power of controlled vocabularies for more effective searching, but such insights are likely to reach the end user only through instruction or system design.

SELECTION

It is generally believed that searchers are likely to focus on just a few familiar databases, even though complementary references or text might be available through smaller or more focused files (MORRIS ET AL.). There does seem to be a growing tendency, however, to go beyond one database (PERDUE & PIOTROWSKI). There are also more databases readily available to users, and as their number continues to grow, so does the problem of selection.

In 1988 BARKER reviewed the use of file-selection features found in the DIALOG, Data-Star, and InfoSearch systems and suggested that user behavior with these features should be studied. MEYER & RUIZ (1990a, 1990b, 1990c; RUIZ & MEYER) responded to this challenge by monitoring use of Telebase's EasyNet Scan feature throughout the year. Given a search request and a user-selected broad subject category, Scan lists the postings from 10–20 files in that subject category. Users are also given the format (e.g., reference, abstract, full text) of the databases and an indication of the recommended database(s) in that subject area. The user can then select any databases that have at least one posting.

Meyer and Ruiz presented results on the databases selected by end users without controlling for how often those databases were displayed with postings. Nonetheless, the results do show which databases with which characteristics were actually searched after using Scan. There was considerable consistency among different subject areas in the extent of searches done in the most frequently used database (27–29%) and in the top four (63–71%). In almost all subject areas, the recommended database was the one most frequently selected for searching. Having a database name that conveyed the content of the database did not seem to affect database selection. We suspect that this might not be the case when using a printed directory for selection because one could not rely on a software feature such as Scan. Also there was no discernible preference for full text over reference or abstract files.

BASCH (1992) points out that the concept of separate and distinct databases is blurred by automatic cross file searching, such as that permitted with NEXIS's OMNI or ALL file searching. She reports that according to Mead Data Central, intermediaries and end users alike prefer the broad approach. She groups the factors involved in source selection into categories of relevance (subject focus, comprehensiveness and coverage, publication types) and accessibility (cost, availability, and design).

Researchers continue to propose expert systems for database selection, either in front-end or integrated software packages. Among the expert retrieval systems that have been implemented are Answerman (WATERS), CANSEARCH (POLLITT), and ORA (HAWKINS, 1988). TRAUTMAN & VON FLITTNER developed a microcomputer-based system for selection by pooling the subject indexes of subject directories, a gateway service, and a vendor's term-frequency index and then developing a classification system for databases. The prototype Online-Expert system of ZAHIR & CHANG for business databases uses database content, type, geographic coverage, currency and cost, and user needs to construct a decision model that ranks databases and hosts in order of preference.

In the Internet environment, the number of potential databases to be searched is enormous. Databases as defined for this chapter are also not generally considered as distinct from other available information resources, such as file archives, online journal article repositories, and information servers; thus, the selection issue becomes more compelling. In this environment, the term "resource discovery" is used to cover both the identification of resources, which can then be browsed for a database of interest, and support for the process of selecting an appropriate database according to subject need. Internet resource discovery tools are covered earlier, so here we focus on developments in the area of selection.

LYNCH & PRESTON (1992) note that the specification of data elements and classification schemes to be used are a significant challenge, and they describe some possible models. The Coalition for Networked Information's (CNI) TopNode project is also concerned with the issue of how to describe resources. OBRACZKA ET AL. compare a number of Internet resource discovery systems, indicating how they can be used and the level of document (e.g., files, file names, directories) which they search. Lynch and Preston also identify the level of document which is described, or the collection granularity, as an important issue and point out the need for the unit of analysis to be consonant with the level of specificity of both the classification scheme used and the user's query.

The National Library of Medicine (NLM) recognized the Internet selection problem early on, within its Unified Medical Language System (UMLS) program (HUMPHREYS & LINDBERG; LINDBERG ET AL., 1993a). The Information Systems Map (ISM) is a descriptive file of databases within the broad area of biomedicine and includes extensive descriptions of each file in terms of subject coverage. Several institutions have developed software for using the ISM; Yale University's

Information Sources Directory uses the subject descriptors to identify potentially useful databases while allowing the user to restrict the search to a particular database format, category of availability (e.g., "free at Yale"), and category of purpose (e.g., patient care) (CLYMAN ET AL.). NLM hopes to extend ISM to include thousands of databases and is planning for entries to be based on producer input.[1]

MANAGEMENT OF DATABASE ACCESS

Libraries have many different choices when deciding how to provide bibliographic access. Databases can be provided in the form of print on paper or in computer readable form accessed on a stand-alone workstation, on a LAN within the library, on a campus network, or over the Internet. Further, those databases and their associated software can be built and maintained locally, purchased elsewhere, or provided by other libraries or vendors. The implications for the management of end-user search programs vary with the options chosen.

A broad perspective on the management of end-user search programs, at least for CD-ROM systems, is given by WELCH. Her report compiles material from different ARL libraries on access, instruction, publicity, staff procedures, and job descriptions along with the results of a survey on other management issues.

R.W. MEYER (1990) describes the library management issues associated with locally mounted databases for Clemson University, including: (1) selection of hardware, software, and databases; (2) development of the system; and (3) user response. Clemson chose the BRS Search software to create a single interface for several databases, one modeled on the NOTIS system used to search Clemson's library catalog.

WOODSMALL ET AL. present case studies on the implementation of a single database (MEDLINE) in various CD-ROM formats (e.g., SilverPlatter, Aries, Cambridge) in a number of institutions. They describe both the management issues and the impact that these installations had on users. Along with others, the libraries described in this report saw a significant shift in staff activities away from mediated searching to the development and maintenance of end-user search programs.

HURD & DAVIDSON describe the use of the CAS Online Academic Plan, a special program for access to Chemical Abstracts Service's online search service that is widely used by academic libraries. Reporting on results of a survey, they discuss equipment and facilities, funding, and training. Librarians believe that the program improved access

---

[1]Personal communication from Naomi Miller, National Library of Medicine, April 22, 1994.

to the chemical literature, decreased per-search costs, and increased cooperation between academic departments and the library.

Analysis of Library Options

Given the number of database options available, a significant problem is choosing from among them. Libraries must begin with the issue of which databases in which subject areas are desired (O'DELL). At least with bibliographic databases, users are generally familiar enough with the printed indexes to have a database preference. Once a desired database is identified, questions of content and coverage have to be addressed. Beyond that, other technological and managerial issues need to be considered in choosing a method of access.

This issue has best been addressed in the area of CD-ROMs. In 1990, 18 of 68 reporting ARL libraries stated that they had CD-ROM selection policies, and four examples were given (WELCH). Various factors to be considered in choosing among CD-ROM versions of MEDLINE, for example, are reflected in WOODSMALL ET AL.; here there is a heavy emphasis on the different interfaces.

A number of papers compare two access methods—e.g., print and online (PITERNICK) and online and CD-ROM (NAHL-JAKOBOVITS & TENOPIR; WILLIAMSON). As new access methods become available, these comparisons provide approaches and models for extending the library analysis.

Attention must also be given in identifying database access methods for the variety of offerings that are available. One argument for using locally mounted systems is that they provide a consistent interface (FAYEN). A vendor system also uses a consistent interface for access to many databases. CD-ROM systems require little investment to purchase and maintain, and access can be provided from individual or networked workstations. Many libraries use a combination of approaches to providing bibliographic databases, and it is expected that there will be more literature on the analysis of alternatives in the years ahead.

Library Instruction

The role of end-user training and approaches to carrying it out have been frequent topics in the library literature during the past seven years. While libraries have always provided some instruction in the use of their resources, the volume and complexity of this activity have increased significantly with the institution of end-user search programs. Thus, although less time is spent on mediated searching, more time is spent on user instruction.

According to MARSHALL & ALLAN, "user training is generally considered to be a major obstacle to the widespread dissemination and use of publicly accessible electronic databases" (p. 38). These authors go on to describe the increasing amounts of end-user training and to review the attendant questions of who, what, when, where, and how. They distinguish between procedural (how-to-do-it) and model-based (how-it-works) training and predict that the former will become less important as systems continue to improve. STEFFEN, in a balanced review of the training issues in an environment of multiple access methods, makes a similar distinction between skill-oriented and conceptual training.

SAULE, writing about user instruction for humanists, suggests ways in which database instruction can be tailored to this group's particular needs (e.g., for extensive browsing). She believes that terminological issues are a particular problem with humanities databases, because the humanist often searches across a number of time periods, languages, and disciplines. A similar type of analysis could be done in other fields to identify particular instructional needs.

ENGEL discusses some of the special issues associated with training users how to use the Internet, including the formidable problem of choosing among multiple systems. She stresses the need to convey the complementarity of local and Internet resources and to help users determine which to use in particular circumstances.

GLITZ describes the training situation in the medical field, where there is heavy emphasis on a single database—MEDLINE—which is available in many forms. This situation leads to various training classes on both the different forms and ways of selecting from among them. It also leads, Glitz notes, to an additional role for librarians—viz., consulting with vendors on how to improve their systems for users.

Searching and Use of the Primary Literature

End-user searching of bibliographic databases through libraries has a perceptible impact on the use of the primary literature, a fact that has been quantitatively demonstrated in a few cases. At Pennsylvania State University, introduction of the NTIS CD-ROM led to a nearly three-fold increase in use of the technical reports described by the database (MUSSER & CONKLING). At Texas A&M University, Wilson's Multi-Database Access was loaded into the university's NOTIS catalog, and preliminary results showed four to five times more use of the locally held journals covered by these databases (ROBBINS & HARER).

It is also believed that increased end-user searching leads to increased interlibrary loan (ILL), although not all of the available evidence supports this conclusion. At Texas A&M, use of the Wilson databases had little impact on ILL, which is understandable since the university owns 86–95% of the titles in the three Wilson indexes. At Moravian College, the introduction of PsycLIT on CD-ROM was followed by a small decrease in ILL of titles covered by the database. CRAWFORD believes this to be the result of an extensive program of user training, which stresses the use of local journals before resorting to ILL. By contrast, REESE reports a trebling in ILL since the introduction of CD-ROM databases at Vanderbilt University, and KELSEY & COHN also show dramatic increases at the County College of Morris.

In addition to increases in the traditional journal services, there is growing interest on the part of users in obtaining articles by other means and libraries are responding with new programs. These include use of electronic full-text systems such as ADONIS (RICHARDSON) and greater use of fax, electronic transmission, and commercial document delivery services to speed ILL. A small but growing number of journals are published online, and these too provide users with a source for electronic full text of articles.

ECONOMICS

The economics associated with end-user searching presents very different issues to vendors, libraries, and the users themselves. The vendor literature on economics focuses primarily on pricing. Database pricing structures generally vary according to format, with fixed prices for print and CD-ROM products and per-search and citation charges for many online systems. These differences in pricing make it difficult to compare the different formats. As NELSON points out, database producers and vendors are also concerned about the different prices charged for different formats, especially as users migrate from print to various online formats.

ROSEN, at the Institute for Scientific Information (ISI), offers a glimpse of the pricing process, when she describes the types of costs involved in developing a new search product and the tradeoffs in using three models: market penetration, skimming (the cream off the top), and competitive pricing.

Vendors do try new models for pricing, and users also suggest possible approaches. O'LEARY (1991b) asserts that the "excessive and unpredictable cost" of online searching has significantly limited database use; he describes various departures from this standard and uses the case of CD-ROM and locally mounted databases to argue that subscription pricing should be the norm. LEVIN proposes differential CD-ROM pricing based on the number and types of potential users.

Prices are also modified as products change. With the advent of networking, there have been changes in the pricing of CD-ROM and other locally mounted systems, and many products are currently priced on the basis of the maximum number of simultaneous users permitted. In the face of CD-ROM availability at fixed prices, some online vendors have provided fixed-price access packages.

Libraries are usually concerned with the comparative costs of access to a particular database in different formats. Comparative CD-ROM and online costs for the ERIC database are worked out in some detail by ERKKILA. HUANG & MCHALE look at comparisons of print and online searching of frequently used sources of business and financial information and calculate a threshold of use over which the fixed print subscription cost is less than online charges.

R.W. MEYER (1993) describes the results of cost comparisons of various forms of several databases used at Trinity College, demonstrating how the total cost and an average cost per search can be calculated for each database and form. The total cost, and its potential variability, are important factors in library budgeting. Calculating the cost per use is a reasonable way to make comparisons across forms that will be used to different extents—e.g., comparing a CD-ROM that is available only in the library with a locally mounted system available on the campus network. Unfortunately, with many options it is very difficult to predict and/or measure the amount of use. A few papers, such as that by DAVIDSON & HURD, do present use data that may be beneficial to other institutions considering similar programs. HAYNES ET AL. (1991) go beyond the comparison of cost per search and, in an interesting controlled experiment, calculate the cost per relevant citation of 12 versions of MEDLINE, finding a considerable range.

Beyond these cost comparisons is the more difficult question of how to make purchasing decisions between bibliographic search products and the primary literature that is subsequently requested by users. This has been mentioned (e.g., LARSEN) but not yet carefully analyzed.

Searches can be paid for from library funds, either grants or regular budgets, and user fees (ZARNOSKY). The choice seems to be related to the method of access; in general, academic and public libraries charge for mediated searching but not for CD-ROM access. However, at least one institution, Kent State University, purchased fixed-rate CD-ROM products and passed these costs on to users with a per-minute search charge. SCHLOMAN ET AL. state that this system was workable but not desirable, and as funds became available, fees were discontinued. Libraries are taking various approaches to funding both locally mounted systems and Internet use, and it seems likely that strategies for funding these types of access will be covered in future *ARIST* chapters.

End users frequently express a preference for "free" searching and are likely to make greater use of database products that are provided without charge. This was demonstrated in an experiment in which physicians in clinical settings were trained in using GRATEFUL MED and then put into two groups—one was required to pay for search costs and the other group searched without fees. A greater percentage of the group that did not pay continued searching, and members of that group who searched conducted twice as many searches as those in the paying group (HAYNES ET AL., 1991). At the same time, convenience causes at least some end users to opt to pay for searching rather than use free services (CLARK & GOMEZ).

USE AND USERS

Who Uses Databases and When

Our discussion of database users is informed by the 1986 *ARIST* review by DERVIN & NILAN that signaled a major shift in the way that we examine users, their needs, and their behaviors. As they rightly point out, this shift is of paradigmatic proportion, yet the number of studies that fully conform to these new models is growing slowly. The information retrieval literature, often largely experimental, frequently presages the literature in more applied settings. While we refer to experimental studies as appropriate, we have concentrated primarily on studies that attempt to examine the behavior of users in the library or information center settings, using systems that are operational and available.

This section is divided into two parts. Discussion of database use focuses on who uses databases and to what extent, while our discussion of users focuses on questions of how the databases are used.

There are few studies of the extent to which end-user searching has penetrated the CD-ROM market. This may be simply because it seems unnecessary to document what is obvious to even casual users of information centers. For example, BELL & HALPERIN found that students were switching from end-user online systems to CD-ROM systems. This is not surprising since the CD-ROM was provided free of charge, but the extent to which students adopted the new technology (nearly a ten-fold increase in the number of searches) suggests that it was not simply economics alone that accounted for the popularity of direct user access to CD-ROMs. Virtually any anecdotal report of CD-ROMs in libraries, for example, describes the enthusiasm with which users have greeted these products.

Personal experience and discussions with colleagues suggest that the improvements in database accessibility have resulted in dramatic increases in the number of people searching and the total number of end-user searches. Modeling the use of different MEDLINE alternatives under consideration at Columbia University suggested that total searching by the institution might vary from 10,000 searches per year (use of online systems only) to 28,000 (online plus networked local system) (RODERER & BARNES). At Yale University, the estimated number of MEDLINE searches performed was 5,000 in 1987/1988 (online only), 19,000 in 1986/1987 (online and locally mounted subset), 44,000 in

1991/1992 (online, locally mounted subset, and local CD-ROM), and nearly 100,000 in 1993/1994 (online and locally mounted full file).

HALPERIN calls for more comprehensive measurement of the extent of database use. Statistics on the number of databases available to the end user, regardless of format, are readily available (WILLIAMS, 1994), but statistics on their use are far more difficult to obtain. Some libraries collect data on the number of mediated searches but not on end-user searches. In addition to the lack of agreement about the definition of a search, the ability to capture interactions with systems is not available consistently across all media.

ABATE ET AL. describe methods for recording and evaluating online searches using a personal computer. A similar approach is suggested by BURKE and SILVER & DENNIS for monitoring the use of CD-ROM databases. Capturing data through user logs not only provides quantitative data but also yields insights into users' search patterns, the errors they commit while searching, and their interaction with specific software or interface features.

There are few longitudinal studies of the adoption of end-user searching, but IKEDA & SCHWARTZ performed a four-year follow-up to determine the impact of end-user search training on pharmacy students. HART & RICE (1991) studied end users in four settings: (1) medicine, (2) law, (3) banking, and (4) aerospace research and development. The decision to access a database directly or through an intermediary was associated with database type (bibliographic, full text, or numeric). Both studies indicated that active end users are likely to be familiar with computer technology and enjoy using it, view themselves as relatively self-sufficient, and need to obtain information on a regular basis. Such individuals do not like to depend on an intermediary, do not wish to pay for such services, and require a search often enough to maintain their skills. Also, they want to conduct their own searching if they plan to download the results for future analysis or manipulation.

When information retrieval needs are not routine, users are more likely to delegate the search to an intermediary; if users are requesting a search in an unfamiliar subject area, they are likely to rely on an intermediary to assess the quality of the search. End-user searches tend to be limited to the current literature, whereas intermediary searches are more likely to require the use of multiple files, including backfiles, and employ more complex strategies (due either to request or searcher preference).

The impact of easy, convenient, and economic access to databases and productivity in a variety of fields was recently reviewed by KOENIG, but little hard data were reported. Prompted by a perceived increase in the number of clinical vs. research questions being searched in MEDLINE, NLM used a critical-incident technique to investigate how MEDLINE was being used in clinical care and to determine the effect of search results on patient outcome (LINDBERG ET AL., 1993b). Although the study included both mediated and end-user access, an important conclusion was that rapid and effective access to the medical literature favorably influenced patient outcomes. VEENSTRA also found that clinicians use both mediated and direct searching. It will be interesting to observe the extent to which and the circumstances under which end-user searching will supplant mediated searches in the clinical setting.

DALRYMPLE (1990a) reported on MEDLINE CD-ROM systems in clinical settings and found that clinicians appreciated the ease and convenience of immediate and direct access to information. In addition their clinical information requests were more focused and practical than those brought to the library. The ability to access full-text information directly rather than through a bibliographic citation was seen as desirable.

MARSHALL & ALLAN studied the implementation of end-user online searching by health professionals, noting that many end users quickly learn that the convenience of personal access to databases and high-quality retrieval are not always related. HAYNES ET AL. (1990) tried to determine the effect when unlimited access to the medical literature through GRATEFUL MED was made available to clinicians. One interesting finding was that about half the searches stemming from patient problems affected clinical decisions. In many cases, there apparently was no perceived need to go beyond the abstract to the full text of an article.

SIEGFRIED ET AL. reported a two-year project that provided humanities scholars with unlimited subsidized access to DIALOG's online databases. The authors found that while the scholars managed to retrieve their search results reasonably well, direct access to online resources was not yet a staple of their activities. In 1991 TIBBO reviewed information systems for the humanities and noted that while humanists' use of computer technology is rapidly increasing, much of that use is concentrated in areas such as computer-assisted textual analysis and computer modeling rather than on database use as defined in this chapter.

CARTER gives one of the few reported examples of end-user access to online systems in schools, in this case for 9-16-year-old students in a British school. Interestingly, the students learned the search commands more quickly than the staff. MARCHIONINI also studied young end users, grade-school students searching a full-text encyclopedia on CD-ROM. They performed adequate searches and used a highly interactive style.

Search Process

Many studies have been done to gain a better understanding of user behavior so that system design or user instruction can be improved. MARSHALL used multivariate analysis to identify three dimensions of task complexity in database searching (intellectual, technical and system-related tasks). She suggests that while better interface design is important for maximizing results, end users need help in formulating their requests to optimize use of the system. JACOBSON ET AL. analyzed interactions between users and the NEXIS database. They too concluded that users failed to take full advantage of the feedback features of the system. KERR observed searchers operating in five different versions of a single database to determine whether a mental model of a system affected such variables as perceived level of difficulty, satisfaction, and enjoyment. He concluded, however, that it is very difficult to create generic models that can help new end users understand higher-order search issues, such as how retrieval engines work.

In her study of end users of PaperChase, an online system designed for end users in health care, N. S. KING found that searchers used few of the features on the system; they conducted rather simple searches with a few search statements. Many studies indicate that users have only a rudimentary understanding of the power of the *OR* operator (SIEGFRIED ET AL.; WILDEMUTH ET AL., 1991). When they do generate synonyms, they often mistakenly use the *AND* operator, which limits or eliminates retrieval. When systems provide links to other vocabulary terms or a list of terms, such as PaperChase and Knowledge Finder, the searcher is more likely to take advantage of this feature, thus increasing retrieval. The "explode" feature on systems providing access to MEDLINE is an example of how research on the search process has aided system designers. Other ways to address this need are through adjustments in indexing policy (MILSTEAD). Indeed, many writers (DALRYMPLE & YOUNGER; LANCASTER ET AL.; MILSTEAD) suggest that improved vocabulary systems and/or better ways to access the power of the vocabularies that already exist are key factors in helping users achieve success.

The degree to which users interact with a system and pay attention to the clues it offers through direct and indirect feedback are also of interest to researchers who are studying the search process. In an exploratory study of online bibliographic searches SHENOUDA found that users reformulated their searches when they received new information (e.g., additional terms) by interacting with the system. Nine new search process variables were proposed by HSIEH-YEE in her study of bibliographic searching; they concerned term selection, search monitoring, and search formulation and modification. Surprisingly, experienced searchers did not exploit the feedback by examining the relevant records for clues to expand the search. MARCHIONINI, however, found that young searchers used a highly interactive style, and rather than planning an advance strategy, they used feedback to reformulate their searches and even to judge the relevance of the material retrieved. LANCASTER ET AL. observed that experienced searchers are more able to use the thesaurus structure to generate terms, a strategy variously known as TRACE (BATES, 1979) or "retrieval by reformulation" (DALRYMPLE, 1990b).

The amount of time spent during a search session or the number of statements entered during a search can also be used to characterize a searcher's use of the database. These measures originated in research on online bibliographic databases; when they are applied to full text, for example, they may need to be regarded differently. MARCHIONINI ET AL. suggest that full-text databases may be more conducive to highly interactive searches like browsing, in contrast with more efficient, carefully planned strategies which are considered optimal in traditional, online bibliographic systems.

Marchionini et al. report that subject experts who searched full-text databases spent more time and paid more attention to the materials retrieved than did search experts. The subject experts suggest that this is because the information itself is the object of their activity and they can judge its usefulness immediately, especially in full-text databases or those that offer abstracts. Search experts must rely on other clues, such as indexing terms or journal title and date. Marchionini et al. conclude that while subject knowledge affects the search process, it is neither a necessary nor sufficient condition for search success.

Understanding how end users search full-text databases is a growing area of concern, not only because these databases are becoming more common but also because information seekers are more likely to search them directly rather than through an intermediary. In reports on users searching full-text databases, WILDEMUTH ET AL. (1991; 1993) identified three factors associated with full-text searching: (1) term selection, (2) use of feedback to improve term selection, and (3) efficiency (time and intensity of interaction). These are similar to those described earlier for bibliographic searching. Building on insights from bibliographic searching, Wildemuth et al. identified five common search approaches that could be incorporated into instruction and interface design. These approaches are combinations of search tactics. Three of the approaches combine browsing, specifying, selecting and revising. The other two approaches start with exhaust (including most or all of the elements of the query in the initial search formulation) and include combinations of browsing, specifying, and revising. They noted that more research is needed to determine whether schemes that can identify search tactics of professional intermediaries are transferrable to searches conducted by end users and whether search process variables generated in bibliographic retrieval can be transferred to fact-based searches. TENOPIR & SHU also looked at the strategies of students and faculty while they searched full-text magazine databases.

Search Outcomes

Virtually any study dealing with searching addresses the paramount issue of whether users find what they want. The extent to which the system designer and user must shoulder the burdens of effort and cost has shifted over the years, but the concern remains the same. Studies aimed primarily at evaluating search results have traditionally used precision and recall as criteria of success, but other measures have also been introduced. For example, in a study of searches performed by human intermediaries, SU found that the users' evaluations of the search results as a whole was the best single measure of system performance. She considered the human intermediary as a part of the overall system.

A critical issue in precision and recall is relevance; for further understanding of relevance and its effect on calculations of precision and recall, the reader should consult FROEHLICH (1994). See also the chapter on Relevance and Information Behavior in this volume (SCHAMBER).

In evaluating search outcomes and search process, a common method is to compare the search results and the process by which they were obtained with those obtained by expert searchers; although other variables may be introduced, precision and recall are calculated for both sets of searches. SULLIVAN ET AL. found that end users retrieved fewer items than experts and that the retrieval was more precise. When HAYNES ET AL. (1994) and LANCASTER ET AL. compared the results of searches done by librarians with those done by end users, they found that librarian searches tend to be of higher quality (i.e., fewer false drops and higher recall) and were done more efficiently. On the other hand, end users usually retrieve at least some relevant items, although there is lower recall and more false drops. MCKIBBON ET AL. found that when experienced end-user searches were compared with librarian searches, the results were the same in recall, but higher in precision for librarians.

In order to study the system features of 27 online and CD-ROM MEDLINE systems, HAYNES ET AL. (1994) compared the results of a search conducted by clinicians, by experienced librarians, and by vendors' representatives and concluded that end users achieved less precise results (i.e., more irrelevant citations). The clinicians conducted simple searches, and although they retrieved some relevant items, they also retrieved many that were not. The librarians, on the other hand, tended to conduct very focused searches and to retrieve mostly relevant citations. This finding appears to agree with Lancaster's study in which end users missed a number of articles they wished they might have seen. Haynes et al. also noted that end users retrieved more irrelevant articles.

Many studies of search results involving both experienced librarians and end users have noted that different searchers find different items. Those items that they find in common are called overlap. This was noted by SARACEVIC & KANTOR in their study of intermediaries. MCKIBBON ET AL. also found that different searchers retrieve different citations. Studies that examine the differences among searchers may use search overlap to determine the common items retrieved. The relationship of relevance to overlap is discussed by PAO. In full-text databases, where searches are done to obtain a particular fact, calculations of precision and recall may need to be adjusted. See WILDEMUTH ET AL. (1991) and TENOPIR & SHU for examples.

Improving End-User Searching

The promise of expert systems to assist end users has not been borne out in our review. An in-depth discussion of the role of expert systems as intermediaries is provided in the recent *ARIST* review by DRENTH ET AL. Attempts to improve the results of end-user searches have generally focused on three areas: (1) increasing use by providing financial and convenience incentives; (2) improving understanding through instruction; and (3) facilitating searches through improved system design.

Findings on the effect of increased use/experience have been mixed. This may be due in part to different definitions of experience and to a lack of consistency in how the interaction between experience and instruction is handled. In her study of PaperChase, N.S. KING found that, in general, experience with the system did not tend to increase searchers' use of important system features. MCKIBBON ET AL. found that with experience and practice, clinicians could improve their results. Although these two studies differed in their focus (McKibbon et al. concentrated on results and use, King on search strategy), research on the effect of experience is inconclusive. It is difficult to discern whether some searchers reach a threshold beyond which they are neither willing nor able to proceed.

HSIEH-YEE examined the effects of both subject knowledge and search experience on end-user online searches of ERIC. She found that subject knowledge affected the ability of searchers to generate synonyms and include them in searching by using the *OR* operator; experience (and knowledge of searching) seemed to make them more aware of the importance of doing so. The benefits of subject knowledge applied only to experienced searchers, suggesting that knowledge of the technical aspects of searching is a threshold that must be crossed before the searcher can tap his or her subject knowledge. Further, when MARSHALL examined the extent to which the perceived complexity of database searching affected its adoption by health care professionals, she concluded that while certain routine tasks can be simplified or even eliminated by good interface and system design, users still need help to understand the process of searching in such areas as query formulation and search strategy.

SUMMARY

Beginning with the introduction of easy gateways and user-friendly interfaces, and continuing through the development of online catalogs and databases available on CD-ROM, the opportunities, motivation, and necessity for information seekers to interact directly with electronic databases has increased substantially. In many environments today, information is available electronically, through campus-wide networks, CD-ROMs, and the Internet, and a special access code or password is no longer necessary. Further, the technology has advanced to a point where knowledge and skills are not as essential to retrieving at least some useful information in a search. The degree to which system design can or should replace the skills of an intermediary to exploit the system's command language and index structure remains an open question. Nevertheless, the rapid rate of change and growth in the world of electronic information indicates that a large proportion of the population can now access some sort of electronic information system.

Since the MISCHO & LEE *ARIST* chapter in 1987 many studies have focused on variables related to the search process and its outcomes. Most of the research has been done on bibliographic databases either in libraries or library-related settings. More research is needed to investigate the variables in nonbibliographic databases—full-text as well as image, numeric, and multimedia. Many of the insights gained from research thus far give us a greater understanding of how individuals search for information when they are strongly motivated, often when the information need is related to school or work. However, we have little understanding of whether and how these processes change when people interact informally, at home, in the lab, and away from work, school, or library. Through the Internet, a vast array of databases of all types will be delivered to users in many different settings, some of which will not be associated with work or school. Research here is in its infancy and is needed to improve the ways in which these information resources are created and used. Finally, although the literature of database access systems seems to have been dominated by investigations in the medical and scientific areas, a body of research is beginning to accumulate from other fields. We can expect this research to expand as more databases become available and as access continues to grow.

BIBLIOGRAPHY

ABATE, MARIE A.; SHUMWAY, JAMES M.; JACKNOWITZ, ARTHUR I.; SINCLAIR, GEORGE. 1989. Recording and Evaluating End-User Searches on a Personal Computer. Bulletin of the Medical Library Association. 1989 October; 77(4): 381-383. ISSN: 0025-7338.

ALI, S. NAZIM. 1990. Retrieval Commands of CD-ROM Databases: A Comparison of Selected Products. CD-ROM Professional. 1990 May; 3(3): 28-33. ISSN: 1049-0833.

ALI, S. NAZIM; YOUNG, HAROLD C. 1992. Information Access through CD-ROM and Its Impact upon Faculty Research Output: A Case of a University in Third World Countries. Microcomputers for Information Management. 1992; 9(3): 177-189. ISSN: 0742-2343.

ALLEN, GILLIAN. 1989. Patron Response to Bibliographic Databases on CD-ROM. RQ. 1989 Fall; 29(1): 103-110. ISSN: 0033-7072.

ALLEN, GILLIAN. 1990. Database Selection by Patrons Using CD-ROM. College and Research Libraries. 1990 January; 51(1): 69-75. ISSN: 0010-0870.

ANDERS, VICKI; JACKSON, KATHY M. 1988. Online vs. CD-ROM: The Impact of CD-ROM Databases upon a Large Online Searching Program. Online. 1988 November; 12(6): 24-32. ISSN: 0146-5422.

BANKS, JANE L. 1989. End User Access to Medical Information: Databases, Networks and Bulletin Boards. In: Nixon, Carol; Padgett, Lauree, comps. Proceedings of the 10th National Online Meeting; 1989 May 9-11; New York, NY. Medford, NJ: Learned Information, Inc.; 1989. 27-31. ISBN: 0-938734-34-2.

BARKER, F.H. 1988. Does Any One of the "User Friendly" Systems Deserve a Prize? In: Online Information 88: Proceedings of the 12th International Online Information Meeting:Volume 1; 1988 December 6-8; London, England. Oxford, England: Learned Information Ltd.; 1988. 121-137. ISBN: 0-904933-68-7.

BASCH, REVA. 1992. Decision Points for Databases. Database. 1992 August; 15(4): 46-50. ISSN: 0162-4105.

BASCH, REVA. 1993. Annual Review of Database Developments: 1993. Database. 1993 December; 16(6): 29-41. ISSN: 0162-4105.

BATES, MARCIA J. 1979. Information Search Tactics. Journal of the American Society for Information Science. 1979 July; 30: 205-214. ISSN: 0002-8231.

BATES, MARCIA J. 1988. How to Use Controlled Vocabularies More Effectively in Online Searching. Online. 1988 November; 12(6): 45-56. ISSN: 0146-5422.

BATES, MARCIA J.; WILDE, DEBORAH N.; SIEGFRIED, SUSAN 1993. An Analysis of Search Terminology Used by Humanities Scholars: The Getty Online Searching Project Report Number 1. Library Quarterly. 1993 January; 63(1): 1-39. ISSN: 0024-2519.

BEHESHTI, JAMSHID. 1991. Retrieval Interfaces for CD-ROM Bibliographic Databases. CD-ROM Professional. 1991 January; 4(1): 50-53. ISSN: 1049-0833.

BELL, STEVEN J.; HALPERIN, MICHAEL. 1989. Making End-Users: Does Student Online Searching Make a Difference? Online. 1989 November; 13(6): 37-42. ISSN: 0146-5422.

BERNAL, NANCY E. 1991. Local Holdings Availability Messages on CD+ MEDLINE: Impact on Users and Interlibrary Loan Patterns. CD-ROM Professional. 1991 May; 4(3): 26-28. ISSN: 1049-0833.

BERUL, LAWRENCE H. 1969. Document Retrieval. In: Cuadra, Carlos A.; Luke, Ann W., eds. Annual Review of Information Science and Technology: Volume 4. Chicago, IL: Encyclopaedia Britannica, Inc. for the American Society for Information Science; 1969. 203-227. ISSN: 0066-4200; ISBN: 0-85229-147-7.

BICHTELER, JULIE. 1987. End User Database Searching in Geoscience. In: Bier, Robert A., Jr., ed. The User and Geoscience Information: Proceedings of the 21st Meeting of the Geoscience Information Society; 1986 November 10-13; San Antonio, TX. Alexandria, VA: Geoscience Information Society; 1987. 45-53. ISBN: 0-934485-14-3.

BLEICH, HOWARD L.; JACKSON, J.D.; ROSENBERG, H.A. 1985. PaperChase: A Program to Search the Medical Literature. MD Computing. 1985 March-April; 2(2): 54-58. ISSN: 0724-6811.

BOEHM-DAVIS, DEBORAH A.; HOLT, ROBERT W.; KOLL, MATTHEW. 1989. Effects of Different Data Base Formats on Information Retrieval. Human Factors. 1989 October; 31: 579-592. ISSN: 0018-7208.

BONIME, ANDREW. 1992. Sony's Data Discman: A Look at These New Portable Information Machines and What They Mean for CD-ROM Developers. CD-ROM Professional. 1992 September; 5(5): 55-65. ISSN: 1049-0833.

BORGMAN, CHRISTINE L. 1986. Why Are Online Catalogs Hard to Use? Lessons Learned from Information Retrieval Studies. Journal of the American Society for Information Science. 1986 November; 37(6): 387-400. ISSN: 0002-8231.

BORGMAN, CHRISTINE L. 1987. Information Retrieval from CD-ROM: Status Quo or a Revolution in End-User Access? Canadian Journal of Information Science. 1987; 12(3/4): 43-53. ISSN: 0380-9218.

BOWERS, RICHARD A. 1986. The Optical/Electronic Publishing Directory, 1986. Carmel Valley, CA: Information Arts; 1986. ISBN: 0-937665-00-2.

BRANDT, KERRYN A. 1993. The GDB Human Genome Data Base: A Source of Integrated Genetic Mapping and Disease Data. Bulletin of the Medical Library Association. 1993 July; 81(3): 285-292. ISSN: 0025-7338.

BRUNNING, DENNIS R.; MACHOVEC, GEORGE S.; PLAZA, JOYCE. 1989. Searching under Multiple Options: Patterns of Database Use in a Mixed Information Environment. In: Online Information 89: Proceedings of the

13th International Online Information Meeting; 1989 December 12-14; London, England. Oxford, England: Learned Information Ltd.; 1989. 49-57. ISBN: 0-904933-72-5.

BURKE, DAVID L. 1991. CD-ROM Master: A Complete CD-ROM Statistics Gathering Program. CD-ROM Professional. 1991 November; 4(6): 58-65. ISSN: 1049-0833.

CAHAN, MITCHELL AARON. 1989. GRATEFUL MED: A Tool for Studying Searching Behavior. Medical Reference Services Quarterly. 1989 Winter; 8(4): 61-79. ISSN: 0276-3869.

CARTER, CAROLYN. 1989. From John the Baptist to Knee Replacements: The Use of Online in Schools. Education Libraries Journal. 1989 Autumn; 32(3): 35-45. ISSN: 0957-9575.

CARTER, ROBERT; JACKSON, KATHY M. 1992. Speech Synthesizer and Screen Reading Software Make CD-ROM Databases Accessible to Visually Impaired Library Users. CD-ROM Professional. 1992 January; 5(1): 129-131. ISSN: 1049-0833.

CHERRY, JOAN M. 1990. Methods of Studying Database Users: The Role of Surveys, Laboratory Studies, and Field Studies. Canadian Journal of Information Science. 1990 July; 15(2): 17-29. ISSN: 0380-9218.

CLARK, KATHARINE E.; GOMEZ, JONI. 1990. Faculty Use of Databases at Texas A&M University. RQ. 1990 Winter; 30(2): 241-248. ISSN: 0033-7072.

CLYMAN, JEFFREY I.; POWSNER, SETH M.; PATON, JOHN A.; MILLER, PERRY L. 1993. Using a Network Menu and the UMLS Information Sources Map to Facilitate Access to Online Reference Materials. Bulletin of the Medical Library Association. 1993 April; 81(2): 207-216. ISSN: 0025-7338.

CORMACK, ERIN, ed. 1989. The CD-ROM Directory. 3rd edition. London, England: TFPL Publishing; 1989. ISBN: 1-870889-11-8.

CRAWFORD, GREGORY A. 1992. The Effects of Instruction in the Use of PsycLIT on Interlibrary Loan. RQ. 1992 Spring; 31(3): 370-376. ISSN: 0033-7072.

CREA, KATHLEEN; GLOVER, JAN; HELENIUS, MAJLEN. 1992. The Impact of In-House and End-User Databases on Mediated Searching. Online. 1992 July; 16(4): 49-53. ISSN: 0146-5422.

CUADRA, CARLOS A. 1990. Historical Overview of Database Development and Use. In: Raitt, David I., ed. Proceedings of the 1st East-West Online Information Meeting; 1989 October 11-13; Moscow, USSR. Oxford, England: Learned Information Ltd.; 1990. 9-18. ISBN: 0-904933-73-3.

CUADRA, CARLOS A. 1991. Portable Databases: Bridging the Gap between Online and Local Databases. Information Today. 1991 January; 8(1): 15-16. ISSN: 8755-6286.

CUADRA ASSOCIATES. 1979. Directory of Online Databases. Santa Monica, CA: Cuadra Associates; 1979 Fall. ISSN: 0193-6840.

DALRYMPLE, PRUDENCE W. 1990a. CD-ROM MEDLINE Use and Users: Information Transfer in the Clinical Setting. Bulletin of the Medical Library Association. 1990 July; 78(3): 224-232. ISSN: 0025-7338.

DALRYMPLE, PRUDENCE W. 1990b. Retrieval by Reformulation in Two Library Catalogs: Toward a Cognitive Model of Searching Behavior.

Journal of the American Society for Information Science. 1990 June; 41(4): 272-281. ISSN: 0002-8231.

DALRYMPLE, PRUDENCE W.; COX, RENE. 1992. An Examination of the Effects of Non-Boolean Enhancements to an Information Retrieval System. In: Williams, Martha E., comp. Proceedings of the 13th National Online Meeting; 1992 May 5-7; New York, NY. Medford, NJ: Learned Information, Inc.; 1992. 75-81. ISBN: 0-938734-63-6.

DALRYMPLE, PRUDENCE W.; YOUNGER, JENNIFER. 1991. From Authority Control to Informed Retrieval: Framing the Expanded Domain of Subject Access. College and Research Libraries. 1991 March; 52: 139-149. ISSN: 0010-0870.

DAVID, MANODARSHANI; MARTIN, GILLIAN. 1989. The ADONIS Experiment. . . Supplying Full-Text Journals on CD-ROM. Health Libraries Review. 1989 December; 6(4): 193-199. ISSN: 0265-6647.

DAVIDSON, LLOYD A.; HURD, JULIE M. 1987. A Study of the Use of CAS Online at an Academic Research Institution under the Conditions of Free Access: Data from an Analysis of Monthly Billing Invoices. In: Chen, Ching-chih, ed. ASIS '87: Information: The Transformation of Society: Proceedings of the American Society for Information Science (ASIS) 50th Annual Meeting: Volume 24; 1987 October 4-8; Boston, MA. Medford, NJ: Learned Information, Inc. for ASIS; 1987. 46-53. ISSN: 0044-7870; ISBN: 0-938734-19-9.

DERVIN, BRENDA; NILAN, MICHAEL S. 1986. Information Needs and Use. In: Williams, Martha E., ed. Annual Review of Information Science and Technology: Volume 21. White Plains, NY: Knowledge Industry Publications for the American Society for Information Science; 1986. 3-33. ISSN: 0066-4200; ISBN: 0-86729-209-1.

DESMARAIS, NORMAN. 1993. CD-ROM Market Study. CD-ROM World. 1993 May; 8(1): 59-62. ISSN: 1066-274X.

DOU, HENRI; HASSANALY, PARINA; LA TELA, ALBERT; QUONIAM, LUC. 1990. Advanced Interfaces to Analyse Automatically Online Database Set of Answers. Information Services and Use. 1990; 10(3): 135-145. ISSN: 0167-5265.

DRENTH, HILARY; MORRIS, ANNE; TSENG, GWYNETH. 1991. Expert Systems as Information Intermediaries. In: Williams, Martha E., ed. Annual Review of Information Science and Technology: Volume 26. Medford, NJ: Learned Information, Inc. for the American Society for Information Science; 1991. 113-154. ISSN: 0066-4200; ISBN: 0-938734-55-5.

DUGGAN, MARY KAY. 1987. A Look at Dialog's First CD-ROM Product. Optical Information Systems. 1987 November/December; 7(6): 401-405. ISSN: 0886-5809.

DUTTON, BRIAN. 1989. End-User Searching—What Are the Implications? Aslib Proceedings. 1989 April; 41(4): 149-157. ISSN: 0001-253X.

EAST, HARRY; FORREST, VICKI. 1988. Indicators of Online Use. In: Online Information 88: Proceedings of the 12th International Online Information Meeting; 1988 December 6-8; London, England. Oxford, England: Learned Information Ltd.; 1988. 91-102. ISBN: 0-904933-68-7.

EGER, ARTHUR J. 1988. Analysis of the Acceptance Behaviour of Medical Librarians and Their Patrons with Regards to Medline on CD-ROM. Online Review. 1988 December; 12(6): 341-348. ISSN: 0309-314X.

ELGHEIM, H.R. 1987. The Psychology of the Database User. In: Online Information 87: Proceedings of the 11th International Online Information Meeting; 1987 December 8-10; London, England. Oxford, England: Learned Information Ltd.; 1987. 359-365. ISBN: 0-904933-62-8.

EMARD, JEAN-PAUL, comp. 1988. CD-ROMs in Print: 1988-1989: An International Guide. Westport, CT: Meckler Corporation; 1988. ISBN: 0-88736-274-5.

ENGEL, GENEVIEVE. 1991. User Instruction for Access to Catalogs and Databases on the Internet. Cataloging and Classification Quarterly. 1991; 13(3/4): 141-156. ISSN: 0163-9374.

ERKKILA, JOHN E. 1990. CD-ROM vs. Online: Implications for Management from the Cost Side. Canadian Library Journal. 1990 December; 47(6): 421-428. ISSN: 0008-4352.

FAYEN, EMILY GALLUP. 1990. Locally Loaded Databases: Some Factors to Consider. Library Acquisitions: Practice and Theory. 1990; 14(4): 347-353. ISSN: 0364-6408.

FROEHLICH, THOMAS J. 1991. Ethical Considerations in End-User Searching and Training End Users to be Self Searchers of CD-ROM and Online Databases. In: Williams, Martha E., ed. Proceedings of the 12th National Online Meeting; 1991 May 7-9; New York, NY. Medford, NJ: Learned Information, Inc.; 1991. 93-98. ISBN: 0-938734-51-2.

FROEHLICH, THOMAS J., ed. 1994. Special Topic Issue: Relevance Research. Journal of the American Society for Information Science. 1994 April; 45(3): 124-217. ISSN: 0002-8231.

FRYER, REGINA KENNY; BARATZ, NANCY; HELENIUS, MAJLEN. 1991. Important Full-Text Databases for the Health Sciences. CD-ROM Professional. 1991 November; 4(6): 92-96. ISSN: 1049-0833.

GECHMAN, MARVIN C. 1972. Machine-Readable Bibliographic Data Bases. In: Cuadra, Carlos A.; Luke, Ann W., eds. Annual Review of Information Science and Technology: Volume 7. Washington, DC: American Society for Information Science; 1972. 323-378. ISSN: 0066-4200; ISBN: 0-87715-206-3.

GLITZ, BERYL. 1989. The Role of Medical Libraries in End-User Searching: Teaching the MEDLINE Database to Health Care Professionals. Science and Technology Libraries. 1989 Fall; 10(1): 47-54. ISSN: 0194-262X.

GOLDBERG, MARTIN. 1992. CD-ROM Periodical Indexes: Better Evaluation Necessary. Indexer. 1992 April; 18(1): 11-15. ISSN: 0019-4131.

GOODWIN, BRYAN. 1989. A Problem on the Horizon: The Proliferation of User Interfaces for CD-ROM Databases. Resource Sharing and Information Networks. 1989; 4(2): 27-30. ISSN: 0737-7797.

HALPERIN, MICHAEL. 1993. What Counts? Measuring Machine Readable Database Use. Database. 1993 April; 16(2): 10-12. ISSN: 0162-4105.

HANCOCK-BEAULIEU, MICHELINE, ed. 1992. Information Systems for End-Users: Research and Development Issues. London, England: Taylor-Graham; 1992. 85p. ISBN: 0-947568-57-3.

HARMAN, DONNA. 1992. Evaluation Issues in Information Retrieval. Information Processing and Management. 1992; 28(4): 439-440. ISSN: 0306-4573.

HART, PAUL J.; RICE, RONALD E. 1987. Online Organizational Information: Tasks, Usage and Evaluation. In: Chen, Ching-chih, ed. ASIS '87: Information: The Transformation of Society: Proceedings of the the American Society for Information Science (ASIS) 50th Annual Meeting: Volume 24; 1987 October 4-8; Boston, MA. Medford, NJ: Learned Information, Inc. for ASIS; 1987. 99-105. ISSN: 0044-7870; ISBN: 0-938734-19-9.

HART, PAUL J.; RICE, RONALD E. 1991. Using Information from External Databases: Contextual Relationships of Use, Access Method, Task, Database Type, Organizational Differences, and Outcomes. Information Processing and Management. 1991; 27(5): 461-479. ISSN: 0306-4573.

HAWKINS, DONALD T. 1981. Online Information Retrieval Systems. In: Williams, Martha E., ed. Annual Review of Information Science and Technology: Volume 16. White Plains, NY: Knowledge Industry Publications, Inc. for the American Society for Information Science; 1981. 171-208. ISSN: 0066-4200; ISBN: 0-914236-90-3.

HAWKINS, DONALD T. 1988. Applications of Artificial Intelligence (AI) and Expert Systems for Online Searching. Online. 1988 January; 12(1): 31-43. ISSN: 0146-5422.

HAYNES, R. BRIAN; MCKIBBON, K. ANN; WALKER, CYNTHIA J.; RYAN, NANCY; FITZGERALD, DOROTHY; RAMSDEN, MICHAEL F. 1990. Online Access to MEDLINE in Clinical Settings: A Study of Use and Usefulness. Annals of Internal Medicine. 1990; 112(1): 78-84. ISSN: 0003-4819.

HAYNES, R. BRIAN; RAMSDEN, MICHAEL F.; MCKIBBON, K. ANN; WALKER, CYNTHIA J. 1991. Online Access to MEDLINE in Clinical Settings: Impact of User Fees. Bulletin of the Medical Library Association. 1991 October; 79(4): 377-381. ISSN: 0025-7338.

HAYNES, R. BRIAN; WALKER, CYNTHIA J.; MCKIBBON, K. ANN; JOHNSTON, MARY E.; WILLAN, ANDREW R. 1994. Performances of 27 MEDLINE Systems Tested by Searchers with Clinical Questions. Journal of the American Medical Informatics Association. 1994 May/June; 1(3): 285-295. ISSN: 1067-5027.

HECK, A. 1992. Astronomical Databases: A User Approach. In: Data Analysis in Astronomy IV. New York, NY: Plenum Press; 1992. 21-28. ISBN: 0-306-44106-3.

HINNEBUSCH, MARK. 1991. Z39.50: A Path for Implementation. Computers in Libraries. 1991 September; 11(8): 30-31. ISSN: 1041-7915.

HOGAN, TOM. 1991. Westlaw Users Gain "Seamless" Access to Dialog. Information Today. 1991 January; 8(1): 2, 10. ISSN: 8755-6286.

HOLLOWAY, CARSON; JACKSON, MARGARET W. 1988. Using the Microcomputer to Keep Statistics on the Use of CD-ROM. Laserdisk Professional. 1988 September; 1(3): 67-69. ISSN: 0896-4149.

HOROWITZ, GARY L.; BLEICH, HOWARD L. 1981. PaperChase: A Computer Program to Search the Medical Literature. New England Journal of Medicine. 1981 October 5; 305(16): 924-930. ISSN: 0028-4793.

HSIEH-YEE, INGRID. 1993. Effects of Search Experience and Subject Knowledge on the Search Tactics of Novice and Experienced Searchers. Journal of the American Society for Information Science. 1993 April; 44(3): 161-174. ISSN: 0002-8231.

HUANG, SAMUEL T.; MCHALE, TERRENCE J. 1990. A Cost Effectiveness Comparison between Print and Online Versions of the Same Frequently-Used Sources of Business and Financial Information. In: Williams, Martha E., ed. Proceedings of the 11th National Online Meeting; 1990 May 1-3; New York, NY. Medford, NJ: Learned Information, Inc.; 1990. 161-168. ISBN: 0-938734-44-X.

HUMPHREYS, BETSY L.; LINDBERG, DONALD A.B. 1993. The UMLS Project: Making the Conceptual Connection between Users and the Information They Need. Bulletin of the Medical Library Association. 1993 April; 81(2): 170-177. ISSN: 0025-7338.

HURD, JULIE M.; DAVIDSON, LLOYD A. 1987. CAS Online Usage in Academic Chemistry Libraries: Report of a Survey. In: Chen, Ching-chih, ed. ASIS '87: Information: The Transformation of Society: Proceedings of the American Society for Information Science (ASIS) 50th Annual Meeting: Volume 24; 1987 October 4-8; Boston, MA. Medford, NJ: Learned Information, Inc. for ASIS; 1987. 116-118. ISSN: 0044-7870; ISBN: 0-938734-19-9.

IKEDA, NAOMI R.; SCHWARTZ, DIANE G. 1992. Impact of End-User Search Training on Pharmacy Students: A Four Year Follow-Up Study. Bulletin of the Medical Library Association. 1992 April; 80(2): 124-130. ISSN: 0025-7338.

INFORMATION TODAY. 1991. UMI Unveils Networked Image Database System. Information Today. 1991 September; 8(8): 28-29. ISSN: 8755-6286.

INGWERSEN, PETER. 1992. Information Retrieval Interaction. London, England: Taylor Graham; 1992. 246p. ISBN: 0-947568-54-9.

JACOBSON, THOMAS L.; FUSANI, DAVID S.; YAN, WENJIE. 1993. Q-Analysis of User Database Interaction. International Journal of Man-Machine Studies. 1993 May; 38(5): 787-803. ISSN: 0020-7373.

JACSÓ, PETER. 1987. The Unsqueezed Juice of Online: A User's Plea for New Features. In: Online Information 87: Proceedings of the 11th International Online Information Meeting; 1987 December 8-10; London, England. Oxford, England: Learned Information, Ltd.; 1987. 343-348. ISBN: 0-904933-62-8.

JACSÓ, PETER. 1993. Searching for Skeletons in the Database Cupboard Part I: Errors of Omission. Database. 1993 February; 16(1): 38-49. ISSN: 0162-4105.

JACSÓ, PETER. 1994. OVID/MEDLINE: A Gourmet Choice. Database. 1994 February; 17(1): 31-34. ISSN: 0162-4105.

KAHN, PAUL. 1988. Making a Difference: A Review of the User Interface Features in Six CD-ROM Database Products. Optical Information Systems. 1988 July; 8(1): 169-183. ISSN: 0886-5809.

KANTOR, ANDREW. 1994. Making On-Line Services Work for You. PC Magazine. 1994 March 15; 13(5): 110-114, 116-118, 120, 122, 126, 128, 143-144, 148-150, 158. ISSN: 0888-8507.

KELSEY, ANN L.; COHN, JOHN M. 1987. The Impact of Automation on Interlibrary Loan: One College Library's Experience. Journal of Academic Librarianship. 1987 July; 13: 163-166. ISSN: 0099-1333.

KERR, STEPHEN T. 1990. Wayfinding in an Electronic Database: The Relative Importance of Navigational Cues vs. Mental Models. Information Processing and Management. 1990; 26(4): 511-523. ISSN: 0306-4573.

KESSELMAN, MARTIN; WATSTEIN, SARAH B. eds. 1988. End-User Searching: Services and Providers. Chicago, IL: American Library Association; 1988. 230p. ISBN: 0-8389-0488-2.

KING, ALAN. 1992. Take Two Disks and Call Me in the Morning: A Look at Medical Databases on CD-ROM. Database. 1992 February; 15(1): 85-87. ISSN: 0162-4105.

KING, NATALIE SCHOCH. 1991. Search Characteristics and the Effects of Experience on End Users of PaperChase. College and Research Libraries. 1991 July; 52(4): 360-374. ISSN: 0010-0870.

KITTLE, PAUL W. 1992. Networking the Light Fantastic: CD-ROMs on LANs. CD-ROM Professional. 1992 January; 5(1): 30-37. ISSN: 1049-0833.

KOENIG, MICHAEL E.D. 1990. Information Services and Downstream Productivity. In: Williams, Martha E., ed. Annual Review of Information Science and Technology: Volume 25. Amsterdam, The Netherlands: Elsevier Science Publishers for the American Society for Information Science; 1990. 55-86. ISSN: 0066-4200; ISBN: 0-444-88531-5.

KOREN, JUDITH. 1992. Providing Access to CD-ROM Databases in a Campus Setting. Part II: Networking CD-ROMs via a LAN. CD-ROM Professional. 1992 September; 5(5): 83-94. ISSN: 1049-0833.

KOVACS, DIANE K. 1992. Government Printing Office CD-ROMs: Where to Find Information and Access to Government CDs. CD-ROM Professional. 1992 July; 5(4): 23-28. ISSN: 1049-0833.

KUBLI, MARY K. 1989. Choices in Online Newsletter Retrieval: NewsNet versus the PTS Newsletter Database. Database. 1989 February; 12(1): 39-46. ISSN: 0162-4105.

LABORIE, TIM; GARSON, KEN. 1988. End User Search Systems: Access to Library and Information Science Literature. Library Trends. 1988 Spring; 36(4): 805-823. ISSN: 0024-2594.

LAGUARDIA, CHERYL; HUBER, CHUCK; DOYLE, CAROL. 1991. CD-ROM Networking in ARL Academic Libraries: A Survey. CD-ROM Professional. 1991 March; 4(2): 36-39. ISSN: 1049-0833.

LANCASTER, F. WILFRID; ELZY, CHERYL; ZETER, MARY JO; METZLER, LAURA; LOW, YUEN-MAN. 1994. Searching Databases on CD-ROM: Comparison of the Results of End-User Searching with Results from Two Modes of Searching by Skilled Intermediaries. RQ. 1994 Spring; 33(3): 370-386. ISSN: 0033-7072.

LARSEN, SUZANNE T. 1991. An Evaluation of a Free, Unlimited Online Searching Program in a University Geology Library: Who Is Using It, What Does It Cost, and Is It Worth It. In: Dvorzak, Marie, ed. Geological Societies and Information Transfer in the Electronic Age: Proceedings of the 25th Meeting of the Geoscience Information Society; 1990 October 29-

November 1; Dallas, TX. Alexandria, VA: Geoscience Information Society; 1991. 119-126. ISBN: 0-934485-18-6.

LATHROP, ANN, comp. 1989. Online and CD-ROM Databases in School Libraries: Readings. Englewood, CO: Libraries Unlimited; 1989. 375p. ISBN: 0-87287-756-6.

LE BAS, M.J.; DURHAM, J. 1989. Scientific Communication of Geochemical Data and the Use of Computer Databases. Journal of Documentation. 1989 June; 45(2): 124-138. ISSN: 0022-0418.

LEIGH, SHARON A. 1991. The Use of Natural Language Processing in the Development of Topic Specific Databases. In: Williams, Martha E., ed. Proceedings of the 12th National Online Meeting; 1991 May 7-9; New York, NY. Medford, NJ: Learned Information, Inc.; 1991. 209-213. ISBN: 0-938734-51-2.

LEVIN, CAROL SIMON. 1990. CD-ROM Pricing: Time for Some New Ideas: A Proposal for a Radical Restructuring of the Pricing of Library CD-ROM Products. CD-ROM Professional. 1990 November; 3(6): 8-9. ISSN: 1049-0833.

LINDBERG, DONALD A.B.; HUMPHREYS, BETSY L.; MCCRAY, ALEXA T. 1993a. The Unified Medical Language System. Methods of Information in Medicine. 1993 August; 32(4): 281-291. ISSN: 0026-1270.

LINDBERG, DONALD A.B.; SIEGEL, ELLIOT R.; RAPP, BARBARA A.; WALLINGFORD, KAREN T.; WILSON, SANDRA R. 1993b. Use of MEDLINE by Physicians for Clinical Problem Solving. JAMA, The Journal of the American Medical Association. 1993 June; 269(24): 3124-3129. ISSN: 0098-7484.

LUEDKE, JAMES A., JR.; KOVACS, GABOR J.; FRIED, JOHN B. 1977. Numeric Data Bases and Systems. In: Williams, Martha E., ed. Annual Review of Information Science and Technology: Volume 12. White Plains, NY: Knowledge Industry Publications, Inc. for the American Society for Information Science; 1977. 119-181. ISSN: 0066-4200; ISBN: 0-914236-11-3.

LYNCH, CLIFFORD A. 1988. Developments in Database Management System Technology and Their Impact on Information Retrieval. In: ASIS '88: Information and Technology: Planning for the Second Fifty Years: Proceedings of the American Society for Information Science (ASIS) 51st Annual Meeting: Volume 25; 1988 October 23-27; Atlanta, GA. Medford, NJ: Learned Information, Inc. for ASIS; 1988. 190-194. ISBN: 0-938734-29-6.

LYNCH, CLIFFORD A. 1991. Nonmaterialized Relations and the Support of Information Retrieval Applications by Relational Database Systems. Journal of the American Society for Information Science. 1991 July; 42(6): 389-396. ISSN: 0002-8231.

LYNCH, CLIFFORD A.; PRESTON, CECILIA M. 1990. Internet Access to Information Resources. In: Williams, Martha E., ed. Annual Review of Information Science and Technology: Volume 25. Amsterdam, The Netherlands: Elsevier Science Publishers for the American Society for Information Science; 1990. 263-312. ISSN: 0066-4200; ISBN: 0-444-88531-5.

LYNCH, CLIFFORD A.; PRESTON, CECILIA M. 1992. Describing and Classifying Networked Information Resources. Electronic Networking: Research, Applications and Policy. 1992 Spring; 2(1): 13-23. ISSN: 1051-4805.

MARCACCIO, KATHLEEN YOUNG, ed. 1993. Gale Directory of Databases. Detroit, MI: Gale Research Inc.; 1993 January. 2 volumes. ISBN: 0-8103-5476-1.

MARCACCIO, KATHLEEN YOUNG, ed. 1994. Gale Directory of Databases. Detroit, MI: Gale Research Inc.; 1994. 2 volumes. ISBN: 0-8103-5747-X.

MARCHIONINI, GARY. 1989. Information-Seeking Strategies of Novices Using a Full-Text Electronic Encyclopedia. Journal of the American Society for Information Science. 1989 January; 40(1): 54-66. ISSN: 0002-8231.

MARCHIONINI, GARY; MEADOW, CHARLES T.; DWIGGINS, SANDRA; LIN, XIA; WANG, JIABIN; YUAN, WEIJING 1991. A Study of User Interaction with Information Retrieval Interfaces: Progress Report. Canadian Journal of Information Science. 1991 December; 16(1): 42-59. ISSN: 0380-9218.

MARSHALL, JOANNE G. 1987. The Perceived Complexity of Database Searching among End-Users: A Multivariate Analysis. Canadian Journal of Information Science. 1987; 12(3/4): 89-97. ISSN: 0380-9218.

MARSHALL, JOANNE G.; ALLAN, SANDRA. 1990. Training and Assistance Techniques for Database Users. Canadian Journal of Information Science. 1990 July; 15(2): 38-51. ISSN: 0380-9218.

MCCAIN, KATHERINE W.; WHITE, HOWARD D.; GRIFFITH, BELVER C. 1987. Comparing Retrieval Performance in Online Data Bases. Information Processing and Management. 1987 December; 23(6): 539-553. ISSN: 0306-4573.

MCCARN, DAVIS B. 1978. Online Systems—Techniques and Services. In: Williams, Martha E., ed. Annual Review of Information Science and Technology: Volume 13. White Plains, NY: Knowledge Industry Publications, Inc. for the American Society for Information Science; 1978. 85-124. ISSN: 0066-4200; ISBN: 0-914236-21-0.

MCKIBBON, K. ANN; HAYNES, R. BRIAN; DILKS, C.J.; RAMSDEN, MICHAEL F.; RYAN, NANCY C.; BAKER, L.; FLEMMING, T.; FITZGERALD, D. 1990. How Good Are Clinical MEDLINE Searches? A Comparative Study of Clinical End-User and Librarian Searches. Computers and Biomedical Research. 1990; 23: 583-593. ISSN: 0010-4809.

MCKININ, EMMA JEAN; SIEVERT, MARYELLEN. 1989. A Comparison of Full-Text and Abstracts for Information Retrieval in Clinical Medicine. In: Nixon, Carol; Padgett, Lauree, comps. Proceedings of the 10th National Online Meeting; 1989 May 9-11; New York, NY. Medford, NJ: Learned Information, Inc.; 1989. 295-301. ISBN: 0-938734-34-2.

MEADOW, CHARLES T. 1988. OAKDEC: A Program for Studying the Effects on Users of a Procedural Expert System for Database Searching. Information Processing and Management. 1988; 24(4): 449-457. ISSN: 0306-4573.

MEYER, DANIEL E.; RUIZ, DEN. 1990a. End-User Selection of Databases. Part I: Science/Technology/Medicine. Database. 1990 August; 13(4): 21-23, 26-29. ISSN: 0162-4105.

MEYER, DANIEL E.; RUIZ, DEN. 1990b. End-User Selection of Databases. Part II: Business/Law. Database. 1990 August; 13(4): 35-42. ISSN: 0162-4105.

MEYER, DANIEL E.; RUIZ, DEN. 1990c. End-User Selection of Databases. Part IV: People/News/General Reference. Database. 1990 October; 13(5): 65-67. ISSN: 0162-4105.

MEYER, RICHARD W. 1990. Management, Cost, and Behavioral Issues with Locally Mounted Databases. Information Technology and Libraries. 1990 September; 9(3): 226-241. ISSN: 0730-9295.

MEYER, RICHARD W. 1993. Selecting Electronic Alternatives. Information Technology and Libraries. 1993 June; 12(2): 173-180. ISSN: 0730-9295.

MILLER, STUART W. 1991. NOTIS' Multiple Access System: Providing Enhanced Information Services with a Single User Interface. In: Williams, Martha E., ed. Proceedings of the 12th National Online Meeting; 1991 May 7-9; New York, NY. Medford, NJ: Learned Information, Inc.; 1991. 281-289. ISBN: 0-938734-51-2.

MILSTEAD, JESSICA L. 1992. Methodologies for Subject Analysis in Bibliographic Databases. Information Processing and Management. 1992; 28(3): 407-431. ISSN: 0306-4573.

MISCHO, WILLIAM H.; LEE, JOUNGHYOUN. 1987. End-User Searching of Bibliographic Databases. In: Williams, Martha E., ed. Annual Review of Information Science and Technology: Volume 22. Amsterdam, The Netherlands: Elsevier Science Publishers for the American Society for Information Science; 1987. 227-263. ISSN: 0066-4200; ISBN: 0-444-70302-0.

MOORE, CAROLINE. 1989. Survey of CD-ROM Users in the UK. Program. 1989 October; 23(4): 385-393. ISSN: 0033-0337.

MORRIS, ANNE; TSENG, GWYNETH; NEWHAM, GODFREY. 1988. The Selection of Online Databases and Hosts: An Expert System Approach. In: Online Information 88: Proceedings of the 12th International Online Information Meeting: Volume 1; 1988 December 6-8; London, England. Oxford, England: Learned Information Ltd.; 1988. 139-148. ISBN: 0-904933-68-7.

MUSSER, LINDA R.; CONKLING, THOMAS W. 1991. Impact of NTIS CD-ROM on the Use of a Technical Report Collection. College and Research Libraries News. 1991 February; 52(2): 110-111. ISSN: 0099-0086.

NAHL-JAKOBOVITS, DIANE; TENOPIR, CAROL. 1992. Databases Online and on CD- ROM: How Do They Differ? Let Us Count the Ways. Database. 1992 February; 15(1): 42-50. ISSN: 0162-4105.

NELSON, MICHAEL L. 1987. High Database Prices and Their Impact on Information Access: Is There a Solution? Journal of Academic Librarianship. 1987 July; 13(3): 158-162. ISSN: 0099-1333.

NESBIT, KATHRYN W. 1990. CD Plus Medline. CD-ROM Professional. 1990 May; 3(3): 61-65. ISSN: 1049-0833.

NICHOLLS, PAUL T. 1988. Statistical Profile of Currently Available CD-ROM Database Products. Laserdisk Professional. 1988 November; 1(4): 38-45. ISSN: 0896-4149.

NICHOLLS, PAUL T. 1990. A Buyer's Guide to CD-ROM Selection: CD-ROM Product Directories and Review Tools. CD-ROM Professional. 1990 May; 3(3): 13-21. ISSN: 1049-0833.

NICHOLLS, PAUL T. 1991. A Survey of Commercially Available CD-ROM Database Titles. CD-ROM Professional. 1991 March; 4(2): 23-28. ISSN: 1049-0833.

NICHOLLS, PAUL T. 1992a. CD-ROM Databases: A Survey of Commercial Publishing. Database. 1992 February; 15(1): 36-41. ISSN: 0162-4105.
NICHOLLS, PAUL T. 1992b. United States History on CD-ROM: A Buyer's Guide. CD-ROM Professional. 1992 May; 5(3): 72-74. ISSN: 1049-0833.
NICHOLLS, PAUL T. 1993a. 15 Quick Tips for Navigating the CD-ROM Literature. CD-ROM Professional. 1993 January; 6(1): 93-98. ISSN: 1049-0833.
NICHOLLS, PAUL T. 1993b. The State of the Union: CD-ROM Titles in Print in 1992. CD-ROM Professional. 1993 January; 6(1): 60-64. ISSN: 1049-0833.
NICHOLLS, PAUL T.; SUTHERLAND, TRISH. 1992. CD-ROM Databases: A Survey of Commercial Publishing Activity. Database. 1992 February; 15(1): 36-41. ISSN: 0162-4105.
NICHOLLS, PAUL T.; VAN DEN ELSHOUT, RIA. 1990. Survey of Databases Available on CD-ROM: Types, Availability, and Content. Database. 1990 February; 13(1): 18-23. ISSN: 0162-4105.
NISTA, ANN S.; ALBERT, KAREN M.; LEWIS, BETH M. 1991. Cost Recovery and Usage Tracking of CD-ROM Databases with Menuing Software. Medical Reference Services Quarterly. 1991 Winter; 10(4): 15-28. ISSN: 0276-3869.
O'CONNOR, MARY ANN. 1992. Markup, SGML, and Hypertext for Full-Text Databases. CD-ROM Professional. Part I: 1992 May; 5(3): 112-113. Part II: 1992 July; 5(4): 123-125. ISSN: 1049-0833.
O'DELL, JUDITH E. 1988. Factors Used in Selecting Online Databases. In: Williams, Martha E.; Hogan, Thomas H., comps. Proceedings of the 9th National Online Meeting; 1988 May 10-12; New York, NY. Medford, NJ: Learned Information, Inc.; 1988. 287-291. ISBN: 0-938734-26-1.
O'LEARY, MICK. 1990. Databases of the Nineties: The Age of Access. Database. 1990 April; 13(2): 15-21. ISSN: 0162-4105.
O'LEARY, MICK. 1991a. Database Review: New Car Showroom Selects Right(?) Car. Information Today. 1991 October; 8(9): 13-14. ISSN: 8755-6286.
O'LEARY, MICK. 1991b. Pricing Breaks Through: Placing the Keystone for Online's Future. Online. 1991 March; 15(2): 6-8. ISSN: 0146-5422.
OBRACZKA, KATIA; DANZIG, PETER B.; LI, SHIH-HAO. 1993. Internet Resource Discovery Services. Computer. 1993 September; 26(9): 8-22. ISSN: 0018-9162.
OJALA, MARYDEE. 1993. Statistical and Numeric Databases for Businesses. Database. 1993 June; 16(3): 99-101. ISSN: 0162-4105.
OJALA, MARYDEE; BATES, ELLEN. 1986. Business Databases. In: Williams, Martha E., ed. Annual Review of Information Science and Technology: Volume 21. White Plains, NY: Knowledge Industry Publications, Inc. for the American Society for Information Science; 1986. 87-117. ISSN: 0066-4200; ISBN: 0-86729-209-1.
ONSI, PATRICIA W.; CAPODAGLI, JAMES A.; HAWKINS, DIANE K. 1992. Dial-in Access to CD-ROM Databases: Beyond the Local Area Network. Bulletin of the Medical Library Association. 1992 October; 80(4): 376-379. ISSN: 0025-7338.
PAISLEY, WILLIAM; BUTLER, MATILDA. 1987. The First Wave: CD-ROM Adoption in Offices and Libraries. Microcomputers for Information Management. 1987 June; 4(2): 109-127. ISSN: 0742-2343.

PAO, MIRANDA LEE. 1994. Relevance Odds of Retrieval Overlaps from Seven Search Fields. Information Processing and Management. 1994 May/June; 30(3): 305-314. ISSN: 0306-4573.

PERDUE, BOB; PIOTROWSKI, CHRIS. 1991. Online Database Use in Psychology: A Survey of Academic Libraries. Collection Management. 1991; 14(1/2): 133-137. ISSN: 0146-2679.

PHILLIPS, GARY LEE. 1992. Z39.50 and the Scholar's Workstation Concept. Information Technology and Libraries. 1992 September; 11(3): 262-270. ISSN: 0730-9295.

PIETY, JOHN. 1992. The Anatomy of a Decision: Tape vs. CD-ROM—Which Product and Why? Online. 1992 September; 16(5): 62-65. ISSN: 0146-5422.

PITERNICK, ANNE B. 1990. Decision Factors Favoring the Use of Online Sources for Providing Information. RQ. 1990 Summer; 29(4): 534-544. ISSN: 0033-7072.

POLLITT, A. STEVEN. 1987. CANSEARCH: An Expert Systems Approach to Document Retrieval. Information Processing and Management. 1987; 23: 119-138. ISSN: 0306-4573.

POLLY, JEAN ARMOUR; LYON, ELAINE. 1992. Out of the Archives and into the Streets: American Memory in American Libraries. Online. 1992 September; 16(5): 51-57. ISSN: 0146-5422.

PUTTAPITHAKPORN, SOMPORN. 1990. Interface Design and User Problems and Errors: A Case Study of Novice Searchers. RQ. 1990 Winter; 30(2): 195-204. ISSN: 0033-7072.

RADECKI, TADEUSZ. 1988. Trends in Research on Information Retrieval: The Potential for Improvements in Conventional Boolean Retrieval Systems. Information Processing and Management. 1988; 24(3): 219-227. ISSN: 0306-4573.

RAPP, BARBARA A.; SIEGEL, ELLIOT R.; WOODSMALL, ROSE MARIE; LYON-HARTMANN, BECKY. 1990. Evaluating MEDLINE on CD-ROM: An Overview of Field Tests in Library and Clinical Settings. Online Review. 1990 June; 14(3): 172-186. ISSN: 0309-314X.

REESE, JEAN. 1989. CD-ROM Technology at Vanderbilt University: Impact on Library Staff and the Educational Community. Optical Information Systems. 1989 January/February; 9: 38-43. ISSN: 0886-5809.

RICHARDSON, JOHN. 1991. Library User Trials with a CD-ROM Database: Users Evaluate ADONIS, a CD-ROM Database of Biomedical Journal Articles. Computers in Libraries. 1991 April; 11: 28-34. ISSN: 1041-7915.

RIETDYK, RON J. 1988. Creation and Distribution of CD-ROM Databases for the Library Reference Desk. Journal of the American Society for Information Science. 1988; 39(1): 58-62. ISSN: 0002-8231.

RITCHIE, JO ANN. 1990. Methods of Studying Users. Canadian Journal of Information Science. 1990 July; 15(2): 30-37. ISSN: 0380-9218.

ROBBINS, RACHEL; HARER, JOHN B. 1991. The Impact of the Wilson Multi-Database Access Product on ILL Requests and Current Periodical Use. Journal of Interlibrary Loan and Information Supply. 1991; 1(4): 17-30. ISSN: 1042-4458.

RODERER, NANCY K.; BARNES, SUSAN. 1988. MEDLINE Alternatives. In: Greenes, Robert A., ed. Proceedings of the 12th Symposium on Computer

Applications in Medical Care; 1988 November 6-9; Washington, DC. New York, NY: IEEE; 1988. 540-544. ISSN: 0195-4210; ISBN: 0-8186-0881-1.
ROSEN, THERESA H. 1986. The Impact of Emerging Technologies upon the Economics of Database Production. In: Williams, Martha E.; Hogan, Thomas H., comps. Proceedings of the 7th National Online Meeting; 1986 May 6-8; New York, NY. Medford, NJ: Learned Information, Inc.; 1986. 389-392. ISBN: 0-938734-12-1.
RUIZ, DEN; MEYER, DANIEL E. 1990. End-User Selection of Databases. Part III: Social Science/Arts & Humanities. Database. 1990 October; 13(5): 59-64. ISSN: 0162-4105.
SACKS, LINDA R. 1989. Trends and Directions in the Distribution and Use of Inhouse Bibliographic Databases: A Producer's View. In: Nixon, Carol; Padgett, Lauree, comps. Proceedings of the 10th National Online Meeting; 1989 May 9-11; New York, NY. Medford, NJ: Learned Information, Inc.; 1989. 383-385. ISBN: 0-938734-34-2.
SARACEVIC, TEFKO; KANTOR, PAUL B. 1988. A Study of Information Seeking and Retrieving. III. Searchers, Searches, and Overlap. Journal of the American Society for Information Science. 1988 May; 39(3): 197-216. ISSN: 0002-8231.
SAULE, MARA R. 1992. User Instruction Issues for Databases in the Humanities. Library Trends. 1992 Spring; 40(4): 596-613. ISSN: 0024-2594.
SCHAMBER, LINDA. 1994. Relevance and Information Behavior. In: Williams, Martha E., ed. Annual Review of Information Science and Technology: Volume 29. Medford, NJ: Learned Information, Inc. for the American Society for Information Science; 1994. 3-48. ISSN: 0066-4200; ISBN: 938734-91-1
SCHIPMA, PETER B. 1975. Generation and Use of Machine-Readable Data Bases. In: Cuadra, Carlos A.; Luke, Ann W.; Harris, Jessica L., eds. Annual Review of Information Science and Technology: Volume 10. Washington, DC: American Society for Information Science; 1975. 237-271. ISSN: 0066-4200; ISBN: 0-87115-210-1.
SCHLOMAN, BARBARA F.; GATTEN, JEFFREY N.; BYERLY GREG. 1990. Fee-Based CD-ROMs at Kent State University. In: Stewart, Linda; Chiang, Katherine S.; Coons, Bill, eds. Public Access CD-ROMs in Libraries: Case Studies. Westport, CT: Meckler; 1990. 207-216. ISBN: 0-88736-516-7.
SCHWARTZ, CANDY. 1991. Knowledge Finder Version 1.5. CD-ROM Professional. 1991 March; 4(2): 40-44. ISSN: 1049-0833.
SCHWERIN, JULIE B. 1988. CD-ROM: Potential Markets for Information. Journal of the American Society for Information Science. 1988 January; 39: 54-57. ISSN: 0002-8231.
SHARRATT, BERNARD. 1994. Please Touch the Paintings. The New York Times Book Review. 1994 March 6; 99: 3; column 1. ISSN: 0028-7806.
SHAW, DEBORA. 1991. The Human-Computer Interface for Information Retrieval. In: Williams, Martha E., ed. Annual Review of Information Science and Technology: Volume 26. Medford, NJ: Learned Information, Inc. for the American Society for Information Science; 1991. 155-195. ISSN: 0066-4200; ISBN: 0-938734-55-5.
SHENOUDA, WAGIH. 1990. Online Bibliographic Searching: How End-Users Modify Their Search Strategies. In: ASIS '90: Proceedings of the American

Society for Information Science (ASIS) 53rd Annual Meeting: Volume 27; 1990 November 4-8; Toronto, Canada. Medford, NJ: Learned Information, Inc. for ASIS; 1990. 117-128. ISSN: 0044-7870; ISBN: 0-938734-48-2.

SHNEIDERMAN, BEN; BRETHAUER, DOROTHY; PLAISANT, CATHERINE; POTTER, RICHARD. 1989. Evaluating Three Museum Installations of a Hypertext System. Journal of the American Society for Information Science. 1989 May; 40(3): 172-182. ISSN: 0002-8231.

SIEGFRIED, SUSAN L.; BATES, MARCIA J.; WILDE, DEBORAH N. 1993. A Profile of End-User Searching Behavior by Humanities Scholars: The Getty Online Searching Project Report No. 2. Journal of the American Society for Information Science. 1993 June; 44: 279-291. ISSN: 0002-8231.

SILVER, HOWARD; DENNIS, SHARON. 1990. Monitoring Patron Use of CD-ROM Databases Using SignIn-Stat. Bulletin of the Medical Library Association. 1990 July; 78(3): 252-257. ISSN: 0025-7338.

SMITH, PHILIP J.; KRAWCZAK, DEBORAH; SHUTE, STEVEN J. 1987. Bibliographic Information Retrieval Systems: Increasing Cognitive Compatibility. Information Services and Use. 1987; 7(4/5): 95-102. ISSN: 0167-5265.

SOLOMON, PAUL. 1993. Children's Information Retrieval Behavior: A Case Analysis of an OPAC. Journal of the American Society for Information Science. 1993 June; 44(5): 245-264. ISSN: 0002-8231.

STANFILL, CRAIG; THAU, ROBERT. 1991. Information Retrieval on the Connection Machine: 1 to 8192 Gigabytes. Information Processing and Management. 1991; 27(4): 285-310. ISSN: 0306-4573.

STEFFEN, SUSAN SWORDS. 1990. Teaching End Users: Content, System, and Database Choices. In: Online/CD-ROM '90 Conference Proceedings; 1990 November 5-7; Washington, DC. Weston, CT: Online, Inc.; 1990. 159-163. Available from: Online, Inc., 462 Danbury Road, Wilton, CT 06897.

STEFFEY, RAMONA J.; MEYER, NIKKI. 1989. Evaluating User Success and Satisfaction with CD-ROM. Laserdisk Professional. 1989 September; 2(5): 35-45. ISSN: 0896-4149.

STERN, BARRIE T. 1977. Evaluation and Design of Bibliographic Data Bases. In: Williams, Martha E., ed. Annual Review of Information Science and Technology: Volume 12. White Plains, NY: Knowledge Industry Publications, Inc. for the American Society for Information Science; 1977. 3-30. ISSN: 0066-4200; ISBN: 0-914236-11-3.

SU, LOUISE T. 1992. Evaluation Measures for Interactive Information Retrieval. Information Processing and Management. 1992 July/August; 28(4): 503-516. ISSN: 0306-4573.

SULLIVAN, MICHAEL V.; BORGMAN, CHRISTINE L.; WIPPERN, DOROTHY. 1990. End-Users, Mediated Searches, and Front-End Assistance Programs on Dialog: A Comparison of Learning, Performance, and Satisfaction. Journal of the American Society for Information Science. 1990 January; 41(1): 27-42. ISSN: 0002-8231.

TENOPIR, CAROL. 1984. Full-Text Databases. In: Williams, Martha E., ed. Annual Review of Information Science and Technology: Volume 19. White Plains, NY; Knowledge Industry Publications, Inc. for the American Society for Information Science; 1984. 215-246. ISSN: 0066-4200; ISBN: 0-86729-093-5.

TENOPIR, CAROL. 1992. Full Text on CD-ROM. Library Journal. 1992 July; 117(12): 50-51. ISSN: 0363-0277.

TENOPIR, CAROL; SHU, MAN EVENA. 1989. Magazines in Full Text: Uses and Search Strategies. Online Review. 1989 April; 13(2): 107-118. ISSN: 0309-314X.

TIBBO, HELEN R. 1991. Information Systems, Services, and Technology for the Humanities. In: Williams, Martha E., ed. Annual Review of Information Science and Technology: Volume 26. Medford, NJ: Learned Information, Inc. for the American Society for Information Science; 1991. 287-346. ISSN: 0066-4200; ISBN: 0-938734-55-5.

TILLEY, CAROLYN B. 1990. Medical Databases and Health Information Systems. In: Williams, Martha E., ed. Annual Review of Information Science and Technology: Volume 25. Amsterdam, The Netherlands: Elsevier Science Publishers; 1990. 313-382. ISSN: 0066-4200; ISBN: 0-444-88531-5.

TRAUTMAN, RODES; VON FLITTNER, SARA V. 1989. An Expert System for Microcomputers to Aid Selection of Online Databases. Reference Librarian. 1989; 23: 207-238. ISSN: 0276-3877.

VALAUSKAS, EDWARD J. 1993a. Newspapers as Databases: The San Jose Mercury News and the Mercury Center. Database. 1993 October; 16(5): 88-90. ISSN: 0162-4105.

VALAUSKAS, EDWARD J. 1993b. One-Stop Internet Shopping: NCSA Mosaic on the Macintosh. Online. 1993 September; 17(5): 99. ISSN: 0146-5422.

VEENSTRA, ROBERT J. 1992. Clinical Medical Librarian Impact on Patient Care: A One-Year Analysis. Bulletin of the Medical Library Association. 1992 January; 80(1): 19-22. ISSN: 0025-7338.

VOGES, MICKIE A. 1988. Information Systems and the Law. In: Williams, Martha E., ed. Annual Review of Information Science and Technology: Volume 23. Amsterdam, The Netherlands: Elsevier Science Publishers for the American Society for Information Science; 1988. 193-216. ISSN: 0066-4200; ISBN: 0-444-70543-0.

WALKER, CYNTHIA J.; MCKIBBON, K. ANN; HAYNES, R. BRIAN; RAMSDEN, MICHAEL F. 1991. Problems Encountered by Clinical End Users of MEDLINE and GRATEFUL MED. Bulletin of the Medical Library Association. 1991 January; 79(1): 67-69. ISSN: 0025-7338.

WALKER, GERALDENE. 1990. Searching the Humanities: Subject Overlap and Search Vocabulary. Database. 1990 October; 13(5): 37-46. ISSN: 0162-4105.

WALSH, BRENDAN. 1987. Get in Touch with Those Public Databases. Accountancy. 1987 April; 99(1124): 137-141. ISSN: 0001-4664.

WANGER, JUDITH. 1979. Education and Training for Online Systems. In: Williams, Martha E., ed. Annual Review of Information Science and Technology: Volume 14. White Plains, NY: Knowledge Industry Publications, Inc. for the American Society for Information Science; 1979. 219-245. ISSN: 0066-4200; ISBN: 0-914236-44-X.

WATERS, S.T. 1986. Answerman, the Expert Information Specialist: An Expert System for Retrieval of Information from Library Reference Books. Information Technology and Libraries. 1986; 5: 204-212. ISSN: 0730-9295.

WELCH, C. BRIGID, ed. 1990. Management of CD-ROM Databases in ARL Libraries. Washington, DC: Association of Research Libraries, Office of Management Services; 1990. 147p. (SPEC Kit 169). ISSN: 0160-3582.

WIBERLEY, STEPHEN E., JR.; DAUGHERTY, ROBERT ALLEN; DANOWSKI, JAMES A. 1990. User Persistence in Scanning Postings of a Computer-Driven Information System: LCS. Library and Information Science Research. 1990 October/December; 12(4): 341-353. ISSN: 0740-8188.

WILDE, DANIEL U. 1976. Generation and Use of Machine-Readable Data Bases. In: Williams, Martha E., ed. Annual Review of Information Science and Technology: Volume 11. Washington, DC: American Society for Information Science; 1976. 267-298. ISSN: 0066-4200; ISBN: 0-87715-212-8.

WILDEMUTH, BARBARA M.; JACOB, ELIN K.; FULLINGTON, ANGELA; DE BLIEK, RUTH; FRIEDMAN, CHARLES P. 1991. A Detailed Analysis of End-User Search Behaviors. In: Griffiths, José-Marie, ed. ASIS '91: Proceedings of the American Society for Information Science (ASIS) 54th Annual Meeting: Volume 28; 1991 October 27-31; Washington DC. Medford, NJ: Learned Information, Inc. for ASIS; 1991. 302-312. ISSN: 0044-7870; ISBN: 0-938734-56-3.

WILDEMUTH, BARBARA M.; DE BLIEK, RUTH; FRIEDMAN, CHARLES P. 1993. Measures of Searcher Performance: A Psychometric Evaluation. Information Processing and Management. 1993 September-October; 29(5): 533-550. ISSN: 0306-4573.

WILLIAMS, MARTHA E. 1974. Use of Machine-Readable Data Bases. In: Cuadra, Carlos A.; Luke, Ann W., eds. Annual Review of Information Science and Technology: Volume 9. Washington, DC: American Society for Information Science; 1974. 221-284. ISSN: 0066-4200; ISBN: 0-87715-209-8.

WILLIAMS, MARTHA E. 1994. The State of Databases Today: 1994. In: Marcaccio, Kathleen Young, ed. Gale Directory of Databases. Detroit, MI: Gale Research Inc.; 1994. xvii-xxviii. ISBN: 0-8103-5747-X.

WILLIAMS, MARTHA E.; ROUSE, SANDRA H., eds. 1976. Computer-Readable Bibliographic Databases: A Directory and Data Sourcebook Washington, DC: American Society for Information Science; 1976. 1 volume. ISBN: 0-87715-114-8.

WILLIAMSON, ROBIN. 1990. CD-ROM and On-line Compared. Libri: International Library Review. 1990 March; 40(1): 19-27. ISSN: 0024-2667.

WOODSMALL, ROSE MARIE; LYON-HARTMANN, BECKY; SIEGEL, ELLIOT R., eds. 1989. MEDLINE on CD-ROM: National Library of Medicine Evaluation Forum; 1988 September 23; Bethesda, MD. Medford, NJ: Learned Information, Inc.; 1989. 498p. ISBN: 0-938734-36-9.

YOUNG, IAN R. 1992. The Use of a General Periodicals Bibliographic Database Transaction Log as a Serials Collection Management Tool. Serials Review. 1992; 18(4): 49-60. ISSN: 0098-7913.

ZAHIR, SAJJAD; CHANG, CHEW LIK. 1992. Online-Expert: An Expert System for Online Database Selection. Journal of the American Society for Information Science. 1992 June; 43(5): 340-357. ISSN: 0002-8231.

ZARNOSKY, MARGARET R. 1992. Knowledge Served on a Silver Platter: Planning and Paying for CD-ROMs. RQ. 1992 Fall; 32(1): 75-84. ISSN: 0033-7072.

III

Applications

Section III includes four chapters. "Health Informatics" is covered by Jennifer MacDougall, an information consultant from the Republic of Ireland, and J. Michael Brittain of the University of South Australia. Ann O'Brien of Loughborough University reviews the status and relatively recent changes in online catalogs in a chapter entitled "Online Catalogs: Enhancements and Developments." Patricia D. Fletcher and Deborah Otis Foy, both of the University of Maryland's Baltimore County campus, have written the first *ARIST* chapter on "Managing Information Systems in State and Local Government." Dianne Rothenberg of the ERIC Clearinghouse on Elementary and Early Childhood Education at the University of Illinois has reviewed the status of "Information Technology in Education."

Jennifer MacDougall and J. Michael Brittain have written the first *ARIST* chapter entitled "Health Informatics." Prior chapters have covered the general application area. In 1990 Carolyn Tilley wrote on medical databases and health information systems, and much earlier chapters on information science applications in medicine appeared in *ARIST* (Caceres et al. and Levy and Cammarn).

MacDougall and Brittain use the term health informatics to describe healthcare information management through the interdisciplinary application of information technology and communications for the benefit of patients, practitioners, and the general public. Their chapter provides an overview of recent developments and issues in health informatics from an historical and global perspective. Various health applications from different countries are cited. Systems in the United Kingdom, United States, and Australasia especially are reviewed with reference to the changing environment, competition, integration, and communication. Developments in the training and education of staff in health informatics are highlighted, and future trends are discussed in relation to international developments and global cooperation.

Ann O'Brien in her chapter on "Online Catalogs: Enhancements and Developments" reviews the research, development, and practical applications of the past three years. She covers a selection of the literature of bibliographic data, i.e., bibliographic standards and record supply, as well as certain problem areas associated with online catalogs, namely, subject access (efforts to improve the matching of search queries to controlled subject headings and keyword searching). Recent developments in search refinement and catalog record enrichment are discussed in detail. The ability to study user searching behavior on a long-term basis is examined. She observes that as catalogs become established, there is a need to include nonbibliographic materials, and an obligation to cater to people with special needs both of physical access and multilingual requirements. Some new interface developments are reviewed.

In their chapter on "Managing Information Systems in State and Local Government," Patricia D. Fletcher and Deborah Otis Foy of the University of Maryland, Baltimore County, note that the proper management of information and information technologies in state and local government is a critical issue in the 1990s. Government is the major provider of information in the United States. State and local governments are in the direct line of citizen services, receiving federal mandates to provide more and new services while not experiencing any increases in funding for such services. Information technologies are increasingly being viewed as tools to manage the administrative paperwork burden and offer services to citizens. The use of information technologies is no longer a question in government; it is the norm.

Over the past 15 years there have been many changes in the use and management of information technologies in state and local governments. The issues of locus of control, policy development, long-range planning for information systems, information professionals, and innovative information system applications are discussed in this review. A history of the evolution of information technology use and management is provided.

Dianne Rothenberg of the ERIC Clearinghouse on Elementary and Early Childhood Education at the University of Illinois reviews the situation regarding "Information Technology in Education." She notes that as schools move away from the information accumulation model of education to the learning-by-doing model, the use of information technologies in education is considered an essential part of school reform. In technology-rich schools, use of MS-DOS and Macintosh hardware and software has accompanied the trends toward local area networking, introduction of sophisticated hardware and software in increasingly lower grades, integrated curriculum and database construction, and use across the curriculum. Virtually all schools now use microcomputers, most use CD-ROM, about half have local area networks, and many use the Internet to enhance teaching and professional development.

The interest and ability of teachers and other school personnel to use the Internet are major changes. Many school library media centers are taking part in multitype library networks, using the Internet and broadening the concept of bibliographic instruction to include information skills across the curriculum. Media specialists are faced with many challenges, including the need for increased staff and financial resources, to adapt their collections, practices, and services to the changing school environment. Their future will be closely linked to their flexibility in adapting to a technology-dominant education environment.

5 Health Informatics

JENNIFER MACDOUGALL
Researcher and Information Consultant

J. MICHAEL BRITTAIN
University of South Australia, Adelaide

INTRODUCTION

This chapter examines recent developments and issues in health informatics from an historical and global perspective. The types of information involved and areas of information technology (IT) application are illustrated with reference to the literature from many countries. Information systems and strategies from the United Kingdom, United States, and Australasia in particular are reviewed, with reference to the changing environment, competition, integration, and communication patterns. Developments in the training and education of staff in health informatics are highlighted, and future trends are discussed in relation to international developments and global cooperation.

Definition

There has been much confusion and misunderstanding over the terms "medical informatics" and "health informatics." Health informatics is the new term for healthcare information management, originating in the systematic use of data to manage and provide health services. Medical informatics, in the strict sense of the term, has a longer history, involving the use of IT and computing for the diagnosis and treatment of disease (e.g., x-rays, imaging, magnetic resonance, scanning magnetic techniques, molecular design and receptor site modeling, electrophysiology). ZIMMERMAN ET AL. (p. 139) provide a useful plan for medical informatics computer systems that illustrates this distinction.

Annual Review of Information Science and Technology (ARIST), Volume 29, 1994
Martha E. Williams, Editor
Published for the American Society for Information Science (ASIS)
By Learned Information, Inc., Medford, N.J.

Previous chapters in *ARIST* by LEVY & CAMMARN and TILLEY have also considered aspects of health informatics with respect to information systems applications in medicine and medical databases and health information systems. In a paper on the origins of medical informatics, COLLEN provides a detailed history of the terminology, showing how the term informatics originated from the French *informatique* or the Russian *informatika.* He defined medical informatics at the Third World Conference on Medical Informatics (MEDINFO) in 1977 as "the application of computer technology to all fields of medicine" (p. 779).

According to LUNIN & BALL, the definitions of health informatics vary, but most of them "emphasize broad information-related issues" (p. 365). Although there is no consensus on a suitable definition, health informatics should contain elements of "acquisition, organization, analysis, evaluation, synthesis, management, communication, and dissemination of information as well as technological literacy" (p. 365).

Concern has been expressed that although health informatics aims to deliver improved healthcare at reduced cost, it does not receive sufficient attention in the healthcare community (WITTENSTROM). The tendency has been to represent health informatics in terms of IT solutions alone, whereas a more comprehensive scientific, social and behavioral approach to patient care is really the aim. When the term informatics first appeared, it was coupled with "medical," tending therefore to limit its meaning. This is partly due to a difference of interpretation—viz., in Europe "medical" tends to include the full range of health professions, but in the United States, it usually refers to physicians only. As BALL ET AL. (p. 345) state, "'health informatics' is being used to describe the field not specific to medicine, but supportive of the full spectrum of health sciences." At the same time, they point out, the present trend is toward the use of terms that differentiate among the various healthcare professions, such as dental informatics and nursing informatics.

Although the concepts of health informatics and medical informatics overlap, this review focuses on the literature relating to the management of information through the interdisciplinary application of information science and technology for the overall benefit of patients, staff, scientists, managers and caregivers involved in the whole range of healthcare activity.

HISTORICAL AND GLOBAL PERSPECTIVE

The years following World War II saw the beginning of a massive increase in the amount of information needed to run efficient health services. The introduction of mainframe computers in the 1960s enabled large amounts of data to be processed quickly (e.g., payrolls). As GREENES & SHORTLIFFE note, the initial impact of IT was largely in the background—in offices, medical records departments, and laboratories. As a number of writers have commented, however, healthcare services have generally been slow to adopt the new technologies compared with other businesses and industries. WALKER makes this point in an editorial, describing why computers must be made "irresistible" to healthcare practitioners. He provides a concise explanation of the overall changes in healthcare and the implications for health professionals, the ways in which computer technology can assist healthcare delivery, and the rewards to be gained.

In the United Kingdom (U.K.), the publicly owned, financed, and administered National Health Service (NHS) has operated a system of statistics gathering since its inception in 1949. However, the greatest impact for health informatics came in the 1980s with the establishment of the STEERING GROUP ON HEALTH SERVICES INFORMATION, which standardized minimum data requirements. As charted by MACDOUGALL & BRITTAIN, these developments led to the implementation of a general management function in NHS, based on business practices, and eventually, in 1989, to the introduction of the internal market which entailed a split along commercial lines between purchasers and providers of healthcare. These reforms began one year later in Scotland, where a slightly differently organized NHS operates, as described by WARDEN (1993a). These developments were information intensive and depended on the systematic collection and processing of information at all levels of healthcare provision.

In the U.K., as documented by LEE, there has been a centralized national responsibility for policy and resourcing of the health service. By contrast, in the United States the development of a decentralized and fragmented healthcare system has meant relatively little control of a national healthcare policy or financing by the federal government. As LINDBERG & SCHOOLMAN (p. 786) have reported, however, the National Library of Medicine (NLM) was set up over 150 years ago and given the mandate to "assist the advancement of medical and related sciences, and to aid in the dissemination and exchange of scientific and other information important to the progress of medicine and to the public health." Among its many roles and services NLM has had a unique role in the advancement of medical informatics (as opposed to health informatics), with the publication of *Index Medicus* (*IM*), the creation of the MEDLARS online service and MEDLINE (the database corresponding to *IM*), and the establishment of the Regional Medical Library network. Nevertheless NLM has funded a few research and training programs in other health informatics areas, such as nursing and biotechnology.

LUNIN & BALL note that the 1970s were devoted to the development of information systems in financial, statistical, and clinical areas;

in the 1980s the attention moved to decision support systems, and in the 1990s the emphasis is on integration and networking. COLAIANNI, for example, refers to the increasing importance of outreach programs, providing health professionals, wherever they may be, with instant access to the world's published knowledge through computer workstations.

YAMADA describes the growth of information systems in Canada, where, as in the United States and the U.K., most development has occurred in the larger acute-treatment hospitals, evolving from systems for payroll, personnel, and accounts, to laboratory, pharmacy, and nursing activity. These systems were department-oriented, or, as GREENES & SHORTLIFFE (p. 1115) describe it, "task-oriented or 'vertical'." Thus, a few highly skilled users in specific departments could deal efficiently with their particular system. The problems of integration and wider use of these early information systems are now being met by the developers of healthcare workstations and networking programs in North America, Europe, and Australia, as this review illustrates.

Many countries experienced basic changes in the structure and funding of their health services during the late 1980s. As already noted, the NHS in the U.K. has undergone a fundamental review and restructuring, and the United States has recently begun such a process. In the Netherlands, as LEE describes, a review proposing major changes in the healthcare system, like the U.K., based on the motivation of market forces was published in 1987. Reforms are also under way, for example, in Russia, Sweden, and Hungary (LEE, p. 23). In Sweden, for example, a new national healthcare information management system has been developed, that provides systematic and objective information for health providers. A new health structure act came into force in Germany on January 1, 1993, which seeks to curb the rise in healthcare costs. Ironically, these measures have led to enormous rises in the cost of statutory health insurance. As VON STILLFRIED & ARNOLD report, a rigid budget will control expenditures across all areas of healthcare in Germany. However, no priorities or scheme for rationing treatment have so far been set. An analysis of the financing of healthcare in the United States, Canada, and Germany by PFAFF compares the different expenditures among similar healthcare systems.

Australia has a state system of healthcare, with an overall national (i.e., Commonwealth) Department of Health, Housing, Local Government and Community Services, which is responsible for national projects and healthcare policy development. The increasing use of case-mix classification systems (a method of classifying treatments for contracting), such as Diagnosis Related Groups (DRG), developed in the United States, has raised awareness in Australia of the necessity of accurate health information (DRAPER). New Zealand is reorganizing its health service along lines similar to the U.K., by separating the purchasing and providing functions, but not without concerns as to the commercialization of the service (BUCHAN).

The recent growth of professionalization in the health informatics field is evidenced by the increasing number of new associations and journals for health information workers in the U.K., Australia, and the United States. New associations are the Australian Health Informatics Association and the American Health Information Management Association; new journals include the *British Journal of Healthcare Computing, Informatics in Healthcare Australia,* the *Journal of Health Information Management Research,* and the *Journal of the American Medical Informatics Association.*

TYPES OF INFORMATION AND AREAS OF IT APPLICATION

Information systems now pervade almost all aspects of the administration and delivery of healthcare. Health informatics covers an enormous range of types of information and areas of IT application. This section indicates the diverse nature and complexity of the field, with reference to issues and developments in different countries.

A modern health service requires that many different types of information run efficiently and effectively. For clarity these are categorized as: (1) scientific, clinical, and health services information, (2) patient-generated clinical data, (3) corporate activity management information, and (4) information for patients, caregivers, and the public. These categories are not mutually exclusive and incorporate both textual and numerical information.

Scientific, Clinical, and Health Services Information

This type of information is mainly textual rather than numerical and includes information in journal articles, abstracts and indexes, reports, computer-based knowledge systems, databases, reference books, and the "grey literature"—i.e., documents, letters, and circulars not published through conventional outlets.

In the United States in the 1960s, NLM recognized that fundamental changes were needed to access scientific and medical information and thus instituted the MEDLARS online system and MEDLINE database. These, in turn, have led to the widespread use of numerous specialized online databases (GREENES & SHORTLIFFE). An early assessment of NLM and its contribution to medical informatics is provided by LINDBERG & SCHOOLMAN.

WYATT (1991a; 1991b) has eloquently described the sources of medical knowledge and computer-based systems used by physicians in the U.K. He reviews current systems, such as medical knowledge bases on floppy disk (e.g., the London Dysmorphology Database) and CD-ROMs (e.g., OncoDisc). Online information services include MEDLINE, CancerLit, Toxline, and so on. The dial-up knowledge base called the Edinburgh Poisons Information System provides updated chemical and clinical information on the whole range of poisons. The introduction of clinical computing in U.K. general practice and hospitals is investigated by BENSON. He shows how more positive role models in the form of demonstration projects are critical in the successful adoption of clinical systems.

The issues involved in clinical information delivery and the new role of the librarian are discussed by MARSHALL. She stresses the need to assess the impact of information services in terms of cost-effectiveness and the development of quality improvement programs. Other applications of information systems in this category include teaching programs that provide simulated patient models to help students learn about dynamic relations among body systems (WYATT, 1991a, p. 1432). Medical-decision aids also provide patient models that allow a physician to explore alternative treatments at no risk to the patient. GRAVES describes A Research-Knowledge System ARKS, which stores, manages, and models scientific knowledge specifically for nursing practice; this program aims to conceptualize research knowledge for the nurse.

Nursing information forms a large portion of the literature in this review, reflecting a general concern that nursing staffs not be left behind in the computerization of healthcare management. ROMANO, in a paper examining the theoretical underpinnings of the adoption and implementation of new technologies, states that up to 35% of a nurse's time is consumed in information-related activities. Nursing information systems must collect, store, process, retrieve, display, and communicate information that nurses need to manage and administer care. ROMANO & HELLER assert the importance of recognizing the nurse as an emerging Nursing Information Systems (NIS) specialist. The role and work of the NIS specialist is discussed in relation to curriculum design and course content for a prototype educational program. Training and education issues in relation to health informatics are discussed in the final section of this chapter.

GASSERT (p. 53) reports that although computerized nursing information systems were well established in the United States by 1989, nurses were often not included in the selection, planning, or development of these systems, with the result that the systems are frequently incompatible with the needs of nursing care. Gassert offers a framework of requirements for such systems in the form of a graphic model with five element outputs: (1) nursing information functions, (2) nursing information processing requirements, (3) nursing system outputs, (4) nursing data requirements, and (5) nursing system benefits. A survey conducted in Australia studied the level of computerization in nursing departments in acute-care hospitals and their plans for the future. AXFORD & MCGUINESS report that only stand-alone microcomputers were being used, thus limiting the nurses' ability to access data. This situation reduced the nurse's influence in clinical decision making and undervalued the role of nursing information generally. The ultimate goal of nursing informatics, states SIMPSON (1992a, p. 26), is "to help nurses make better-quality clinical decisions through more effective management of accurate, timely, and complete patient care information."

This chapter can refer to only a fraction of the scientific and clinical informatics programs and systems currently in existence worldwide. The long-term aim in health informatics is to integrate the systems dealing with medical knowledge with those dealing with the management of healthcare. In the U.K. the emphasis recently has been on the clinician as manager. Since the early 1980s the pressure on doctors and healthcare practitioners to become involved in management has been growing, as CHANTLER (p. 634) explains: "all those who are involved in the delivery of service should contribute to the management of it." Clinicians, therefore, require both medical/scientific information and patient-generated data as well as hospital activity data and management information. The integration of information systems is reviewed in more detail later in this chapter.

The need for improved clinical information systems in Australia is discussed by MOREY, who asserts that the mere presence of quality assurance programs and accreditation of healthcare facilities in that country did not necessarily indicate that the information available was adequate for health planning and resource allocation. Clinical data systems in the areas of specific services (e.g., accident and emergency), outcomes of medical practices, regional variations in clinical practice, and disease surveillance information all needed improvement. A number of initiatives to improve the quality of clinical information are mentioned, such as the Information Task Force and a new Strategic Direction for Information Systems. Strategic planning and integration of systems are the next logical but difficult steps in the overall improvement of health informatics, and a more detailed examination of the literature on information strategies and planning for health informatics is provided in a later section of this chapter.

Patient-Generated Clinical Data

This type of data, also called clinical information documentation, is often statistical or numerical in format and is based on patients' medical records. It may include details on symptoms, medical history, diseases, occupations, examinations, diagnostic and preventive procedures, operative and therapeutic procedures, drug use, and the like. Clinical data also encompass information on treatment regimes, pathology tests, prognosis, screening, clinical outcome, followup procedures, as well as call and recall facilities for patient checkups and appointments. As reported by MACDOUGALL & BRITTAIN, apart from the immediate use in the treatment and prevention of illness, these data are used in various ways and for different purposes—e.g., in epidemiological surveys to assess trends and the spread of disease and in morbidity statistics to provide both local and/or national pictures of disease patterns. Patient-generated clinical data are also vital in research and teaching and are essential for successful medical audits and the development of outcome and performance indicators.

In 1990 YAMADA noted that Florence Nightingale would see little change in medical record keeping in the 127 years since she compiled her notes on hospitals. Yamada describes the development in Canada of mission-critical integrated systems, which are centered around patients rather than administrative functions. "Their primary purpose is to capture meaningful information to assist the physician in diagnosis and in providing the most effective treatment for the patient" (YAMADA, p. 100). Important economic factors have influenced the development of these systems with, for example, the introduction in the United States in the 1980s of Diagnosis Related Groups (DRG), an analysis and coding system that uses statistically generated categories to group patients with similar or related conditions.

The development of DRG strategies in the different states of Australia is described by DUCKETT ET AL. Canada and Germany have developed Case Mix Groups along similar lines. DRG involves a fixed payment for the treatment of a particular condition. This means that if a more efficient or cheaper method of treatment can be used, the hospital or unit benefits from money saved, but if the treatment is longer and more costly than the fixed rate, the hospital loses money. Efficient and accurate patient information becomes paramount when, as DUCKETT (p. 44) states, "DRGs are probably the best measure of inpatient activity." The role of DRGs and some of the theoretical issues relating to their use in the context of the U.K. health service are examined by ROYCE. The steep learning curve required in using DRGs to contract services is identified as the key issue. The role of U.K. purchasers is much more complex than that of their counterparts in the U.S.A., and yet they have less sophisticated tools with which to carry it out. A pilot DRG project in Wales is described by ROYCE & SAIT. The approach is to emphasize the importance of the economic motivation while considering the contribution that DRGs may have to other areas such as medical audit.

In the U.K., the recent NHS reforms placed the responsibility for buying and providing health services on local health authorities and hospitals. The emphasis on accountability, medical audit and quality assurance, as well as effectiveness assessment of all healthcare, has meant an overall review of the structure, management, and standardization of medical records and all data collection. In 1986 the NHS Management Board's publication, *A National Strategic Framework for Information Management in the Hospital and Community Health Services* (GREAT BRITAIN. NATIONAL HEALTH SERVICE (NHS). MANAGEMENT BOARD) set out as one of its main requirements the need for agreed common standards. This initiative led to a comprehensive program of data modeling, beginning with data definition and moving on to the Common Basic Specification (CBS). CBS involved the development of a set of business, process, and data models to form the basis of future design and purchase specifications for information systems. This has important implications for Hospital Information Support Systems (HISS) as CBS will ensure the improved development and increased consistency in patient-generated data. Examples of more recent activity of the NHS Management Executive are described in the later section on information systems and strategies.

NEAME stresses the importance of including patient care systems based on medical records in hospital information systems. He argues that patient data are central to the effective administration, strategic planning, and proactive management of the health service. Failure to record crucial information on patients and their treatment, which can be computer coded and classified, means that there can be no coherent approach to effective HISS. The international concern with the "seriously deficient medical record systems" is discussed by WILSON (p. 53), who discusses the way forward in relation to the role of the Australian Council on Healthcare Standards (ACHS) and its hospital accreditation program. Despite the establishment of the accreditation program nearly 20 years ago along with many improvements in medical record keeping, the recent rapidly increasing sophistication of information systems and the complexity of hospital management and accountability have meant that the information in virtually all medical records is still inadequate for modern requirements. Some records that are parts of medical studies may be adequate for all uses.

CHANTLER describes many ways, however, in which new information systems for patient records should directly improve patient care.

The direct scheduling of outpatients by clinicians through computerized patient information systems means that all relevant information is available at the consultation, which reduces clerical time and generates standard discharge summaries and outpatient letters. Computer links to laboratories and wards and resource management data are easily added to such a system.

Advances in electronic data interchange technology have allowed the development of smart cards for the transfer of patient information among general practitioners (GPs), hospitals, and all other healthcare practitioners. However, as REGAN argues, there are serious confidentiality and cost problems involved, for GPs in particular, in implementing the new technology required. In contrast, KARA takes a more positive view in describing the benefits of smart cards in Australia: "They can effectively provide cheap, portable, secure computerised management of medical records at points where computer network connections are unavailable" (p. 30).

Management Information

This type of information is mainly internally generated throughput data, often numerical, plus some externally produced statistics (e.g., by governments). Examples include: (1) patient administration systems (PAS), which provide the vital records of hospital admissions and procedures; (2) contract and service specifications (information for managers to enable them to make informed decisions); (3) statistical information on service utilization and costs, waiting lists, bed-occupancy rates, operating-theater schedules, and so forth; (4) numbers, costs, and use of drugs; (5) financial and personnel information; (6) demographic and epidemiological reports; and (7) other survey data and reports produced by various organizations.

As FOSTER & MCBRIDE reported in 1992, more than half of British acute-care hospitals planned to have executive information systems (EISs) implemented within two years. These systems are designed to gather data from a number of internal and external sources and present them in an accessible and understandable format that is relevant to managers' needs. There are three categories of EIS: (1) front-end tools that enhance the presentation of output from existing systems; (2) internal consolidation tools that take data from internal sources, store them in a central database, and present them to users; and (3) front ends that integrate data from internal and external data. EISs facilitate access to all types of information, both textual and statistical/numerical, and enable users to communicate easily with each other. Foster and McBride explain how an EIS can meet managers' information requirements, and they detail the benefits to be gained from their use.

DUCKETT discusses the information needs of regional health authorities and explains the different needs of hospitals and regions. Although hospitals in Australia are normally centrally funded as in the U.K., there will always be differences in perspective and objectives among individual hospitals and between the regional health authority and hospitals.

NORDIN examines the growth of healthcare services sited outside hospitals, or "alternate site healthcare" (ASHC), and the implications for information systems. The increase in ASHCs is a result of the combination of rising costs and improved medical standards and technology, requiring a need for both traditional and new applications of IT. Examples of ASHC in the United States include home infusion therapy and physical therapy centers, ambulatory care centers, and patient home monitoring. NORDIN provides a business model of an ASHC information resources methodology overview. This is implemented with a "hybrid strategy of decentralized and centralized applications and hardware platforms" (p. 17). All locations are linked through wide-area networks (WANs) and supported by on-site operators, backed up by a corporate information resources group, including technical expertise.

Contracting for healthcare services has become an increasingly complex operation, requiring systems to manipulate financial and clinical information into a usable format. HARD (p. 50) describes advanced systems under development in the United States to track patient information from "physicians' offices across the continuum of care." These systems involve computer links between off-site physicians and hospitals, called physician–hospital venturing. A number of obstacles have to be overcome, in particular the problems of incompatible systems and the logistics of setting up the computer links. The importance of conducting a needs assessment is stressed before making any commitment to new systems.

In the U.K. the recent government reforms have emphasized the importance of "seamless" healthcare, and attention is focused on the computerization of GPs to enable them to link up with the other parts of the health service and to facilitate better management of their practices. A survey conducted in Wales by GOVES ET AL. revealed that computerization of GPs was steadily increasing and would reach 80% by 1992. The government's decision to partially refund the cost of GP computerization has been encouraging. Small practices, however, find the increased workload and costs to be major problems, and many have deferred computerization.

SILLINCE & FROST have done a major review of the effects of rapid expansion of information systems in U.K. primary healthcare. They describe how primary healthcare has always had to take a back seat to other sections of the health service even though it consumes about one-fourth of the NHS budget. This is partly due to the problems of management and communication within a system involving 90 Family Health Service Authorities (FHSAs), 192 District Health Authorities (DHAs) and 20,000 general practices. According to the NHS primary care reforms of 1991, GPs were to manage their own budgets and purchase services from hospitals; however, these reforms were implemented with no supporting information infrastructure. Sillince and Frost review the current information systems available for GPs and discuss the critical success factors for primary care systems. These factors include: (1) timeliness, such as rapid feedback from consultants; (2) security of patient information; (3) accessibility and availability; (4) flexibility; (5) accuracy and comprehensiveness; and (6) relevance. The NHS Information Management Group (GREAT BRITAIN. DEPARTMENT OF HEALTH, 1992) has recognized many of these needs and has outlined the basis of an IT infrastructure that requires, for example, that information systems be patient based and that common clinical codes be used to ensure compatibility; networks will be established to allow exchange of clinical data, make appointments, receive referral and dismissal summaries, and obtain information on waiting lists and service quality.

The Healthcare Management Information Consortium (HMIC) provides a forum in the U.K. for promoting the coordination and development of healthcare management library and information services. The consortium comprises a group of quasi-national library and information services that cooperates to ensure comprehensive coverage of nonclinical information, to make efficient use of resources, and to encourage the development of a national healthcare information strategy. Another important aim is coordinating the contribution of U.K. data to international databases and information networks.

Information for Patients, Caregivers, and the Public

Consumer health information (CHI) is the fastest growing area in healthcare information. It is a direct response to increasing public demand and pressure from governments for health organizations to be more open and accountable. The publication in the U.K. of *The Patient's Charter* (GREAT BRITAIN. DEPARTMENT OF HEALTH, 1991) was a recognition of this trend and set out the basic rights of healthcare consumers, including access to detailed information on health services. Patients and caregivers are demanding increasingly sophisticated information about the range of health services, illness, treatments, side effects, and self-help and support groups. In addition, the public wants information on how to improve and maintain health. There is also a growing awareness of the need for more information aimed at specific groups such as ethnic minorities, the disabled, and children. GANN provides a fascinating history of consumer health information, beginning with Hippocrates, continuing with the development of health information services in the United States, and chronicling the first consumer health information services in the U.K. in the 1970s. Gann illustrates the range and types of information services, from the sophisticated British Association of Cancer United Patients, which is run by a voluntary agency with an extensive database of information, to patient information resource centers in hospital wards.

The role of libraries in the provision of CHI in the United States is described by DAHLEN. The problems relating to the dissemination of health information within the current complex environment of social issues, structured pricing and IT are discussed. The author stresses the need for libraries to foster and maintain links with community and state organizations which produce and distribute information resources. It is important that libraries take a proactive approach to collecting and disseminating information. The lack of a centralized system to coordinate a national CHI program is the reason for underutilization of existing resources and is affecting patients' choice through limited access to information.

The increasing influence of healthcare consumers in the United States is emphasized by RUFFIN in a paper describing the customer goals of a leading regional healthcare system. The "vision" of a fully integrated computer-based patient record system, with patients' clinical and demographic information available online from all healthcare service points, is described. This is the vision defined by representatives of the customers—patients, relatives, and caregivers, as well as employers and government contributors—under Presbyterian Healthcare Services; it manifests the demands of consumers to contribute to the organization and financing of healthcare. This theme is continued in a symposium collection edited by HAFNER, which includes four papers on medical libraries and patient information services. Hafner stresses the role of the individual in assuming greater responsibility for maintaining health and preventing disease. He argues that the more well-informed consumers are, the better their decision making will be and that increased access to medical information benefits both consumers and practitioners.

One of the issues most prominent in recent publications is the confidentiality of personal health information. As SOUTHGATE observes, consumers want access to their medical records for various reasons—e.g., to check for errors, to be aware of what is in the record, and as a mechanism for holding healthcare professionals accountable. In a paper presented at a conference of the Medical Record Association in Australia, DRAPER discusses the interests of health consumers in aggregated health information. She asserts that consumers have an important role in ensuring the accuracy of basic information in medical records used for DRGs, monitoring procedures and outcomes, and in quality assurance programs. It is vital that consumers of healthcare have full access to information on their health records to enable them to make the right decisions. In the past, healthcare practitioners have not been keen to reveal this information because of fears that patients would not understand the medical terminology and it could be harmful to them.

An important issue related to access to health records is privacy. Personal information is demanded by a range of organizations and individuals, including healthcare workers, insurance companies, and government departments such as social services. The patient or consumer cannot give informed permission unless he or she is fully aware of the information concerned. The Australian advisory body, the Health Services Review Council, takes the view that while information in health records is not the consumer's personal property, access should be allowed on the basis that it is the consumer's right to protect his or her own interests (SOUTHGATE, p. 24).

The coordination of consumer health information services is a vital factor in developing standards and providing unified support for the Consumer's right to information. In the U.K. this role is undertaken by the Consumer Health Information Consortium (CHIC) as described by GANN & NEEDHAM. One of the consortium's main aims is to develop a consistent approach in the quality and standard of information provision to healthcare consumers.

INFORMATION SYSTEMS AND STRATEGIES

This section discusses some of the issues involved in the development and implementation of information systems and strategies, including national strategies in the U.K., competition and the changing environment, developmental difficulties, integration and communication, and the role of the World Health Organization (WHO).

Information Strategies in the U.K.

The Information Management Group of the NHS Management Executive (previously the Management Board) set the scene for the total review of information management strategy for healthcare in the U.K. Following the previously cited publication, *A National Strategic Framework for Information Management in the Hospital and Community Health Services* (GREAT BRITAIN. NATIONAL HEALTH SERVICE. MANAGEMENT BOARD), other publications were issued to implement the government reform program in information terms. *A Framework for Information Systems* (GREAT BRITAIN. DEPARTMENT OF HEALTH, 1990) was produced as a working paper following the government's major reform legislation, *Working for Patients* (GREAT BRITAIN. DEPARTMENT OF HEALTH, 1989). The *Framework* set out to provide an overall view of how the new requirements for information systems could be developed. Short-term goals for all purchasers and providers of healthcare were specified, including the categories of data that had to be improved. Long-term aims included the need to concentrate on resource management and full medical audit, with integrated HISS to facilitate these requirements. This was followed by *A Framework for Information Systems: Next Steps* (GREAT BRITAIN. DEPARTMENT OF HEALTH. NATIONAL HEALTH SERVICE, 1990), which describes the main aims of the District Information Support Systems (DISS); these involve each health authority's having its own integrated set of operational and management systems, with links to systems in other NHS organizations. A series of publications was issued to help District Health Authorities prepare for their new role as set out in the government review of the health service, *Working for Patients*. The emphasis of *Purchasing Intelligence* (GREAT BRITAIN. NATIONAL HEALTH SERVICE. MANAGEMENT EXECUTIVE, 1991) was on the integration of all types of information (or "intelligence"), including routine, ad hoc, local and national, textual and numerical, which would be needed to support needs assessment, service evaluation and monitoring, and contracting and management procedures. A report on the project called Developing Information Systems for Purchasers was published by the NHS Information Management Group in 1992 (GREAT BRITAIN. NATIONAL HEALTH SERVICE. MANAGEMENT EXECUTIVE. INFORMATION MANAGEMENT GROUP, 1992a). The project aimed to develop functional and technical specifications for integrated operational systems in collaboration with different commercial suppliers in order to benefit other purchasers in the development of their own systems.

One of the main initiatives arising from the *National Strategic Framework for Information Management* was the move toward a Common Basic Specification (CBS), as mentioned earlier. A major part of the CBS program, as reported by JONES, was the Public Health Information Specification (PHIS) Project, completed in July 1992. Its main objective was to produce a model of the activities and information processes of public health medicine. Jones states that the PHIS model has been used in several different contexts, including strategy development, the purchasing of healthcare, the producing of reports, teaching, as a standard for auditing the performance of health needs assessment, for intervention planning and outcome monitoring, and as a basis for specifying requirements for the locally controlled development of healthcare (JONES, p. 17).

In 1992 the NHS Information Management Group launched its new information management and technology (IM&T) strategy, *Getting Better with Information* (GREAT BRITAIN. NATIONAL HEALTH SERVICE. MANAGEMENT EXECUTIVE. INFORMATION MANAGEMENT GROUP, 1992b). Its main aim is to improve the nation's health by supporting care and communication through IM&T. As LEANING remarks, the strategy was welcomed because it set clinical objectives for information technology in NHS. The strategy is based on five basic principles: (1) information should be person based; (2) systems should be integrated; (3) management information should be derived from operational clinical systems; (4) data should be secure and confidential; and (5) data should be shared across NHS. The success of the strategy will depend on how useful healthcare practitioners find the new systems. It is essential, therefore, that clinical staff be involved in the design and evaluation of information systems.

Competition and the Turbulent Environment

As already noted, the situation in the United States is completely different from that in the U.K. for various historical, economic, and geographic reasons. The use of information systems in healthcare has been dictated mainly by individual large hospitals that need to capture accurately all healthcare episodes and charge for them. KETTELHUT describes how this competitive environment has changed dramatically over the past ten years, and he identifies other effective uses of information systems. The changing competitive factors in healthcare involve changes in customer requirements, technology, competitors, economic structure, and legislation. All these changes add up to the "turbulent healthcare environment" in which information systems must operate. The three main requirements for hospital systems are: (1) they must continue to support traditional tasks (e.g., tracking patients, charging, and paying staff); (2) they must increase hospital marketing effectiveness; and (3) they must measure and improve hospital efficiency. However, MORIARTY notes that the healthcare service has lagged behind industry and business in the strategic application of information systems. He argues that healthcare managers need to think of information systems as tools for implementing and modifying corporate strategy, not simply as systems to support operational functions. When considering strategic information systems, it is vital to distinguish between their ability to change how healthcare services are provided and how they simply support operations. The importance of competitive advantage as a benefit of strategic information systems is emphasized. Moriarty stresses that many healthcare organizations are losing important opportunities due to a lack of strategic planning for information systems.

These issues are also raised by ALLEN & CARMICHAEL, who discuss the contribution of management consultants to the development of corporate information strategies within U.K. hospitals in the new NHS.

A clinician's view of developing a hospital information strategy is given by BUNCH, who describes the importance of clinical staff in this process. The increasing involvement of clinicians in the new management structures of NHS is also discussed by SILLINCE & FROST, who ask what the priorities should be for primary health care. U.K. government strategies have concentrated on prioritizing particular diseases, with the result that issues such as low income, education, and unemployment have been neglected. The importance of involving clinicians in the development of hospital information systems (HISs) as a "competitive weapon" is also stressed by KIM & MICHELMAN, who also give a short review of the literature on this aspect of information systems technology. They contend that the new economic environment has caused changes in clinicians' behavior and that this is a barrier to the integration of HISs. For many clinicians information systems are only a way to monitor and report on their activities. Thus, a dialog must be established between clinicians and managers to overcome these barriers.

Developmental Difficulties

The development of healthcare information systems has not been without its problems. As already discussed, political resistance to the introduction and integration of HISs, such as organizational restructuring, changes in work flow, communications, and reporting relationships, are a real threat to their successful implementation. Moreover, other major failures have led to vast economic losses; in a number of cases in the U.K. money has been wasted on HIS investments. CROSS reports that a consortium of three health authorities in the West Midlands spent £21 million on a Hospital Information Support System (HISS) that now has only a few minor elements operating. The reasons for the failure were partly technical but were mainly the result of poor timing and politics. An even larger "scandal" occurred in the Wessex Regional Health Authority, where a £50 million investment was lost when the integrated computerization project failed. One of the earliest NHS projects, it was abandoned in 1990 after six years work, a victim of "the twin enthusiasms for devolved management and information technology" (WARDEN, 1993b, p. 1292). This fiasco involved a lack of control by the health authority, which allowed suppliers and consultants to dictate the services they provided and resulted in insider dealing, huge payoffs, charges of fraud, and a multimillion pound civil court action.

These early pilot projects suffered from a lack of control that encouraged an open-checkbook approach. The projects were more complicated and much more expensive than anticipated—i.e., suppliers were faced with demanding specifications and little experience of British hospital systems. The only positive result is that lessons have been learned and future HIS investments will be more thoroughly scrutinized.

One direct result of the early difficulties encountered in the development of integrated HISs was the concern to improve collaboration between suppliers and healthcare units on procurement. According to SCOTT, total integration requires close cooperation on the information systems strategy, procurement, and implementation stages. He argues that "the role of modern systems as a critical part of healthcare should be part of the national strategy of healthcare" (p. 29). He describes a U.K. study jointly funded by NHS and suppliers of computer systems to develop a model of the procurement process, using value-process modeling. By working together, much progress has been made toward a totally integrated healthcare system.

Systems procurement in the United States has developed in response to market demands and has evolved through several generations of information systems, resulting in a process that is relatively sophisticated. MELLING explains that the American procurement process is similar to the one developed in the U.K. but varies among the different types of hospitals (e.g., private, community, city, state) and their size and complexity. Standard checklists and requests for proposals (RFPs) from vendors provide hospital-tailored specifications so that suppliers that cannot meet requirements can quickly be eliminated. This saves time, effort, and costs. The U.S. system allows for more flexibility and relies on a pragmatic common approach and the sharing of information.

Hospitals in the United States recognize that there are many points of similarity among them and therefore systems have a common core. At the same time, suppliers can ensure that system performance fits the individual hospital's requirements. Managers realize that lower prices are not always the most cost-effective or beneficial in the long term. Hospitals generally purchase so-called "turnkey systems" where staff simply turn the key and begin using the equipment, theoretically. This solution is regarded as low risk at reasonable cost.

Integration and Communication

The present decade is one of assessment and accountability for all healthcare services (CUDDEBACK). The concentration on costs of services is being replaced with an equally strong emphasis on quality of outcome at the lowest cost. The old management methods cannot meet these new demands; new standards of quality in data and healthcare information are required for total quality management, also known as continuous quality improvement. The new healthcare management methods rely on a teamwork approach and the total care process, with the emphasis on data-driven decision making. There are far-reaching implications for integration of information systems. Although many systems have been running efficiently in support of individual departmental processes, they were not designed to run as part of larger integrated systems. Central systems tend to be restricted to charging functions rather than coordinating and uniting the departmental systems. Cuddeback provides a lucid description of the changes in management attitudes and system design needed to achieve the continuous quality improvement model.

The problems encountered in clinical computing and specifically the implementation of Integrated Clinical Workstations (ICWS) in the U.K. are addressed by ORR. He argues that a solid basis of clinical computing, using the new thesaurus of clinical terms being developed by the NHS Centre for Coding and Classification, is an essential prerequisite for the implementation of the national information management strategy. The ICWS project aims initially to help local initiatives to solve local problems through the involvement of clinicians in a drive to achieve seamless healthcare.

KIM & MICHELMAN also describe the frustration felt by many healthcare managers at the proliferation of independent information systems within their organizations, resulting in data from different systems that are incompatible and cannot be linked to other facilities. This situation is largely a result of the historical evolution of information systems management and technology in healthcare services. These authors examine successful applications and use case studies to illustrate important factors that managers must consider when developing competitive integrated systems—e.g., overcoming political barriers to integration, integrating independent transaction-processing systems and information-reporting systems, and the importance of strategic planning.

A major initiative in the integration of healthcare information systems is the Integrated Academic Information Management Systems (IAIMS) developed in the United States by the National Library of Medicine (NLM). The program is designed to encourage academic medical centers to plan and implement an integrated organizational approach to information management for clinical practice, medical education, and biomedical research. A second related initiative, also developed by NLM, is the Unified Medical Language System (UMLS), a collaborative project to assist integration of online information resources, with emphasis on the lexical terminology used by different systems to describe medical concepts. MILLER ET AL. report on a prototype information environment to link networked information resources in an integrated way. They describe how the prototype demonstrates the relationship between the IAIMS and UMLS projects and how they can be combined to improve access to many different information sources.

In the European Union (EU) the emphasis has been on: (1) improving the overall standards of healthcare; (2) widening access to and knowledge of services; (3) establishing standards in hardware, software, and terminology; and (4) efficient communication of medical records and information through integrated health systems. In a useful paper on the European situation, MANTAS provides an overview of EU's Advanced Informatics in Medicine (AIM) program, which ran from 1989 until 1994. One of AIM's main tasks was the integration of decision-support systems with HIS, the integration of medical informatics generally with communication concepts and systems, and the development of the telemedicine concept. The enormous range of services now available from healthcare units demands more sophisticated communications networks, while increasing the levels of data exchange and integration are essential. The integrated broadband communication (IBC) service will be introduced in 1996. IBC is a new multimedia communications network to facilitate improved integration of European healthcare services and increased exchange of healthcare data. IBC will be integrated with HIS to facilitate these new developments in Europe. The development of the telematics technology reflects the increasing trend toward alternate-site healthcare, as discussed earlier. The shift to primary and home care increases the role of effective communication among patients, medical practitioners, and healthcare units. Telecommunications also has a major role in the continuing education and updating of information for healthcare professionals through such means as distance learning and remote consultation and conferencing as well as in supporting collaborative treatment programs. Through telemedicine it is hoped that multimedia information for patients and the public on health promotion and the latest advances in the diagnosis and treatment of such diseases as AIDS may be transmitted easily and effectively to a wide and disparate population.

The importance of standardization as an integral part of telematics development is stressed by DE MOOR, who describes the user requirements of healthcare services and provides an overview of the EU situation. He describes the progress made by the European Standardization Committee, Technical Committee on Healthcare Informatics, and its relation to the AIM European Research Programme. A useful appendix lists the current projects in these two programs.

An Australian perspective is supplied by MORE & MORE in a paper on the challenges in health communication and information raised by technological change. These authors consider the vast range of new tools available to healthcare professionals and review the key factors affecting the implementation of effective health communication systems. They also include a useful review of the recent literature on the subject, as does MASSO in a discussion on quality assurance. Masso concentrates on the nursing profession but provides a wide-ranging overview of the literature on assessing healthcare quality generally. The importance of integrating quality assurance programs with management information systems is a major concern.

Integration of healthcare data from a variety of sources also has important implications for employers. CAUDRON reports that a number of large self-insured companies in the United States are in the forefront of developments in integrated health data management systems (IHDMS). These systems comprise a series of health-related databases linked by software that can retrieve information and identify relationships and correlations. This facility allows companies to develop a strategic approach to the management of health benefits rather than the ad hoc methods used previously. IHDMS will provide the way to measure the effectiveness of certain healthcare processes according to treatment outcomes. Thus, the least successful and more expensive treatments can be withdrawn from healthcare plans in favor of the cost-effective ones. Databases, both internal and external, will be integrated and accessed to supply the information required. In this way, companies expect to cut costs and improve healthcare quality. The complex issues of development and implementation are also discussed.

Recent developments in the application of IT to all aspects of healthcare were described at the triennial conference of the International Medical Informatics Association in 1992 (LUN ET AL.). International communication networks were discussed, with reference to the important developments for medical and scientific research in the Internet and JANET computer network systems. An account was given of satellite technology in the form of HEALTHNET, which allows doctors and researchers in remote areas to access international communication networks from a personal computer and receiver.

The practicality of integrating healthcare systems is discussed in a short paper by PALMER ET AL., who relate the manager's difficulties in implementing an integrated system. Although integration can be beneficial, it is costly to achieve and can limit choice and flexibility. The authors argue that integration should be attempted only when it is of obvious benefit and when the issues are completely understood.

Role of the World Health Organization

The role of the World Health Organization (WHO) and the impact of informatics on healthcare in third world countries is discussed in a paper by MANDIL. He reports that many of these countries are developing health informatics programs but that most of them began doing this in the absence of a national health informatics policy or strategy. Mandil gives examples of healthcare informatics in several countries—e.g., videotext applications in Brazil. Some developing countries (Egypt, India, Mexico, and the Philippines) have many informatics professionals who undertake large software development contracts from western countries. It is vital that these countries recognize the need for health applications and that their professionals be recruited to improve local healthcare services. ELMANDJRA asserts that poor countries must adopt the most advanced informatics and telematics technologies in order to advance; progress will be impossible with "adapted" technologies. Models should be developed according to the local political, social, and cultural environment rather than as imitations of programs in developed countries.

MANDIL states that WHO is supporting and promoting informatics in healthcare and is engaged in several collaborative projects with member countries. The WHO secretariat itself is a heavy user of informatics, but many difficulties must still be overcome in relation to developing countries. Apart from the usual problems faced in developing integrated systems, some obstacles are: making IT support available in local languages, providing telelinks to remote areas, and drawing up appropriate legislation for accessing and using medical data.

In a more recent account, MAURICE reports on a U.N. initiative, in collaboration with Swedish and Canadian R&D agencies, to promote research on healthcare in third world countries. The Council on Health Research for Development (COHRED) was established in 1993 to encourage governments to make local research a high priority in terms of healthcare policy. Local working parties will be set up, including all those involved in planning healthcare, to decide on research priorities. The council will also act as a broker to channel funds from western donor countries for research in developing countries. WHO is criticized for not doing enough to help governments build up the necessary expertise in healthcare management and informatics.

As part of its commitment to the holistic view of health, WHO launched a major campaign in 1978 aimed at "Health for All by the Year 2000," with targets designed to improve the factors that affect public health. The Healthy Cities Project was set up as the vehicle to promote these targets and test their application locally. Hundreds of cities worldwide (650 in Europe) are now involved, with national and regional networks working toward five key goals: (1) building healthy public policy; (2) creating supportive environments; (3) strengthening community action; (4) developing personal skills; and (5) reorienting urban health services. For example, in the Republic of Ireland the Dublin

Healthy Cities Project is actively involved in various campaigns, such as reducing smoking in the workplace and controlling the amount of refuse and noise on beaches; community-based projects include encouraging participation in health awareness and a more active lifestyle through activities like those recommended in the Health, Environment, Lifestyles Projects (HELP). These and other projects are described in publications issued by the Dublin Healthy Cities Project; for example, HAYES ET AL., in a position statement, describe the current state of health in Dublin and how it is affected by mortality, morbidity, lifestyles, health promotion, and the social and the physical environment.

The implications of WHO's Healthy Cities Project for healthcare information networks and telecommunications are immense. GOUMANS has studied the structure and organization of national Healthy Cities networks in Europe. In Latin America, a research program begun in 1992 is investigating information and communication technologies (ICT) in public and private health services management. The aims of the research, as described by FINQUELIEVICH, include: (1) identification of current practice in the use of ICT; (2) evaluation of the impact of ICT in terms of benefits for users, quality of life, efficiency of use, cooperation with other organizations, staff training, and so forth; and (3) proposing of policies for ICT application for healthier cities. This work exemplifies the impact and importance of the correct and efficient use of healthcare information technology and communications in such a wide-ranging and diverse project.

TRAINING AND EDUCATION

The management of healthcare is likely to remain information intensive, and because an increasing proportion of the health service workforce is already involved with information systems, education and training assume added importance. At present there is, and will remain for at least a decade in most countries, a lot of catching up to do in terms of training and education in information work and health informatics. However, health authorities are beginning to take seriously the need to invest in the education and training of their staff.

The U.K.'s NHS has suffered from a general lack of staff training and education in IM&T. As shown by BRITTAIN (1991) this has led to a serious underexploitation of the new technology as well as inappropriate or misapplied investment in IT. The equal lack of awareness and training among healthcare managers is highlighted by BROWN & WARREN, who outline the concerns of the NHS Training Directorate and other NHS officials. To improve the situation, an *IMT Strategy for Training and Staff Development* was drawn up by the Training Directorate (then known as the Training Authority) in conjunction with the NHS

Information Management Group (GREAT BRITAIN. NATIONAL HEALTH SERVICE. TRAINING AUTHORITY & INFORMATION MANAGEMENT GROUP). This was followed by a series of guidelines, infrastructure support measures, training products, and publications on training in many areas of NHS, including IMT organization and training issues (GREAT BRITAIN. NATIONAL HEALTH SERVICE. TRAINING DIRECTORATE). The IM&T Training Programme, financed since 1989, currently runs over 30 individual projects with an annual budget of around £4 million, and is probably the most comprehensive and substantial program of its kind in Europe. A major new area of work, described by Adams,[1] involves training and education in IM&T specifically for doctors, nurses, and allied professions at pre- and post-qualification levels. TOWNSEND & ADAMS provide an earlier review of the work of the IM&T Training Programme.

BRITTAIN & ABBOTT have edited a comprehensive guide to education and training for IM&T in healthcare, which sets out the scope and range of IM&T training in the U.K. and elsewhere. Contributions include papers from the United States, Australia, and New Zealand and represent the knowledge and experience of professionals from the spectrum of healthcare IM&T training in the U.K. EU's AIM program has set up a concerned action group, with representatives from each member state, to address the specific education and training issues associated with health informatics. A comprehensive survey of the state of the art in healthcare informatics education and training throughout Europe has been conducted, and a core curriculum has been developed for use in Europe.[2]

A number of writers have argued for a new kind of information professional to assemble, analyze, manage, and present the expanding range and diversity of information required to run an efficient health service. HEPWORTH lists the skills and knowledge needed by a "well rounded professional," including techniques for identification of information needs, organization of text and numeric data, development of an information system, ability to search databases, proactive information dissemination, and liaison with IT personnel. One of the major obstacles in the U.K. is the need to persuade senior managers of the need to commit resources to the training and education of information staff in healthcare organizations, even though the IM&T Training Programme, financed centrally by the NHS Management Executive, is

[1]Personal communication from Paul Adams, Director, IM&T Training Programme, NHS Training Directorate, St. Bartholomew's Court, 18 Christmas St., Bristol BS1 5BT, England.

[2]Personal communication from Paul Adams, Director, IM&T Training Programme, NHS Training Directorate, St. Bartholomew's Court, 18 Christmas St., Bristol BS1 5BT, England.

probably one of the largest in the world. The program is encouraging NHS staff to move into information work by facilitating the development of local IM&T programs. In addition, postgraduate diplomas and master's degrees in healthcare information management and informatics are offered at universities in the U.K. One such new program at the University of Manchester Health Services Management Unit is described by ATKINSON & PEEL.

In the United States, as documented by BALL & DOUGLAS, the concern has been to train physicians, dentists, and pharmacists in information-handling techniques. The authors review the slowly changing attitudes of healthcare practitioners toward the role of informatics, but they assert that more education is needed to make them more effective practitioners. The challenges include the need to build on the basic skills of professionals, training them to use the computer as a tool in decision making and problem solving. Further, it is necessary to reach beyond the traditional classroom and convince those practicing in the community of the benefits of informatics.

WOODS & COGGAN describe a medical informatics education program to support the Florida Health Information Network. Training has targeted both library staff and users of the Florida Health Science Center. The paper explains how the program has developed, including a service to remote users. CARTER outlines a curriculum in medical information science suitable for an internal medical residency program. He considers a number of issues, including the relevance of medical informatics to primary care practice, how graduate medical education should be changed to accommodate training in medical informatics, and the development and support of information systems for office-based practitioners.

A review of the literature on the training of nurses in informatics reveals a large body of work. One study on nurses' knowledge of computers was conducted as long ago as 1982 by HARDIN & SKIBA. The difficulties encountered by American nurse educators in relating computer studies to specific clinical applications are described by SINCLAIR, who discusses the experience gained in teaching nursing informatics. A summer institute on informatics applications for nurse managers, held in the Netherlands in 1988, 1989, and 1990, is described by ABRAHAM ET AL. Participants were able to learn theoretically and practically about computer systems that support the organization and delivery of nursing services. It is suggested by ABRAHAM ET AL. that the institute represents a model of continuing education for nursing management in western Europe and North America.

New career opportunities in healthcare informatics comprise the focus of papers by SIMPSON (1992b) and BRITTAIN (1992). Simpson reports on typical job descriptions for careers in nursing informatics and discusses the kind of person most suitable for these positions. Brittain reviews the current shortage of persons with information-handling skills in the U.K.'s NHS. He estimates almost 6,000 available jobs in information work in England and Wales; this figure does not include the increasing number of openings in health promotion and consumer health information services.

THE FUTURE

The future for health informatics encompasses a wide range of exciting challenges in terms of the enormous technical advances and information management expertise that are required to facilitate the new initiatives being developed worldwide. With the development of appropriate continuing education and training courses for staff, health informatics is developing a clearer identity and brighter prospects.

BONINE describes the role of new technology in future healthcare—e.g., improvements in biotechnology and electrotechnologies, in-home "test and treatment kits," and home-based computers that are linked to local area medical networks. Many hospitals will close, but those that remain open will become regional centers of excellence for high-tech care of complex conditions and diseases. General healthcare will rely primarily on integrated computer systems that link widely spaced care networks, which will generate enormous scope for even greater healthcare IT developments, particularly with the growth in artificial intelligence (AI) systems. Bonine predicts that cost will continue to be a major concern but that those who seek to restrain new technology are merely postponing the advent of cheaper, more user-friendly technologies. He suggests that while nurses will continue to be the primary caregivers, they will be backed up by voice-activated AI computing systems that will act as "expert" information resources.

New information systems designed to slow the escalating costs of healthcare constitute one of the greatest concerns of healthcare providers in the United States. American businesses, which provide employee healthcare, are adopting new measures to contain rising costs, as noted earlier. CHRISTINE reports on the development of health-oriented telecommunication (HOT) systems, which would reduce costs through enhanced information processing, such as, for example, automatic claims processing and record-keeping software, and improvements in healthcare strategies. It is also claimed that consumers would have more power over their own care. A HOT system would comprise a national intelligent information system linking patients, healthcare practitioners, companies, and insurers in a single network. The main obstacle to implementation is the lack of a national infrastructure to accommodate the system. This is currently the subject of several pieces of legislation and national networking projects. In the meantime, a number of HOT applications are being used by American companies, such as health risk assessment (HRA) and the health listing and systems review (HH).

In the U.K. much progress has been made in the design and implementation of a national IT infrastructure, although a lot remains to be done. The Department of Health, working with NHS, has recognized the need for a flexible approach, as stated by the Junior Health Minister, ROGER FREEMAN. The difficulties of coordination and cooperation are proving hard to overcome, but IT and information systems are key to the transformation of healthcare delivery.

Fundamental reform of healthcare services is becoming a global phenomenon, as this chapter has illustrated. The vision of an internationally integrated healthcare system is discussed by KLEIN, who reviews a model of healthcare financing and organization advanced by the National Economic Research Associates (NERA). The model is claimed to have universal applicability while also accommodating particular situations in individual countries. It is based on market competition and universal comprehensive coverage provided by competing private insurance schemes. Unfortunately, however, as Klein argues, the model is too good to be true. When it is applied to the U.K.'s NHS, a number of flaws are revealed. Depending, as it does, on the assumption that all healthcare will be funded by the insurance companies, the model ignores the fact that all governments must control, to some extent at least, the cost of healthcare, regardless of who funds it. One of the main incentives of the health reforms of President Clinton is the rising cost of health insurance premiums and incomplete coverage. NERA's model would be unlikely to work in either the United States or the U.K. in the present economic and political climate.

Over the next few years several countries will be implementing new healthcare informatics models applicable to their own health systems, whether financed through insurance schemes or taxation. Much will be learned about the effects of implementation and integration of healthcare information systems regionally, nationally, and internationally. It is hoped that the opportunity for cooperative evaluation and sharing of experience will be used to benefit the countries concerned and those still struggling to adapt to the new age of healthcare informatics.

CONCLUSION

The full impact of healthcare informatics is just beginning to be realized worldwide. The fact that so many activities in medicine and healthcare are information intensive makes the implementation of IT and communication essential. A new generation of information systems specifically designed for healthcare will be implemented during the next few years, facilitating efficiency and reducing costs of healthcare generally. The development and implementation of international standards for data exchange and definition, coding of medical terminology, and effective electronic networking will enhance global cooperation and sharing of expertise. Equally, the application of performance indicators for healthcare services will ensure the cost-effectiveness and consumer satisfaction now demanded by healthcare users and providers. These factors, together with new university courses in healthcare informatics, will guarantee the emergence of well-educated and experienced health informatics personnel over the next decade. While many issues remain to be resolved, the developments described here will transform the delivery of healthcare at all levels, benefiting health consumers and leading to improved health for all.

BIBLIOGRAPHY

ABRAHAM, IVO; EVERS, GEORGES; HASMAN, ARIE; TANGHE, HUIBERT; SILKENS, REINHILDE; HEIN, FRANSJE. 1991. A Summer Institute on Computer Applications for Nursing Management: Background, Curriculum, and Evaluation. The Journal of Continuing Education in Nursing. 1991; 22(4): 136-142. ISSN: 0022-0124.

ALLEN, RICHARD; CARMICHAEL, IAN. 1992. Strategic Weapons. British Journal of Healthcare Computing. 1992; 9(3): 25-28. ISSN: 0265-5217.

ALTER, JOANNE; HOLZMAN, DAVID. 1992. Putting Outcomes Research to Work: Special Report on Business and Health. Kenilworth, NJ: Schering Laboratories; 1992.

ATKINSON, C.; PEEL, VICTOR. 1992. New Breed. British Journal of Healthcare Computing 1992; 9(1): 17-28. ISSN: 0265-5217.

AXFORD, RITA; MCGUINESS, BILL. 1992. Australian Journal of Advanced Nursing. 1992; 9(2): 34-39. ISSN: 0813-0531.

BALL, MARION J.; DOUGLAS, JUDITH V. 1992. Preparing Medical Informaticians: A Cross-Disciplinary Approach. Computers in Healthcare. 1992 July; 13(7): 38-41. ISSN: 0745-1075.

BALL, MARION J.; DOUGLAS, JUDITH V.; LUNIN, LOIS F. 1988. Informatics and Education in the Health Professions. Journal of the American Society for Information Science. 1988; 39(5): 344-347. ISSN: 0002-8231.

BENSON, TIM. 1993. The Rise of Clinical Computing. British Journal of Healthcare Computing. 1993; 10(2): 35-39. ISSN: 0265-5217.

BLOOMFIELD, BRIAN P.; COOMBS, ROD. 1992. Information Technology, Control and Power: The Centralisation and Decentralisation Debate Revisited. Journal of Management Studies. 1992 July 4; 29: 459-484. ISSN: 0022-2380.

BONINE, BRUCE R. 1990. Alternative Futures in Health Care. Health Care Strategic Management. 1990 January; 8(1): 12-15. ISSN: 0742-1478.

BRITISH JOURNAL OF HEALTHCARE COMPUTING. 1984-. Brown, Peter, ed. Weybridge, Surrey England: B.J.H.C. Ltd. ISSN: 0265-5217.

BRITTAIN, J. MICHAEL. 1991. Distributed Training. British Journal of Healthcare Computing. 1991; 8(2): 26-30. ISSN: 0265-5217.

BRITTAIN, J. MICHAEL. 1992. The Emerging Market for Information Professionals in the U.K. National Health Service. International Journal of Information Management. 1992; 12(4): 261-271. ISSN: 0268-4012.

BRITTAIN, J. MICHAEL; ABBOTT, WILLIAM, eds. 1993. Information Management and Technology in Healthcare: A Guide to Education and Training. London, England: Taylor Graham; 1993. 388p. ISBN: 0-947568-59-X.

BROWN, PETER; WARREN, LIZ. 1992. Age of Enlightenment. British Journal of Healthcare Computing. 1992 February; 9(1): 14-15. ISSN: 0265-5217.

BUCHAN, HEATHER. 1993. New Zealand's Health Care Reforms. British Medical Journal. 1993; 307: 635-636. ISSN: 0959-8146.

BUNCH, CHRISTOPHER. 1992. Developing a Hospital Information Strategy: A Clinician's View. British Medical Journal. 1992; 304: 1033-1036. ISSN: 0959-8146.

CALVANO, MARGARET. 1991. Consumer Health Information and the Not-for-Profit Health Agency. Bulletin of the Medical Library Association. 1991; 79(2): 189-194. ISSN: 0025-7338.

CARTER, JEROME H. 1991. Medical Informatics in Postgraduate Training. Journal of General Internal Medicine. 1991 July/August; 6: 349-354. ISSN: 0884-8734.

CAUDRON, SHARI. 1993. Use Facts, Not Probability, to Design Benefits. Personnel Journal. 1993 April; 72: 136-149. ISSN: 0031-5745.

CHANTLER, CYRIL. 1992. Management and Information. British Medical Journal. 1992; 304: 632-635. ISSN: 0959-8146.

CHRISTINE, BRIAN. 1992. The Future of Health Care Technologies. Risk Management. 1992; 39(11): 14-16. ISSN: 0035-5593.

COLAIANNI, LOIS ANN. 1992. That Vision Thing. Bulletin of the Medical Library Association. 1992; 80(1): 1-8. ISSN: 0025-7338.

COLLEN, MORRIS F. 1986. Origins of Medical Informatics. The Western Journal of Medicine. 1986; 145(6): 778-785. ISSN: 0093-0415.

CROSS, MICHAEL. 1992. Boo HISS. Health Service Journal. 1992; 102(5302): 13. ISSN: 0952-2271.

CUDDEBACK, JOHN K. 1993. Integration of Health Care Information Systems. RadioGraphics. 1993; 13(2): 445-456. ISSN: 0271-5333.

DAHLEN, KAREN HACKLEMAN. 1993. The Status of Health Information Delivery in the United States: The Role of Libraries in the Complex Health Care Environment. Library Trends. 1993; 42(1): 152-179. ISSN: 0024-2594.

DE MOOR, G.J.E. 1992. Telestroika in Healthcare Informatics: A Challenge for Standardisation in Europe. Medical Informatics. 1992; 17(2): 133-140. ISSN: 0307-7640.

DEAN, ROBERT L.; JOHNSON, DALE. 1991. Designing an Information System for a Health Care Organization. Journal of Systems Management. 1991 January; 23-31. ISSN: 0022-4839.

DICK, RICHARD S.; STEEN, ELAINE B., eds. 1991. The Computer-Based Patient Record: An Essential Technology for Health Care. Washington, DC: National Academy Press; 1991. 190p. (IOM Study Report). LC: 91-023584.

DRAPER, MARY C. 1992. For Whose Eyes Only? Health Records, Access and Privacy. Paper Presented at the 14th Conference for the Medical Record Association of Australia; 1991 October 29-November 1; Brisbane, Australia. Australian Medical Record Journal. 1992; 22(1): 7-9. ISSN: 0817-3907.

DUCKETT, STEPHEN. 1991. Clinical Resource Management: The Information Needs of Regional Health Authorities. Australian Health Review. 1991; 14(1): 43-45. ISSN: 0156-5788.

DUCKETT, STEPHEN; BARRETT, TERRY; SAYERS, RAY; WHITE, JAN. 1988. DRGs: How Far Have We Come? Hospital and Healthcare Australia. 1988; 19(5): 19-22.

ELMANDJRA, MAHDI. 1989. Informatics and Telematics: The Future. World Health. 1989 August/September; 28-29. ISSN: 0043-8502.

FINQUELIEVICH, SUSANA. 1993. Information Technologies as Tools for Healthier Cities: Policies for the 1990s in Latin America. Research for Healthy Cities. 1993 April; 4: 5. Available from: WHO/EURO Healthy Cities Project, 8 Scherfigsvej, 2100 Copenhagen, Denmark.

FOSTER, KEITH; MCBRIDE, N. 1992. Management Information Systems—Green Light for Better Info. Health Service Journal. 1992 February 27; 102 (5291): 27-30. ISSN: 0952-2271.

FREEMAN, ROGER. 1990. Information—Lifeblood of the NHS. Health Service Journal. 1990 March 1; 100(5190): 332-333. ISSN: 0952-2271.

GANN, ROBERT. 1991. Consumer Health Information: The Growth of an Information Specialism. Journal of Documentation. 1991; 47(3): 284-308. ISSN: 0022-0418.

GANN, ROBERT; NEEDHAM, GILLIAN, eds. 1992. Promoting Choice: Consumer Health Information in the 1990s: Report of a Conference; 1991 September 28-30; Loughborough, England. Winchester, England: Consumer Health Information Consortium; 1992. Available from: Consumer Health Information Consortium, c/o Gill Needham, Milton Keynes Health Authority, Standing Way, Milton Keynes, MK6 5LD, England.

GASSERT, CAROLE A. 1990. Structured Analysis: Methodology for Developing a Model for Defining Nursing Information System Requirements. Advances in Nursing Science. 1990; 13(2): 53-62. ISSN: 0161-9268.

GLADSTONE, JOHN. 1993. Real World RM. British Journal of Healthcare Computing. 1993; 10(1): 25-26. ISSN: 0265-5217.

GOUMANS, M. 1992. What about Healthy Networks? Maastricht, The Netherlands: Research for Healthy Cities Clearing House; 1992. 100p. (RHC Monograph Series No. 3). ISBN: 90-74590-03-9. Available from: Research for Healthy Cities Clearing House, University of Limburg, P.O. Box 616, 6200 MD, Maastricht, The Netherlands.

GOVES, JOHN R.; DAVIES, T.; REILLY, TERRY. 1991. Computerisation of Primary Care in Wales. British Medical Journal. 1991; 303: 93-94. ISSN: 0959-8146.

GRAVES, JUDITH RAE. 1990. A Research-Knowledge System (ARKS) for Storing, Managing, and Modelling Knowledge from the Scientific Literature. Advances in Nursing Science. 1990; 13(2): 34-35. ISSN: 0161-9268.

GREAT BRITAIN. DEPARTMENT OF HEALTH. 1989. Working for Patients. London, England: Her Majesty's Stationery Office; 1989. Available from: HMSO, P.O. Box 276, London SW8 5DT, England.

GREAT BRITAIN. DEPARTMENT OF HEALTH. 1990. Working for Patients: Framework for Information Systems: Overview. London, England: Her Majesty's Stationery Office; 1990. (Working Paper 11). Available from: HMSO, P.O. Box 276, London, SW8 5DT, England.

GREAT BRITAIN. DEPARTMENT OF HEALTH. 1991. The Patient's Charter. London, England: Her Majesty's Stationery Office; 1991. Available from: HMSO, P.O. Box 276, London, SW8 5DT, England.

GREAT BRITAIN. DEPARTMENT OF HEALTH. 1992. Handbook for IM&T Specialists: An Information Management and Technology Strategy for the NHS in England. London, England: Department of Health, National Health Service Management Executive, Information Management Group; 1992.

GREAT BRITAIN. DEPARTMENT OF HEALTH. NATIONAL HEALTH SERVICE. 1990. Working for Patients: Framework for Information Systems: Next Steps. London, England: Her Majesty's Stationery Office; 1990. Available from: HMSO, P.O. Box 276, London, SW8 5DT, England.

GREAT BRITAIN. NATIONAL HEALTH SERVICE. MANAGEMENT BOARD. 1986. A National Strategic Framework for Information Management in the Hospital and Community Health Services. London, England: National Health Service; 1986. Available from: HMSO P.O. Box 276, London, SW8 5DT, England.

GREAT BRITAIN. NATIONAL HEALTH SERVICE. MANAGEMENT EXECUTIVE. 1991. Purchasing Intelligence: DHA Project Team. London, England: National Health Service; 1991. Available from: HMSO, P.O. Box 276, London, SW8 5DT, England.

GREAT BRITAIN. NATIONAL HEALTH SERVICE. MANAGEMENT EXECUTIVE. INFORMATION MANAGEMENT GROUP. 1992a. Developing Information Systems for Purchasers. London, England: Department of Health; 1992. Available from: HMSO, P.O. Box 276, London, SW8 5DT, England.

GREAT BRITAIN. NATIONAL HEALTH SERVICE. MANAGEMENT EXECUTIVE. INFORMATION MANAGEMENT GROUP. 1992b. Getting Better with Information: IM&T Strategy Overview. London, England: National Health Service Management Executive; 1992. Available from: HMSO, P.O. Box 276, London, SW8 5DT, England.

GREAT BRITAIN. NATIONAL HEALTH SERVICE. TRAINING AUTHORITY & INFORMATION MANAGEMENT GROUP. 1989. IMT Strategy for Training and Staff Development. London, England: National Health Service; 1989. Available from: HMSO, P.O. Box 276, London, SW8 5DT, England.

GREAT BRITAIN. NATIONAL HEALTH SERVICE. TRAINING DIRECTORATE. 1992. Information Management and Technology: Developing Information Systems for Purchasers: Organisation and Training Issues. Bristol, England: NHS Training Directorate; 1992. Available from: NHS Training Directorate, St. Bartholomew's Court, 18 Christmas Street, Bristol, BS1 5BT, England.

GREENES, ROBERT A.; SHORTLIFFE, EDWARD H. 1990. Medical Informatics. Journal of the American Medical Association. 1990; 263(8): 1114-1120. ISSN: 0098-7484.

HAFNER, ARTHUR W., ed. 1994. Symposium: Medical Libraries and Patient Information Services. Bulletin of the Medical Library Association. 1994; 82(1): 43-66. ISSN: 0025-7338.

HARD, ROB. 1992. Well-Managed Information Vital to Effective Managed Care Contracting. Hospitals. 1992 June 5; 66: 50. ISSN: 0018-5973.

HARDIN, RICHARD C.; SKIBA, DIANE J. 1982. A Comparative Analysis of Computer Literacy Education for Nurses. In: Blum, B.I., ed. Proceedings of the 6th Annual Symposium on Computer Applications in Medical Care; 1982 October 30-November 2; Washington, DC. New York, NY: IEEE Computer Society Press; 1982. 525-530. ISSN: 0195-4210.

HAYES, CATHERINE; DOORLEY, PAT; BATESON, RAY. 1992. Dublin 1992—A Healthy City? A Position Statement. Dublin, Ireland: Dublin Healthy Cities Project; 1992. 103p. Available from: Carmichael House, North Brunswick Street, Dublin 7, Republic of Ireland.

HEPWORTH, JOHN. 1991. IT Training: Through the Training Maze. Health Service Journal. 1991 December 12; 101(5282): 33-34. ISSN: 0952-2271.

JONES, TIM. 1992. The Public Health Information Specification (PHIS) Model. Information for the Management of Healthcare Newsletter. 1992; 3(4): 15-18. Available from: Information Resource Centre, Nuffield Institute for Health Services Studies, 71-75 Clarendon Road, Leeds, LS2 9PL, England.

KARA, GEORGE. 1991. The Low-down on High Tech Health Information Systems. Health Issues. 1991 March; 26: 28-30. Available from: Centre for Technology Policy & Management, Royal Melbourne Institute of Technology, Melbourne, Australia.

KETTELHUT, MICHAEL C. 1992. Strategic Requirements for IS in the Turbulent Healthcare Environment. Journal of Systems Management. 1992 June; 43: 6-9. ISSN: 0022-4839.

KIM, K. KYU; MICHELMAN, JEFFREY E. 1990. An Examination of Factors for the Strategic Use of Information Systems in the Healthcare Industry. Management Information Systems Quarterly. 1990 June; 14(2): 201-215. ISSN: 0276-7783.

KLEIN, RUDOLF. 1993. Health Care Reform: The Global Search for Utopia. British Medical Journal. 1993; 307: 752. ISSN: 0959-8146.

LEANING, M.S. 1993. The New Information Management and Technology Strategy of the NHS. British Medical Journal. 1993 July 24; 307: 217. ISSN: 0959-8146.

LEE, KENNETH. 1991. Competition Versus Planning in Health Care: Implications for Corporate and Individual Incentives, Efficiency and Control. Australian Health Review. 1991; 14(1): 9-34. ISSN: 0156-5788.

LEVY, A.H. 1977. Is Informatics a Basic Medical Science? In: Shires, D.B.; Wolf, H., eds. MEDINFO-77. Amsterdam, The Netherlands: North-Holland; 1977. 979-981.

LEVY, RICHARD P.; CAMMARN, MAXINE R. 1968. Information Systems Applications in Medicine. In: Cuadra, C.A., ed. Annual Review of Information Science and Technology: Volume 3. Chicago, IL: Encyclopaedia Britannica Inc. for the American Society for Information Science; 1968. 397-428. LC: 66-25096.

LINDBERG, DONALD A.B.; SCHOOLMAN, HAROLD M. 1986. The National Library of Medicine and Medical Informatics. The Western Journal of Medicine. 1986 December; 145: 786-790. ISSN: 0093-0415.

LUN, K.C.; DEGOULET, P.; PIEMME, T.E.; RIENHOFF, O., eds. 1992. Proceedings of the 7th World Congress on Medical Informatics; 1992 September 6-10; Geneva, Switzerland. Amsterdam, The Netherlands: North-Holland; 1992. 1637p. ISBN: 0-444-89668-6.

LUNIN, LOIS F.; BALL, MARION J. 1989. Perspectives on Information Science and Health Informatics Education: Introduction and Overview. Journal of the American Society for Information Science. 1989; 40(5): 365-367. ISSN: 0002-8231.

MACDOUGALL, JENNIFER; BRITTAIN, J. MICHAEL. 1992. The Use of Information in the National Health Service. London, England: British Library Board; 1992. 70p. (Library and Information Research Report 92). ISBN: 0-7123-3275-8.

MANDIL, SALAH. 1989. Health Informatics. World Health. 1989 August/September; 2-5. ISSN: 0043-8502.

MANTAS, JOHN. 1992. The Application of Advanced Information Technology in Medicine and Healthcare: A European Approach. International Journal of Technology Management. 1992; 7(6-8): 560-571. ISSN: 0267-5730.

MARSHALL, JOANNE G. 1993. Issues in Clinical Information Delivery. Library Trends. 1993; 42(1): 83-107. ISSN: 0024-2594.

MASSO, MALCOLM. 1989. The Quality Assurance Dilemma. Australian Journal of Advanced Nursing. 1989; 7(1): 12-22. ISSN: 0813-0531.

MAURICE, JOHN. 1993. Agency to Improve Health Policy in Third World. British Medical Journal. 1993 April 3; 306: 880-881. ISSN: 0959-8146.

MCDONALD, CLEMENT J. 1991. Delivering X-ray Images on Hospital Computer Networks. M.D. Computing. 1991; 7: 348-350. ISSN: 0724-6811.

MELLING, JON. 1991. Informed Decisions: America. Health Service Journal. 1991 August 29; 101(5267): 31. ISSN: 0952-2271.

MILLER, PERRY L.; PATON, JOHN A.; CLYMAN, JEFFREY I.; POWSNER, SETH M. 1992. Prototyping an Institutional IAIMS/UMLS Information Environment for an Academic Medical Center. Bulletin of the Medical Library Association. 1992; 80(3): 281-287. ISSN: 0025-7338.

MORE, ELIZABETH; MORE, DAVID. 1990. Changing Environments in Healthcare Communication Systems: The Technological Imperative. Australian Journal of Communication. 1990; 17(3): 22-37. ISSN: 0811-6202.

MOREY, SUE. 1990. The Need for Better Clinical Information Systems. Australian Medical Record Journal. 1990; 20(4): 159-161. ISSN: 0817-3907.

MORIARTY, DANIEL D. 1992. Strategic Information Systems Planning for Health Service Providers. Health Care Management Review. 1992; 17(1): 85-90. ISSN: 0361-6274.

NEAME, RODERICK. 1990. Keeping an Open Mind. Health Service Journal. 1990 July 19; 100(5210): 1077-1080. ISSN: 0952-2271.

NORDIN, JOHN R. 1992. Systems Implications of Alternate Site Healthcare. Journal of Systems Management. 1992 June; 43: 13-41. ISSN: 0022-4839.

ORR, STEWART. 1993. Alone on a Wide, Wide Sea. British Journal of Healthcare Computing. 1993; 10(8): 14-15. ISSN: 0265-5217.

PALMER, GUY; CRUICKSHANK, JOHN; BEALE, PHIL. 1991. Making the IT Jigsaw Fit. Health Service Journal. 1991 January 31; 101: 29-30. ISSN: 0952-2271.

PFAFF, M. 1990. Differences in Health Care Spending across Countries: Statistical Evidence. Journal of Health Politics, Policy and Law. 1990; 15(1): 1-23. ISSN: 0361-6878.

REGAN, BRIAN G. 1991. Computerised Information Exchange in Health Care. The Medical Journal of Australia. 1991; 154: 140-144. ISSN: 0025-729X.

ROMANO, CAROL A. 1990. Diffusion of Technology Innovation. Advances in Nursing Science. 1990; 13(2): 11-21. ISSN: 0161-9268.

ROMANO, CAROL A.; HELLER, BARBARA R. 1990. Nursing Informatics: A Model Curriculum for an Emerging Role. Nurse Educator. 1990; 15(2): 16-19. ISSN: 0363-3624.

ROYCE, ROBERT. 1993. DRGs and the Internal Market. British Journal of Healthcare Computing. 1993; 10(1): 27-28. ISSN: 0265-5217.

ROYCE, ROBERT; SAIT, JEAN. 1993. DRGs and the Internal Market: A Welsh Pilot Study. British Journal of Healthcare Computing. 1993; 10(2): 32-34. ISSN: 0265-5217.

RUCK, ANDREW. 1993. Only Connect. British Journal of Healthcare Computing. 1993; 10(7): 23-26. ISSN: 0265-5217.

RUFFIN, MARSHALL. 1993. Medical Informatics. Healthcare Forum Journal. 1993 March/April; 36(2): 47-50. ISSN: 0899-9287.

SCOTT, TONY. 1991. Informed Decisions. Health Service Journal. 1991; 101(5267): 29-31. ISSN: 0952-2271.

SHORTLIFFE, EDWARD H. 1991. Medical Informatics and Clinical Decision Making: The Science and the Pragmatics. Medical Decision Making. 1991; 11(Supplement): S2-S14. ISSN: 0272-989X.

SILLINCE, J.A.A.; FROST, C.E.B. 1993. Management Information Systems in U.K. Primary Health Care: The Need for a Strategy. International Journal of Information Management. 1993; 13(6): 425-437. ISSN: 0268-4012.

SIMPSON, ROY L. 1992a. Informatics: Nursing's Newest Speciality. Nursing Management. 1992; 23(8): 26. ISSN: 0744-6314.

SIMPSON, ROY L. 1992b. The New Careers in Nursing Informatics. Nursing Management. 1992; 23(10): 26-27. ISSN: 0744-6314.

SINCLAIR, VAUGHN G. 1989. Addressing Challenges in Nursing Informatics Instruction. Journal of Nursing Education. 1989; 28(2): 82-84. ISSN: 0022-3158.

SOUTHGATE, JAN. 1991. For Your Eyes Only? Health Records, Access and Privacy. Health Issues. 1991; 26: 24-27.

STEERING GROUP ON HEALTH SERVICES INFORMATION. 1982. First Report to the Secretary of State. London, England: HMSO; 1982. Available from: HMSO, P.O. Box 276, London, SW8 5DT, England.

TILLEY, CAROLYN B. 1990. Medical Databases and Health Information Systems. In: Williams, Martha E., ed. Annual Review of Information Science and Technology: Volume 25. Amsterdam, The Netherlands: Elsevier

Science Publishers for the American Society for Information Science; 1990. 313-382. ISSN: 0066-4200; ISBN: 0-444-88531-5.

TOWNSEND, CHRISTINA; ADAMS, PAUL. 1991. Training Matters. British Journal of Healthcare Computing. 1991 October; 8(8). ISSN: 0265-5217.

VON STILLFRIED, DOMINIK; ARNOLD, MICHAEL. 1993. What's Happening to Health Care in Germany? British Medical Journal. 1993; 306: 1017-1018. ISSN: 0959-8146.

WALKER, DON. 1993. Editorial: To Succeed, Computers Need to Be "Irresistible". Informatics in Healthcare Australia. 1993; 2(5): 5-6. ISSN: 1037-308X.

WARDEN, JOHN. 1993a. Scotland Catches Up with Health Reforms. British Medical Journal. 1993; 306: 882. ISSN: 0959-8146.

WARDEN, JOHN. 1993b. The Wessex Fiasco. British Medical Journal. 1993; 306: 1292. ISSN: 0959-8146.

WARREN, LIZ. 1993. Double Jeopardy. British Journal of Healthcare Computing. 1993; 10(2): 27-28. ISSN: 0265-5217.

WILLIAMSON, MAURICE. 1992. New Health Reforms Need Support of Appropriate Information Systems. New Zealand Health and Hospital. 1992 November/December; 9-14. ISSN: 0114-3727.

WILSON, LIONEL. 1991. Looking to Solutions for Deficiencies in Medical Records. Australian Medical Record Journal. 1991; 21(2): 53-57. ISSN: 0817-3907.

WITTENSTROM, JOHN C. 1991. Requirements for Realizing the Full Potential of Informatics in the Field of Health Care. Journal of Dental Education. 1991; 55(4): 254-256. ISSN: 0022-0337.

WOODS, SUSAN E.; COGGAN, JANET M. 1994. Developing a Medical Informatics Education Program to Support a Statewide Health Information Network. Bulletin of the Medical Library Association. 1994; 82(2): 147-152. ISSN: 0025-7338.

WYATT, JEREMY. 1991a. Computer-Based Knowledge Systems. The Lancet. 1991 December 7; 338: 1431-1436. ISSN: 0140-6736.

WYATT, JEREMY. 1991b. Use and Sources of Medical Knowledge. The Lancet. 1991 November 30; 338: 1368-1372. ISSN: 0140-6736.

YAMADA, RONALD H. 1990. Mission Critical Health Care Systems. Business Quarterly. 1990 Summer; 55: 99-104. ISSN: 0007-6996.

ZIMMERMAN, JOHN L.; VAN BEMMEL, JAN H.; RIENHOFF, OTTO. 1988. Medical Informatics Education. Journal of the American Society for Information Science. 1988; 39(2): 138-141. ISSN: 0002-8231.

6 Online Catalogs: Enhancements and Developments

ANN O'BRIEN
Loughborough University

INTRODUCTION

In the past decade, the catalog emerged from the back room to take a central place in the library once again. Of course, it always has been central, but online access has given the catalog a particularly high profile and even a sense of liberation. In the past year or two, however, new factors (principally remote access to multiple networked resources) have begun to threaten to edge the catalog into the shadows again. BUCKLAND ET AL. (1992) distinguish among the paper library, the automated library, and the electronic library. At present we are in the automated stage, moving toward the electronic stage. It is possible to see the catalog in this context because it has moved from a manual to an automated tool but is not yet fully electronic.

This review deals with online catalog enhancements over the past two to three years. It takes for granted those features that are now standard and mainly discusses issues related to problem areas, in particular, subject access and user-searching behavior, as well as new developments that directly impinge on its future—i.e., new interface developments and network access and resources. Many of the topics covered are very broad and widely covered in the literature. This review covers each topic by highlighting recent developments and treats in depth those issues that are currently concerned with developing and redefining the online catalog.

Information retrieval (IR) is only effective when the people involved share common knowledge structures. The match of concepts among user, intermediary, and system then has some chance of success. In

Annual Review of Information Science and Technology (ARIST), Volume 29, 1994
Martha E. Williams, Editor
Published for the American Society for Information Science (ASIS)
By Learned Information, Inc., Medford, N.J.

online catalogs, the intermediary is no longer a factor, and the tension between system and end user is even more crucial. Much of the short history of online catalogs has consisted of concern as to whether or not a set of manual standards has been transferred to an online environment. The chronology is described by HILDRETH as the evolution of three generations of systems, but a parallel reading might be as follows: automate the card catalog; accept user approval; notice search failures and inadequacy of access points; and accept improvement due to keyword searching linked with a high degree of user satisfaction. This takes us up to Hildreth's second generation of catalog development. The third involves recognition that better efforts are needed to understand user behavior, to solve the most pressing problems of too few or too many items retrieved, and at the same time to keep pace with novel retrieval techniques and the emerging role of the catalog as just one of many databases that can be accessed by the same workstation.

It is clear that users were often better helped in their interaction with manual catalogs precisely because of the catalogs' limitations. The subject catalog was usually full of cross references, and library staff supplemented internal aids with assistance. There was an implicit sense that serious catalog users would familiarize themselves with the various constraints of the manual catalog and then benefit by their diligence. The perception now is that we cannot expect users to bring the same degree of application to a self-contained, self-service system, and most evaluations of such systems confirm this. As such, much thought and effort have been devoted to problem areas in an effort to offer improved access (INTNER). The principal areas in which users have difficulties are search formulation and searching for subjects. Most of the discussion of efforts to enhance or improve online catalogs addresses these two areas.

BIBLIOGRAPHIC STANDARDS

To enhance access to online catalogs, the first responsibility should be to improve existing systems and standards and make them function more effectively. The standards we are heavily invested in are AACR2 (Anglo-American Cataloging Rules, 2nd ed.), MARC (machine-readable cataloging), classification schemes, and Library of Congress Subject Headings (LCSH), although the last is not widespread as a standard in Europe. No determination has been made regarding adoption of these standards. The dominant view is that we are committed to these standards by vested interests and should make the most of them. At the other end of the opinion scale is a more radical approach that sees these standards as by no means immutable. Bibliographic records have tied catalogs to a particular form that has not taken advantage of other record structures. This has left us with a flat two-dimensional record that is not entirely suitable for an online environment. MARC format also shows its manual origins but at the same time has a significant amount of data that has not been fully utilized in catalogs. Classification and LCSH are central to subject access, and although usable, they pose enormous problems in application and retrieval.

Cataloging Rules

The major contribution of AACR2 to online catalogs is that it provides standard, predictable bibliographical elements in short-, medium-, or full-record displays. It is doubtful if this in itself is of any concern to users. There has been a continuous examination of the role of cataloging rules (BIERBAUM; BRUNT; JEFFREYS; LEWIS; WINKE), especially in the early euphoria of online access when it was believed that very few of the complexities need remain. Whatever theoretical basis the rules have was ignored rather than reexamined, but some shift in attitudes is noticeable. Fewer people have to apply the rules since centralized cataloging agencies predominate, but some reconsideration of the rules is beginning to be heard. As catalog databases become larger, control is increasingly needed to cope with large sets of retrieved documents. For example, since simple alphabetical filing of the works of some authors results in the separation of many related works, collocation of the works of prolific authors is becoming a problem in most catalogs. Uniform titles are being reexamined in this respect, especially as catalogs include more and more non-monographic items. TILLETT (1991) gives a timely reassessment of bibliographic relationships in the online catalog.

There is a predictable tension between those who desire to simplify cataloging procedure and those who believe that bibliographic records need to be more informative. KNUTSON (1993) reports on various initiatives, based mostly on the need to reduce costs, while HORNY describes current trends and practice. However, ill-thought out cost-cutting initiatives can be poor economies because libraries often have to add local data to the records to make them usable and compatible in their own catalogs (PREECE & FOX), or the initiative may have to be reversed, as in the case of the British Library that dropped LCSHs from their records in 1987 only to have to reintroduce them in 1994 because of customer pressure (BRITISH LIBRARY. NATIONAL BIBLIOGRAPHIC SERVICE). Name searching has been improved greatly by good authority control in online catalogs. This topic has received much attention in recent years, and TILLETT (1989) offers a comprehensive survey.

MARC

A detailed study of developments in MARC formats is outside the scope of this chapter, but we mention one or two important recent issues. MARC remains mainly unchallenged for much the same reasons as AACR2. Conversion software offers relative ease of transfer between one version of the format and another. Also some elements hitherto ignored (especially fixed-field information codes) are now being used to help limit searches (see below). Although it is common to remark that catalog records are poor in subject information, there is also some truth in the fact that some of these data have been underused in terms of which fields are permitted to be searched. MARC has also been extended for various materials—i.e., for electronic texts and items in unconventional catalog databases (ALIPRAND, 1993; BROWNRIGG & BUTLER; LLORENS & TRENOR).

BIBLIOGRAPHIC RECORD SUPPLY

Provision of bibliographic records to libraries is still a fairly straightforward matter. Records usually come from one of the bibliographic utilities, such as a cooperative or national agency—e.g., OCLC and the British Library. This state of affairs is the result of a fairly simple development. As the major cooperatives became national and even international providers, smaller, local cooperatives were formed to provide catalog records economically. As a result, a library may receive data from several sources and not need to create any original records itself. Issues of quality also emerged in the 1980s (O'NEILL ET AL.). Some databases gained reputations for variable quality cataloging and unnecessary duplicate records. Some larger university and research libraries both in the United States and the United Kingdom found it necessary to form consortia to ensure maintenance of their standards.

Further diversification has occurred with the huge growth in retrospective conversion in the past decade. The largest bibliographic databases offer customer-tailored retrospective services. Again, several sources may be used by any library for record provision. Linked to this, the advent of CD-ROM-based bibliographic records has had an important effect. Libraries or groups of libraries may buy or subscribe to a CD-ROM service and download records. If good coverage can be ensured, this may be a highly effective means of providing good quality records even if not always in a timely manner.

Bibliographic Records and the Book Trade

In the U.K., in recent years, another player has emerged in supplying records—viz., the book trade. The various nonlibrary sectors of the book trade have always had a small but significant role in record provision, but with recent advances in automation, new possibilities are appearing.

Many libraries have automated acquisitions systems which include ordering from book suppliers or publishers. Since a bibliographic record of some type is necessary for ordering material, these minimal records often provide the basis for the subsequent full catalog record. It would be ideal for libraries to acquire as full a record as possible at the time of publication. Also, prepublication and publication data are increasingly available through various branches of the book trade. Booksellers, book suppliers, and publishers maintain their own databases, some for internal use and some for public use. In the U.K. these databases are becoming more important in bibliographic record supply. The Book Industry Communication (BIC), a group of interested agencies that promotes convergence of similar initiatives in database production, promotes cooperative efforts among the Publishers Association, the Booksellers Association, and the Library Association to harmonize various activities, including bibliographic record creation and supply. DEMPSEY gives an overview of these developments for a possible "all through system."

The 1990 report of the Book Trade Electronic Data Interchange Standards (BEDIS) Committee deals with this reality (TALLIM). The various working groups looked at standardization among various sectors of the book trade. Working Party 1 examined bibliographic data to arrive at a set of recommended data elements for minimal-level bibliographic description. The widespread use of MARC was accepted and incorporated into the result. The working party came up with a list of bibliographic data elements under three headings: (1) mandatory, (2) highly desirable, and (3) optional; although the headings included elements particular to the book trade, they also included those elements necessary for a basic MARC format.

SUBJECT ACCESS

Subject access is the most problematic area of online catalogs. Controlled searching via systems such as LCSH has been difficult because it involves typing long strings of artificial language; the result can often be failure. Free-text or keyword searching is much more successful but prone to problems that are now increasingly evident to the user. There has been much effort to improve the situation by either enhancing the bibliographic record by adding subject-rich terms, by increasing browsing features, or by allowing keyword searching on the controlled heading string (CONNELL; LANCASTER ET AL.). Most methods for improvement assume that one must simplify methods of access because one cannot expect serious efforts from most catalog users.

Connell suggests that before embarking on major catalog enhancement, it is sensible to study improvements that are likely to increase retrieval of relevant information. Some modifications may not warrant extra effort and expense. Her study involved manipulating the grammar of LCSH and accessing parts of fields not normally accessed directly. The result was a 20% increase in recall in the sample. She also found that both precision and recall can be increased if keyword matching is allowed in name fields.

Subject searching is accomplished either through controlled subject systems—i.e., classification schemes and subject headings of which LCSH is the standard—or by keyword or free-text searching on titles and other parts of the bibliographic record. Keyword access is a liberating byproduct of computerized retrieval, while controlled systems are a legacy of manual catalogs, which are two-dimensional browsing systems.

In the U.K., the situation has not been so predictable. Subject approach (manual) is often via the classified catalog from which a subject term is chosen; if it is an accepted term, a classification number is found, which is subsequently searched in the classified sequence, or more likely on the shelves. Locally generated subject indexes are common and have been mounted in online catalogs with varying success and commitment. In order for this type of index to be viable, it needs to contain at least 15,000–20,000 unique, nonrotated records, and indexes of over 40,000 terms are likely to perform well. The result is nonstandard subject searching, which generates heavy reliance on free-text or keyword searching (CRAWFORD & POWLES; CRAWFORD ET AL.).

Keyword Searching

Catalog users generally do not make much distinction between keyword and controlled subject searching. Librarians are aware of the vital difference but are as yet unsure of the final role of each. Early catalogs did not offer keyword access, but now it is the norm, although how it is presented to users differs significantly from one catalog to another. BATES (1989) discusses some of the problems. Keyword search may be done on the title field alone or on several fields; it may be called "title" search rather than "keyword," having the effect of making a title search more flexible or less exact, depending on one's point of view. Equally likely, it may be called "subject" search, and one would perform a search on title alone or on controlled subject headings alone or possibly both. Keyword search may allow only single terms to be searched, may allow string searching, or more likely may involve an implicit Boolean search. All of these variations makes a general evaluation difficult, but there is no doubt that this form of searching using natural language is increasingly preferred by users. LARSON (1991c), in a long-term study, has recorded a significant move from controlled subject term searching to keyword searching.

One of the most radical effects of keyword searching on controlled subject fields is that it undermines the structure of a controlled system such as LCSH by allowing access to any term in what may be a long heading consisting of a main heading and a number of subdivisions. This affects the specificity of retrieved items, making things highly unstructured in that it loses the embedded links in the linear display which gives each term its context. It is successful in that it is more likely to find documents and thus increases recall, which is regarded as preferable to not retrieving any items. The tension here is between getting no matches when searching using a controlled term and getting too many with highly flexible keyword searching. This situation is linked to the inescapable facts that: (1) any controlled subject system using nonnatural language will be difficult to use especially without extensive aids online, and (2) even with natural language, people do not use the same terms to describe or search for the same concepts. BATES (1989, p. 409) also reported that "the average likelihood that any two people will use the same term for a concept or a book, or that a searcher and an information system will use the same term for a concept, is in the range of 10 to 20 percent."

Library of Congress Subject Headings (LCSH)

Of the many drawbacks to LCSH in online catalogs, two of the most important are: (1) it is not capable of the specificity necessary for large online catalogs because a heading traditionally has been chosen to encompass the whole subject of the book, and (2) the existing linear structure (i.e., the main heading followed by subdivision(s)) is unsuitable for online retrieval. As very few subject headings are assigned to monographic records, one suggestion to improve retrieval is to increase the number of headings included and to cover more specific elements within the text rather than the overall subject. This would require substantial changes in policy by the cataloging agencies, and there is no definite evidence that retrieval would be significantly improved (BATES, 1989).

Browsing. The ability to browse subject headings has greatly improved the ability to refine a subject search. As yet, however, browsing is fairly two dimensional and usually consists of paging through lists of titles, subjects, and/or authors. However, there are problems associated with this. STUDWELL discusses the premise that LCSH offers too much horizontal specificity—i.e., too many subdivisions in its linear headings are redundant. He offers as a possible solution the establishment of two levels of headings. A subject heading is assigned and given a marker as to how it might be split. This allows each library to choose between an abbreviated short heading or the full second-level heading. A study in the same area (MCGARRY & SVENONIUS) suggests that there is redundancy in (vertical) lengthy lists of subject headings that are displayed to searchers. Redundancy can be avoided by using compression techniques, so that if there are more than ten occurrences of a heading, it can be reduced to one. The study also deals with the problem of how entries are ordered within a subject heading display. The authors found that in their sample 53% of subject headings were lengthy (i.e., their extensions by subdivisions, phrases, inversions, or parenthetical qualifiers numbered more than 60—i.e., two or more display screens). ALLEN developed a similar hierarchical browsing interface to help reduce excessive scanning without reducing the number of potentially relevant headings found.

Helping users with LCSH. If LCSH is a barrier to retrieval, one of the simplest approaches is to encourage users to learn more about LCSH and how to make good searches. Another school of thought is that the user should not become bogged down in complex preparations but that the system should help in the most transparent way possible (CARSON). While this is certainly the long-term aim, many catalogs have to find an interim solution that accommodates the users' imperfect knowledge of subject searching. Several catalogs will advise alternative strategies automatically after a zero-hit search. A study at the University of Toronto Library (CHERRY) explored (with positive results) the possibility of converting zero-hit subject searches into various types of keyword searches using the original query.

Subject authority control. The availability of LCSH online as an authority control system promises to make it a more useable instrument. LCSH-mr (machine-readable) provides many of the missing cross references that can lead users' natural-language queries to acceptable terms, and it offers many related terms to aid further. There are, however, considerable limitations. LCSH-mr is not a true thesaurus and so does not provide consistent vocabulary links. Also LCSH-mr does not fully echo the headings as used in an online catalog, which includes many subdivisions and even main headings built from "pattern" headings and locally applied subdivisions. It may, however, be the source of a locally developed subject authority file.

Thesauri. Although not common in large online catalogs, the relative success of thesauri in searching online databases makes them worthy of interest. While the highly structured nature of thesauri is an advantage in logical coherent searching, their drawbacks are many, the most inescapable being the lack of a multisubject general thesaurus.

As specialized thesauri are increasingly used in CD-ROM searching, the necessity to move in and out of the thesaurus while searching is a major drawback. BATES (1991) describes the development of a thesaurus for the Los Angeles Department of Water and Power. Although it was specialized, it involved a multimillion records-management database and faced all the problems of possible large retrieval sets as well as the various difficulties of using a thesaurus (detailed above). The thesaurus solves many of the traditional problems and makes it possible for unskilled users to find and search with good terms by offering a selection from which users can refine their needs without having to move in and out of the search interface. JACKSON proposes that geographic access in online catalogs could be improved by organizing and structuring geographic data through thesaurus hierarchies that could be presented to the user in graphic displays for easier retrieval.

Natural-language front ends to subject headings and thesauri. With the difficulty of finding the correct term or assembling long linear headings in using thesauri and subject headings, there is a move to develop some mediating device between the user's natural-language query and the controlled system. One such system is described by LE LOARER, who discusses a front end to the French Minitel Guide des Services and the Annuaire Electronique (French electronic phone book) and makes the case for its application to online catalogs. The front end analyzes queries by: (1) word recognition, including inflection rules, spell checking, and disambiguation (removal of ambiguity among various grammatical categories, such as the noun "watch" and the verb "watch"), (2) syntactic analysis of the sentence, and (3) semantic analysis. This analysis helps with many problems from null retrieval to the elimination of irrelevant items and ambiguities. This work is an extension of the procedure used by Okapi (WALKER, 1988) in processing queries. Another approach is to use statistical relationships between title words and LCSH. Larson's Cheshire experimental catalog uses this technique based on a listing, in ranked order, of the classification numbers most likely to correspond to the user's search (LARSON, 1991b).

Multiple Vocabularies

While we are attempting to make LCSH more effective in online catalogs, the coming reality of information retrieval in our libraries means access to many databases, local and remote, from the same terminal. Each database may bring its own highly developed subject thesaurus and, although until recently it has been acceptable to search each one separately (thus having to use each individual search language and subject system), this is unlikely to be the future of such searching as users cease to differentiate between the library catalog and other sources (DALRYMPLE & YOUNGER). More sophisticated strategies need to be devised. WEINTRAUB describes the use of LCSH and Medical Subject Headings (MeSH) in the same catalog. Subject headings are indexed separately, and each index is accessed individually from the main menu. Inevitably, users sometimes choose the inappropriate option for a search, but overall reaction is favorable. MANDEL deals with this and other problems in her review of four approaches: (1) segregated bibliographic files, each representing one vocabulary, (2) mixed vocabularies in a single bibliographic file, (3) integrated vocabularies in which various editorial techniques are applied to provide an integrated access structure, and (4) navigation of multiple vocabularies through computer-assisted techniques. Some of these approaches—e.g., amalgamation of thesauri—are established techniques in commercial IR systems. Searching across databases with a single search language can result in a loss of some advanced features particular to some databases. This has led to the development of front-end interfaces that can be used with multiple different databases (MISCHO & COLE).

Classification

Traditional classification systems are used in online searching in a number of ways (WALKER, 1991). For example, in a direct classification search the user enters a class mark and the system displays relevant records for documents entered by that number or near it. In another method (common in online catalogs in the U.K.) classification is used as a pivotal or linking device—i.e., a suitable subject heading or term is found from the subject index, then the class number attached to the heading is shown and used to find and display bibliographic records. Classification can also be used as a type of primitive relevance feedback device to find related works by a further search on the classmark of the item displayed (KINSELLA). In the case of Dewey Decimal Classification (DDC), because the classification schedules and index are themselves a list of subject descriptions, it was worth testing whether or not DDC could form a base for searching (MARKEY & DEMEYER).VIZINE-GOETZ describes a way to adapt the machine-readable DDC into an online classifier's tool, although this does not yet make it suitable for public use.

In a different approach, LARSON (1991b) showed how classification clustering combined with probabilistic retrieval techniques could provide an effective natural-language search technique. Generally the class number of a particular item in online public access catalogs (OPACs) is treated as just another keyword assigned to that item. In this project, however, class numbers extracted from MARC records are used to increase the number of terms associated with an individual record, the additional terms being analogous to "use" and "RT" (related term) references in a thesaurus, directing the user to the controlled "vocabulary" of concepts represented by the class numbers. Thus, the "class clusters" function somewhat like a front-end thesaurus.

REFINING SEARCHES

As catalogs get larger, the problem of retrieving excessive numbers of items, even using fairly specific terms, is becoming acute (HUSAIN & O'BRIEN; LARSON, 1991a). This is particularly true for subject searching but also happens with author searches. We are all familiar with messages that tell us our search is not permitted because it is too general. Most solutions to this problem have been crude—i.e., making the user try again with more specific terms or allowing searches in a subset of the catalog, as in the case of MELVYL (the University of California's OPAC). The possibility of limiting the items retrieved from a search is common in searching online databases and CD-ROMs but has only recently been taken up by online catalog designers. Inevitably such limiting features will have to be general, unlike those available to some of the specialized online databases. It makes their effect less focused, but when supplemented by the ability to limit with another search term, they do indicate the beginning of a welcome search refinement.

For limiting, use has been made of the Fixed Field Information Codes of the MARC record. This feature allows limiting by several categories that correspond to fixed fields in MARC records, the most common of which are date, language, format, and place of publication. Another common limiting factor is location (e.g., by library, reading room). These limiting features are useful but not always the most appropriate. They have little to do with the subject content of the documents and are really mechanical devices that are not always the most sympathetic to a search.

In OASIS, a front-end interface to the MELVYL catalog, BUCKLAND ET AL. (1992; 1993) describe an approach that makes the catalog "adaptive" in that it tries to retrieve the preferred number of the preferred records regardless who the user may be, what the query is and what the database is. This represents a welcome reappraisal of conventional searching and makes good use of existing bibliographic data. One feature of OASIS, "filter," uses conventional limiting devices to subdivide the retrieved items into many subsets that can be ranked by the searcher. Another feature, "fewer," engages a default list of search limiters that can be modified by the user for the duration of the session. The "summarize" feature activated on subject will cause the list of subject terms from the retrieved set to be printed in decreasing frequency order. Evaluation of these enhanced features is eagerly awaited.

Other principles of search refinement have moved across from the online searching environment. One with a good deal of potential is relevance feedback. As mentioned above, it is now fairly common to be able to find other similar works from the display of a retrieved record (the system searches on the classmark or subject headings of the current record). This represents an elementary effort to build on the relevance of an initial search. A more comprehensive version is seen in Okapi, the experimental online catalog based at City University, London (WALKER, 1988). Here the user can select relevant records from the retrieved set and the system will automatically add terms from these records to the initial search, thus enriching the existing search terms if a further search is made.

ENRICHING THE CONTENTS OF BIBLIOGRAPHIC RECORDS

There is no doubt that subject indexing of monographs is both superficial and inadequate, particularly the lack of in-depth treatment of edited compilations. It seems that a move to at least consider adding information from tables of contents, back-of-book indexes, and analytical entries for individual items is being seriously considered. FRANTZ suggests that libraries are concentrating on providing access to materials not owned by the library while much of the monographic stock is lacking subject coverage. He discusses possible solutions, including the expansion of the Essay and General Literature Index as a companion to the catalog. In a review of the literature, VAN ORDEN advocates the use of contents-enriched records to increase recall with a possible decrease in precision.

Researchers at Carnegie-Mellon (MICHALAK) established criteria for works that would benefit from enhancement—e.g., books with citable references, exhibition catalogs concerning 25 or fewer artists, and chapter titles that improve on title subject information. Excluded were proceedings of scientific and technical conferences (mainly because they tend to be lengthy and require considerable data input), books for which sufficient keyword and subject information already exist, and exhibition catalogs that contain illustrations for 26 or more artists. As a result, 7.85% (851 from a total of 10,835) of the books were enhanced in the first stage of the project. No systematic evaluation of effectiveness was available at this stage

At OCLC, Inc. a small experiment was conducted to measure the effectiveness of searching a database containing abstracts and tables of contents (DILLON & WENZEL). Artificially constructed queries were devised and searched over four levels of contents: (1) title and subject headings; (2) title, subject headings, and table of contents; (3) title, subject headings, and abstracts; and (4) title, subject headings, contents, and abstracts. Recall and precision were measured, precision based on relevance judgments made on a scale of 1 to 3 by "experts in the field." The greatest precision was achieved at the first level—i.e., title and subject headings. The experiment and its methodology were limited, so the findings are only indicative.

KNUTSON (1991) reports an experiment in adding extra subject headings and contents notes to books (essay collections and conference proceedings) that had been in the library for two or three years. The 291 records were divided into three groups: (1) one with subjects and contents notes, (2) one with full contents notes added, and (3) a control group with no additions. Over the period of a year, 19.6% of the titles circulated at least once, of which the group enhanced with subject headings and contents notes accounted for just over 50%. BEATTY gives an account of a project at the Australian Defence Academy. Here 40,000 records (out of 210,000 titles) have had terms added from the tables of contents or back-of-the-book indexes, so that an average of 73 words or 20 phrases have been added to each MARC record. Evaluation shows that retrieval (recall) is improved to some extent although (inevitably) precision suffers a bit. COUSINS describes a study, part of which involved adding terms to bibliographic records. In this case, terms chosen from contents pages and indexes were translated into PRECIS (Preserved Context Indexing System) terminology. This adds the dimension of mapping controlled headings as opposed to seminatural language. PRECIS performed well in some controlled retrieval experiments, but natural-language enhanced records performed slightly better in the same experiments.

Enhancing bibliographic records is one possible route to improve subject retrieval. It helps to enrich our superficially indexed monograph collections in both depth and exhaustivity. However, more access points would result in even more items' being retrieved, thus adding another problem associated with catalogs.

UNDERSTANDING CATALOG USERS

Methods for evaluating online catalogs is a large area of research. It encompasses those methods that study the system and those that study the users' reactions. The latter usually involves surveys and interviews (i.e., individual case studies and impact studies). The former can include surveys but has the advantage of transaction analysis that can give major insight into what users of systems actually do when searching. Lots of data have been gathered from transaction log analysis, which has informed research and development for new systems. Long-term studies are starting to show patterns of user behavior, indicating their increasing familiarity as well as continuing problems. LARSON (1991c) reports a small but significant decline in controlled subject searching over ten years in favor of keyword searching. This helps to confirm other data that indicate the difficulty of subject searching and the solutions users bring to the problem.

User studies abound, but few evaluate anything deeper than initial reaction and satisfaction. Studies on online catalogs and also with mediated online searches have raised questions about the relationship between users' expectations and the effectiveness of their search. ANKENY reports a study of end users of online services that shows that although high levels of "satisfaction" with a search were recorded, this did not reflect true success rate. Most early surveys measured only satisfaction with searches or the catalog in general. More rigorous measurement is very difficult as one reviews the variation in success in relevance or precision in mediated online searches over the past 40 years. People who use online catalogs do so for various reasons that are hard to pin down. Their information needs range from highly specific to very general ones, and the relevance of retrieved items is even more volatile (O'BRIEN). It is possible to detect in a large proportion of catalog users a growth of computer literacy or at least familiarity with computers. This does not necessarily mean that these users will perform better as searchers. It is equally likely that they have higher expectations from catalogs of easy and fruitful searching.

More comprehensive studies have been conducted on end users, although the majority have used online databases rather than catalogs. SIEGFRIED ET AL. report a study of end-user searching by humanities scholars at the Getty Center for the History of Art and the Humanities. Although the scholars were not expert searchers, the findings of the study echo earlier results reporting that mainly single terms are used (63%) and that simple searching is the norm. WILDEMUTH ET AL. studied in detail the searching behavior of medical students in a factual database, but again the results show that students made only a few distinct moves and that their selection of these moves varied by individual and by search stimulus.

BELKIN ET AL. combined transaction log analysis, online questionnaires, nonparticipant observation, and detailed interview methods to discover the "goals, tasks and behaviors of users of libraries and library catalogs." This technique takes evaluation beyond the catalog and on to the bookshelves with the readers. Preliminary results showed browsing behavior at the shelves that seems to support the need to include tables of contents and/or indexes. This methodology has characterized the work of HANCOCK-BEAULIEU.

SPECIAL MATERIALS AND SPECIAL NEEDS

Most of the above discussion implies that online catalogs are full of standard monographs, and although this is true, catalogs are beginning to accommodate special materials and serve nonstandard needs. For example, a museum catalog must reflect the museum's desire to express details about objects, whole/part relationships, provenance, and dating. Many of these items used to be standard catalog features, but now they are not necessarily emphasized in system design (STARR). BURBANK & HENIGMAN and TROUTMAN discuss the implications for music, which can be both helped and hindered by uniform titles.

GRANT & JONES discuss accessibility to catalogs for the disabled, much of which involves interface developments—i.e., speech synthesis. Such systems are beginning to be available (MATES) and recognized as an essential next step for public access.

MULTILINGUAL ACCESS

As online catalogs become the norm, users have begun to expect access to materials in their original language. The implications are: (1) bibliographic records recorded in the language and script of the text, and (2) full access to those materials in the preferred language of the catalog user. A number of issues are involved, such as the ability to display and search using diacritical marks and non-Roman scripts as well as bilingual/multilingual access where appropriate.

The bibliographic record needs to be reassessed for its ability to store and manipulate text that includes non-English characters and symbols. If the texts are in Roman-based alphabets, the extra characters may be accents, cedillas, and so forth; if they are in a non-Roman alphabet, all the characters may be different. In any case, an extended character set is needed. These are available, but only recently has a universal standard been needed. Recent reviews of these developments are given by ALIPRAND (1992) and PERUGINELLI ET AL. Despite the lack of an agreed upon standard, the library world is increasingly planning its complex systems with these developments in mind. BUTCHER describes current developments in the new British Library online catalog, while JAMIESON discusses network access to Oriental-language materials.

ROLLAND-THOMAS & MERCURE (p. 146) define the "ideal bilingual OPAC" as follows:

> In order that an OPAC be considered bilingual, it must allow the user to search in the language of his/her choosing. The authority control with reciprocal references must be available in the same file. The ideal situation would include one bilingual subject heading list or thesaurus for searching in either language with retrieval under other subject headings or terms used both in the "other" language or in the language used for searching. The least that can be expected is multilingual authority files which include equivalent forms

> from one language to the others. Moreover, searching in any language must allow retrieval of the whole collection and not be limited to items matching the language of the search.

At the same time these authors acknowledge that as yet no online catalog has achieved all of these aims. In some cases this is because fully linked authority control is considered unnecessary, as in several Canadian systems where the expectation that users perform two similar searches is regarded as reasonable; in others it is the difficulty involved in multilingual equivalences that prevents a fully integrated system.

INTERFACE DEVELOPMENTS

Most of the developmental research in interface design is being done outside the library and information field. Many personal computer users take a step backward when they move from their Mac or Windows graphical user interfaces (GUIs) to use an online catalog. In this respect online catalogs are firmly a generation behind. There is a growing lobby that believes that GUIs are easier to learn and are more forgiving, although this theory is not without its detractors. We await the appearance of GUIs as installed mainstream catalog software. The hypertext interface of MICCO uses icons and graphics to enable complex searches to be simplified. After typing in a search term, the user can point to another search type or a modification routine to assemble a complex search statement that would be exceedingly difficult to get right in a command language-based environment where considerable typing would be necessary. The system also involves several enhancements discussed earlier: (1) the database of 18,000 records has been enriched with tables of contents terms; (2) over one million "see" and "see also" cross references from natural language to the controlled subject headings have been input; and (3) subject headings have been linked to class numbers to enable users to break down large sets of retrieved items. This experimental system thus brings together a number of current concerns in a single system. No user studies have yet been reported, but they are awaited eagerly.

BERGER (p. 155) sees a GUI as:

> more than just an improvement in display technology; it is a change in the way the interface is viewed by both designers and users. The interface goes beyond sequential processing of a single application or application task to become an asynchronous window on multiple applications.

MELVYL designers are planning to support a range of multitasking user interfaces. For those who use the Internet, it is currently possible to access the same remote service in several ways using different interfaces from the same microcomputer. Navigation and response time can vary considerably depending on the interface used.

The attraction of a front-end system such as OASIS (BUCKLAND ET AL., 1992) is that it can incorporate new interface developments and at the same time do much of the sophisticated processing, thus making a standard catalog more powerful and easier to use without extensive further development.

BEYOND THE ONLINE CATALOG

As access to other or remote information sources becomes increasingly available alongside the catalog, will the catalog lose ground as a primary information source? If databases of journal articles are readily available that are more specifically targeted and better indexed than catalogs, is catalog use likely to diminish?

BERGER describes this environment of easily accessible remote and local databases as a "mosaic of loosely connected systems" and suggests that for MELVYL the way forward is to process the search in all reasonable information sources and return an informed display of items retrieved. This will require even more sophisticated approaches to display, ranking, and feedback procedures than currently available.

As more and more library users work from personal workstations and access global networks, they will be able to carry out a variety of activities from their workstations: send and receive e-mail, download and reformat records, order and pay for documents, and eventually have documents delivered electronically. The distinctions between the catalog and the online database will become quickly blurred. With the advent of the ANSI (American National Standards Institute) Z39.50 standard "search and retrieve" protocol, it is feasible for vendors to provide a single view of multiple databases and enable users to search several sources through a single interface, without the need to log on to the remote system (CARSON & FREIVALDS; CRAWFORD, 1993). Users of remote systems need to be studied further. SLOAN gives some general characteristics of remote access and reports that remote users of ILLINET (the Illinois state-wide network) are over 30% more likely to search the online catalog by author or title than are system users as a whole. Subject searches are only initiated half as much by remote users and the rate of invalid commands by remote users is double that of the more generic system user. These are interesting findings but need to be supported by more detailed research.

The ability to link the outcomes of searches in noncatalog databases to the local library holdings has a positive effect. It makes those resources seem to act as backup to the controlling local library, but these links must be set up and maintained. As more and more text is held electronically, the catalog could eventually act as the central access point to the electronic library.

CONCLUSIONS

Online catalogs still seem to be highly imperfect systems. If the user matches a request with the database, the result will be some sort of success. Such success may be interpreted differently by the non-expert end user and the librarian/expert intermediary. The latter feels a need to ensure that most, if not all, of the relevant records for that search be retrieved. The former is likely to be pleased with a lot less. Catalog users then have a poor sense of what the ideal outcome might be but perhaps that is just as well; our catalogs are getting so large that if users were to retrieve all possible items, they would be overwhelmed.

Most libraries that have implemented an online catalog do not fully understand what their users need. Users are coming to express less "satisfaction" and becoming more demanding. This change will become more apparent when users' personal computing environment will have easier, more flexible, and enjoyable interfaces than the library catalog.

As more experimental systems are developed, we move further away from the "card metaphor" as CRAWFORD (1992) calls it. The need to deliver a more individually tailored set of bibliographic records to end users demands a catalog that resembles less the traditional manual model, not just in how it displays information but more critically in how it searches. Future developments, on the model of OASIS, although probably stuck with the traditional apparatus of the bibliographic record (AACR2 and MARC), will be able to offer pliant front ends that are both effective and reassuring.

BIBLIOGRAPHY

ALIPRAND, JOAN M. 1992. Nonroman Scripts in the Bibliographic Environment. Information Technology and Libraries. 1992 June; 11(2): 105-119. ISSN: 0730-9295.

ALIPRAND, JOAN M. 1993. Linkage in USMARC Bibliographic Records. Cataloging & Classification Quarterly. 1993; 16(1): 2-37. ISSN: 0163-9374.

ALLEN, BRYCE. 1993. Improved Browsable Displays: An Experimental Test. Information Technology and Libraries. 1993 June; 12(2): 203-209. ISSN: 0730-9295.

ANKENY, MELVON L. 1991. Evaluating End-User Services: Success or Satisfaction? Journal of Academic Librarianship. 1991; 16(6): 352-356. ISSN: 0099-1333.

BATES, MARCIA J. 1989. Rethinking Subject Cataloging in the Online Environment. Library Resources & Technical Services. 1989; 33(4): 401-412. ISSN: 0024-2527.

BATES, MARCIA J. 1991. OPAC Use and Users: Breaking Out of the Assumptions. In: Van Pulis, Noelle, ed. Think Tank on the Present and Future of the Online Catalog: Proceedings; 1991 January 11-12; Chicago, IL. Chicago, IL: Reference and Adult Services Division, American Library Association; 1991. 49-58. (Reference and Adult Services Division (RASD) Occasional Papers, Number 9). ISBN: 0-8389-7520-8.

BEATTY, SUE. 1992. Subject Enrichment Using Contents or Index Terms: The Australian Defence Force Academy Experience. In: Ra, Marsha, ed. Advances in Online Public Access Catalogs: Volume 1. Westport, CT: Meckler; 1992. 93-113. ISSN: 1063-2255; ISBN: 0-8873-6775-5.

BELKIN, NICHOLAS J.; CHANG, SHAN-JU; DOWNS, TRUDY; SARACEVIC, TEFKO; ZHAO, SHUYUAN. 1990. Taking Account of User Tasks, Goals and Behavior for the Design of Online Public Access Catalogs. In: Henderson, Diane, ed. ASIS '90: Information in the Year 2000: From Research to Applications: Proceedings of the American Society for Information Science (ASIS) 53rd Annual Meeting: Volume 27; 1990 November 4-8; Toronto, Canada. Medford, NJ: Learned Information for ASIS; 1990. 69-79. ISSN: 0044-7870; ISBN: 0-938734-48-2.

BERGER, MICHAEL G. 1992. The MELVYL System: The Next Five Years and Beyond. Information Technology and Libraries. 1992 June; 11(2): 146-157. ISSN: 0730-9295.

BIERBAUM, ESTHER GREEN. 1994. A Modest Proposal: No More Main Entry. American Libraries. 1994 January; 25: 81-84. ISSN: 0002-9769.

BRITISH LIBRARY. NATIONAL BIBLIOGRAPHIC SERVICE. 1993. Return of the Subject Headings. Select: Newsletter, National Bibliographic Service. 1993 Summer; 10: 5. ISSN: 0960-1570.

BROWNRIGG, EDWIN; BUTLER, BRETT. 1990. An Electronic Library Communications Format: A Definition and Development Proposal for MARC III. Library Hi Tech. 1990; 31(3): 21-26. ISSN: 0737-8831.

BRUNT, RODNEY M. 1985. In Defence of Bibliographic Standards. Aslib Proceedings. 1985 May; 37(4): 213-219. ISSN: 0001-253X.

BUCKLAND, MICHAEL K. 1992. Redesigning Library Services: A Manifesto. Chicago, IL: American Library Association; 1992. 82p. ISBN: 0-8389-0590-0.

BUCKLAND, MICHAEL K.; BUTLER, MARK H.; NORGARD, BARBARA A. 1992. OASIS: A Front-End for Prototyping Catalog Enhancements. Library Hi Tech. 1992; 10(4): 7-22. ISSN: 0737-8831.

BUCKLAND, MICHAEL K.; NORGARD, BARBARA A.; PLAUNT, CHRISTIAN. 1993. Filing, Filtering, and the First Few Found. Information Technology and Libraries. 1993 September; 12(3): 311-319. ISSN: 0730-9295.

BURBANK, RICHARD; HENIGMAN, BARBARA D. 1992. Music Symbols and Online Catalogs: A Survey of Vendors and an Assessment of Retrieval Capabilities. Information Technology and Libraries. 1992 September; 11(3): 203-209. ISSN: 0730-9295.

BUTCHER, ROGER. 1993. Multi-lingual OPAC Developments in the British Library. Program. 1993 April; 27(2): 165-171. ISSN: 0033-0337.

BYRNE, ALEX; MICCO, MARY. 1988. Improving OPAC Subject Access: The ADFA Experiment. College & Research Libraries. 1988 September; 49: 432-441. ISSN: 0010-0870.

CARSON, ELIZABETH. 1985. OPACs: The User and Subject Access. Canadian Library Journal. 1985 April; 42: 65-70. ISSN: 0008-4352.

CARSON, SYLVIA MACKINNON; FREIVALDS, DACE I. 1993. Z39.50 and LIAS: Penn State's Experience. Information Technology and Libraries. 1993 June; 12(2): 230-237. ISSN: 0730-9295.

CHERRY, JOAN M. 1992. Improving Subject Access in OPACs: An Exploratory Study of Conversion of Users' Queries. Journal of Academic Librarianship. 1992 May; 18(2): 95-99. ISSN: 0099-1333.

CONNELL, TSCHERA HARKNESS. 1991. Techniques to Improve Subject Retrieval in Online Catalogs. Information Technology and Libraries. 1991 June; 10(2): 87-98. ISSN: 0730-9295.

COUSINS, SHIRLEY ANNE. 1992. Enhancing Subject Access to OPACs: Controlled Vocabulary vs Natural Language. Journal of Documentation. 1992 September; 48(3): 291-309. ISSN: 0022-0418.

CRAWFORD, JOHN C.; POWLES, JOHN A. 1991. In-House (Locally Generated) Subject Indexes Mounted on Academic Library OPACs. Library Review. 1991; 40(1): 29-36. ISSN: 0024-2535.

CRAWFORD, JOHN C.; THOM, LINDA C.; POWLES, JOHN A. 1993. A Survey of Subject Access to Academic Library Catalogues in Great Britain. Journal of Librarianship and Information Science. 1993 June; 25(2): 85-93. ISSN: 0961-0006.

CRAWFORD, WALT. 1992. Starting Over: Current Issues in Online Catalog User Interface Design. Information Technology and Libraries. 1992 March; 11(1): 62-76. ISSN: 0730-9295.

CRAWFORD, WALT. 1993. The Future Online Catalog: A Single View of Multiple Databases. Information Technology and Libraries. 1993 June; 12(2): 253-254. ISSN: 0730-9295.

DALRYMPLE, PRUDENCE WARD; YOUNGER, JENNIFER. 1991. From Authority Control to Informed Retrieval: Framing the Expanded Domain of Subject Access. College & Research Libraries. 1991 March; 52: 139-149. ISSN: 0010-0870.

DELSEY, TOM. 1990. Retrospective Conversion in a Bilingual Context. IFLA Journal. 1990; 16(1): 46. ISSN: 0340-0352.

DEMPSEY, LORCAN. 1991. Publishers and Libraries: An All Through System for Bibliographic Data? International Cataloguing & Bibliographic Control. 1991 July/September; 20(3): 37-41. ISSN: 1011-8829.

DILLON, MARTIN; WENZEL, PATRICK. 1990. Retrieval Effectiveness of Enhanced Bibliographic Records. Library Hi Tech. 1990; 31(3): 43-46. ISSN: 0737-8831.

DWYER, JIM. 1991. Bibliographic Records Enhancement: From the Drawing Board to the Catalog Screen. Cataloging & Classification Quarterly. 1991; 13(3-4): 29-51. ISSN: 0163-9374.

FRANTZ, PAUL. 1990. A Gaping Black Hole in the Bibliographic Universe: In the Flurry to Explore Access Frontiers, Books Have Been Left Out; One Librarian Has a Plan for Getting at Those Chapters Lost in Space. American Libraries. 1990 July/August; 21: 632-633. ISSN: 0002-9769.

GRANT, WALLACE T.; JONES, DOROTHY E. 1993. The Three T's for a Talking Online Catalog: Technology, Teamwork, Teaching. Information Technology and Libraries. 1993 June; 12(2): 193-202. ISSN: 0730-9295.

HANCOCK-BEAULIEU, MICHELINE. 1990. Evaluating the Impact of an Online Library Catalogue on Subject Searching Behaviour at the Catalogue and at the Shelves. Journal of Documentation. 1990 December; 46(4): 318-338. ISSN: 0022-0418.

HILDRETH, CHARLES R. 1991. Advancing toward the E^3OPAC: The Imperative and the Path. In: Van Pulis, Noelle, ed. Think Tank on the Present and Future of the Online Catalog: Proceedings; 1991 January 11-12; Chicago, IL. Chicago, IL: Reference and Adult Services Division, American Library Association; 1991. 39-48. (Reference and Adult Services Division (RASD) Occasional Papers, Number 9). ISBN: 0-8389-7520-8.

HORNY, K. 1991. Cataloguing Simplification: Trends and Prospects. International Cataloguing & Bibliographic Control. 1991 April/June; 20: 25-28. ISSN: 1011-8829.

HUSAIN, SHABAHAT; O'BRIEN, ANN. 1992. Recent Trends in Subject Access to OPACs: An Evaluation. International Classification. 1992; 19: 140-145. ISSN: 0340-0050.

INTNER, SHEILA S. 1993. Enhancing OPACs. Technicalities. 1993 March; 13(3): 4-6. ISSN: 0272-0884.

JACKSON, PHILIP. 1991. A Thesaurus for Enhanced Geographic Access. LASIE, Library Automated System Information Exchange. 1991 November/December; 22(3): 49-60. ISSN: 0047-3774.

JAMIESON, R.C. 1992. Oriental Language Materials in Online Public Access Catalogues. In: Ra, Marsha, ed. Advances in Online Public Access Catalogs: Volume 1. Westport, CT: Meckler; 1992. 136-159. ISBN: 0-88736-775-5.

JEFFREYS, ALAN. 1993. AACR2 after 1978. In: Byford, John; Trickey, Keith V.; Woodhouse, Susi, eds. AACR, DDC, MARC and Friends: The Role of Catalogue and Indexing Group (CIG) in Bibliographic Control. London, England: Library Association; 1993. 49-60. ISBN: 1-85604-023-2.

KINSELLA, JANET. 1992. Classification and the OPAC. Catalogue & Index. 1992 Autumn/Winter; 105-106: 1-10. ISSN: 0008-7629.

KNUTSON, GUNNAR S. 1991. Subject Enhancement: Report on an Experiment. College & Research Libraries. 1991 January; 52(1): 65-79. ISSN: 0010-0870.

KNUTSON, GUNNAR S. 1993. The Year's Work in Descriptive Cataloging, 1992. Library Resources & Technical Services. 1993 July; 37(3): 261-275. ISSN: 0024-2527.

LANCASTER, F. W.; CONNELL, TSCHERA HARKNESS; BISHOP, NANCY; MCCOWAN, SHERRY. 1991. Identifying Barriers to Effective Subject

Access in Library Catalogs. Library Resources & Technical Services. 1991 April; 35(2): 377-391. ISSN: 0024-2527.

LARSON, RAY R. 1991a. Between Scylla and Charybdis: Subject Searching in the Online Catalog. In: Advances in Librarianship: Volume 15. San Diego, CA: Academic Press; 1991. 175-236. ISSN: 0065-2830; ISBN: 0-12-024615-5.

LARSON, RAY R. 1991b. Classification Clustering, Probabilistic Information Retrieval and the Online Catalog. Library Quarterly. 1991; 61(2): 133-173. ISSN: 0024-2519.

LARSON, RAY R. 1991c. The Decline of Subject Searching: Long-Term Trends and Patterns of Index Use in an Online Catalog. Journal of the American Society for Information Science. 1991; 42(3): 197-215. ISSN: 0002-8231.

LARSON, RAY R. 1992. Evaluation of Advanced Retrieval Techniques in an Experimental Online Catalog. Journal of the American Society for Information Science. 1992; 43(1): 34-53. ISSN: 0002-8231.

LE LOARER, PIERRE. 1993. OPAC: Opaque or Open, Public, Accessible and Co-operative? Some Developments in Natural Language Processing. Program. 1993 July; 27(3): 251-268. ISSN: 0033-0337.

LEWIS, PETER. 1993. AACR2: Policies and Politics in Catalogue Revision. In: Byford, John; Trickey, Keith V.; Woodhouse, Susi, eds. AACR, DDC, MARC and Friends: The Role of Catalogue and Indexing Group (CIG) in Bibliographic Control. London, England: Library Association; 1993. 33-47. ISBN: 1-85604-023-2.

LLORENS, JOSE; TRENOR, ASUNCION. 1993. MARC and Relational Databases. The Electronic Library. 1993 April; 11: 93-97. ISSN: 0264-0473.

MANDEL, CAROL A. 1987. Multiple Thesauri in Online Library Bibliographic Systems: A Report Prepared for Library of Congress Processing Services. Washington, DC: Cataloging Distribution Service, Library of Congress; 1987. 94p. ERIC: ED 291390; LC: 87-3997.

MARKEY, KAREN; DEMEYER, A. N. 1986. Dewey Decimal Classification Online Project: Evaluation of a Library Schedule and Index Integrated into the Subject Searching Capabilities of an Online Catalog: Final Report to the Council on Library Resources. Dublin, OH: OCLC; 1986. 520p. ERIC: ED 269021.

MATES, BARBARA T. 1991. Library Technology for Visually and Physically Impaired Patrons. Westport, CT: Meckler; 1991. 190p. ISBN: 0-88736-704-6.

MCGARRY, DOROTHY; SVENONIUS, ELAINE. 1991. More on Improved Browsable Displays for Online Subject Access. Information Technology and Libraries. 1991 September; 10(3): 185-191. ISSN: 0730-9295.

MICCO, MARY. 1991. The Next Generation of Online Public Access Catalogs: A New Look at Subject Access Using Hypermedia. In: Tyckoson, David A., ed. Enhancing Access to Information: Designing Catalogs for the 21st Century. New York, NY: Haworth Press; 1991. 103-132. ISBN: 1-56024-219-1.

MICHALAK, THOMAS J. 1990. An Experiment in Enhancing Catalog Records at Carnegie Mellon University. Library Hi Tech. 1990; 31(3): 33-40. ISSN: 0737-8831.

MISCHO, WILLIAM H.; COLE, TIMOTHY W. 1992. The Illinois Extended OPAC: Library Information Workstation Design and Development. In:

Ra, Marsha, ed. Advances in Online Public Access Catalogs: Volume 1. Westport, CT: Meckler; 1992. 38-57. ISBN: 0-88736-775-5.

NORGARD, BARBARA A.; BERGER, MICHAEL G.; BUCKLAND, MICHAEL K.; PLAUNT, CHRISTIAN. 1993. The Online Catalog: From Technical Services to Access Service. In: Advances in Librarianship: Volume 17. San Diego, CA: Academic Press; 1993. 111-148. ISSN: 0065-2830; ISBN: 0-12-024617-1.

O'BRIEN, ANN. 1990. Relevance as a Measure of Evaluation in OPACs. Journal of Information Science. 1990 August; 16(4): 265-271. ISSN: 0165-5515.

O'NEILL, EDWARD T. ; ROGERS, SALLY A.; OSKINS, W. MICHAEL. 1993. Characteristics of Duplicate Records in OCLC's Online Union Catalog. Library Resources & Technical Services. 1993 January; 37(1): 59-71. ISSN: 0024-2527.

PERUGINELLI, SUSANNA; BERGAMIN, GIOVANNI; AMMENDOLA, PINO. 1992. Character Sets: Towards a Standard Solution? Program. 1992 July; 26(3): 215-223. ISSN: 0033-0337.

PREECE, BARBARA G.; FOX, MARY ANN. 1992. Preliminary LC Records for Monographs in OCLC. Information Technology and Libraries. 1992 March; 11(1): 3-9. ISSN: 0730-9295.

ROLLAND-THOMAS, PAULE; MERCURE, GERARD. 1989. Subject Access in a Bilingual Online Catalogue. Cataloging & Classification Quarterly, 1989; 10(1-2): 141-163. ISSN: 0163-9374.

SIEGFRIED, SUSAN; BATES, MARCIA J.; WILDE, DEBORAH N. 1993. A Profile of End-User Searching Behavior by Humanities Scholars: The Getty Online Searching Project Report No. 2. Journal of the American Society for Information Science. 1993; 44(5): 273-291. ISSN: 0002-8231.

SLOAN, BERNARD G. 1991. Remote Access: Design Implications for the Online Catalog. In: Tyckoson, David A., ed. Enhancing Access to Information: Designing Catalogs for the 21st Century. New York, NY: Haworth Press; 1991. 133-140. ISBN: 1-56024-219-1.

STARR, DANIEL. 1993. Comparative Solutions: Responses to the Special Needs of the Museum Library OPAC. Art Documentation. 1993 Summer; 12: 52-54. ISSN: 0730-7187.

STUDWELL, WILLIAM E. 1990. Cataloging Forum: Subject Access Theory No. 11: Bilevel Headings: A Proposal to Modify the Architecture of LC Subject Headings. Technicalities. 1990 November; 10(11): 7-8. ISSN: 0272-0884.

TALLIM, PAULA. 1991. The Work of the BEDIS Committee in the UK. IFLA Journal. 1991; 17(3): 333-334. ISSN: 0340-0352.

TILLETT, BARBARA B., ed. 1989. Authority Control in the Online Environment: Considerations and Practices. New York, NY: Haworth Press; 1989. 169p. ISBN: 0-86656-871-9.

TILLETT, BARBARA B. 1991. A Taxonomy of Bibliographic Relationships. Library Resources & Technical Services. 1991 April; 35(2): 150-158. ISSN: 0024-2527.

TROLL, DENISE A.; RICHARDS, BARBARA GEISLER. 1992. From Vision to Reality: Implementing the Distributed Electronic Library. In: Shaw, Debora, ed. ASIS '92: Proceedings of the American Society for Information Science (ASIS) 55thAnnual Meeting: Volume 29; 1992 October 26-29; Pittsburgh,

PA. Medford, NJ: Learned Information for ASIS; 1992. 144-149. ISSN: 0044-7870; ISBN: 0-938734-69-5.

TROUTMAN, LESLIE A. 1992. The Online Public Access Catalog and Music Materials: Issues for System and Interface Design. In: Ra, Marsha, ed. Advances in Online Public Access Catalogs: Volume 1. Westport, CT: Meckler; 1992. 9-37. ISBN: 0-88736-775-5.

VAN ORDEN, RICHARD. 1990. Content-Enriched Access to Electronic Information: Summaries of Selected Research. Library Hi Tech. 1990; 31(3): 27-32. ISSN: 0737-8831.

VIZINE-GOETZ, DIANE. 1992. The Dewey Decimal Classification as an Online Classification Tool. In: Williamson, Nancy J.; Hudon, Michele, eds. Classification for Knowledge Representation and Organization: Proceedings of the 5th International Study Conference on Classification Research; 1991 June 24-28; Toronto, Canada. Amsterdam, The Netherlands: Elsevier; 1992. 373-380. ISBN: 0-444-89343-1.

WALKER, STEPHEN. 1988. Improving Subject Access Painlessly: Recent Work on the Okapi Online Catalogue Projects. Program. 1988 January; 22(1): 21-31. ISSN: 0033-0337.

WALKER, STEPHEN. 1991. Views on Classification as a Search Tool on a Computer. In: Computers in Libraries International; 1991 February 4-6; London, England. Westport, CT: Meckler; 1991. 131-139. ISBN: 0-88736-754-2.

WEINTRAUB, TAMARA S. 1992. The Dual-Thesaurus Catalog: MeSH and LCSH. Technicalities. 1992 December; 12(12): 10-12. ISSN: 0272-0884.

WILDEMUTH, BARBARA M.; DE BLIEK, RUTH; HE, SHAOYI; FRIEDMAN, CHARLES P. 1992. Search Moves Made by Novice End Users. In: Shaw, Debora, ed. ASIS '92: Proceedings of the American Society for Information Science (ASIS) 55th Annual Meeting: Volume 29; 1992 October 26-29; Pittsburgh, PA. Medford, NJ: Learned Information for ASIS; 1992. 154-161. ISSN: 0044-7870; ISBN: 0-938734-69-5.

WINKE, R. CONRAD. 1993. Discarding the Main Entry in an Online Cataloging Environment. Cataloging & Classification Quarterly. 1993; 16(1): 53-70. ISSN: 0163-9374.

7

Managing Information Systems in State and Local Government

PATRICIA D. FLETCHER and
DEBORAH OTIS FOY
University of Maryland, Baltimore County

INTRODUCTION

According to the U.S. Bureau of the Census, in 1992 there were 86,743 nonfederal governments in the United States: 50 state governments, 3,043 county governments, and the rest of the 83,649 being municipalities, townships, and special districts (see Table 1). In the past decade the services provided by these levels of government have increased while budgetary problems also increased. These services are extensive, wide ranging, and rapidly changing.

Information technologies, such as optical storage for data, shared databases, and the use of automated teller machines (ATM) for distribution of welfare or Veterans Administration (VA) benefits, have enabled states, counties, municipalities, and the like to meet these growing service needs without increasing the number of full-time government employees. According to two recent, large-scale research projects carried out by the School of Information Studies at Syracuse University, expenditures for information technologies and services, excluding personnel, at the state level of government were \$15.6 billion a year for fiscal year (FY) 1987 (CAUDLE ET AL., 1989) and at the county level were \$23.4 billion for FY 1991 (FLETCHER ET AL.). Given this substantial investment, it is important to track the patterns of procurement, use, and management of information technologies.

The last *ARIST* review of this literature was done by HEARLE in 1970. Since then there have been many and significant changes in the types and uses of information technologies in state and local govern-

Annual Review of Information Science and Technology (*ARIST*), Volume 29, 1994
Martha E. Williams, Editor
Published for the American Society for Information Science (ASIS)
By Learned Information, Inc., Medford, N.J.

Table 1

Number of Governmental Units: 1967–1992[a]

Type of government	1967	1972	1977	1982	1987	1992
Total	81,299	78,269	79,913	81,831	83,237	86,743
Federal	1	1	1	1	1	1
State	50	50	50	50	50	50
Local	81,248	78,218	79,862	81,780	83,186	86,692
County	3,049	3,044	3,042	3,041	3,042	3,043
Municipal	18,048	18,517	18,862	19,076	19,200	19,296
Township and town	17,105	16,991	16,822	16,734	16,691	16,666
School district	21,782	15,781	15,174	14,851	14,721	14,556
Special district	21,264	23,885	25,962	28,078	29,532	33,131

[a]Source: U.S. Department of Commerce, Bureau of the Census, 1992 Census of Governments.

ments. This review covers the literature from 1980 to 1993. For the most part the literature from the 1970s is excluded due to constraints on time and space. Because of the rapid advances in information technologies that were heralded by the personal computer in 1980 and the changes in the roles and service functions of state and local governments in the 1980s, it is more useful to concentrate on the events of the 1980s and early 1990s. This gives the most current picture of the use of information technologies while at the same time conveying a sense of the development of information technologies and their use and management in state and local governments. The focus is limited to the management of information systems and does not cover the associated policy issues.

We begin with a brief description of public-sector organizations to provide context. The history of information technology use in state and local governments is given to provide a framework. Information technologies include computer hardware and software, voice, data, and video communications devices, and investments in providing library and records management services. A well-developed picture of the current state of the management and use of information technology is also given to show how these technologies are being used to respond to the growing service responsibilities of state and local governments. That overview is also informative for indicating future trends and issues. Finally, we present these topical issues as they relate to information professionals working in state and local governments. These professionals can and should play a leadership role in the management and use of information technologies in their jurisdictions.

PUBLIC-SECTOR ORGANIZATIONS

This section gives a brief review of literature that describes the roles and constraints associated with public organizations. An understanding of the nature of "public" will benefit the reader in the technology sections of this review.

The Nature of Being Public

The similarities and differences between public and private organizations have been the object of much research and deliberation. The main concern over differences/similarities is how management practice affects these two sectors. Critical reviews of the research literature have been done by BOZEMAN, PERRY & RAINEY, and RAINEY ET AL., who make clear that there is no consensus about similarities or differences between public and private sectors. It is agreed that differences do exist and affect management practice. As OSBORNE & GAEBLER assert, there are fundamental differences between the management of government and the management of a business.

A study by CAUDLE ET AL. (1991) found some essential similarities and differences between public-sector and private-sector managers' perceptions of key information systems issues. Important in their findings was the fact that in the public sector, the strategies used to develop information technologies come from middle, not top, management. Political appointees are less likely to initiate new technology development. In another study, BRETSCHNEIDER & WITTMER found that public-sector organizations had a larger investment in information technology than their private-sector counterparts. The information-intensive nature of government, coupled with the need to supplement scarce human resources, might explain this disparity. What the research does show is that any assumptions about public-sector and private-sector similarities or differences will drive the way an organization develops its information technologies. If it is believed that there is no difference, as is commonly held, then generic systems applications, such as finance or personnel systems, can and have been introduced into organizations regardless of sector. Unfortunately, the differences between the public and private sectors make this type of system development disastrous. There are fundamental differences in accountability and decision making that affect what information is collected and where and how it is disseminated. Awareness and understanding of differences are necessary to successfully carry out the management activities and development of information technologies in public organizations.

BOZEMAN & STRAUSSMAN have developed an argument for public/private differences by articulating the notion of political authority. Political authority is instantiated in official policy actions and in government itself. The Constitution, regulations and statutes, elected officials, interest groups, and citizens' belief in the legitimacy of government represent both tangible and symbolic aspects of political authority. Political authority is a dynamic context that changes with elections, new legislation, policy shifts, and public sentiment. As such, it becomes a set of constraints at a given point in time that limits public managers in their ability to develop long-term plans for the use of information technologies. The private sector is not constrained in this manner and can develop more flexible and strategic uses of information technology (BOZEMAN & STRAUSSMAN).

These constraints affect how and what services are provided and the role of information technologies in the administration and delivery of services. BOZEMAN & BRETSCHNEIDER developed the concept of a public management information system (PMIS) to highlight the importance of sector differences for managing information. Their notion of a PMIS takes into account the effects of the constraints imposed on public managers by political authority, time compression, public personnel systems, and public decision making.

State-Level Governments

In the 1980s, state governments experienced a significant and unpredictable shift in their responsibilities (GONA). It was expected that Ronald Reagan's New Federalism would result in the states' taking a "back seat," with the federal government taking the lead in setting policy and being responsible for policy implementation. The growing federal budget deficit made this expectation unrealistic, and the deficit became a main driver of the new directions for state governments. State legislatures were forced to assume greater policy and service initiatives for critical and visible issues such as health care, education, economic development, environmental protection, and social service delivery (JONES). Federal funding declined markedly in the 1980s, but the mandates for service did not. This impelled state governments to take more innovative, entrepreneurial, and pragmatic approaches to policy and implementation.

Fiscal conditions in state governments were actually promising in the 1980s (GONA). During the mid-1980s, the states actually had a 51% increase in general fund expenditures, and a 62% increase in state aid to local governments. But the stock market crash of 1987 and the federal Tax Reform Act of 1986, coupled with depressed local economies and continued growth in state expenditures, have led to a more dismal fiscal picture for the 1990s. GONA reports that serious budget problems will be facing more than half the state governments in the 1990s. This leaves the success of earlier state-level innovations and programs in some jeopardy because the necessary long-term financial support for these new programs cannot be guaranteed.

A 1988 survey by the Council of State Governments detailed the major issues and challenges that were facing states at that time (GONA): education, economic development, the environment, human services, health care, and crime and corrections. While state officials believed that they had and could satisfactorily address some or many of these issues, there was general pessimism about state revenue shortages and instability as well as the growing impact of the federal deficit.

Local-Level Governments

The 1980s proved to be equally if not more difficult for local governments, especially county governments, the main administrative division of states. County governments have become more important because of the demographic shift from urban growth to suburban and rural growth. This has created an increased role in delivery of direct citizen services and new roles and duties inherited from state government (MARANDO & REEVES; MENZEL ET AL.; SCHNEIDER & PARK). The diversity of local governments in size, form, location, population, and roles and responsibilities makes them a hard target for study. This is compounded at the local level by the many governing jurisdictions, such as counties, municipalities, school districts, townships, and special districts, which are stacked on top of one another, with blurred or disputed lines of authority (HERBERS).

Issues that are important to city and county administrators determine their resource allocations and uses of information technologies. A recent study by the INTERNATIONAL CITY MANAGEMENT ASSOCIATION (1990) (ICMA) defined the trends that will be driving city and county government in the future (PAUL): an aging population, a work-force shortage, cultural diversity, the shift to a service-based and information-based economy, data management, access and dissemination, an old and inadequate infrastructure, a dysfunctional criminal justice system, and education and health systems that no longer respond to citizen needs. These issues are corroborated by HERBERS and by THOMAS.

The Importance of Public-Sector Studies

According to CLEVELAND, government and information are synonymous. He states that the raw material of government is information and the product of government is transformed information. The report of the National Performance Review (GORE) underscores the importance of information in government organizations. One of the action items in the report focuses on private-sector partnering with federal, state, and local governments to create a National Spatial Data Infrastructure (NSDI). The NSDI will integrate into a single digital resource that is widely available with environmental, geophysical, land use, and transportation data that are currently collected by dozens of agencies. These data are not only of use to government agencies but have commercial value as well. Funding from the private sector is expected to finance a minimum of 50% of the cost of collecting, storing, and disseminating these data.

The idea of electronic government, i.e., the provision of government services using computer and telecommunications technology, is recognized as the next wave of service delivery by both the National Performance Review and the 1993 report from the Office of Technology Assessment (OTA) (U.S. CONGRESS. OFFICE OF TECHNOLOGY ASSESSMENT). In the GORE report it is recommended that a one-stop "800" calling service be developed and integrated with service delivery "kiosks" and government bulletin boards as a means of efficient and easy access to government services by the public. The OTA report develops the necessary link among the levels of government, using information technologies to provide citizen access to services.

The information technologies themselves are ubiquitous to government, and computers are a standard and accepted office tool (ALTER; BOZEMAN & BRETSCHNEIDER; BRETSCHNEIDER; KRAEMER & KING; NORRIS, 1989; NORTHROP ET AL.). Although automation of routine functions is the most common application, sophisticated and integrated applications that link citizens to services, provide intradepartmental data, and assist with environmental concerns are also being implemented. Management strategies range from use of the budget to control spending to extensive and strategic information resource management (IRM) plans. We can no longer talk about "when government is automated"; we are now at the next level of automated government, moving toward an integration of services and functions across governments via information technologies (NATIONAL ACADEMY OF PUBLIC ADMINISTRATION).

HISTORY OF INFORMATION-TECHNOLOGY MANAGEMENT

A look at the literature over the past 14 years, and taking into account the 1970 *ARIST* review by HEARLE, shows a consistent pattern of development, implementation, and use of information technologies in state and local governments. This pattern is not unlike that in the private sector, although in government it developed much later. The data presented here come primarily from four major national studies of information technology use at the state and local levels and have been substantiated by smaller, more regional or technology-specific research. At the state level, the data come from a national study of IRM conducted by the School of Information Studies at Syracuse University (CAUDLE ET AL., 1989). At the county level, the data are from a national study of information technology management, again done by the School of Information Studies at Syracuse University (FLETCHER ET AL.). The city-level studies were done by the Public Policy Research Organization at the University of California, Irvine's Urban Information Systems (URBIS) Group (KRAEMER & KING).

Development of the Information-Technology Architecture

The acquisition of computer hardware and software has been similar at all levels of government. One of the most striking variables influencing technology investment is size of the jurisdiction: large jurisdictions invest earlier and in greater quantities than smaller ones (CAUDLE ET AL., 1989; FLETCHER ET AL.; KING & KRAEMER; NORRIS, 1984). Large jurisdictions have more computers overall, and very large jurisdictions make extensive use of mainframes while small jurisdictions make extensive use of personal computers (PCs). The type of technology adopted is similar throughout state and local governments, generally being mainframes that run finance and budget applications.

Data obtained from the four studies above show that the earliest adoption of information technology by a state was in 1962, with most states reporting adoption by the early 1980s. By 1969, 7.4% of county governments had at least one computer; by 1975, 59% had computers; by 1985, 97.5% of counties reported having at least one computer. In 1976, large cities (populations more than 50,000) had an average of 2.64 computers per city (including mainframes and minicomputers). It was not until 1983 that small local governments reached a 53.3% rate of adoption.

These dates show that public-sector organizations were slow to adopt the technology. The ENIAC mainframe computer was built in 1946, UNIVAC I was installed in 1951, and in 1964 IBM Corp. introduced the System/360 computer. The minicomputer was introduced in 1965 by

Digital Equipment Corp., but it was not until the mid-1970s that state and local governments began using this second wave of technology. The PC was introduced by IBM in 1981 and had been picked up by most public-sector organizations by the mid-1980s. It enabled many smaller public organizations to enter the computing age.

The number of large (2.5–10 MIPS (million instructions per second)) and very large (10+ MIPS) computers in state government remained relatively stable in the 1980s. Increases in computer hardware investments occurred in the medium-sized to small-sized computers and in minicomputers and PCs. In 1988 there were at least 197,300 PCs in state governments, a 16.7% increase over 1987. This growth continued through the 1980s.

The early applications by state and local governments concerned fiscal, personnel, and property matters. Nearly one-half of the large-sized city computer applications in 1976 were for budget and finance. While smaller jurisdictions adopted later, they too started with financial management applications, processes that are routine and easy to automate. The development of multifunctional information systems that would share data across departments and agencies did not catch on in the 1980s. While state and local governments expressed an interest in these systems, the development of comprehensive, integrated systems that serve many related areas has not occurred. Issues of data ownership and sharing may be an impediment. In general, most state and local applications through the 1980s focused on building large central databases, process control systems, and housekeeping applications.

A major federal funding initiative, during the Nixon administration, in the middle 1970s led to a dramatic increase in criminal justice applications in city and county governments. The Law Enforcement Assistance Administration allocated as much as $50 million annually to assist in the automation of local police jurisdictions through development of information systems.

An area in state government that grew enormously in the 1970s and 1980s was legislative information technology. In 1977 there were seven state government legislative systems, primarily focused on bill tracking and fiscal tracking applications. By the late 1980s, there were at least 30 state legislative systems, a fourfold increase in one decade (NEWKIRK). Along with this growth came a change in the end users. In the 1970s legislative members were twice removed from the legislative systems: the data processing people and the bill status information or bill typists stood between them and the data. Now the members bring computer skills and expectations with them to the state capitals and help support the development of new applications. As the legislative systems grow in size and complexity, the members are confronted with the same management issues that flourish in the executive branch. The question of access to legislative systems is important, as is the concern for access to executive agency databases. The issue of centralized vs. decentralized technology management is also rearing its head. While end users are becoming more sophisticated in their use of the information technologies, the technologies are becoming more complex. Geographic information systems (GIS), networks, the merging of voice, data, and video all require a high level of maintenance that the members may not be able to perform. Legislatures in the 1990s will be tackling these problems and questions as information systems become a basic management tool.

Development of the Management Function

As with the adoption of information technologies, the corresponding management functions developed along very similar lines in state and local governments through the mid-1980s. The initial adoption of large mainframe computers facilitated centralized management control. At first this central control was housed in the finance or taxation departments or in the office of the clerk, all heavy users of financial data. The type of technology and the first-used application led to a dominant framework of centralization.

This was quickly followed by the emergence of a new centralized control function—the data processing department (GURWITT, 1992). At first there was a need for technical expertise to run these novel and complex systems. While it made sense to centralize the control over the early systems, problems quickly grew in state and local governments as a result of the emerging "mainframe priesthood." The data processing departments jealously guarded their territory and made it difficult for other departments and agencies to get their information needs met. After a time, this rigid control worked against the goals of the governments, sustaining data processing fiefdoms that had no idea what went on in their organizations.

With the beginning use of networked minicomputers and microcomputers, and the growing investment in PCs in the mid-1980s, the data processing kingdom began to crumble. End-user departments bought and ran their own PC-based systems and realized initial savings of time and money. This freedom from centralized data processing seemed to be all to the good, but it had and continues to have some serious negative implications (FLETCHER & BERTOT). Departmental systems grew without consideration for organizational needs. Many systems were redundant. Organizations did not know who collected what data and even what data were available at any given time. The individual systems were developed to meet individual needs and reflected individual information-processing biases and preferences; hence, the systems could not interact with each other. Control, standardization, and interoperability went by the wayside. Massive inefficiencies began to emerge as organizations belatedly realized in the early 1990s that they had lost control over their information.

End-user computing with PCs and networks did, however, bring many benefits. Applications for the nonfinance arena began to emerge, data were more accessible, and the data processing function redefined its role, moving from controller to enabler. In order to survive, data processing departments had to become more customer-focused, more attuned to the departmental needs of their organizations. Help desks and hotlines were developed, quality team approaches emerged, and the data processing department, in order to reflect its new image, changed its name to Information Services Department, Information Resources Management, Computer and Information Support Services, and the like (CAUDLE ET AL., 1989; FLETCHER & BERTOT; GURWITT, 1992).

CURRENT INFORMATION TECHNOLOGIES

This section focuses on technology applications and management strategies currently in place in state and local governments. The data range from the statistical variety to theoretical musings on information management practices. While the hardware, applications, and the development of information technology have remained similar in state and local governments, the management of these technologies has differed. Therefore, we present the current picture by level of government to show the management distinctions. Unless otherwise noted, the data come from the two Syracuse studies and the URBIS studies.

The State Government Arena

Information architectures. Today in state government we can find mainframes, minicomputers, and PCs in networked and stand-alone configurations. Budget projections based on 1987 data predicted that states would spend more than $20 billion in 1989 for nonpersonnel information resources for the executive branch of state government (THURMAIER). Using the calculations with a biennial percentage adjustment, approximately $52 billion was spent in 1993. The money is being spent on stand-alone and networked PC purchases and is still increasing. Over half of the operating environments in state government are completely interactive, a change reflecting the impact of end-user computing. This is especially true for criminal justice systems in states. Trends in state expenditures indicate that the adoption of new technologies, the upgrading and replacement of hardware, and networking are where the bulk of the information budget is going (NATIONAL ASSOCIATION OF STATE INFORMATION RESOURCE EXECUTIVES (NASIRE)).

The applications arena shows considerable change from the 1980s. Seventy-three percent of state governments developed some multi-agency information system between 1989 and 1991 (NATIONAL ASSOCIATION OF STATE INFORMATION RESOURCE EXECUTIVES)); most of these are in the areas of human services, health, and welfare. The next most common multi-agency applications are in statewide accounting systems and personnel systems.

Although no one type of innovative application can be discerned from the state data, an overall theme of providing better services to the public through information technology is evident. Innovations are occurring typically in image technology, optical disc storage, and citizen access systems. Some routine functions have been the recipients of innovations to solve work flow problems, slow response time to the public, and red tape burdens. Massachusetts used information technology to lower its Medicaid costs, gain control over the paperwork burden, and better and more efficiently meet client needs. According to the NATIONAL ASSOCIATION OF STATE INFORMATION RESOURCE EXECUTIVES report, the Medicaid costs in Massachusetts had become an uncontrollable fiscal burden that contributed significantly to the state's bond fiscal crisis. The recipients and service providers involved in the Medicaid system found it unmanageable and nightmarish in proportion. The state responded with the development of the Medicaid Recipient Eligibility Verification System to assist in containing costs while providing faster and more accessible service to clients. Kansas has an operational state-of-the-art information system integrating all data from the Office of Vital Statistics, e.g., births, deaths, marriages, and divorces, resulting in reduced system errors, faster response times, and more efficient use of data. Optical storage technology has featured strongly in innovative developments (NATIONAL ASSOCIATION OF STATE INFORMATION RESOURCE EXECUTIVES).

Executive Information Systems (EIS) are also beginning to appear in state government. The New York State Office of General Services began to develop an EIS in 1988 to help provide economical, efficient, effective, and relevant data in a proactive manner (MOHAN ET AL.). The EIS is implemented on a PC with a network to the office's mainframe for data access. A modular development using prototyping techniques and the support of top management were critical success factors for this project. The EIS can provide factual reports with historical data, identify problem areas in the budget, track down the real sources of problems, compare the performances of different office units under their budgetary control, and provide data projections to help detect possible problems before they actually occur. The ease of use of the EIS, low development and implementation costs, and time savings for the users are good reasons for adopting EIS technology in the public sector.

Information management. Even more remarkable than the changes in the types and uses of technologies at the state level is the development of management strategies to maintain them. State governments in the 1980s actively developed and used information resource management (IRM) concepts and practices (CAUDLE ET AL., 1989). Here the state data processing directors played a pivotal role. CAUDLE (1990) characterizes IRM by four measures: (1) the existence of central direction and mandates for an IRM program; (2) a well-structured planning process to identify the mission of the organization; (3) a formal IRM organization to carry out the IRM initiatives; and (4) a formal process for policy development to ensure systems interoperability and organizational information sharing. According to Caudle the main functions of the state-level IRM are centered around planning and budgeting for information resources, policy administration, providing end-user support services, systems operations services, information systems development and maintenance, procurement, and the central coordination and oversight of all agency information systems and resources. This is different from the IRM practices at the federal level. There IRM was mandated by the Paperwork Reduction Act of 1980 and operationalized in Circular A-130 by the Office of Management and Budget (1985). While these espoused the value of information as a resource to government and the necessity for information to flow unimpeded from government to citizen and back, CAUDLE (1988) found that IRM in practice has not become diffused across federal agencies and within federal agencies. Technology management is the dominant paradigm, and management of the information resources and the management processes themselves have not been adopted.

This is not the case, however, in state government. What started out as a data processing function has evolved in a managed and cooperative effort as the directors of the data processing departments began the transition from being technicians to information professionals. They formed their original professional organization in 1969, the National Association for State Information Systems. In 1989, the membership voted to implement a major organizational change, becoming the National Association of State Information Resource Executives. Today this group is composed of information executives and managers from all 50 states, the District of Columbia, and six U.S. territories. The goals of NASIRE are to share information across jurisdictions, to formulate state information policy, and to provide a forum for senior IRM managers to address opportunities and problems relating to information systems (RUFFIN).

The IRM organization that exists today in state government reflects the success of NASIRE in reaching its goals. Data from the 1990-1991

NASIRE report (NATIONAL ASSOCIATION OF STATE INFORMATION RESOURCE EXECUTIVES) describe the current management configuration in state governments; only three states could not list a single person who was responsible for statewide computer services (California, New York, and Michigan). In the other 47 states, this function has been centralized under a career professional. Today 88% of the states also have a central policy agency for IRM, a considerable change over the former lack of policy and numerous independent operational structures. Most of these policy agencies are less than 20 years old; the bulk of them were formed between 1969–1972 and 1981–1990. These policy bodies have clout, 44% of them being regulatory. Another IRM-related development is the inclusion of the telecommunications function under the central state data processing agency; 27 states have made this change since 1984.

Data centers are the main operating organizations in the states. Forty-nine states have at least one data center with an annual budget of at least $5 million (Vermont being the exception). Not content to rest on their laurels, since 1989, 21 states have already reorganized their IRM operations to better control costs, coordinate policy, and increase accountability, efficiency and effectiveness. The functions for which the central IRM organizations are responsible are wide ranging and more extensive and strategic than were those of the former data processing organization. IRM organizations are involved in long-range IRM policy and planning, systems development, budgeting for data processing, database management, training, providing strategic direction to state agencies, operating data centers, providing technical assistance and training to state agencies, and database management activities.

A further point on this role for IRM can be seen in the increase and sophistication of state-level technology plans. These formal planning documents provide short- and long-term IRM direction for state agencies. Notable among these are the Information Technology Master Plan (KANSAS), the State Strategic Plan for IRM (FLORIDA. INFORMATION RESOURCE COMMISSION), Government Data Practices Act (MINNESOTA) and Basic Principles of IRM (UTAH). Their breadth and depth are exemplary. They not only set out the strategic goals for IRM but operationalize these goals in a way that can be measured. There are many other well-developed plans that reflect a commitment to IRM in state government.

What we have at the state level is a well-structured and top-level commitment to maximizing the investments in information technologies. Centralized management and policy development are the norm. Merging the islands of information (computers, telecommunications, records management activities) with the information technology management functions (budgeting, planning, control, and personnel) is the key to state management of its information technologies.

The Local Government Arena

The data for this section come primarily from the Syracuse study of county governments (FLETCHER ET AL.). Literature on current information technology installations and management practices in city governments is nearly nonexistent. There have been no wide-scale, national studies of information technology in city governments since the URBIS studies in the mid-1980s (KRAEMER & KING).

Information architectures. In county governments, mainframes, minicomputers, and PCs are evident across jurisdictions of all sizes. Even small counties (population of fewer than 100,000) have at least one mainframe. Large and very large counties have at least one stand-alone minicomputer, two mainframe computers, and three networked minicomputers. PCs and portables are also used regardless of population size. Portables are now coming into use. County departments are also purchasing and maintaining their own minicomputers and PCs. In general, however, host-centered and local-area network (LAN)-centered networks are owned and operated by the central information system department. This makes sense given the complexity of network management and the high level of skills needed to maintain a network.

The development of software programs for in-house applications is still the norm in county governments; off-the-shelf applications account for only 23% of all software used.

The types of applications already in place in county governments are beginning to reflect a growing interest in providing better citizen services. Voice communications, networking, end-user devices, and communication technologies and services are already in place in more than 50% of all U.S. counties. LANs, WANs, e-mail, fax, and cellular phones are making considerable inroads, helping employees to work faster, and to work in remote locations. An added benefit of electronic networks is a reduction in vehicle traffic congestion. The technologies are also important in geographically large counties, where departments are spread out, and in rural counties.

Municipalities are also experiencing similar trends in the uses of their information technologies. KRAEMER & NORRIS found that there is a shift towards the use of networked PCs in all city governments, regardless of size. While cities have historically used information technology in a limited sense, i.e., for the management of routine data functions, there is an indication that the applications are becoming more external and citizen-focused in the 1990s. There is evidence that municipalities are developing applications such as 24-hour city halls, public conferencing networks, information kiosks, and electronic bill payment systems. The authors also noted a trend toward interconnectivity between municipalities and other governmental and educational institutions, businesses, and industry.

While citizen interaction technologies are currently in place in about 12% of all counties, another 40% plan to obtain these in the next three to five years. Document management technologies reflect the area of most interest for new development for most all counties. Hand-held technologies are also of interest to county governments, which fits in with the need to collect data efficiently at the many field locations that county departments maintain. Departmental desktop publishing is also becoming popular. Its eventual adoption will mean an organizational change for counties, perhaps eliminating a need for central print shops. Multi-agency applications however are not currently a mainstay of county systems. If these do have any impact, it will most likely be seen first in the courts and criminal justice areas.

Information management. While centralization of the information systems operations is the norm, the use of an IRM process to guide it is notably nonexistent in county governments. Further, there is no move to consolidate the various information islands (e.g., data processing, telecommunications, printing, records, and reprographic functions). Most county governments have separate and independent departments for information systems, telecommunications, printing, reprographics, and the like; there is little communication among them and no evidence of plans to coordinate or consolidate them in the near future. Wake County, N.C., Metro-Dade County, Fla., and Larimer County, Colo. are exceptions. In Larimer County, the inclusion of all information functions under one information systems department has proved to be a successful management approach.

The directors of the information systems departments are more involved in operations development and maintenance than in long -range planning or policy development. Strategic plans have been few in number, and polices governing information systems management, use, access, and the information contained in them have not been common. If plans did exist, they were usually one-year and were often tied to the budgets. Los Angeles County, Calif., was an exception, with county executive orders directing the management of information and information technologies.

There have been some novel management structures in place, however, which detailed how different counties structured their information systems departments. One emerging trend is an enterprise approach wherein the information systems department must compete with other vendors for the business of county departments. Their operating budget is derived from fees for service to customers, with a net county cost of zero. This organizational structure is used to increase efficiencies in operations.

Total quality management is also taking hold in county information systems departments in response to the problems created by the data processing fiefdoms. This approach uses work teams comprised of end users, administrators, and information experts to develop, implement, and maintain departmental information systems. It is seen as a better way to provide information for running the county's business and has been successful in Wake County, N.C. ROSENBAUM offers a particularly cogent picture of this management response currently under way in Hennepin County, Minn. The experiences of this county are not unlike what many others are going through in the 1990s.

Outsourcing of the information systems function is an alternative management approach. The practice of contracting out the information technology operation to an outside company that specializes in the development, implementation, and maintenance of information technology is referred to as outsourcing (KEEN). It is generally used to reduce in-house operating costs associated with the information technology function. It is also seen as an efficient way to keep current with the new developments in information technology without having to hire and continuously train information professionals within an organization. Outsourcing can range from contracting out routine data processing transactions to having a private company actually manage the computer facilities. If done well, it results in substantial savings, gives the county access to the latest information technologies, enables it to use computer hardware without buying it, and provides a steady stream of trained, up-to-date information professionals. Prince George's County, Md., is in its third five-year cycle of outsourcing and has realized the above-mentioned benefits. The problem with outsourcing in government organizations lies in the loss of control over one's information systems and information, not an easy hurdle to overcome. Constraints such as civil service, electoral cycles, and annual budget appropriations hinder the use of outsourcing for government.

Although most counties have not adopted IRM approaches, they do not seem to suffer as a result. Rather, they adopt management structures that are relevant to their own jurisdictions. The information systems departments remain the centralized function for mainframe and minicomputer operations and for the implementation of hardware and software standards in the county. There is no corresponding high-level involvement at the state level (FLETCHER & BERTOT).

Special Issues in Information Technology

Along with looking at current information technology according to government level, research and the literature suggest that it can also be examined by topic. There are a few special topic areas where there is consensus about the importance of information technology applications across levels of government. We briefly describe these areas and their potential impact on government organizations.

Geographic information systems (GIS). In the past decade, GIS has emerged as one of the most talked about, and experimented with, information technologies across all levels of government (ROCHELEAU). The combination of database management systems (DBMSs) and computerized mapping is very powerful for government. Spatial information accounts for at least two-thirds of all government information (FELLEMAN). Optimally uses for GIS cut across departmental domains and include decision support, public works, parks and recreation, code enforcement, environmental enforcement, and fire departments.

GIS technology digitizes data that is traditionally stored on maps, tables, charts, or microfiche. Specifically, it stores and organizes spatial information in electronic databases and in geographic images that are computerized models of land area, water, and space. GIS databases house statistics on crime, weather, disasters, infrastructure, permits, and buildings. These statistics are electronically linked to geographic images of specific spatial locations. Examples of digital data stored on GIS are city or county street maps, local parcel maps, demographic data, survey control data, and address-related data.

State and local governments use GIS technology to update critical statistics and geographic images and to analyze "what-if" scenarios, particularly those involving potential disasters and a response. GIS technology reduces the need to update necessary government information stored on several different maps or charts in different locations. GIS also reduces the potential for errors in recording and updating statistics and graphics. Although state and local governments spend considerable money for GIS startup, they believe that the long-term benefits outweigh the initial cost. Most of the money goes for the implementation phase—i.e., digitizing large amounts of data and training personnel (THOMPSON, 1989).

Other important issues for state and local governments interested in GIS technology are measurement standards and quality control, especially in merging data from several locations into a common database; spatial accuracy and appropriate scales must be used. Other related issues, though not discussed here, include privacy, turf, and the importance of GIS to local political agendas.

The state and local uses of GIS technology have grown increasingly sophisticated over the past decade. A common and crucial theme that emerges is the role of planning. A successful GIS takes many years to develop; interdepartmental cooperation and communication as well as legislative oversight are critical success factors; unsuccessful ones come and go. Wisconsin developed and implemented a statewide program to modernize state land information systems (NEIMANN ET AL.). The enabling legislation for this program is the result of more than 20 years of work among local, state, and federal agencies, the state university system, the private sector, and professional associations. Given the large amounts of money the state expected to pay to maintain old land systems ($140 million per year), the development of a GIS was seen as the only possible solution to accommodate the growing land data needs and uses.

The GIS program in Clark County, Nev., began in 1980 as part of a comprehensive planning effort. Clark County experienced rapid and large population growth, and the existing systems could not keep up with the needs of the taxation, public works, fire, and police departments. The GIS Management Office was developed to coordinate and maintain GIS efforts across county departments. County administrators believe that the GIS has already paid for itself. In one instance, it discovered that a local developer was not being assessed for more than $14 million of beach front property, a considerable cost recovery for the county. The County Assessor noted that without the GIS, his office could not keep up with the information required to track more than 20,000 new land parcels a year (FLETCHER ET AL.).

As with other new technologies, along with the expected cost efficiencies comes an emphasis on quality, which ultimately leads to better citizen services (FORESMAN & FAIN). GIS is an innovative technology for state and local governments that is gaining confidence, exposure, and momentum in its varied uses and applications.

Records management. State, county, and municipal governments are also interested in using innovative technologies to help organize the voluminous amounts of data they must collect and store. Records management at the state and local levels is concerned with maintaining and providing documents to state and local officials and citizens accurately and in a timely manner (FLETCHER, 1990a). Imaging technology, which involves scanning documents into digitized images and storing them on computer for later retrieval, allows documents to be retrieved quickly, maintains accuracy, and uses minimal storage space.

The use of innovative and efficient imaging systems for records management does not reflect the role of records management in government. The Syracuse Studies (CAUDLE ET AL., 1989; FLETCHER ET AL.) made clear that while records management is a mandated and well-developed function in state governments, little attention is given to it at the local level. State governments are well organized to control their documents via centralized and agency-level requirements for records development, retention, and disposal. This level of organization rarely is found in local governments.

A related component to records management is records dissemination. There are great differences in how the states and local governments disseminate records. All 50 states have a central agency that provides document services to state employees, officials, and the public. State library agencies maintain state government documents: legislative reference works, state history and genealogy, state archives, and law library documents. The state library agencies also develop programs and policies to meet the information needs of the public. Local government documents rarely receive this kind of attention from any local agency (FLETCHER, 1990b).

About 60% of public libraries collect local documents, but these are often confused with local history materials, which may not be the same. This number has been constant for more than a decade, reflecting the lack of awareness of the importance of local government records collections (CASTONGUAY). The collections that do exist tend to be small, (500 documents or fewer), generally in paper form, and go back 6–25 years. Such collections clearly do not represent the totality of local government documents available.

A team from Syracuse conducted case studies in 13 county governments across the United States and found that all mentioned that they were interested in using imaging technology to improve records management (FLETCHER ET AL.). Using an attitudinal rating scale, county program managers indicated that document management technologies are "very important" to their delivery of services and administration of government. The ability to scan documents and store them on optical discs was viewed as a way to save time and space. Image technology can also solve the massive "paper problem" in government. Vast amounts of space are currently required to house government documents that might be stored on CD-ROM discs or other optical media that take very little office space.

RICHTER (1992) mentions the paper burden that state and local governments face in an age of electronic communication. Storage facilities for paper documents are being exhausted, yet these documents are critical because they track the lives of Americans from birth, through marriage, divorce, death, wills, and everything in between. They also are the legal memory of government organizations, formalizing statutes and legislation, decisions, policy, and operating procedures.

THOMPSON (1990) investigated the use of imaging technology in Autauga County, Ala. He found that although the technology raised legal concerns, it did improve efficiency and delivery of services. Autauga County uses an image processing system to store paper documents such as deeds, birth certificates, and wills on optical disc. The county recognizes concerns about the legal status of documents generated by the imaging system but believes this issue can be addressed with standards.

Delaware has implemented an imaging system for the Division of Corporations. It enables 80 employees to take advantage of workstation-based image flow across locations within the agency. Using remote compatible systems, and PC or fax machines, external authorized users can also access the data (NATIONAL ASSOCIATION OF STATE INFORMATION RESOURCE EXECUTIVES).

A 1988 report (NEW YORK. STATE ARCHIVES AND RECORDS ADMINISTRATION) describes an executive order requiring state agencies to develop records management improvement plans and retention schedules for all records, including machine-readable records. One objective of this order was to ensure that state government programs and operations are adequately documented for legal, fiscal, administrative, and historical purposes. Another objective was to enhance the ability of state agencies to manage and preserve records created with modern information technologies in a format that will be usable and will minimize storage problems.

As with GIS technology, standards and legal issues come into play when image technology is adopted. In Los Angeles County, Calif., an interim policy on imaging standards was issued in 1991 to head off compatibility and use problems. This policy requires the use of an ANSI Structured Query Language DBMS for image indexing, the use of a standard Windows environment, and a Logical Unit 6.2, Open Systems Interconnection, or Transmission Control Protocol for communications integrity.

Citizen public access technologies. The use of information technology to promote access to government information and services is becoming more popular in state and local governments. In many cases, these technologies are placed in libraries, a natural starting place to look for information (DURRANCE). The Public Access Library System in Pasadena, Calif., is just such a facility. Databases on local businesses, statistics, events, organizations and human services, officials, and schools are available and accessible via computer at the public libraries (WEISS). The citizens have the information needs and they can best describe their needs. Pasadena made a concerted effort to involve local organizations, institutions, and community members in the development and maintenance of their system, an important consideration.

Wake County, N.C., also involves end users in the development of citizen access technologies. The Register's Office is legally responsible for maintaining public documents that date back to 1785. The Register developed an online system to provide better and easier 24-hour access between his location and the Clerk of the Courts, the Revenue Collector, the Real Property Lawyers Association, the Surveyors Association, and other interested members of the public. A users' group of these individuals was formed to develop, test, and monitor this new online system. Public access and customer service are combined with information technology to provide a value-added service for the citizens (FLETCHER ET AL.).

Wisconsin has combined the use of a Touch-Tone phone and a credit card to facilitate renewal of auto registrations. This is a labor-intensive, high-volume service for government and a tedious and time-consuming transaction for the citizen. Using a computerized database and a voice-response system, Wisconsin residents now spend only three minutes to complete this process in the comfort of their homes or offices (RICHTER, 1991).

Although the issue of citizen access seems to meet with approval, its implications raise questions (GUTHRIE & DUTTON). Policy choices are embedded in the design of information systems. The services that are made technologically available reflect policy choices. This prompts us to ask several questions: should we use ATM technology to aid in the delivery of welfare or health care; will we offer these public service technologies in the languages of our constituents or only in English; should federal and state governments support local citizen access initiatives, or will only those cities and counties with a healthy tax base be able to support them? Information technologies are not neutral or value free. When we consider citizen access, we need to appreciate the implications of our choices.

THE ROLE OF THE INFORMATION PROFESSIONAL

The definition of an information professional has evolved over the past few decades. From the time of Hearle's review to this one, we have seen a marked change in both the scope of the information professionals' responsibilities in public organizations and in the level of specialization that has developed. There has also been a remarkable change in the relationship of the information professional in government with the end user. This section addresses these characteristics and provides some guidance for future development.

Managing Information and Information Technology

The role of the technical expert has become complex and specialized. This is reflected in the changing job titles that can be seen in state and local personnel. In the past, job titles in state governments included data processing manager, programmer, and systems analyst. Today they are more likely to be GIS manager, information resources manager, office automation administrator, data resources coordinator, technology management officer, or telecommunications coordinator (CAUDLE ET AL., 1989). This change is also reflected in county governments, with job titles ranging from GIS-CADD analyst to network coordinator, distributed systems specialist, communications training officer, systems security specialist, information center analyst, and end-user computing manager (FLETCHER ET AL.).

A recent job title is that of training specialist. State governments in particular are paying attention to training because they realize that end users will not use systems they do not understand. Hand in hand with this development are formal training centers for state employees where they can receive hands-on training at various skill levels.

Another new role for the information systems professional is that of communicator/liaison. In the past, these professionals were content to stay in their offices, programming and analyzing, never coming into contact with their end users. Today, job evaluations for information systems professionals are almost certain to include a section on communication skills. The importance of involvement with the customers, of understanding their information needs, and of constant communication are factors critical to the successful use of information systems (FLETCHER ET AL.).

Records management professionals, archivists, and librarians also play major roles in the management of information resources in state governments. This is less likely to occur at the local level where these functions are accorded less importance.

Related personnel issues are the hiring, retention, and training of information professionals. State and local governments are not particularly good at any of these. This is unfortunate given the level of skills needed to perform information systems jobs. Personnel directors have expressed concern over their inability to master these problems, but solutions are scarce (CAUDLE ET AL., 1989).

One big problem with hiring concerns salary and compensation. A recent survey of information professionals' salaries (*INFORMATION CENTER QUARTERLY REPORTS*) indicates that in the private sector, these are lucrative jobs with a median salary of $44,500. In state government, these salaries range from an average of $13,200 to $21,400 (CAUDLE ET AL., 1989). The figures for county information professionals are more recent and reflect cost-of-living increases not included in the 1987 salaries for state employees. In county government, information professionals' salaries average $25,900–$37,400 (FLETCHER ET AL.).

Another factor contributing to the personnel retention problem in government is the lack of training for information professionals. These employees are knowledge workers and have a high interest in continuous learning. With the rapid advances in information technologies, they also need to learn and use the newest technologies. Governments generally cannot accommodate these needs. There is little funding for continuous learning, and government systems tend to be less than state of the art. Thus, turnover is high, often more than three times greater than that in the private sector.

The Policy and Planning Roles

State policy and planning activities are most often carried out by central policy agencies; 88% of the states have such an entity usually at the cabinet level, agency level, or department level (NATIONAL ASSOCIATION OF STATE INFORMATION RESOURCE EXECUTIVES). Members of the central planning agency include the information resource executives, state management personnel, judicial and legislative personnel, participants from the private sector, higher education, and local governments, and telecommunications directors. These planning bodies are high-level regulatory groups that provide the direction for the use of information technology in their states.

What is not evident is participation by state library professionals. Librarians, archivists, and records managers are notably lacking in these planning and policy groups. A look at the planning activities of 23 state governments shows that a librarian was a member of the group in only two states (FLETCHER, 1990b). The exclusion of representatives from the state library agencies and of top level library administrators is noticeable given the missions of these groups. It is disturbing that these professionals do not play an active role in the IRM policy and planning activities. State library agencies do an exemplary job of strategic planning for their own agencies and constituents who are, in effect, all employees and residents of the state.

In 1990 the Council of State Governments (CSG) took a step to change this. Three national associations of information professionals joined to develop an Information Services Unit of CSG (HORTON). Participants included the chief officers of state library agencies, the National Association of Government Archives and Records Administrators (NAGARA), and NASIRE. This cooperative effort has allowed these three groups to bring their individual skills in policy setting and agenda recognition to a macro level for state government, leading to better identification and tracking of common policy issues. While this does not give librarians and records managers membership in their states' central policy agencies, it is a good first step in recognizing the value of their contributions to statewide IRM.

SUMMARY

Scope of the Literature

One purpose of a review is to orient the reader to the relevant literature. Our search in this arena led to some useful insights. First, until a few years ago, there were no central sources of literature for the convergence of information technology in government. This, however, is changing both in the research and practice domains. With the arrival of journals such as *Government Information Quarterly* and *Informatization in the Public Sector* there is now a forum for the dissemination of academic research. More practitioner-oriented publications such as *Governing, Government Technology,* and *American City and State* offer articles on applied uses of information technologies in government settings.

Second, we found that much information in this arena is contained in reports published by the individual state and local governments. These are not easy to locate, as there is no database that records them. Reports, planning documents, personnel newsletters, even budget documents are a rich source of information for both the researcher and practitioner. They offer a "real world" picture of how the individual jurisdictions manage and use their information technologies and, when aggregated, provide a picture of trends and issues at state and local levels of governments. They can also give a history of technology use when viewed as retrospective data.

Third, while we are beginning to see the emergence of government technology-oriented publications, we found that there were no domain-specific boundaries for the publication of relevant literature. Research could be found in expected journals such as *Public Administration Review* but was just as likely to be in publications such as *Journal of Communication* or *Policy Studies Journal.* Practitioner-oriented articles could be found in *Business Week, Fortune,* and even *Newsweek* or *Time* magazines, as well as the more focused technology publications.

Finally, we found that the professional organizations—i.e., NAGARA, the National Association of Counties (NACo), the International City/County Management Association (ICMA), or NASIRE—publish timely and useful articles on the practice of information technology management (see Table 2). There are many such groups at the state, county, and municipal levels of government that have as at least one focus, the use of information technologies for providing government services and administration. Many of these associations also offer database and electronic services for their members. ICMA has an information system called LEX (Local Exchange), which provides an electronic network, database, and news service for its members. NACo has NACoNet, which uses the joint purchasing power of more than 3,000 counties to provide a one-stop information technology shopping service for members. NASIRE has a toll-free electronic news network for its members to provide easy access to timely and relevant data.

Implications of the Literature Review

What can we conclude about the management and use of information technologies in state and local governments? First, the development of the information technologies and their management occurred at a similar pace for both levels of government, which lagged, however,

Table 2
Professional Organizations Serving State and Local Governments

Academy for State and Local Government
American Library Association
American Planning Association
American Society for Public Administration
Association of Records Managers and Administrators
Cable Television Information Center
Chief Officers of State Library Agencies
Council of State Community Development Agencies
Council of State Governments
Government Finance Officers Association
Government Technology Conference
International City/County Management Association (ICMA)
ICMA Data and Information Services
International Institute of Municipal Clerks
International Personnel Management Association
National Association of Counties (NACo)
NACo Information Technology Administrators
National Association of Government Archives and Records Administrators
National Association of Regional Councils
National Association of State Information Resource Executives
National Association of State Telecommunications Directors
National Association of Towns and Townships
National Conference of State Legislatures
National Council for Urban Economic Development
National Governors' Association
National League of Cities
State Information Policy Consortium
Special Libraries Association
Urban and Regional Information Systems Association (URISA)
U.S. Conference of Mayors

behind that of the private sector. Despite this, many innovative information systems exist today, and they increasingly support citizen service and access.

The management function is most likely to be centralized in the government with large state data centers in control of the operations and policy setting for IRM. Counties are also centralized but do not follow any management model such as IRM. Rather, the centralization offers operational support and sets standards and guidelines in technology procurement and use. Centralization at all levels of government grew out of a need to rein in the multiple, redundant systems that proliferated in the 1980s with the adoption of PCs by departments and agencies. Interoperability, networking, and standards are now viewed as essential tools for efficient and effective information systems.

The adoption of an IRM stance by state government reflects a growing awareness of the importance of information to governments. It also controls costs and unifies state-level technologies so that common systems can provide information or services to multiple user groups.

Applications that offer faster, better, easier-to-access services for the public are the hallmark of the 1990s. Governments are paying more attention to their "customers," as exemplified by their embracing total quality techniques. Customers include the public and the departmental and agency users of information technologies. A focus on both groups is leading to innovative, cost-efficient systems.

The development of state or countywide information policies needs the participation of all information professionals. These policies affect all government employees and citizens and should not remain in the total control of technical experts.

Research on state and local government information technologies is still sparse, and the scale of undertaking such a project can be daunting and expensive. Updates to the four national studies, however, should be done now because reliable baselines for hardware, software, and management practices have been established. Smaller, government-specific research efforts should also be encouraged because they offer valuable insights.

Finally, the value of trade publications such as those mentioned previously and of state and local documents must be emphasized. These contain road maps for development and practice, enabling jurisdictions to use the experiences of government professionals to implement and manage their own information technologies.

BIBLIOGRAPHY

ABOLT, R.E. 1986. Data Processing for the Chief Executive Officer. Public Management. 1986 March; 68: 19-20. ISSN: 0033-3611.

ALTER, ALLAN. 1988. The Art of the State. CIO Magazine. 1988 November; 2(2): 28-39. ISSN: 0894-9301.

ANDERSEN, DAVID F.; DAWES, SHARON S. 1991. Government Information Management. Englewood Cliffs, NJ: Prentice Hall; 1991. 227p. ISBN: 0-13-361866-8.

ASPRAY, WILLIAM. 1991. Review of *Creating the Computer: Government, Industry, and High Technology*, by Kenneth Flamm. The Journal of Economic History. 1991 September; 51: 739-740. ISSN: 0022-0507.

BECKER, TED. 1993. Teledemocracy: Gathering Momentum in State and Local Governance. Spectrum. 1993 Spring; 66: 14-19. ISSN: 0039-0097.

BINGHAM, RICHARD D. 1984. The Wired City: Review Essay. Urban Affairs Quarterly. 1984 December; 20: 265-272. ISSN: 0042-0816.

BOZEMAN, BARRY. 1987. All Organizations Are Public: Bridging Public and Private Organizational Theories. San Francisco, CA: Jossey-Bass Inc.; 1987. 184p. ISBN: 1-55542-036-2.

BOZEMAN, BARRY; BRETSCHNEIDER, STUART I. 1986. Public Management Information Systems: Theory and Prescription. Public Administration Review. 1986; 46: 475-487. ISSN: 0033-3352.

BOZEMAN, BARRY; STRAUSSMAN, JEFFREY D. 1990. Public Management Strategies: Guidelines for Managerial Effectiveness. San Francisco, CA: Jossey-Bass Inc.; 1990. 239p. ISBN: 1-55542-237-3.

BRETSCHNEIDER, STUART I. 1990. Management Information Systems in Public and Private Organizations: An Empirical Test. Public Administration Review. 1990 September/October; 50: 536-543. ISSN: 0033-3352.

BRETSCHNEIDER, STUART I.; WITTMER, DENNIS. 1993. Organizational Adoption of Microcomputer Technology: The Role of Sector. Information Systems Research. 1993 March; 4(1): 88-110. ISSN: 1047-7047.

BULLETIN OF THE AMERICAN SOCIETY FOR INFORMATION SCIENCE. 1991. Government Information Policy. Bulletin of the American Society for Information Science. 1991 October/November; 18(1): 8-20. ISSN: 0095-4403.

BYRD, TERRY ANTHONY; SAMBAMURTHY, V.; ZMUD, ROBERT W.; HALE, WILLIAM M. 1992. Experiences with Information Technology Planning in State Government: A Multiple-Site Based Assessment. Government Information Quarterly. 1992; 9(2): 135-150. ISSN: 0740-624X.

CALHOUN, CRAIG JACKSON. 1986. Computer Technology, Large-Scale Social Integration, and the Local Community. Urban Affairs Quarterly. 1986 December; 22: 329-349. ISSN: 0042-0816.

CASTONGUAY, RUSSELL. 1987. Maintenance and Management of Local Government Documents Collections: Survey Findings. Government Information Quarterly. 1987; 4(2): 167-188. ISSN: 0740-624X.

CAUDLE, SHARON L. 1988. Federal Information Resources Management after the Paperwork Reduction Act. Public Administration Review. 1988 July/August; 48: 790-798. ISSN: 0033-3352.

CAUDLE, SHARON L. 1990. Managing Information Resources in State Governments. Public Administration Review. 1990 September/October; 50: 515-524. ISSN: 0033-3352.

CAUDLE, SHARON L.; GORR, WILPEN L.; NEWCOMER, KATHRYN E. 1991. Key Information Systems Management Issues for the Public Sector. MIS Quarterly. 1991 June; 15: 171-188. ISSN: 0276-7783.

CAUDLE, SHARON L.; MARCHAND, DONALD A.; BRETSCHNEIDER, STUART I.; FLETCHER, PATRICIA T.; THURMAIER, KURT M. 1989. Managing Information Technology: New Directions in State Government. Syracuse, NY: School of Information Studies, Syracuse University; 1989 August. 307p. ISBN: 0-9623807-0-9.

CLEVELAND, HARLAN. 1986. Government Is Information (but Not Vice Versa). Public Administration Review. 1986 November/December; 46: 605-607. ISSN: 0033-3352.

COUNCIL OF STATE GOVERNMENTS. 1990. The Book of the States. Lexington, KY: The Council of State Governments; 1990. 624p. ISBN: 0 87292-955-8.

DANZIGER, JAMES N.; DUTTON, WILLIAM H.; KLING, ROB; KRAEMER, KENNETH L. 1982. Computers and Politics: High Technology in American Local Governments. New York, NY: Columbia University Press; 1982. 280p. ISBN: 0-231-04888-2.

DAVIES, THOMAS R.; HALE, WILLIAM M. 1986. Implementing a Policy and Planning Process for Managing State Use of Information Technology Resources. Public Administration Review. 1986 November; 46: 516-521. ISSN: 0033-3352.

DILLMAN, DON A. 1985. The Social Impacts of Information Technologies in Rural North America. Rural Sociology. 1985 Spring; 50: 1-26. ISSN: 0036-0112.

DUNFORD, RICHARD. 1987. The Suppression of Technology As a Strategy for Controlling Resource Dependence. Administrative Science Quarterly. 1987 December; 32: 512-525. ISSN: 0001-8392.

DURRANCE, JOAN C. 1988. Providing Access to Local Government Information: The Nature of Public Library Activity. Government Information Quarterly. 1988; 5(2): 155-167. ISSN: 0740-624X.

FELLEMAN, JOHN. 1990. There's a GIS in Your Future. Government Information Quarterly. 1990; 7(3): 261-267. ISSN: 0740-624X.

FLETCHER, PATRICIA T. 1990a. Electronic Records Management in State Government: Planning for the Information Age. Records Management Quarterly. 1990 October; 24(4): 26-32. ISSN: 1050-2343.

FLETCHER, PATRICIA T. 1990b. Planning for the Future: The Leadership Role of the State Library Agencies. Government Information Quarterly. 1990; 7(4): 403-414. ISSN: 0740-624X.

FLETCHER, PATRICIA T.; BERTOT, JOHN CARLO. 1994. The Central Information Services Function in County Governments: From Controller to Enabler. Government Information Quarterly. 1994; 11(1): 73-88. ISSN: 0740-624X.

FLETCHER, PATRICIA T.; BRETSCHNEIDER, STUART I.; MARCHAND, DONALD A.; ROSENBAUM, HOWARD; BERTOT, JOHN CARLO. 1992. Managing Information Technology: Transforming County Governments in the 1990s. Syracuse, NY: School of Information Studies, Syracuse University; 1992 August. 213p. ISBN: 0-685-60164-1.

FLORIDA. DEPARTMENT OF STATE. DIVISION OF LIBRARY AND INFORMATION SERVICES. RECORDS MANAGEMENT PROGRAM. 1987. State of Florida Records Center Handbook. Tallahassee, FL: Florida, Department of State; 1987. 23p. Available from: Florida, Department of State, Division of Library and Information Services, Records Management Program.

FLORIDA. INFORMATION RESOURCE COMMISSION (IRC). 1988. State Strategic Plan for Information Resources Management. Tallahassee, FL: Florida IRC; 1988 January. 55p. Available from: Florida IRC.

FORESMAN, TIMOTHY W.; FAIN, MICKEY A. 1991. Taking the Gamble Out of a Parcel Layer: Horizontal Control and Quality Assurance for GIS in the Las Vegas Valley. Geo Info Systems. 1991 July/August; 1(7): 27-40. ISSN: 1051-9858.

GONA, DEBORAH A. 1990. The State of the States, 1988-89. In: The Council of State Governments. The Book of the States. Lexington, KY: The Council of State Governments; 1990. 1-17. ISBN: 0-87292-955-8.

GORE, AL. 1993. Cutting Red Tape. In: From Red Tape to Results: Creating a Government That Works Better & Costs Less: Report of the National Performance Review. Washington, DC: Government Printing Office; 1993. 11-41. SUDOCS: PRVP 42.2: G74; OCLC: 28758524.

GOVERNMENT TECHNOLOGY. 1993. Resource Guide for GIS Geographic Information Systems. A Supplement to Government Technology. Sacramento, CA: GT Publications Inc.; 1993. 80p. ISSN: 1043-9668.

GREENBERGER, MARTIN. 1983. Review of *Computers and Politics; High Technology in American Local Governments*. American Journal of Sociology. 1983 November; 89: 743-745. ISSN: 0002-9602.

GURWITT, ROB. 1988. The Computer Revolution: Microchiping Away at the Limits of Government. Governing. 1988 May; 1(8): 34-42. ISSN: 0894-3842.

GURWITT, ROB. 1989. Happy Machines, Unhappy People: How to Ease the Pain of the Computer Transition. Governing. 1989 May; 2(8): 62-68. ISSN: 0894-3842.

GURWITT, ROB. 1991. The Decision Machine. Governing. 1991 May; 4(8): 50-54. ISSN: 0894-3842.

GURIOTT, ROB. 1992. The Defrocking of the Computer Priesthood. Governing. 1992 April; 5(7): 57-62. ISSN: 0894-3842.

GUTHRIE, K. KENNETH; DUTTON, WILLIAM H. 1992. The Politics of Citizen Access Technology: The Development of Public Information Utilities in Four Cities. Policy Studies Journal. 1992 Winter; 20(4): 574-597. ISSN: 0190-292X.

HEARLE, EDWARD F.R. 1970. Information Systems in State and Local Governments. In: Cuadra, Carlos A.; Luke, Ann W., eds. Annual Review of Information Science and Technology: Volume 5. Chicago, IL: Encyclopaedia Britannica for the American Society for Information Science; 1970. 325-349. ISBN: 0-85229-156-6.

HERBERS, JOHN. 1989. 17th-Century Counties Struggle to Cope with 20th-Century Problems. Governing. 1989 May; 2(8): 42-48. ISSN: 0894-3842.

HEWLETT PACKARD; PUBLIC TECHNOLOGY INC. USER REQUIREMENTS COMMITTEE (URC). 1986. Information Master Planning: A Guidebook for Local Government. 1986 April. 36p. (5954-0260D). Available from: Public Technology Inc., Washington, DC.

HORTON, GAYE. 1991. Government Information Policy: A View from the States. Bulletin of the American Society for Information Science. 1991 October/November; 18(1): 11-12. ISSN: 0095-4403.

HURLEY, MICHAEL W.; WALLACE, WILLIAM A. 1986. Expert Systems As Decision Aids for Public Managers: An Assessment of the Technology and Prototyping As a Design Strategy. Public Administration Review. 1986 November; 46: 563-571. ISSN: 0033-3352.

INFORMATION CENTER QUARTERLY REPORTS. 1992. IC Salary Survey. Boston, MA: Weingarten Publications, Inc.; 1992.

INTERGOVERNMENTAL PERSPECTIVE. 1991. Counties. Intergovernmental Perspective. 1991 Winter; 17(1): 5-51. ISSN: 0362-8507.

INTERNATIONAL CITY MANAGEMENT ASSOCIATION. 1990. The Municipal Year Book. Washington, DC: International City Management Association; 1990. 425p. ISSN: 0077-2186; ISBN: 0-87326-965-9.

INTERNATIONAL CITY MANAGEMENT ASSOCIATION. 1991. The Municipal Year Book. Washington, DC: International City Management Association; 1991. 388p. ISSN: 0077-2186; ISBN: 0-87326-966-7.

INTERNATIONAL CITY/COUNTY MANAGEMENT ASSOCIATION. 1992. The Municipal Year Book. Washington, DC: International City/County Management Association; 1992. 394p. ISSN: 0077-2186; ISBN: 0-87326-967-5.

INTERNATIONAL CITY/COUNTY MANAGEMENT ASSOCIATION. 1993. The Municipal Year Book. Washington, DC: International City/County Management Association; 1993. 394p. ISSN: 0077-2186; ISBN: 0-87326-968-3.

JONES, RICH. 1990. The State Legislatures. In: The Council of State Governments. The Book of the States. Lexington, KY: The Council of State Governments; 1990. 108-117. ISBN: 0-87292-955-8.

KANSAS. DEPARTMENT OF ADMINISTRATION. DIVISION OF INFORMATION SYSTEMS AND COMMUNICATIONS. BUREAU OF INFORMATION RESOURCE MANAGEMENT. 1986. State of Kansas Information Technology Master Plan. Topeka, KS: Bureau of Information Resource Management; 1986 March. 86p. Available from: Kansas, Department of Administration, Division of Information Systems and Communications, Bureau of Information Resource Management.

KEEN, PETER G.W. 1991. Every Manager's Guide to Information Technology. Boston, MA: Harvard Business School Press; 1991. 170p. ISBN: 0-87584-309-3.

KING, JOHN LESLIE; KRAEMER, KENNETH L. 1985. The Dynamics of Computing. New York, NY: Columbia University Press; 1985. 283p. ISBN: 0-231-05432-7.

KONVITZ, JOSEF; ROSE, MARK H.; TARR, JOEL A. 1990. Technology and the City. Technology and Culture. 1990 April; 31: 284-294. ISSN: 0040-165X.

KORN, PETER A. 1989. Video Technology in Local Government: Recent Experience in Council-Manager Communities in New York State. Public Management. 1989 November; 71: 12-14. ISSN: 0033-3611.

KRAEMER, KENNETH L.; KING, JOHN LESLIE. 1986. Computing and Public Organizations. Public Administration Review. 1986; 46: 488-496. ISSN: 0033-3352.

KRAEMER, KENNETH L.; NORRIS, DONALD F. 1994. Computers in Local Government. In: International City/County Management Association. The Municipal Year Book. Washington, DC: International City/County Management Association; 1994. 3-13. ISSN: 0077-2186; ISBN: 0-87326-969-9.

LENO, TONY. 1989. Is GIS Good for Local Government? Public Management. 1989 June; 71: 15-16. ISSN: 0033-3611.

MARANDO, VINCENT L.; REEVES, MAVIS MANN. 1991. Counties as Local Governments: Research Issues and Questions. Journal of Urban Affairs. 1991; 13(1): 45-53. ISSN: 0735-2166.

MARYLAND. DEPARTMENT OF GENERAL SERVICES. RECORDS MANAGEMENT DIVISION. 1984. Records Management Records Disposition Manual. Waterloo, MD: State Records Management Center; 1984. 20p. Available from: Maryland, Department of General Services, Records Management Division.

MCGOWAN, ROBERT P.; LOMBARDO, GARY A. 1986. Decision Support Systems in State Government: Promises and Pitfalls. Public Administration Review. 1986 November; 46: 579-583. ISSN: 0033-3352.

MCMILLAN, SAM. 1984. Office Automation: A Local Government Perspective. Public Administration Review. 1984 January/February; 44: 60-63. ISSN: 0033-3352.

MENZEL, DONALD C.; MARANDO, VINCENT L.; PARKS, ROGER B.; WAUGH, WILLIAM L., JR.; CIGLER, BEVERLY A.; SVARA, JAMES H.; REEVES, MAVIS MANN; BENTON, J. EDWIN; THOMAS, ROBERT D.; STREIB, GREGORY; SCHNEIDER, MARK. 1992. Setting a Research Agenda for the Study of the American County. Public Administration Review. 1992 March/April; 52(2): 173-182. ISSN: 0033-3352.

MINNESOTA. HENNEPIN COUNTY. RECORDS MANAGEMENT INFORMATION SERVICES DEPARTMENT. 1991. Minnesota Government Data Practices Act. Minneapolis, MN: Records Management Information Services Department; 1991 July. 67p. Available from: Minnesota, Hennepin County, Records Management Information Services Department.

MOHAN, LAKSHMI; HOLSTEIN, WILLIAM K.; ADAMS, ROBERT B. 1990. Private vs. Public Systems. MIS Quarterly. 1990 December; 14(4): 435-448. ISSN: 0276-7783.

MORRIS, JOE. 1987. Computer-Mapping the Infrastructure. Office Automation. 1987 April; 32: 50-58. ISSN: 0472-6049.

MOSCO, VINCENT. 1988. Toward a Theory of the State and Telecommunications Policy. Journal of Communication. 1988 Winter; 38: 107-124. ISSN: 0021-9916.

NATIONAL ACADEMY OF PUBLIC ADMINISTRATION. CENTER FOR INFORMATION MANAGEMENT. 1993. The Information Government: National Agenda for Improving Government through Information Technology: Recommendations from a Forum on The Role of Information Technology in Reinventing Government; 1993 April 23-24; Warrenton, VA. 42p. Available from: National Academy of Public Administration, Washington, DC.

NATIONAL ASSOCIATION OF STATE INFORMATION RESOURCE EXECUTIVES. 1990-91. State Information Resource Management, Structure and Activities, July 1991. Lexington, KY: The Council of State Governments; 1990-91. 115p. Available from: The Council of State Governments, Publication No. C-007-91.

NEIMANN, BERNARD J., JR.; MERIDETH, ROBERT W., JR.; MOYER, D. DAVID; CLAPP, JAMES L. 1990. Land Information Systems Modernization in Wisconsin: Government-University-Professional Interactions. Government Information Quarterly. 1990; 7(3): 269-283. ISSN: 0740-624X.

NEW YORK. STATE ARCHIVES AND RECORDS ADMINISTRATION. 1988. A Strategic Plan for Managing and Preserving Electronic Records in New York State Government. Albany, NY: The State Education Department; 1988 August. 36p. Available from: The State Education Department.

NEWKIRK, GLENN M. 1991. Trends in State Legislative Information Technology. Government Information Quarterly. 1991; 8(3): 259-271. ISSN: 0740-624X.

NORRIS, DONALD F. 1984. Computers and Small Local Governments: Uses and Users. Public Administration Review. 1984 January/February; 44: 70-78. ISSN: 0033-3352.

NORRIS, DONALD F. 1989. Microcomputers & Local Government. Washington, DC: International City Management Association; 1989. 143p. ISBN: 0-87326-925-X.

NORTHROP, ALANA; KRAEMER, KENNETH L.; DUNKLE, DEBORA; KING, JOHN LESLIE. 1990. Payoffs from Computerization: Lessons over Time. Public Administration Review. 1990 September/October; 50: 505-514. ISSN: 0033-3352.

OSBORNE, DAVID; GAEBLER, TED. 1992. Reinventing Government: How the Entrepreneurial Spirit Is Transforming the Public Sector. Reading, MA: Addison-Wesley; 1992. 405p. ISBN: 0-201-52394-9.

PAUL, AMY COHEN. 1990. What Is Our Future? In: International City Management Association. The Municipal Year Book. Washington, DC: International City Management Association; 1990. 3-7. ISSN: 0077-2186; ISBN: 0-87326-965-9.

PERRY, JAMES L.; RAINEY, HAL G. 1988. The Public-Private Distinction in Organization Theory: A Critique and Research Strategy. Academy of Management Review. 1988; 13(2): 182-201. ISSN: 0363-7425.

PRICE, RICHARD. 1991. Managing Personal Computer Development. Public Management. 1991 September; 73: 9-11. ISSN: 0033-3611.

RAINEY, HAL G.; BACKOFF, ROBERT W.; LEVINE, CHARLES H. 1976. Comparing Public and Private Organizations. Public Administration Review. 1976 March/April; 36: 233-244. ISSN: 0033-3352.

RAMSEY, WILLIAM A. 1984. Local Government Microcomputer Information Systems. Public Administration Review. 1984 January/February; 44: 68-69. ISSN: 0033-3352.

RICHTER, M.J. 1991. Easing the Burden with Touch-Tone Government. Governing. 1991 November; 5(2): 60. ISSN: 0894-3842.

RICHTER, M.J. 1992. Image Processing: Streamlining the Paper Chase. Governing. 1992 April; 5(4): 41-55. ISSN: 0894-3842.

ROCHELEAU, BRUCE. 1992. Information Management in the Public Sector: Taming the Computer for Public Managers. Public Administration Review. 1992 July/August; 52(4): 398-400. ISSN: 0033-3352.

ROSENBAUM, HOWARD. 1992. Managers and Information Technology: A Case Study of Organizational Change in County Government. In: Shaw, Debora, ed. Proceedings of the American Society for Information Science (ASIS) 55th Annual Meeting: Volume 29; 1992 October 26-29; Pittsburgh, PA. Medford, NJ: Learned Information, Inc. for ASIS; 1992. 55-66. ISSN: 0044-7870; ISBN: 0-938734-69-5.

RUFFIN, JOHN A. 1991. State Information Resources: Management Issues and Approaches. Bulletin of the American Society for Information Science. 1991 October/November; 18(1): 13-14. ISSN: 0095-4403.

SCHNEIDER, MARK; PARK, KEE OK. 1989. Metropolitan Counties As Service Delivery Agents: The Still Forgotten Governments. Public Administration Review. 1989 July/August; 49: 345-352. ISSN: 0033-3352.

SCRIVENS, ELLIE. 1985. Review of *The Computer Revolution in Public Administration: The Impact of Information Technology on Government*. Journal of Social Policy. 1985 July; 14: 451-452. ISSN: 0047-2794.

STEVENS, JOHN M.; LAPLANTE, JOSEPHINE M. 1986. Factors Associated with Financial-Decision Support Systems in State Government: An Empirical Exploration. Public Administration Review. 1986 November; 46: 522-531. ISSN: 0033-3352.

THOMAS, ROBERT D. 1991. Counties in Transition: Issues and Challenges. Intergovernmental Perspective. 1991 Winter; 17(1): 41-44. ISSN: 0362-8507.

THOMPSON, BOYCE. 1989. The Dazzling Benefits (and Hidden Costs) of Computerized Mapping: Geographic Information Systems Are Transforming Governments. Governing. 1989 December; 3(3): 40-46. ISSN: 0894-3842.

THOMPSON, BOYCE. 1990. Image Processing vs. the Ever-Growing Stack of Paper. Governing. 1990 April; 3(7): 50-55. ISSN: 0894-3842.

THURMAIER, KURT. 1990. Information Resources Management Expenditures in the States: A Case for Integrating Accounting and Budgeting Systems. Public Budgeting and Finance. 1990 Winter; 10(4): 28-46. ISSN: 0275-1100.

TIEN, JAMES M.; MCCLURE, JAMES A. 1986. Enhancing the Effectiveness of Computers in Public Organizations through Appropriate Use of Technology. Public Administration Review. 1986 November; 46: 553-562. ISSN: 0033-3352.

U.S. CONGRESS. OFFICE OF TECHNOLOGY ASSESSMENT. 1993. Making Government Work: Electronic Delivery of Federal Services. Washington, DC: Government Printing Office; 1993 September. 178p. ISBN: 0-16-042080-6.

U.S. DEPARTMENT OF COMMERCE. BUREAU OF THE CENSUS. 1992. 1992 Census of Governments. Washington, DC: Government Printing Office; 1992. SUDOC: GP3.22.2:156/992.

U.S. DEPARTMENT OF COMMERCE. ECONOMICS AND STATISTICS ADMINISTRATION. 1993. Statistical Abstract of the United States. Washington, DC: Government Printing Office; 1993. 1009p. ISBN: 0-16-042046-6.

UTAH. OFFICE OF PLANNING AND BUDGET. 1985. Basic Principles: Information Resource Management. Salt Lake City, UT: Utah Office of Planning and Budget; 1985 November. 6p. Available from: Utah Office of Planning and Budget.

VOSS, L.E.; EIKMEIER, DONALD. 1984. Microcomputers in Local Government. Public Administration Review. 1984 January/February; 44: 60-63. ISSN: 0033-3352.

WATSON, CHARLES C. 1992. GIS Aids in Hurricane Planning. GIS World. 1992 July; 46-52. (Special issue). ISSN: 0897-5507.

WEISS, JUDY. 1989. Pasadena's Two-Tiered Technology. Public Management. 1989 November; 71: 10-11. ISSN: 0033-3611.

8 Information Technology in Education

DIANNE ROTHENBERG
University of Illinois, Urbana-Champaign

INTRODUCTION

Since the 1991 *ARIST* chapter on this topic by EISENBERG & SPITZER, the literature on the use of information technology in schools has increased substantially. This chapter discusses information technology in teacher education, teaching, and learning in K–12 education from 1991 through 1993, primarily in the United States, but with as much information about other countries as possible in the space allowed. Information technology here includes computer applications that store, communicate, retrieve, share, disseminate, and manage information from internal and external sources.

The literature discussed in this chapter falls into several overlapping categories that: (1) link information technology to fundamental education reform; (2) describe computer hardware and the increasing number of software applications and electronic resources residing on various media used in schools; (3) discuss instructional uses of information technology; (4) examine electronic networks and their uses by students and teachers; (5) center on school library media centers and information technology; and (6) suggest changing roles for school library media specialists in an era of rapid technological change.

As Congress considered the High Performance Computing Act of 1991, which was intended to provide federal funding for the establishment of the National Research and Education Network (NREN), DOUGHERTY pointed out that school libraries had a key role to play in the development of the network. They would help bridge the growing

Annual Review of Information Science and Technology (*ARIST*), Volume 29, 1994
Martha E. Williams, Editor
Published for the American Society for Information Science (ASIS)
By Learned Information, Inc., Medford, N.J.

gap between the information rich and poor, provide electronic access to resources distant from students and teachers, and facilitate interactive learning projects. Passage of the act was a landmark event for the use of telecommunications in schools. The High Performance Computing and High Speed Networking Act of 1993 amended the 1991 act to establish an interagency program to develop applications of computing and networking for education and other areas.

The appointment of Linda Roberts, a senior analyst at the congressional Office of Technology Assessment (OTA), to the new post of director of educational technology and special advisor on technology to the Department of Education (DOE) in November 1993 was another landmark event. Roberts is to help DOE become "technology-minded" and focus on how technology can be applied in schools (PORIS & BRUDER).

INFORMATION TECHNOLOGY AND SCHOOL REFORM

SOLOWAY (1991b, p. 29) argued that:

> History has dealt computer and information science a special role in the inevitable restructuring of the educational system in the United States. In the coming decade computing and information technology will be the backbone of the most significant change in education in over 100 years. Rather than being an adjunct to learning and teaching, technology is facilitating a fundamental rethinking of what should be learned and how.

The full use of computer capabilities in education is now defined to include "the retrieval, manipulation, and exchange of information" (MCDANIEL ET AL., p. 73). During the years covered by this chapter, school reform and restructuring have been increasingly linked in the literature with school uses of state-of-the-art information technology (CALLISON; EISENBERG & ELY; HUNTER). This reflects the paradigm shift in education from information transmission to information processing, or, as SOLOWAY (1991b) says, from the information-accumulation model to the learning-by-doing model. HAWKINS calls this change "reorganizing schools for thoughtfulness" (p. 6). Along with others who view access to basic telecommunications technology as essential to reform, CLEMENT (1992a) argues that collaborative projects that link educators and students in "real world" experiences are necessary if NREN or NII (National Information Infrastructure) is to be a tool for educational reform on a national scale.

CARLISLE identified technology as one of four driving forces in the movement to improve American education (the others are the education establishment, the educational standards movement, and the school choice movement). Within the educational technology movement itself, most observers agree that information technology supplies a new, powerful set of complex tools that can change teaching and learning dramatically, if not transform it entirely (BRADY; CALLISON; CARLISLE; EISENBERG & ELY). Similar claims have been made in the past about other kinds of educational technologies—educational television, videos, computer-assisted instruction—yet information technologies appear to offer greater promise than these earlier technologies because they offer support for and integration of key reforms in instruction, including more student exploration, interactive instruction, interdisciplinary work, teachers as facilitators, and heterogeneous or mixed-age grouping (MEANS ET AL.).

Despite the repeated failures of earlier technologies to live up to claims that they would fundamentally change education, support for use of technology as one means to reach the goals of the reform movement appears to be higher now than ever before. Technology plays a key role in President Clinton's plan for education reform (as it did in former President Bush's plans), in media and education entrepreneur Chris Whittle's Edison Project (an outside-the-system model for systemic reform), and in bottom-up, grassroots community efforts (BRADY). The New American School Design Corp., which originally funded 11 design teams to create "break-the-mold" schools, noted that the teams intended to use current information technology (BRADY). The Co-Nect (Cooperative Networked Educational Community for Tomorrow) school design project is viewed as the one most oriented toward technology (OLDS & PEARLMAN). In a recent survey of school board members and superintendents (GAUL ET AL.) 91% indicated that their districts were implementing reform in part by implementing "computer instruction programs."

The work of CLYDE and OWEN indicates that the link between information technology and education reform is not merely an American phenomenon. In Australia, England, and other industrialized countries, the same issues of technology use are being considered and discussed. CLYDE points out that many of the discussions deal with "communications, learning media, information access and information retrieval, areas traditionally associated with the school library" (p. 17). Owen links the emphasis on information technology (IT) use in England to the changes taking place in British schools as a result of the creation of a national curriculum. IT is intended to be a change agent in the British National Curriculum, which mandates that students should be able to use information technologies across the curriculum (CLYDE).

USE OF EDUCATIONAL TECHNOLOGY IN SCHOOLS

For the first time, the number of microcomputers in use in K–12 education passed the 2.5 million mark in the United States during the 1991–1992 school year (QUALITY EDUCATION DATA) and reached the 3.9 million mark in 1992–1993.[1] Ninety-nine percent of public and private elementary and secondary schools in the United States had computers in the 1992–1993 school year, with one for about every 15 students in elementary and middle schools and about one for every ten students in high schools (R. ANDERSON; BECKER, 1993).

Computer spending in general rose during 1992–1993 (SOFTWARE PUBLISHERS ASSOCIATION (SPA)), reaching $2.1 billion as compared with $1.6 billion in the United States in 1991–1992. These figures are based on responses from 332 K–12 school districts to a questionnaire distributed in the summer of 1993 by SPA.

Although U.S. schools have more computers per student than those in Austria, Germany, The Netherlands, and Japan, about half of them (49%) are outdated 8-bit machines—Apple IIs (R. ANDERSON). Japan, which only recently added computers to school environments, had the highest median percentage of 16- or 32-bit computers (96%); Austria has 88% of high-end machines, The Netherlands 14%, and the United States, just 7%. As recently as 1991, more new educational software titles were released for the Apple IIe than for any other computer platform, according to an *Electronic Learning* spot survey of 11 of the largest stand-alone educational software publishers. Researchers are concerned that the American lead in the computer–student ratio means little because about half of the equipment is obsolete (R. ANDERSON).

Most of the recent programs, especially multimedia software, depend on the large memory and speed of 16- or 32-bit computers. The growing pressure to take advantage of the new software is driving the move in computer purchases toward a split between Macintosh and MS-DOS machines.

The total number of MS-DOS machines in schools increased to 34% of the installed base, and Macintoshes increased from 4% to 17% in 1992. Schools are moving toward a two-platform world—MS-DOS and Macintosh—and the market is fragmented, with little agreement among software developers as to the features they expect in either system in schools (R. ANDERSON).

While the strongest new trend was toward the purchase of IBM-compatible computers, other technology purchases also increased. CD-ROM use tripled in schools in the past two years. Encyclopedias on CD-ROM have been of special interest in schools (BECKER, 1991), and students have easily learned to use CD-ROM for writing and research

---

[1]Internal survey.

(NEILSEN). Studies on CD-ROM use and its effectiveness are just beginning (MENDRINOS).

According to MARKET DATA RETRIEVAL, INCORPORATED (1993), 44.5% of schools had CD-ROM in 1992-1993 vs. 15.5% in 1990-1991; 41.2% of schools had videodisc technology in 1992-1993 compared with 10.7% in 1990-1991; 49.4% had local area networks (LANs), compared with 21.8% in 1990-1991; and 64.2% of schools had modems during 1992-1993 vs. 48.4% in 1990-1991.

In a related event, Texas has become the first state to legislate that videodisc-based materials can be used in place of a traditional textbook. At least 65% of elementary schools in Texas were reported to have adopted the "Windows on Science" videodisc and supporting materials for elementary science in place of a conventional textbook by 1991 (SOLOWAY, 1991a). Most other educational software producers are following suit: Dynacomp, MECC, EduQuest/IBM, and Apple are among the many who are producing multimedia products for schools. The 1994 edition of the *Multimedia and Videodisc Compendium for Education and Training* (EMERGING TECHNOLOGY CONSULTANTS) contains more than 2,800 descriptions of multimedia products from over 275 producers. The increasing availability of videodisc, multimedia, and other computer equipment and learning materials has led observers to question the effectiveness of traditional curriculum materials with students in ways that would have been unthinkable just half a dozen years ago (NOVEMBER & THORNBURG).

Instructional Uses of Information Technology

Against this general backdrop are several trends that are specific to information technology use.

Local area networking. A major current trend in schools is local area networking (LAN), which usually involves school library media centers, classrooms, and administrative offices and is found in schools of all sizes (HANSON; MANCALL ET AL.). MARKET DATA RETRIEVAL, INCORPORATED (1993) reports that half of U.S. public schools are using LANs to manage their computer resources more efficiently. Networking facilitates the use of CD-ROM resources in classrooms and in the school library media center, and, in technology-rich schools, provides access to video servers in a central location. This trend is likely to gather momentum in the coming years.

Powerful hardware and software in increasingly lower grades. Apple Computer Inc. and other interactive videodisc producers are moving strongly into the preschool and primary school market with hardware to be used with various software including "interactive" books such as *Grandma and Me* (BALLENGER). Interactive books on CD-ROM contain text and characters that can be manipulated by the child in response to keyboard, touch-screen, or mouse-generated commands. Because of the popularity of programs that require these capabilities, many elementary school teachers are beginning to object to receiving low end computers as donations from the upper grades, and some schools are starting to question the wisdom of accepting donations of older computers from local businesses.

Integrated curriculum. Another significant trend is the change from using computers to enhance traditional instruction by delivering information to creating interactive learning environments (SOLOWAY, 1991a) in which students construct and use knowledge, often in ways that cut across curriculum areas. Interactive learning environments provide a means to go beyond framing a task to providing scaffolding (a form of support that bridges the gap between a student's current abilities and the next learning stage). Interactive learning environments can be viewed as part of a larger movement to integrate the curriculum into meaningful, coherent units or projects that include the use of skills in reading and writing, mathematics and scientific concepts (rather than drill and practice of isolated skills). Curriculum integration is a trend in all levels of K–12 education (WISHNIETSKY, 1992).

Integrated curriculum efforts include a schoolwide project to create coloring books for Boston City Children's Hospital by students who scanned drawings, wrote text, and completed the project with desktop publishing software and in-house bookmaking and binding (HOLZBERG). In another example, third graders worked with a state legislator to create a survey and collect data to support a carjacking bill, using e-mail for correspondence. Other projects have involved vocational educators and students in work that had an application in the world beyond school. Some concern is expressed in the professional library literature that library media specialists are not as involved as they should be in curriculum integration efforts (BIAGINI).

Database construction and use across the curriculum. Although not a new trend, the construction and use of databases in science, social studies, geography, and mathematics are increasingly common activities (EHMAN ET AL.). Indeed, the new multimedia programs are also databases, and should be evaluated according to quality, accessibility, and ease of use.

EFFECTS OF INFORMATION TECHNOLOGY USE ON STUDENT ACHIEVEMENT

The effectiveness of instructional technology has been the subject of research since the 1960s. Studies of instructional technologies can be divided into those that: (1) compare effectiveness of the new instructional methods with those of conventional instruction on the basis of student outcomes; (2) focus on the contextual nature of innovations in technology use in the classrooms, often using case studies and not relying on single outcome measures; or (3) studies that experiment with particular innovations and provide information for constructing new applications (MEANS ET AL.). Overall, studies of instructional technologies have found the newer technologies to be either equivalent or superior to conventional instruction in student learning (BIALO & SIVIN). Studies of computer-assisted instruction, interactive videodisc and multimedia technologies in the classroom, and distance learning have usually found novelty effects that boosted student achievement, results equal to student achievement compared with conventional instruction, or, in a few studies, higher student achievement (BIALO & SIVIN).

Studies of the effects of information technologies on student achievement are only now being conducted. HONEY & HENRIQUEZ present some of the most comprehensive data on information technology use and, indirectly, on student achievement. Their data were collected using the contextual approach; they linked use of telecommunications and networking to teacher and student behaviors that support best practice and educational reform and found positive correlations. Only longitudinal studies will be able to provide conclusive evidence on the effects of information technology use on student achievement, but researchers believe that information technology supports "functions that are fundamental if teachers are to provide authentic, active learning experiences as envisioned by education reform goals" (MEANS ET AL., p. 57).

THE NETWORKED SCHOOL

In 1991 DOUGHERTY spoke of schools as still being at the R&D stage in Internet use. A few schools had guest accounts supplied by university contacts or took part in limited research projects to explore Internet use in schools.

CLEMENT (1992a; 1992b; 1992c) reviewed the extent and uses of K–12 computer networking and discussed the significant role that the Consortium of School Networks has played in working to connect schools to the Internet as well as the numerous collaborations between K–12 schools and postsecondary institutions.

In 1993 HONEY & HENRIQUEZ, in the first systematic and large-scale ($N = 550$) survey of how educators use telecommunications, found network use had moved beyond R&D to become a growing component of student and professional development activities, such as finding and using research and discussing issues with colleagues.

Informal estimates of the numbers of teachers, administrators, and support personnel at the school-building level who use the Internet or other commercial or nonprofit networks vary widely, from 50,000 to 250,000. The print literature is not a good source for up-to-date figures and seldom includes school personnel who may be connected through commercial services that offer Internet access.

DYRLI cited estimates that 50,000 teachers use the Internet—a fraction of the estimated nearly 3 million K–12 teachers in the U.S. (NATIONAL CENTER FOR EDUCATION STATISTICS). The experience of some of the state networks provides a basis for gauging the tremendous upsurge of participation of K–12 educators in Internet use. SENDIT, the North Dakota network for the K–12 education community, began operation in late 1990 with a National Science Foundation (NSF) Higher Education grant. As of February 1, 1994, in this mostly rural state, over 2,100 teachers and administrators and 5,200 students were users of the system.[2] During the first year (August 1991–August 1992) of TENET's (Texas Education Network) existence, the Texas Education Agency statewide network for educators signed up 16,000 members of the K–12 community (3,000 had been expected to sign up). TENET now (February 1994) has 28,000 K–12 educators as Internet users.[3] In California, the CORE (California Online Resources for Education) network, which began operation in 1990, currently has 15,000 teachers online and is adding 600 educators per week.[4] Other state networks are active in Florida (FIRN), Michigan (Merit Michnet), Georgia (GC EduNet), and Virginia (PEN), while most other states are planning for widespread Internet access for teachers. Clearly, school library media specialists, teachers, and administrators will take the first step toward becoming Internet users if they are given an opportunity for easy and inexpensive access. The interest in Internet and other network use in schools from teachers, school library media specialists, and administrators is obvious from the literature, which contains numerous articles on Internet and other network use published in the past two years (DECANDIDO; DESCY; ROSENBAUM; THOMPSON). This interest shows no signs of abating. Uses of these networks are discussed in the next section.

Student Network Use

Use of the Internet and other networks is a relatively inexpensive application of educational technology that is supported by grassroots efforts in communities with local bulletin boards, Freenets, and

---

[2]Personal communication, SENDIT program office, February 11, 1994.
[3]Personal communication, Richard Lagow, February 11, 1994.
[4]Personal communication, Keith Vogt, February 11, 1994.

CommunityNets. Children, often avid users of computer bulletin boards, can help their teachers learn to use the equipment and software.

Several recent studies have explored Internet use by teachers and students. COLLIS (1992a) reviewed 45 studies on use of online databases and computer-mediated communication in secondary schools; CLEMENT (1992a; 1992b; 1992c) explored the extent and kinds of uses by teachers and students. Most recently, HONEY & HENRIQUEZ surveyed teachers on how extensively they and their students use the Internet, what they use it for, and what kind of impact it has on teaching. These and other studies (noted below) indicate the following categories of student Internet use.

Researching beyond local libraries. Internet use allows students to expand their basic research beyond the local libraries (EISENBERG & ELY; O'NEIL). Student projects can focus on current events using timely materials available through Internet (O'NEIL; STIX). HARRIS described the use of Telnet software to access information resource collections for elementary and secondary education. HONEY & HENRIQUEZ provide overlapping categories showing that of student learning activities involving services and databases, 57% involve encyclopedia use; 54%, news retrieval services; 48%, ERIC and other education databases; and 39%, science databases.

Expanding student awareness about the world. U.S. students can communicate through electronic pen-pal programs with foreign students more immediately than through traditional overseas mail. Pen-pal exchanges are engaged in by students in 41% of telecommunications-using teachers' classrooms (HONEY & HENRIQUEZ). Second-language learning becomes meaningful when students can talk with their peers in other countries in their own languages (SANAOUI & LAPKIN). WISHNIETSKY (1991) describes the uses of e-mail in schools, and BOSTON ET AL. describe its use to adapt curricula to a global approach (one that is multicultural and international in focus), from kindergarten through high school. Many student uses of the Internet foster the exchange of cultural and social information, both internationally and within the United States (HONEY & HENRIQUEZ).

Engaging in cooperative learning. Networking makes cooperative learning possible by allowing students from different schools or countries to work together on joint projects (O'NEIL; RIEL; STIX). Virtually every study of Internet use includes examples of this kind of collaboration. Telecommunications also facilitate cross-age, cross-network mentoring and team work (LADESTRO; RIEL).

Addressing real-world problems. In recent years John Dewey's theories on learning by practical experience (now called experiential or authentic learning) have been supported by the findings of cognitive research. Telecommunications are being used in 34% of telecommunications-using classrooms to gather and exchange scientific data and in 27% of classrooms for story-writing exchanges (HONEY & HENRIQUEZ). To support intellectually engaging learning, students take part in projects that minimize the distinction between learning in school and in the "real world" and often collaborate with university-based researchers (P. ANDERSON; CLEMENT, 1992a; HONEY & HENRIQUEZ; O'NEIL; POTTER).

About half the students in networked classrooms collect and analyze weather data, share their findings on local recycling efforts or acid rain effects with students in other states, or create and share writings that describe their community to students in other countries. Most "real-world" projects involve communication with other students at other sites via the Internet or a specially created network. Instead of working on written exercises or hypothetical problems, students use technology to address the same issues that concern adults (O'NEIL; SOLOWAY, 1991b).

By providing links between classroom work and ongoing scientific, literary, and other kinds of projects, teachers can introduce authenticity into students' work and reinforce connections between their work and that of the adult world (O'NEIL; STIX).

Meeting special needs. Network use is spread across the grades, across the curriculum from vocational education to advanced placement courses, and among all kinds of students. The literature describes many projects that provide all students with opportunities to use electronic networks. RIEL and others describe telecommunications projects involving at-risk students in inner-city classrooms and homes. Children with special needs benefit from telecommunications projects because physical and mental barriers to electronic communication are minimal. Examples include a pilot electronic mail (e-mail) project for adolescents with and without disabilities (LEFEBVRE), a telecommunications curriculum for elementary school students with physical disabilities (GANDELL & LAUFER), and, at the Florida School for the Deaf and the Blind, a project that helps blind students access information online, the way their sighted peers do.

Changing Teaching through Telecommunications

Internet services are used almost twice as often for professional development as for student learning (HONEY & HENRIQUEZ). Use of the Internet carries with it great potential for change in the day-to-day work of teaching through peer communication in and among organizations. E-mail has been a key feature—the most heavily used feature—of virtually all telecommunications systems adapted or created for use in education (HONEY & HENRIQUEZ). SPROULL & KIESLER (p. 116) discuss the potential impact of this new communication mode:

> Managers are often attracted to networks by the promise of faster communication and greater efficiency. In our view, the real potential of network communication has less to do with such matters than with influencing the overall work environment and the capabilities of employees.

Beginning teachers are particularly vulnerable to the stresses and tensions of teaching. Because one-third to one-half of new teachers leave the profession within the first five years (MERSETH), it is necessary to give them immediate access to support, advice, and assistance. Here networks can reduce isolation and provide support by providing a non-threatening forum for discussion with peers in similar situations (e.g., other new teachers). The most publicized new-teacher network may be BTCN (Beginning Teacher Computer Network) initiated at Harvard Graduate School of Education in 1987 (MERSETH).

HONEY & HENRIQUEZ (p. 25) surveyed educators on how the use of telecommunications changes their teaching. Teachers reported significant gains in the following areas: (1) more time to spend with individual students; (2) greater comfort with allowing students to work independently; (3) less time spent lecturing; and (4) higher expectations of students in pursuing and editing their own work.

Use of e-mail within and among schools significantly reduces a teacher's sense of isolation (COLLIS, 1992b; HONEY & HENRIQUEZ; WATTS & CASTLE) and provides opportunities for professional development, including the acquisition of new knowledge and the dissemination of research. With greater access to both a community of peers and to research, teachers may feel better prepared to play a vital role in accomplishing school reform by starting with their own teaching (CLEMENT, 1992a). Computer networking has become a source of information and support for restructuring and effecting fundamental change in many schools.

A large-scale attempt to help educators use the Internet is AskERIC (ACCESS ERIC), which helps educators negotiate the Internet by providing human-mediated question–answering, guides to Internet resources, assistance in Internet use, and referral services to other educators on the Internet (ACCESS ERIC). Originally targeted to teachers, media specialists, and administrators in three state networks with Internet connections (NYSERNET (New York), TENET (Texas), and SENDIT (North Dakota)) and then expanded in 1993 to ten states, AskERIC is expanding its services rapidly to parents and others interested in education. AskERIC responds to more than 300 information requests per week from U.S. and other educators (ACCESS ERIC).

The ERIC Clearinghouse on Information and Technology at Syracuse University has also created the AskERIC Electronic Library, an online repository of education resources, including curriculum guides, an AskERIC database of "frequently asked questions" (FAQ) and answers, ERIC searches on high-interest topics, and "InfoGuides" to the Internet and print literature on several dozen topics on a publicly accessible Internet Gopher server. Between 7,000 and 9,500 individuals were downloading information each week from the AskERIC Electronic Library using Gopher or FTP (file transfer protocol) by late 1992 (ACCESS ERIC).

Several ERIC clearinghouses and education associations (e.g., the National Education Association (NEA) and the Association for Supervision and Curriculum Development (ASCD)), operate forums or special-interest groups on commercial services on the Internet: K–12 administration (K12 ADMIN), early childhood education (ECENET-L), middle-level education (MIDDLE-L), or school library media centers (LM_NET) (EISENBERG & MILBURY). Hundreds of these groups exist for educators.

One successful telecommunications network for professional development is the NEA School Renewal Network. Based on their experience with this network, WATTS & CASTLE identified six conditions necessary to encourage and facilitate what they called "dialogic networking": (1) the network must encourage the development of affinity groups or self-selecting groups based on similar interests rather than geography; (2) the mechanization of the network needs to be balanced with personalization—i.e., qualified facilitators must be available, including telephone-based technical support for ongoing technical problems and conversational facilitation; (3) local outreach is needed to involve colleagues at the site level; (4) the structure of the network must be empowering to those who take part; (5) the network must take advantage of the principle of distributed expertise; and (6) access to the network must be maximized by keeping costs low and providing the kinds of support listed here.

HAWKINS concurs that "simply hooking teachers to a network is insufficient; engaged discussion and sharing of images with peers at a distance needs to be carefully structured as a social organization of technology use for professional growth" (p. 5). In a discussion of UrbNet, a newly established online forum for teachers in the Urban Sites Writing Network, JERVIS echoes a problem common to many networks: more readers who are not writing on the network than is desirable.

The five-year experiment with the NEA School Renewal Network has enhanced teacher professionalism in participating schools, increased the dialog between researchers and practitioners, brought about greater possibilities for substantive change through the use of information, hastened the destruction of institutional and hierarchical barriers, and helped eliminate barriers of time and place (WATTS & CASTLE).

Another example of networking for professional development is the Mathematics Leadership Project at Bank Street College in New York, which supplied laptop computers and modems to participating teachers involved in a summer institute for mathematics educators who then returned to their schools. Throughout the next school year, the teachers were electronically linked to each other and to expert advisors (HAWKINS).

The first guidelines established by the International Society for Technology in Education (ISTE) Accreditation Committee for standards for teacher education related to computer knowledge and computer skills were approved by NCATE, the National Council for Accreditation of Teacher Education, in September 1991. Two sets of guidelines—computer technology competencies for undergraduates and educational computing and technology leadership guidelines for those receiving graduate degrees—were approved (ABRAMSON).

With these guidelines, ISTE has established fundamental skills in information technology for all preservice teachers and administrators including: (1) demonstrating knowledge of the use of telecommunications to support instruction, and (2) using computer-based technologies to access information (ABRAMSON). The recognition of technology skills and competencies in the accreditation process marks the acceptance of information technology as a basic part of teaching in the United States. The incorporation of information technology into teacher education is an issue in other countries as well. GORNY describes the introduction of information science and technology into West German public schools, focusing on the teacher preservice and inservice education needed to support it.

INFORMATION SERVICES AND TECHNOLOGIES IN SCHOOL LIBRARY MEDIA CENTERS

School library media specialists are as deeply affected by use of information technology as are classroom teachers, and all of the developments mentioned in this article affect school libraries as well as classrooms. School libraries face a number of challenges in technology-rich schools. Research continues to support school library media centers as important contributors to academic achievement, and the presence of more media specialists than in the mid-1980s[5] is a hopeful trend.

[5]Personal communication, Pamela Kramer, American Association of School Librarians, February 14, 1994.

Access to funds for updating collections and library services, however, remains limited.

Data on U.S. school library staffing, budget, collections, technology, and services were collected by the National Center for Education Statistics (NCES) in a fall 1993 survey for the first time since 1985, but the data will not be available until 1995 (AMERICAN LIBRARY ASSOCIATION). In the meantime the U.S. National Commission on Libraries and Information Science (NCLIS) contracted with the American Library Association (ALA) to collect selected statistics from a random sample of 1,300 school library media centers in 12 states in September 1993 (the complete report will be published in early 1994).[6] Preliminary findings indicate that the lack of availability of telephone lines for telecommunications remains a major barrier to the use of online networks. The survey also indicated that CD-ROMs are present in 53.5% of elementary schools and 73.8% of secondary schools.

ZIMMERMAN found that librarians have extremely positive attitudes toward the use of technology, but also that there is a large gap between their attitudes and willingness to use technology and the conditions under which they are able to implement its use. As more information becomes available electronically, school library media centers are rethinking collection development strategies to change the proportion of funds spent on print and electronic information products. KURK, for example, based on a survey of school libraries in five Georgia counties in the Atlanta area, found that school libraries spend 15–30% of their budgets on technology resources compared with 30–40% on book purchases. However, many school library media center budgets leave little room for updating library collections while at the same time acquiring new electronic resources. The NCLIS/ALA survey found that half of all elementary schools have less than $5,494 for all library material purchases, including books and technology, and that half of all secondary schools have less than $9,888 to spend for all materials purchases.

Networking beyond the School

Local area networks have had a great impact on school library media centers, but an even greater impact is experienced when networking extends beyond the school building to connect school libraries to multitype library regional and state networks. Among the trends that MARCHIONINI and others have described as affecting school library

[6] The states involved were Arizona, Arkansas, California, Illinois, Kansas, Kentucky, Massachusetts, Michigan, Oregon, Pennsylvania, Rhode Island, and West Virginia (AMERICAN LIBRARY ASSOCIATION).

media centers in all parts of the country in the 1990s is increased resource sharing and networking.

In Pennsylvania, the state-funded ACCESS PENNSYLVANIA project provides a CD-ROM union catalog of high school, public, academic, and special library collections (EPLER & TUZINSKI) and offers consulting for schools that want to automate their card catalogs. The state library makes available a toll free number and develops materials to help media specialists integrate technology and online catalog use into the curriculum. Participation has become a status symbol for schools. Epler and Tuzinski report that ACCESS PENNSYLVANIA has

> focused attention on school library media centers like nothing else in the past twenty years. Proof of this lies in the fact that many school administrators have chosen to pay the costs involved. . .rather than wait for state funds because they wanted their students and teachers to have the advantages the project has to offer. . . (p. 23)

For many school library media specialists, however, who are responsible for several libraries in a district, lack of funding and staff time prevent focusing on the creation of an electronic card catalog.

Next to a microcomputer, CD-ROM is the most popular form of information technology in the school library media center. In a survey of media specialists in New York State (ZIMMERMAN; N = 1,469), in which the sample was almost equally divided between elementary and secondary school library media specialists, Zimmerman found that 86.7% of schools had a computer in the library media center and 46.2% of library media centers had at least one CD-ROM. Only 14.6% of respondents had an "automated card catalog" (p. 307), and just 21.8% had an automated circulation system. According to ZIMMERMAN (p. 308), "It seems evident that although computers may be used in the library media center as instructional tools, they are not being used to their potential to provide library services or to increase library efficiency." No data are available on the number of online card catalogs in school libraries nationwide. Professional journals tend to feature uses of information technologies in "cutting edge" libraries and media centers (NELSON), but it appears unlikely that more than half of school library media centers use information technology to organize their own collections.

Internet Use

School library media specialists are among the most active K–12 Internet participants, and many are able to be on-site advisors and guides to Internet use for students and teachers in their schools. These specialists use the Internet the way teachers do: (1) to reduce the sense of isolation and share experiences; (2) to find information to solve problems; (3) to share information on current issues (especially Internet use); and (4) to help them do a better job of teaching others (administrators, students, teachers, and support personnel) in their schools to use the Internet (DESCY; EISENBERG & MILBURY). Reducing isolation may be an especially important use of the Internet for media specialists since they are often the only information professionals in their schools.

LM_NET, a listserv (a BITNET program for managing mailing lists) devoted to discussion of issues important to school library media specialists, has 1,600 members and has been extremely popular and influential in the school library community (EISENBERG & MILBURY). DECANDIDO, KOLLASCH, and THOMPSON provide descriptions of the Internet and its uses by school library media specialists.

Information Skills Instruction

Given the dynamic environment for information technology use in schools, many have suggested that bibliographic instruction needs to be reconceptualized more broadly. MANCALL suggests that it be called information skills instruction or "information access/utilization instruction" and draws an analogy between "searching across the curriculum" and the "writing across the curriculum" movement that is popular in elementary and secondary education.

Like writing across the curriculum, searching across the curriculum might be characterized by many approaches but also by a shared goal—developing competencies useful in searching for information by learning to subdivide complex problems into component parts and reorganize them to find solutions. ALA & CERABONA call Boolean searching a new "life skill" that is important for finding precise information without being inundated by irrelevant data.

Searching for information in an electronic environment, either online or on CD-ROM, has become recognized as a meaningful and effective way to develop critical thinking skills in every curricular area (MANCALL ET AL.). The integration of database construction and use into many areas of the curriculum (EHMAN ET AL.) is tacit recognition of the value of this process.

MANCALL ET AL. identify other key information-handling skills that are being viewed as essential to problem solving in all curriculum areas and for all students, college bound or not: (1) identifying needed information; (2) locating and acquiring the identified information; (3) analyzing and synthesizing content; (4) applying and communicating the results; and (5) evaluating one's success or failure and considering how to improve the procedure or enhance the outcome next time (p. 527). IRVING and others have also discussed the importance of the incorporation of a range of information skills across the curriculum.

Looking Ahead

Several trends will become more noticeable in school librarianship over the next few years.

Changing roles. CALLISON argues that a new vision is needed to increase media specialist access to resources for improving school libraries, suggesting that the fostering of telecommunications in schools is a responsibility of school librarians and that the media center mission will continue to change to ensure "that teachers and students, parents and other community members are effective users of information" (p. 414) inside and outside of the school library media center.

Information will continue to be decentralized from the school library to every classroom that has access to the Internet, CD-ROM, or other online resources. In schools where librarians become advisors on technology-related issues, curriculum consultants, database evaluators and selectors, and teachers of "searching-across-the-curriculum" skills, their roles are likely to be seen as valuable and central to schooling.

BARRON & BERGEN, among many others, urge library media specialists to become conversant in the wide range of technologies needed to supply school personnel and students with information, regardless of media, and inside or outside the school library media center.

An increasingly networked future. MANCALL ET AL. (p. 527) see networks in the future as "layers of potential access" to

> collections in local schools and libraries; directories identifying local people who can be contacted for information on specific subjects; remote electronic databases containing reference information, including abstracts, and full text or statistical primary source information; electronic bulletin boards; regional access to additional people and resources when local networks are unable to fill an information request; and national access to an even larger community of people and resources when regional sources cannot produce the requested information.

These layers will be essentially invisible to users because it will be as simple to contact an international organization or individual for information as a local one. Al Gore (quoted in DOUGHERTY) anticipated a time when K–12 students can connect via computer and modem to the resources of the Library of Congress. This vision is already a reality in some schools and needs to be expanded to all schools. The federal government, states, regional network providers, and organizations, such as the Consortium of School Networks (COSN), will play major roles in the realization of that goal.

New developments to influence online catalogs. The knowledge base on the behaviors of young information users continues to grow and is likely to influence the shape of online catalogs in schools in the next decade. ROSENBERG & BORGMAN created a graphically based direct manipulation interface for science materials, called the Science Library Catalog, which was pilot tested in two California elementary schools. SOLOMON explored information access and interface usability for an online catalog in an elementary school, identifying factors that contribute to OPAC (online public access catalog) success. BUSEY & DOERR created Kid's Catalog, a graphical user interface with point-and-click capability. MOORE & ST. GEORGE describe the information retrieval process used by New Zealand sixth graders and explore the cognitive difficulties they encountered. JACOBSON & JACOBSON studied cognitive learning theories and bibliographic instruction in a case study of end-user searching in a high school library in Illinois.

CONCLUSION

The use of information technologies in schools is viewed by parents, teachers, administrators, and policy makers as an essential part of improving education. The link between reform and technology is significant because it means increased support for sophisticated information technologies at all levels of schooling. Technology-rich schools reflect the increasing emphasis on information processing, integrated curriculum, and the connecting of school work to the world of work outside the school.

The number of teachers, media specialists, and administrators connected to the Internet by the end of 1993 was increasing very rapidly. The explosion of telecommunications use is expected to fundamentally change the educational process and the roles of all those involved in education.

School library media specialists are reallocating budgets, rethinking collection development and networking needs, and broadening their concept of information skills, often in the face of insufficient resources. Many are consciously reshaping their role to become leaders, advisors, and consultants on technology or Internet use in their schools as they face the challenge of an education environment in which information technology plays a major role.

BIBLIOGRAPHY

ABRAMSON, GERTRUDE W. 1993. Technology and the Teacher Education Accreditation Process. Ed-TECH Review. 1993 Autumn/Winter; 27-30. ISSN: 1065-6901.

ACCESS ERIC. 1993. 1992 Annual Report: Summarizing the Recent Accomplishments of the Educational Resources Information Center. Washington, DC: Office of Educational Research and Improvement, U.S. Department of Education; 1993 July. 29p. Available from: ACCESS ERIC, Aspen Systems Corporation, 1600 Research Boulevard, Rockville, MD 20850-3172.

ALA, JUDY; CERABONA, KATHY. 1992. Practically Speaking: Boolean Searches—A Life Skill. School Library Journal. 1992 November; 38(11): 42. ISSN: 0362-8930.

AMERICAN LIBRARY ASSOCIATION. 1994. NCLIS/ALA School Library Media Center Statistics Project. Fact Sheet. Chicago, IL: American Library Association; 1994 January. 2p. Available from: American Library Association, 50 East Huron St., Chicago, IL 60611.

ANDERSON, PEGGY. 1993. Connecting with the "Real World." Momentum. 1993 February-March; 24(1): 26-27. ISSN: 0026-914X.

ANDERSON, RONALD. 1993. Computers in American Schools 1992: An Overview. Minneapolis, MN: International Association for the Evaluation of Educational Achievement; 1993 December. 178p. Available from: IEA Computers in Education Study, 909 Social Sciences Building, 267 19th Ave. S., University of Minnesota, Minneapolis, MN 55455.

BALLENGER, MARCUS. 1992. Software for the Classroom. Childhood Education. 1992 Winter; 69(2): 118-119. ISSN: 0009-4056.

BARRON, DANIEL; BERGEN, TIMOTHY, JR. 1992. Information Power: The Restructured School Library for the Nineties. Phi Delta Kappan. 1992 March; 73(7): 521-525. ISSN: 0031-7217.

BECKER, HENRY JAY. 1991. Encyclopedias on CD-ROM: Two Orders of Magnitude More Than Any Other Education Software Has Ever Delivered Before. Educational Technology. 1991 February; 31(2): 7-20. ISSN: 0013-1962.

BECKER, HENRY JAY. 1993. Teaching with and about Computers in Secondary Schools. Communications of the ACM. 1993 May; 36(5): 69-72. ISSN: 0001-0782.

BIAGINI, MARY K. 1994. Curriculum Integration: What's Our Role? School Library Media Quarterly. 1994 Winter; 22(2): 77. ISSN: 0278-4823.

BIALO, E.; SIVIN, J. 1990. Report on the Effectiveness of Microcomputers in Schools. Washington, DC: Software Publishers Association; 1990. 25p. ERIC: ED 327177.

BOSTON, JANE; CHAN, ADRIAN; MUKAI, GARY. 1991. Classroom Technology and Its Global Connections. Media & Methods. 1991 January-February; 27(3): 18, 48-49, 54. ISSN: 0025-6897.

BRADLEY, BERNARD. 1992. JEDI: The Power of CD-ROM Technology. Science Scope. 1992 September; 16(1): 40-43. ISSN: 0887-2376.

BRADY, HOLLY. 1992. Who Will Rebuild America's Schools? Technology & Learning. 1992 September; 12(1): 52, 54-57. ISSN: 1053-6728.

BUSEY, PAULA; DOERR, TOM. 1993. Kid's Catalog: An Information Retrieval System for Children. Journal of Youth Services in Libraries. 1993 Fall; 7(1): 77-84. ISSN: 0894-2498.

BUTTERWORTH, MARGARET. 1992. Online Searching and CD-ROM in British Schools. Education for Information. 1992 March; 10(1): 35-48. ISSN: 0167-8329.

CALLISON, DANIEL. 1993. The Impact of New Technologies on School Library Media Center Facilities and Instruction. Journal of Youth Services in Libraries. 1993 Summer; 6(4): 414-419. ISSN: 0894-2498.

CARLISLE, KENNETH E. 1993. The Politics of Educational Reform. Educational Technology. 1993 May; 33(5): 43-47. ISSN: 0013-1962.

CLEMENT, JOHN. 1992a. K-12 Networking: Constructing the K-12 Collaboratory on the NREN. EDUCOM Review. 1992 May-June; 27(3): 18-20. ISSN: 1045-9146.

CLEMENT, JOHN. 1992b. Surveying K-12 and Postsecondary School Networking Partnerships. EDUCOM Review. 1992 July-August; 27(4): 44-46. ISSN: 1045-9146.

CLEMENT, JOHN. 1992c. Where We Are in Networking for K-12 Education: A First Annual Review. EDUCOM Review. 1992 September-October; 27(5): 20-23. ISSN: 1045-9146.

CLYDE, ANNE. 1992. New Technology, Information Access and Educational Outcomes. Emergency Librarian. 1992 January-February; 19(3): 8-14, 16-18. ISSN: 0315-8888.

COLLIS, BETTY. 1992a. Supporting Educational Uses of Telecommunication in the Secondary School: Part I. An Overview of Experiences. International Journal of Instructional Media. 1992; 19(1): 23-44. ISSN: 0892-1815.

COLLIS, BETTY. 1992b. Supporting Educational Uses of Telecommunication in the Secondary School: Part II. Strategies for Improved Implementation. International Journal of Instructional Media. 1992; 19(2): 97-109. ISSN: 0892-1815.

CRANE, BEVERLY. 1993. Information Technology: Stepping Stone to the Future. Social Studies Review. 1993 Winter; 32(2): 44-49. ISSN: 1056-6325.

CRANE, BEVERLY; MARKOWITZ, NANCY L. 1993. Online Searching, Critical Thinking, and Curriculum. The Computing Teacher. 1993 October; 20(2): 19-21. ISSN: 0278-9175.

DECANDIDO, GRACEANNE A. 1993. School Librarians on Internet: An Online Story. School Library Journal. 1993 January; 39(1): 10-11. ISSN: 0362-8930.

DESCY, DON E. 1993. All Aboard the Internet. TechTrends. 1993 January/February; 38(1): 29-34. ISSN: 8756-3894.

DOUGHERTY, RICHARD M. 1992. Balancing the E and R in the NREN: The Educational Imperative. In: Proceedings of FLICC Forums on Federal Information Policies: Combined Summaries of Proceedings of Access Is the Key; 1990 March 20; Washington, DC; and Building Information Superhighways: Supercomputing Networks and Libraries. 1991 March 21; Washington, DC. Washington, DC: Federal Library and Information Center Committee; 1992. 72-73. ISSN 1061-1485; ERIC: ED 349021.

DOYLE, DENIS; LEVINSON, ELIOT. 1993. Doing More with Less. American School Board Journal. 1993 March; 180(3): 26-29. ISSN: 0003-0953.

DYRLI, ODVARD EGIL. 1993. The Internet: Bringing Global Resources to the Classroom. Technology & Learning. 1993 October; 20(2): 51-58. ISSN: 1053-6728.

EHMAN, LEE H.; GLENN, ALLEN D.; JOHNSON, VIVIAN; WHITE, CHARLES S. 1992. Using Computer Databases in Student Problem Solving: A Study of Eight Social Studies Teachers' Classrooms. Theory and Research in Social Education. 1992 Spring; 20(2): 179-206. ISSN: 0093-3104.

EISENBERG, MICHAEL B.; ELY, DONALD P. 1993. Plugging into the 'Net. The ERIC Review. 1993 Winter; 2(3): 2-9. ISSN: 1065-1160.

EISENBERG, MICHAEL B.; MILBURY, PETER G. 1993. LM-NET: The School Library Media Electronic Community. Information Searcher. 1993; 5(2): 1-2. ISSN: 1055-3916.

EISENBERG, MICHAEL B.; SPITZER, KATHLEEN L. 1991. Information Technology and Services in Schools. In: Williams, Martha E., ed. Annual Review of Information Science and Technology: Volume 26. Medford, NJ: Learned Information, Inc. for the American Society for Information Science; 1991. 243-285. ISSN: 0066-4200; ISBN: 0-938734-55-5.

ELY, DONALD P. 1992. Response 1 to Ann Irving. School Library Media Annual. 1992; 10: 46-47. ISSN: 0739-7712.

EMERGING TECHNOLOGY CONSULTANTS. 1994. Multimedia and Videodisc Compendium for Education and Training. St. Paul, MN: Emerging Technology Consultants; 1994. 125p. Available from: Emerging Technology Consultants, P.O. Box 120444, St. Paul, MN 55112 .

EPLER, DORIS M.; TUZINSKI, JEAN H. 1991. A System for Statewide Sharing of Resources: A Case Study of ACCESS PENNSYLVANIA. School Library Media Quarterly. 1991 Fall; 20(1): 19-23. ISSN: 0278-4823.

GANDELL, TERRY S.; LAUFER, DOROTHY. 1993. Developing a Telecommunications Curriculum for Students with Physical Disabilities. Teaching Exceptional Children. 1993 Winter; 25(2): 26-28. ISSN: 0040-0599.

GAUL, THOMAS H.; UNDERWOOD, KENNETH E.; FORTUNE, JIM C. 1994. Reform at the Grass Roots. American School Board Journal. 1994 January; 181(1): 35-40. ISSN: 0003-0953.

GORNY, PETER. 1991. Fundamental Informatics in Teacher Education in West Germany. Computers and Education. 1991; 16(1): 37-42. ISSN: 0360-1315.

HALE, ROBERT G. 1992. It Ain't Just Paint. Emergency Librarian. 1992 January/February; 19(3): 23-25. ISSN: 0315-8888.

HANSON, CHARLES D. 1992. Commitment to Access: Resource Sharing in Public and School Libraries. Library Administration & Management. 1992 Winter; 6(1): 21-25. ISSN: 0888-4463.

HARRIS, JUDI. 1993. Using Internet Know-How to Plan How Students Will Know. The Computing Teacher. 1993 May; 20(8): 35-40. ISSN: 0278-9175.

HAWKINS, JAN. 1993. Technology and the Organization of Schooling. New York, NY: Center for Children and Technology, Bank Street College; 1993. 10p. (Technical Report no. 28). ERIC: ED 359933.

HEZEL, RICHARD T. 1991. Statewide Planning for Telecommunications in Education: Some Trends and Issues. TechTrends. 1991; 36(5): 17-20. ISSN: 8756-3894.

HOLZBERG, CAROL S. 1993. Solving Real-World Problems with Technology. Technology & Learning. 1993 November/December; 14(3): 10-18. ISSN: 1053-6728.

HONEY, MARGARET; HENRIQUEZ, ANDRES. 1993. Telecommunications and K-12 Educators: Findings from a National Survey. New York, NY: Center for Technology in Education, Bank Street College; 1993. 95p. ERIC: ED 359923.

HUNTER, BEVERLY. 1992. Linking for Learning: Computer-and-Communications Network Support for Nationwide Innovation in Education. Journal of Science Education and Technology. 1992; 1(1): 23-34. ISSN: 1059-0145.

IRVING, ANN. 1992. Information Skills across the Curriculum. School Library Media Annual. 1992; 10: 38-45. ISSN: 0739-7712.

JACKSON, LINDA; SQUIRE, DEBORAH L. 1993. Integrating Science Databases across the Curriculum. Information Searcher. 1993; 55(2): 22-27. ISSN: 1055-3916.

JACOBSON, FRANCES F.; JACOBSON, MICHAEL J. 1993. Representative Cognitive Learning Theories and BI: A Case Study of End User Searching. Research Strategies. 1993 Summer; 11(3): 124-137. ISSN: 0734-3310.

JERVIS, KATHE. 1992. The Birth of UrbNet: A New Medium for Teacher Talk. Quarterly of the National Writing Project and the Center for the Study of Writing and Literacy. 1992 Spring; 14(2): 12-14, 17. ISSN: 0896-3592.

KEAN, DEBRA M.; KEAN, DONALD K. 1992. Using Model Technology. Middle School Journal. 1992 May; 23(5): 44-45. ISSN: 0094-0771.

KEARSLEY, GREG. 1993. Education@Internet. ED-TECH Review. 1993 Autumn/Winter; 43-46. ISSN: 1065-6901.

KINNAMAN, DANIEL E. 1993. Making Professional Development Pay Off. Technology & Learning. 1993 January; 13(4): 51-52. ISSN: 1053-6728.

KOLLASCH, MATTHEW. 1993. School Media Matters: Modem Operandi. Wilson Library Bulletin. 1993 May; 67: 65-66. ISSN: 0043-5651.

KUHLTHAU, CAROL COLLIER 1992. Response 2 to Ann Irving. School Library Media Annual. 1992; 10: 48-51. ISSN: 0739-7712.

KURK, GAYLE. 1993. The Impact of Technology on the High School Media Center Budget. Atlanta, GA: Georgia State University; 1993. 67p. ERIC: ED 355923.

LADESTRO, DEBRA. 1991. A Tale of Two Cities. Teacher Magazine. 1991 May/June; 2(8): 47-51. ISSN: 1046-6193.

LEFEBVRE, ARLETTE. 1992. Ability Online: Promoting Social Competence and Computer Literacy in Adolescents with Disabilities. Rehabilitation Digest. 1992; 23(1): 3-6. ISSN: 0048-7139.

LEVINSON, ELIOT; DOYLE, DENIS. 1993. Doing the Productivity Three-Step. America's Agenda. 1993 Fall; 3(2): 29-31. ISSN: 1055-1247.

MANCALL, JACQUELINE C. 1991. (Un)changing Factors in the Searching Environment: Collections, Collectors, and Users. School Library Media Quarterly. 1991 Winter; 19(2): 84-89. ISSN: 0278-4823.

MANCALL, JACQUELINE C.; LODISH, ERICA K.; SPRINGER, JUDITH. 1992. Searching across the Curriculum. Phi Delta Kappan. 1992 March; 73(7): 526-528. ISSN: 0031-7217.

MARCHIONINI, GARY. 1991. Technological Trends and Implications: Toward the New Millennium. School Library Media Annual. 1991; 9: 182-187. ISSN: 0739-7712.

MARKET DATA RETRIEVAL, INCORPORATED. 1992. The Survey of Microcomputers in Schools. Shelton, CT: Market Data Retrieval, Inc.; 1992. 55p. ERIC: ED 352930.

MARKET DATA RETRIEVAL, INCORPORATED. 1993. Educational Mailing List and Market Guide: 1993-94. Shelton, CT: Market Data Retrieval, Inc.; 1993. 56p. Available from: MDR, 16 Progress Dr., Shelton, CT 06484.

MARKUSON, CAROLYN A.; MANCALL, JACQUELINE C. 1991. A Perspective on Contemporary Collection Development in School Libraries. School Library Media Quarterly. 1991 Winter; 19(2): 83. ISSN: 0278-4823.

MCCARTHY, ROBERT. 1993. CD-ROM Spins into Schools: How These Shiny Little Discs Will Revolutionize Education. Electronic Learning. 1993 October; (special edition): 10-17. ISSN: 0278-3258.

MCDANIEL, ERNEST; MCINERNEY, WILLIAM; ARMSTRONG, PENNY. 1993. Computers and School Reform. Educational Technology, Research and Development. 1993; 41(1): 73-78. ISSN: 1042-1629.

MEANS, BARBARA; BLANDO, JOHN; OLSON, KERRY; MIDDLETON, TERESA; MOROCCO, CATHERINE COBB; REMZ, ARLENE R.; ZORFASS, JUDITH. 1993. Using Technology to Support Education Reform. Washington, DC: U.S. Department of Education, Office of Educational Research and Improvement, Office of Research; 1993 September. 110p. Available from: U.S. Government Printing Office, Superintendent of Documents, Mail Stop: SSOP, Washington, DC 20402-9328.

MENDRINOS, ROXANNE B. 1992. CD-ROM Technology for Reference in Secondary School Library Media Centers. School Library Media Annual. 1992; 10: 158-163. ISSN: 0739-7712.

MERSETH, KATHERINE K. 1992. First Aid for First-Year Teachers. Phi Delta Kappan. 1992 May; 73(9): 678-683. ISSN: 0031-7217.

MOORE, PENELOPE A.; ST. GEORGE, ALISON. 1991. Children as Information Seekers: The Cognitive Demands of Books and Library Systems. School Library Media Quarterly. 1991 Spring; 19(3): 161-168. ISSN: 0278-4823.

MOURSUND, DAVE. 1993. Networking the World. The Computing Teacher. 1993 August/September; 20(1): 4. ISSN: 0278-9175.

NATIONAL CENTER FOR EDUCATION STATISTICS. 1993. Digest of Education Statistics, 1993. Washington, DC: U.S. Department of Education, Office of Educational Research and Improvement; 1993 October. 571p. (NCES-93-292). ISBN: 0-16-042052-0.

NEILSEN, LINDA. 1991. Writing and Research Using CD-ROM. Writing Notebook: Creative Word Processing in the Classroom. 1991 January-February; 8(3): 35-36. ISSN: 0749-2537.

NELSON, NANCY M. 1993. Editorial: Technology in School Libraries. Computers in Libraries. 1993 March; 13(3): 4. ISSN: 1041-7915.

NEWMAN, DENIS; BERNSTEIN, S.L.; REESE, P.A. 1992. Local Infrastructures for School Networking; Current Models and Prospects. New York, NY: Center for Technology in Education, Bank Street College; 1992. 30p. (Technical Report no. 22). ERIC: ED 349957.

NOVEMBER, ALAN; THORNBURG, DAVID. 1993. Has Technology Made the Curriculum Obsolete? Electronic Learning. 1993 September; 13(1): 16-17. ISSN: 0278-3258.

O'NEIL, JOHN. 1993. Using Technology to Support "Authentic" Learning. ASCD Update. 1993 October; 35(8): 1, 4-5. Available from: ASCD, 1250 N. Pitt St., Alexandria, VA 22314-1403.

OLDS, HENRY F., JR.; PEARLMAN, ROBERT. 1992. Designing a New American School. Phi Delta Kappan. 1992 December; 74(4): 296-298. ISSN: 0031-7217.

OWEN, GAVIN. 1992. Whole School Management of Information Technology. School Organisation. 1992; 12(1): 29-40. ISSN: 0260-1362.

PEZZULO, JUDY. 1993. The Human Interface with Technology. Computers in Libraries. 1993 May; 13(5): 20-23. ISSN: 1041-7915.

PORIS, JIM; BRUDER, ISABELLE. 1993. US DOE Appoints Director of Technology. Electronic Learning. 1993 November/December; 13(3): 6. ISSN: 0278-3258.

POTTER, ROSEMARY LEE. 1992. Using Telecommunications in Middle School Reading. Bloomington, IN: Phi Delta Kappa Educational Foundation; 1992. 48p. (PDK Fastback no. 335). ISBN: 0-87367-335-2; ERIC: ED 350996.

QUALITY EDUCATION DATA. 1992. Ed Tech Trends, 1992-93. Denver, CO: Quality Education Data; 1992 December. Available from: QED, 1600 Broadway, Suite 1200, Denver, CO 80202.

RIEL, MARGARET. 1992. Making Connections from Urban Schools. Education and Urban Society. 1992 August; 24(4): 477-488. ISSN: 0013-1245.

ROBLYER, M.D. 1992. Electronic Hands across the Ocean: The Florida-England Connection. The Computing Teacher. 1992 February; 19(5): 16-19. ISSN: 0278-9175.

ROSENBAUM, HOWARD. 1993. Educators and the Internet: What's Out There and How to Get Some of It. Indiana Media Journal. 1993 Summer; 15(4): 1-13. ISSN: 0164-7660.

ROSENBERG, JASON B.; BORGMAN, CHRISTINE L. 1992. Extending the Dewey Decimal Classification via Keyword Clustering: The Science Library Catalog Project. In: Shaw, Debora, ed. ASIS '92: Proceedings of the American Society for Information Science (ASIS) 55th Annual Meeting: Volume 29; 1992 October 26-29; Pittsburgh, PA. Medford, NJ: Learned Information, Inc. for ASIS; 1992. 171-184. ISSN: 0044-7870; ISBN: 0-938734-69-5.

ROTH, EMERY, II. 1992. ScrapBook USA: Writing 'Cross Grade, 'Cross Curriculum, 'Cross Country. The Computing Teacher. 1992 December/January; 20(4): 33-37. ISSN: 0278-9175.

SADOSKI, BEV. 1991. The High School Library and Technology. The Sourdough. 1991 Summer; 28: 23-24. ISSN: 0002-4570.

SAKS, JUDITH. 1993. Going On-Line. American School Board Journal. 1993 June; 180(6): 17-19, 22-23. ISSN: 0003-0953.

SANAOUI, RAZIKA; LAPKIN, SHARON. 1992. A Case Study of an FSL Senior Secondary Course Integrating Computer Networking. Canadian Modern Language Review. 1992 April; 48(3): 525-552. ISSN: 0008-4506.

SOFTWARE PUBLISHERS ASSOCIATION. 1992. SPA K-12 Market Study Report. Washington, DC: Software Publishers Association; 1992 Spring. 50p. Available from: SPA, 1730 M Street, NW, Washington, DC 20036.

SOLOMON, PAUL. 1991. Information Systems for Children: Explorations in Information Access and Interface Usability for an Online Catalog in an Elementary School Library. College Park, MD: University of Maryland; 1991. 354p. (Ph.D. dissertation). Available from: University Microfilms, Ann Arbor, MI. (UM order no. 9133166).

SOLOWAY, ELLIOT. 1991a. How the Nintendo Generation Learns. Communications of the ACM. 1991 September; 34(9): 23-26. ISSN: 0001-0782.

SOLOWAY, ELLIOT. 1991b. Quick, Where Do the Computers Go? Communications of the ACM. 1991 February; 34(2): 29-33. ISSN: 0001-0782

SOLOWAY, ELLIOT. 1993. Reading and Writing in the 21st Century. EDUCOM Review. 1993 January-February; 28(1): 26-29. ISSN: 1045-9146.

SPROULL, LEE; KIESLER, SARA. 1991. Computers, Networks, and Work. Scientific American. 1991 September; 265(3): 116-123. ISSN: 0036-8733.

STANZIONE, DOMINICK; THOMPSON, NEAL. 1993. What's Tech Got to Do with It? America's Agenda. 1993 Fall; 3(2): 22-24, 26-27. ISSN: 1055-1247.

STEARNS, MARIAN S.; DAVID, JANE L.; HANSON, SUSAN G.; RINGSTAFF, CATHY; SCHNEIDER, S.A. 1991. Cupertino-Fremont Model Technology Schools Project Research Findings: Teacher-Centered Model of Technology Integration: End of Year 3. Menlo Park, CA: SRI International; 1991. 41p. ERIC: ED 332326.

STIX, GARY. 1993. Domesticating Cyberspace: Trends in Communications. Scientific American. 1993 August; 269(2): 100-110. ISSN: 0036-8733.

SWISHER, ROBERT; SPITZER, KATHLEEN L.; SPRIESTERSBACH, BARBARA; MARKUS, TIM; BURRIS, JERRY M. 1991. Telecommunications for School Library Media Centers. School Library Media Quarterly. 1991 Spring; 19(3): 153-160. ISSN: 0278-4823.

THOMPSON, BETTY. 1993. The TENET [Texas Education Network] and T-STAR Networks: An Answer to Edgewood v. Kirby? Texas Library Journal. 1993 Summer; 69(2): 55-58. ISSN: 0040-4446.

TROTTER, ANDREW. 1993. Planning for Multimedia. Executive Educator. 1993 June; 15(6): 18-21. ISSN: 0161-9500.

WATTS, GARY D.; CASTLE, SHARI. 1992. Electronic Networking and the Construction of Professional Knowledge. Phi Delta Kappan. 1992 May; 73(9): 684-689. ISSN: 0031-7217.

WHITNEY, KAREN A. 1992. Response 3 to Ann Irving. School Library Media Annual. 1992; 10: 52-55. ISSN: 0739-7712.

WILLIAMS, ROBERT A. 1992. The Effectiveness of the Online Card Catalog for Sixth, Seventh, and Eighth Grade Students at Sailorway Middle School Library: A Survey. Kent, OH: Kent State University; 1992. 44p. ERIC: ED 355956.

WISHNIETSKY, DAN H. 1991. Using Electronic Mail in an Educational Setting. Bloomington, IN: Phi Delta Kappa Educational Foundation; 1991. 39p. (PDK Fastback no. 316). ISBN: 0-87367-316-6; ERIC: ED 333865.

WISHNIETSKY, DAN H. 1992. Hypermedia: The Integrated Learning Environment. Bloomington, IN: Phi Delta Kappa Educational Foundation; 1992. 37p. (PDK Fastback no. 339). ISBN: 0-87367-339-5; ERIC: ED 354877.

ZIMMERMAN, NANCY P. 1993. Compromise in the Information Age: The Attitudes of School Library Media Specialists toward Technology. Journal of Youth Services in Libraries. 1993 Spring; 6(3): 305-311. ISSN: 0894-2498.

ZORFASS, JUDITH M.; REMZ, ARLENE R. 1992. Successful Technology Integration: The Role of Communication and Collaboration. Middle School Journal. 1992 May; 23(5): 39-43. ISSN: 0094-0771.

IV

The Profession

Section IV includes a chapter by Alan Poulter, Anne Morris and Julie Dow. Alan Poulter and Anne Morris are both from Loughborough University, England, and Julie Dow is from the University of South Australia. These authors have collaborated to produce the first *ARIST* chapter dealing with knowledge engineering. Their chapter is entitled "LIS Professionals as Knowledge Engineers."

A knowledge engineer is one who builds expert systems, and an expert system is a knowledge-based system that emulates the performance of a human expert in a particular task or domain. The knowledge-based system possesses, as data, human knowledge consisting of facts and heuristics (rules of thumb) about the task or domain. In their chapter Poulter, Morris and Dow introduce the history of knowledge engineering as a background to its adoption by library and information science (LIS) professionals. They point out that knowledge engineering for expert systems is a specialized category of artificial intelligence. They show how LIS professionals have fared as knowledge engineers and how their involvement relates to the perception of LIS professionals as knowledge engineers. Poulter et al. discuss the tools and techniques of knowledge engineering as they have been applied to the LIS domain, and they also look at the involvement of LIS professionals in knowledge engineering outside LIS.

Poulter, Morris and Dow focus on the years 1989-1993. They investigate the methods used in knowledge acquisition, the types of knowledge representation used, the user modeling performed, the tools used to build expert systems, user interface considerations, the development status of knowledge engineering and expert system projects, and the evaluation techniques employed for them. The authors find that the amount of activity and research in the LIS expert system field is surprisingly large and observe that the majority of the work deals with the domains of reference and online intermediaries but that some work extends beyond these. In general the work is contributing to the understanding of the functions of these elements in the systems. Poulter, Morris and Dow are encouraged by the willingness of LIS professionals to venture into the challenging area of knowledge engineering and to use their expertise in solving real world problems and increasing the efficiency of their own work.

9 LIS Professionals as Knowledge Engineers

ALAN POULTER and
ANNE MORRIS
Loughborough University

JULIE DOW
University of South Australia, Magill

INTRODUCTION

A knowledge engineer is a person who participates in building expert systems. An expert system is a knowledge-based system that possesses as data human knowledge, consisting of facts and heuristics (rules of thumb) about a task or a domain (HAYES-ROTH ET AL.). An expert system should possess knowledge derived from human experts, and its performance should emulate that of the human expert. This chapter deals with the knowledge engineering of expert systems, not the broader field of knowledge-based systems. WECKERT & COOPER (p. 284) claim that it is incorrect to use the term knowledge-based system as a synonym for expert system. They explain that:

> While expert systems are knowledge-based, so are other AI applications. Natural language processing systems, for example, often require large knowledge-bases in order to make sense of the language which they are asked to process. We see expert systems, then, as just one type of knowledge-based system.

L.C. SMITH (1987, p. 51) clarifies this further, explaining that knowledge systems may be able to "reason about and apply knowledge," but unlike expert systems they are not intended to "mimic human experts." Smith further notes that expert systems: "preserve otherwise perishable human expertise; distribute otherwise scarce expertise; reduce costs of mediocre or poor human performance; and provide help to humans trying to access information and use computers" (p. 51). Expert systems

Annual Review of Information Science and Technology (ARIST), Volume 29, 1994
Martha E. Williams, Editor
Published for the American Society for Information Science (ASIS)
By Learned Information, Inc., Medford, N.J.

are generally considered to be advice givers or decision-support systems that can explain their reasoning to users.

Knowledge engineers are specialists in eliciting knowledge from experts rather than necessarily being experts in the domain itself. Their role in attempting to understand and represent in machine form the nature of the problem-solving strategies of experts is central to the success of any system. Library and information professionals have taken a keen interest in the knowledge engineering role, both as knowledge engineers themselves and as cooperating experts, and they have done a substantial amount of work in exploring and extending the boundaries of knowledge engineering within library and information studies (LIS).

History and Development

Knowledge engineering has its roots in early artificial intelligence (AI) research, which was looking for general problem-solving techniques that had universal application. A classic example of this research was the GPS (General Problem Solver), which tried to solve mathematical problems by reducing them into successively smaller problems until a solution was found. This partial solution could then recursively unwind to solve the original problem (ERNST & NEWELL; NEWELL & SIMON). This approach contradicted human problem-solving behavior, in which heuristics found shortcuts to a solution. It also was unable to help solve real-world problems.

The direction taken by research switched, to look at specialist knowledge and the facts and heuristics that were specific to particular problems or domains (FEIGENBAUM). This approach led to the development of seminal expert systems, the names of some of which are DENDRAL (LINDSAY ET AL.), PROSPECTOR (GASCHNIG), and MYCIN (BUCHANAN & SHORTLIFFE; SHORTLIFFE) for deriving molecular structures, for geological exploration, and for medical diagnosis, respectively.

The announcement of the Japanese fifth-generation computer development project, which commenced in 1981, gave a massive boost to research in expert systems and their applications around the world, as the United States and Europe strove to keep up with Japan. This research effort percolated into LIS.

Aims and Objectives

This chapter is concerned with knowledge engineering, which is the process of designing and building expert systems, and includes the following elements that L.C. SMITH identified (1987, p. 51):

knowledge acquisition, knowledge system design, knowledge programming (implementation of a knowledge base and inference engine), and knowledge refinement.

Knowledge engineering for expert systems is a specialized category of artificial intelligence, which was discussed in an *ARIST* chapter for the first time in 1980 (L.C. SMITH, 1980). In a subsequent chapter SOWIZRAL gave an overview of emerging expert system research in LIS. This was followed by an analysis of AI techniques in information retrieval (L.C. SMITH, 1987) and the function of expert systems as information intermediaries (DRENTH ET AL.). These authors discussed aspects of knowledge engineering as it pertained to their subject matter.

This chapter aims to investigate how LIS researchers have fared as knowledge engineers and how their involvement relates to the perception of LIS professionals as potential knowledge engineers. To this end this chapter examines two areas: first, in the section entitled "LIS Professionals as Knowledge Engineers within LIS", it considers the tools and techniques of knowledge engineering as they have been applied within the LIS domain; second, in the section entitled "LIS Professionals as Knowledge Engineers outside LIS", it examines the involvement of LIS professionals in knowledge engineering outside of LIS.

The focus of the chapter is on knowledge engineering in LIS, over the years 1989 to 1993 chiefly. This is covered in the first section by investigating in detail all areas involved: the methods employed in knowledge acquisition, the types of knowledge representation used, the user modeling performed, the tools used to build expert systems, user interface considerations, the development status of projects and the evaluation techniques harnessed. General material is covered only as an introduction to particular efforts in LIS.

This chapter does not attempt to summarize progress in specific application areas within LIS (e.g., the use of expert systems as online intermediaries to commercial systems). For this approach the reader should consult such guides as ALBERICO & MICCO, GAUCH and MORRIS (1992a).

LIS PROFESSIONALS AS KNOWLEDGE ENGINEERS WITHIN LIS

A comprehensive collection of papers on knowledge engineering within LIS prior to 1989 was built up through online searches and general research. A DIALOG search was performed to identify examples of knowledge engineering performed in LIS from 1989 to 1993. A DIALINDEX search identified databases with the most frequent occurrences of the terms knowledge engineering, knowledge acquisition, and knowledge representation, combined with any term covering information science. These sources were searched and yielded many items that discussed libraries of software routines used to develop expert systems in information fields outside of LIS but failed to locate some known LIS publications. Retrieval under the broader "expert systems" term was necessary. This approach reflects the publishing pattern, especially in earlier papers, as authors tended only to give overviews of systems, devoting small sections of their papers to each aspect of the system that concerned them. More recently, as specific elements of expert system development have attracted the attention of researchers, papers are becoming more specialized and are likely to be retrieved under more specific terminology. Predictably the most relevant sources were combed from the known information science databases within DIALOG.

A total of 195 papers was found by the DIALOG search and by general research. They detailed the development, features, and functions of 139 expert system projects in the LIS domain. A database was set up to hold information for each project relating to:

- LIS application area
- application type
- project status
- knowledge acquisition techniques
- knowledge representation methods
- expert system construction tools used
- development methodology used
- user modeling
- user interface
- evaluation

Each category was held in the database as a list of possible values. For example for the category "application type" the possible values were "Advisor," "Tutor," "Other," and "Not known." The tables and statistics included in this chapter are derived from this database.

Scope of Expert Systems in LIS

Notwithstanding the existence of a substantial literature on knowledge engineering in LIS, one must ask how suitable the LIS domain is for the application of knowledge engineering. A suitable domain should have clearly circumscribed borders and contain a limited number of entities and relationships (SOWA; WELBANK). With respect to just a subdomain of LIS, namely information retrieval, BROOKS makes clear:

> The "world" of the intelligent IR system would be a wide one, including as it must users and their problems, documents and their descriptions, and retrieval heuristics. In other words, the domain is neither narrow nor discrete nor homogeneous and involves a great many objects and relations. (p. 375)

SPARCK JONES agrees. Not surprisingly then, no one expert system covers the range of expertise an LIS professional ought to possess.

Systems are usually grouped in the literature by the subdomain (online intermediary, reference work, cataloging, indexing, classification) that they address. Some particular LIS subdomains have received relatively little attention (e.g., abstracting) while others (e.g., acquisition of new stock) are hardly represented at all.

In the database developed for this chapter, 80% of the projects were intended for one LIS subdomain. Of the projects based in one LIS subdomain, their breakdown by subdomain was: 32% reference work; 28% online retrieval; 12% indexing, cataloging, or classification; 7% library management applications; and 1% abstracting.

Within each subdomain, systems tend to be restricted to even more limited domains to avoid problems associated with ill-defined borders and large numbers of entities and relationships.

PLEXUS (VICKERY & BROOKS) is limited by subject to gardening and by client group to public library clients, while POINTER (K.F. SMITH) is limited to U.S. government publications.

The modality of a system (i.e., whether it tutors, offers advice, or performs the task unaided) adds further specialization. By far most expert system applications in LIS reported in the literature are advisory. For example, ERCEGOVAC (1990) describes the expert system MAPPER, which advises novice map catalogers. While this approach is ideal for tackling those materials requiring specialized cataloging experience, it is only useful for a few awkward items like maps and is not for the much more numerous mundane items. From the database 69% of the projects were advisory only and 3% were tutor systems only. Some 9% of the projects operated in both modes; as many as 19% of projects were classified as operating in some other mode. One project that overlaps these categories is REFSIM (PARROTT, 1989), which offers a consultation mode, a simulation-based coach, and a Socratic tutor. Here one system has been designed to function in multiple roles.

KNOWLEDGE ACQUISITION

A knowledge engineer is a specialist in eliciting knowledge from experts rather than an expert in the domain itself. Knowledge acquisition or the process of transferring human expertise to an expert system permeates all stages of development. HAYES-ROTH & WECKERT identify five stages in the design of a knowledge system: (1) identification: definition of the scope and characteristics of the problem area; (2) conceptualization: finding key ideas, relationships, and ways to represent the knowledge; (3) formalization: designing a structure to represent the knowledge as demanded by a selected expert-building tool; (4)

implementation: formalizing the knowledge into rules that can be tested; (5) testing: validating the rules within the prototype and amending them until the system's performance is compatible with the excellence demanded by the domain experts. Testing locates areas of weakness in the early stages of the cycle. The knowledge engineer may need to revert to knowledge acquisition at all stages of development to achieve expert performance.

Knowledge acquisition is the most challenging and important element in expert system development. It is the process of eliciting knowledge from experts and converting it into facts and rules that are compatible with the knowledge representation form of the chosen development tool. Much of the expertise in all knowledge domains is within the minds of human experts. It has developed from experience, and only some components are included in publications (ALBERICO & MICCO).

A recurring problem in knowledge acquisition is how to extract and represent the heuristics of the expert and build into the system the knowledge that comprises real expertise. Frequently experts are not consciously aware of their decision-making processes and need to be prompted to explain their actions. The challenge for the knowledge engineer is to use various strategies to extract this knowledge and to try to represent it in a way that replicates expert human behavior. ALBERICO (1992, p. 199) observes:

> One of the major obstacles to knowledge acquisition is the tendency of human experts to compile knowledge, i.e., to compress all the steps required to solve a complex problem into a single mental construct. It is difficult to decompose the knowledge of human experts, breaking down an approach to problem solving into the separate steps required by the computer.

Given this complexity, CHIGNELL & PETERSON explain some of the pitfalls in knowledge acquisition: (1) collecting knowledge from the first available or most convenient rather than the best source; (2) collecting irrelevant knowledge; (3) insufficient exploration of the range and flexibility of the expert's knowledge; and (4) the difficulties inherent in observing behavior. Chignell and Peterson say that knowledge acquisition is the most time consuming and expensive aspect of expert system development, accounting for perhaps 50% of the system's total cost (DOS SANTOS ET AL.). DOS SANTOS ET AL. propose a mathematical model to help developers analyze their costs and determine when it is better to use a single source rather than multiple sources to maximize knowledge acquisition in terms of quality, cost, and elimination of unnecessary overlap. A related issue is the identification of experts who are willing to commit sufficient time.

Human experts understand the boundaries of their expertise and do not attempt to solve problems beyond their scope (CHIGNELL & PETERSON). They have an in-depth store of specialized domain knowledge but also draw on an extensive common-sense knowledge of the world that is too broadly based to build into a small system and impossible to represent in a large system. Within a very narrow problem area, good expert system performance can be achieved by limiting the system to "problem-specific" knowledge (TRAVIS). It is difficult, however, to place precise restrictions around the particular domain, and the system may be asked for advice outside this narrow focus. This is brittleness and is a major problem in system development.

The classic model of knowledge engineering for the development of an expert system begins with a thorough understanding of the skills and knowledge possessed by a human expert. For any expert system, human experts are the preeminent source of knowledge. They must agree both on how to solve problems and on the correct answers.

Eliciting knowledge through interviews with experts is the most common way of developing a knowledge base (O'NEILL & MORRIS, 1989b). Interviews, whether structured or semistructured, have limitations and must be planned carefully to ensure their validity (ERCEGOVAC, 1992). Knowledge engineers often supplement the shortcomings of interviews by observing the expert in the process of completing relevant tasks, asking for verbal reports (verbal protocols) of problem-solving activities, asking the expert to complete written questionnaires, and using the published literature in the domain. The last is common in reference expert systems.

Knowledge acquisition is a two-way process that is iterative and evolutionary (HAYES-ROTH & WECKERT). It is also intense and requires extended consultations between the knowledge engineer and the expert (WATERMAN). Sometimes the roles of both the domain expert and the knowledge engineer are taken by the same person, though this is not a recommended practice. As WATERMAN explains, experts are unable to articulate clearly the nature of their expertise and are known to offer plausible explanations for their decision-making processes that do not accord with or explain how they solve problems.

To take one subdomain of LIS, expertise in being an online intermediary essentially involves knowledge of clients and their problems, knowledge of the search subject domain and its databases with their information content, and knowledge of searching facilities and how retrieved items relate to problems. There are problems here for knowledge acquisition. First, because these tasks cover such a wide territory, the expertise of an online intermediary is diffuse and hard to specify. Investigation of that expertise is hampered by acquisition techniques that omit nonverbal communication and tacitly held assumptions.

Second, knowledge of the search subject domain, even if the domain is specific, involves the recognition of many concepts and the relationships among them. This knowledge does not come just from the expert but also from the resources of the subject domain. Developers of expert intermediary systems (MARCUS; PAICE; POLLITT, 1986; SHOVAL) have replaced direct investigation of human experts with that of the resources of subject domains. There is a choice to be made in allocating knowledge acquisition efforts. Table 1 illustrates the choices of knowledge acquisition methods reported in the literature stored in the database. The table shows the preponderance of reliance on printed sources; perhaps this is a reflection on the nature of the LIS domain.

Personal Experience

The broad knowledge and concept base of most subdomains within LIS may help to explain why these experts sometimes choose to become their own knowledge engineers, especially when they wish to develop an in-house prototype system. The reference staff of the McKinney Engineering Library at the University of Texas answer over 50,000 engineering reference questions per year (ARDIS). Questions about patents are time consuming, and when the reference desk is very busy, these queries sometimes receive only cursory attention. Ardis reports on the development of the Patent Information Assistant to guide users in online patent searching. The patent reference experts examined and logically structured their own heuristics and wrote explanations to instruct searchers in appropriate strategies. Ardis gives some insight into the knowledge engineering of the system by including the menus for each of the modules together with helpful details on the functions within each component. Although the reference staff tested its knowledge base, it became apparent after two years of use in the library that many users needed additional guidance to distinguish between patents and trademarks before they began their search. This failure can be explained by knowledge remaining unidentified that must have been

Table 1
Percentages (%) of the Projects Using Certain Knowledge-Acquisition Techniques

	Used	Not Used	Not Known
Printed sources	50	4	46
Interviewing	28	9	63
Personal experience	12	18	70
Observation	7	16	77
Protocol analysis	6	17	77
Multidimensional sorting	4	18	78

used routinely and perhaps unconsciously by the reference staff in face-to-face interviews with users.

HALL discusses the disadvantages of being a knowledge engineer and having a stake in knowledge base construction, particularly within an interview, when neutrality and objectivity are necessary. He recommends using an interview outline and including a second knowledge engineer from another discipline to maintain balance and focus. The constraints were less apparent in being a participant when applying protocol analysis to the principles for selecting journals for the academic library in which he worked.

Interviews

ERCEGOVAC (1992) provides a literature review of interviewing theory and highlights problems surrounding the validity of the interview process. The decisions relating to choice of methodology for Ercegovac's research provide helpful guidance to others in LIS using this method for eliciting knowledge.

After assessing the literature on collection building, SOWELL found a list of selection criteria but little advice on how to weight these criteria or evaluate the relationships among them. A recorded, transcribed in-depth interview with a subject bibliographer and two follow-up sessions did little more than provide rudimentary knowledge needed for the Monograph Selection Advisor, an expert system which is restricted to classical Latin literature (SOWELL). The interview questions were based on material inspired by the literature of selection criteria. The researchers sought to identify the kinds of decisions made in selection, establish the depth of knowledge of the expert, obtain information about the research and teaching needs of the faculty, the budget, and the scope of Latin literature. The expert was able to consult a range of selection criteria simultaneously in making decisions about selection but experienced difficulty in explaining the exact method of working to reach those decisions. The great problem here is that the selection criteria are not clearly delineated within the literature, and experts use heuristics extensively with few measures of their success beyond meeting expressed demands for materials.

In another study GUNNING reports that the library reference staff was interviewed to collate the knowledge base for an expert system called Reference Expert. Reference and library systems staff, working as knowledge engineers, clearly recognized the experts' difficulty in articulating their knowledge and the limits of the software in representing the complexity of that knowledge. To encourage ongoing input, they developed prototypes, left them in the work area for experimentation with a log for comments, and on the basis of this feedback from the experts, incrementally extended the knowledge base.

Protocol Analysis

In protocol analysis, the knowledge engineer seeks to ascertain the protocol (the set of actions and responses) that the human expert uses. This involves getting the experts to talk through what they are doing; a recording can later be combed for clues as to the nature of the protocol. P.J. SMITH ET AL. used protocol analysis in designing EP/X. After interviewing experienced searchers they videotaped them helping users and helping investigators who were playing the role of users. This technique revealed the importance of communication in resolving ambiguity and in helping the user formulate search statements.

Observation

Observation is almost the same technique as protocol analysis except that human experts need not talk through their actions; they just proceed as normal. A recording of their activities is then analyzed by the knowledge engineer. Observation can involve the logging of online activities. DEBROWER & JONES report that direct observation of the selection process for accepting or rejecting donations to a library, accompanied by the expert talking through the decision process, proved to be a very effective knowledge-acquisition method. This technique followed interviews with the expert and examination of manual decision slips that recorded the outcomes. Observation revealed the weighting of the decision factors and the relationships among them in different areas of the collection.

Multidimensional Sorting

Multidimensional sorting attempts to get the human expert to build a concept map of the domain of expertise. A human expert might, for example, be asked to sort concepts on cards into groups according to different criteria that the human expert devises. This method was used successfully by MORRIS ET AL. (1988) to get online searchers to rate the selection criteria they used for host and database selection.

Printed Sources

Within some areas of LIS, published materials include an extensive body of knowledge used as sources of information by LIS professionals. Bibliographies, for example, list sources used to answer reference questions, and there are monographs that summarize the major sources in many categories of knowledge. Even so books do not provide the knowledge needed to answer all reference questions (CHIGNELL &

PETERSON). Nonetheless, some knowledge engineers apply knowledge acquisition to printed sources for knowledge about reference information, although it is advisable to supplement the knowledge gleaned by talking to human experts.

The compilers of Technical Writing Assistant, for example, used standard reference tools in the relevant subject fields and the library catalog to create a knowledge base designed to help students find suitable reference resources to complete a technical writing course at Texas A&M University (BUTKOVICH ET AL.).

Online Reference for Expertise in Opera (ORFEO) recommends sources to answer questions about opera. It contains a knowledge base developed from one major bibliography of 700 items, plus some items added by GERBER. Like Kiwinet (A. SMITH, 1991), this system is based on the "given and wanted" notion of reference theory and is purely a prototype. Gerber argues that with different sources, the knowledge categories of ORFEO are sufficiently general to be applied to drama and with some adjustment could also work for art. Gerber's argument is exemplified by Anything Goes! (METZGER) which uses ORFEO as a model but answers questions on American musical theater. TRAUTMAN & VON FLITTNER used a range of sources for their system for aiding selection of online databases. They used the same sources—database directories (e.g., MARCACCIO), a textbook, and DIALINDEX (a term-frequency index for databases)—that an online searcher would use in database selection.

The literature of collection building lists a range of criteria to apply when selecting sources for libraries. JOHNSTON & WECKERT (1990), in exploring the development of an expert system to choose materials for an academic library, considered the literature of selection principles and developed their initial criteria from one article. They modified the criteria on the basis of one other publication and in consultation with one of those authors. These criteria became the basis for a series of studies exploring appropriate forms of knowledge representation for this purpose.

An essential part of LIS are thesauri and classification schemes for many domains, and it is tempting to redeploy them as knowledge bases. Thesauri have successfully served as de facto knowledge bases. For example POLLITT (1988) used the MeSH thesaurus of medical subject headings to build a browser for MEDLINE. The AGROVOC keyword vocabulary and the CAB thesaurus have been used for both CAIN (FRIIS), which aids indexing of material for AGREP (Inventory of Agricultural Research Projects) and AGRIRES (KONIG), which assists in retrieval from agricultural databases. However, there is skepticism over whether most thesauri and classification schemes are suitable for use as knowledge bases (PAICE; SORMUNEN & ALKULA).

Machine Learning

Knowledge engineers have attempted to develop systems of machine learning for automatic knowledge acquisition, although none has been especially successful to date. JOHNSTON & WECKERT (1991) used listings of titles from publishers' catalogs and asked professional librarians to evaluate items for library selection (as discussed above) on a weighted scale for each criterion. The knowledge engineers were dissatisfied with the librarians' basis for deciding the weightings in an apparently ad hoc manner. To test the relative importance of the various criteria, they logged these scores and, using a derivative of the ID3 algorithm devised by QUINLAN, automatically induced rules about which items to select. They concluded, as they predicted, that the machine weighted the criteria differently from the librarians. This method seems to have promise for item selection and could be applied to the electronic data held by publishers to assist with selection. CIMINO & BARNETT have attempted to extract medical knowledge by analyzing citations in the National Library of Medicine's (NLM) MEDLINE database. They used co-occurrence information for keywords to build semantic relationships among medical concepts. Using a set of 504 rules that look for patterns in keyword distributions in 673 MEDLINE citations, they produced 2,795 "facts" about medical concepts. While they found their system especially useful in constructing semantic networks, they recognize that they are relying on the structure and controlled vocabulary of MEDLINE.

KNOWLEDGE REPRESENTATION

Once human knowledge has been extracted (e.g., through interviews, observation, or protocol analysis) from experts or other sources, it must be organized and structured for use in a knowledge base. Knowledge acquisition and representation form the core of the knowledge engineer's expertise.

In a knowledge base it is possible to use one or more knowledge-representation schemes—viz., typically production rules, frames, and semantic nets (BARR & FEIGENBAUM). The chief criteria for the scheme are applicability and efficiency in the target domain/task (LEVESQUE & BRACHMAN).

Production rules alone were used (see Table 2) by 21% of projects, while 14% used production rules in conjunction with another method. These figures must be treated cautiously due to the high percentage of "not knowns." Frames alone were used by 8%, while 12% used frames in conjunction with another method. Semantic nets alone were used by 5% of projects, while 12% used semantic nets in conjunction with another method.

Table 2
Percentages (%) of Knowledge-Representation Techniques Used

	Used	Not Used	Not Known
Production rules	35	11	54
Frames	20	15	65
Semantic nets	17	17	66
Predicate calculus	4	24	72

Production Rules

In expert systems, production rules consist of conditions and conclusions. Typically all the conditions have to be satisfied to prove the conclusion. Each condition is an *IF* statement, which gets a Boolean value from either questioning the user or from the already proven conclusions of other production rules. Each conclusion is a *THEN* statement of a known fact or condition. Production rules are reasonably overt in their representation and can be easily amended, at least until large numbers of them are involved. Production rules also have other problems in use, and COSGROVE & WEIMANN have proposed an improved scheme, which embeds production rules into a hierarchical data structure that allows inheritance. They suggest that the improved scheme could be applied to library classification.

At first, cataloging looks like an ideal domain for expert systems because it is already based on sets of rules. D. SMITH ET AL., for example, include a disk with sets of production rules directly generated from AACR2 rules for added entries. However, ERCEGOVAC (1986) considers cataloging a "pseudo-formalized" task, in that although it appears to be rule governed it is not mechanical but draws on a cataloger's knowledge of previous examples or analogies. Rules by themselves are not enough; they must be supplemented by human knowledge. The knowledge engineering needed for this task may be far deeper than that demanded by a restatement of cataloging rules into an expert system. FENLY agrees with Ercegovac that the adoption of existing knowledge bases expressed as rules is often an unsatisfactory method of knowledge representation. He judges attempts to convert AACR2 rules into expert systems as "unconvincing," largely because experienced catalogers use heuristics to interpret the rules and to identify appropriate choices. Novices lack this private knowledge of cataloging rule interpretation which may not be built into the system when the rule base is converted. Instead of looking for ready-made rules in selecting suitable knowledge engineering projects, Fenly recommends examining characteristics of the knowledge domain against appropriate criteria for a good expert system. He provides readers with a methodology by citing as examples the demands of descriptive cataloging of monographic series and the creation of unique Cutter numbers for shelf listing at the Library of Congress.

A. SMITH (1992) used the shell EXSYS to develop a production rule-based advisor to help library assistants locate appropriate reference material to answer questions on New Zealand. NZRef is based on Jahoda's notion that a reference question is composed of a given—the information known by the client—and a wanted—the information required by the client. Smith judged the rule structure to be a limited but useful way to represent knowledge about sources. One difficulty he noted was that certain combinations of rules used for particular reference tasks created unsuitable recommendations and, to suppress these, special rules had to be added to the knowledge base. Another difficulty was that not all members of a class of information sources could have a general set of rules applied. He argues that frames would provide better representation where differences are important.

Frames

A frame is a data structure that contains "slots," attributes of the entity represented by the frame as a whole. There can be restrictions on which slots have to be filled and on the contents of slots. It is possible to include a complete frame in a slot of another frame so that inheritance hierarchies can be constructed. Frames lower in the hierarchy inherit features of those frames higher in the hierarchy.

WHITE is perhaps the earliest example of someone in LIS who used frames as a model for the reference process. PARROTT (1989) used frames in REFSIM, an expert system for the reference process. Each dialog with a client was driven by the need to fill in slots in types of frames. Types of transactions were directional (i.e., where is a particular library service), holdings, ready reference, and substantive. There were also frames for the librarian and the client.

In a different domain, indexing, HUMPHREY (1992) used frames to represent elements in the MeSH thesaurus. In this system the thesaural linking information for elements is subsumed, but inheritance links are also added. It is these links that the MedIndEx system uses as a prescriptive indexing aid and that sets it apart from a standard thesaurus.

Within cataloging, DAVIES considers that frames could provide satisfactory representation of the rules for describing items as required by AACR2 and the assigning of MARC codes. These frames could be linked to other administrative modules such as acquisitions and circulation. Additionally, the hierarchical nature of frames could help with cataloging problems related to examples of similar resources in the same format. BAILEY ET AL. continue the theme of using frames, in their case to represent the bibliographic records of reference sources in Index Expert. The hierarchical structure of the frame allows for efficient representation and maintenance of the knowledge base, which was written in TURBO PROLOG, using the Knowledge Base Management system. This allows the use of a fully featured editor to update and to change the knowledge base, which could be reloaded into the system for error checking.

Semantic Nets

A semantic net is a set of linked concepts. The links among the concepts, known as arcs, express the relationships. Relationships are named to show their nature (e.g. "is-a," "contains"). A semantic net can provide a compact graphical overview of a domain.

Semantic networks tend to be costly to develop, so BRUANDET has attempted to generate one automatically for a domain using production rules to control generation and linking of new items. COHEN & KJELDSEN report a unique application of semantic networks for information retrieval; their GRANT system tries to match funding agencies with research projects. Although it performs well in trials, the semantic network of 4,500 nodes took four person-months of effort to construct. They recommend the construction of a system like Bruandet's to offset this disadvantage. The system of TAN ET AL. is another example of an information retrieval system that uses a semantic net as a browsing resource.

Predicate Calculus

Predicate calculus is a system of knowledge representation based on logic. Predicates are logical statements about variables and the relationships between them. Predicates are usually defined and interrogated by a logic programming language, such as PROLOG. Specialist programming and design skills are needed to derive the rigorous logical structure that is required for knowledge representation. An example of one of these, CODER (FOX), uses µ-PROLOG exclusively to build a complex, multitiered system for document retrieval. It required a team of graduate students to build a working prototype. LUCARELLA & MORARA have attempted to extend the representative power of PROLOG by building with it a document retrieval system, FIRST (Fuzzy Information Retrieval SysTem), which uses fuzzy instead of Boolean logic.

Hybrids

Production rules, frames, and semantic nets have been used in combination. To an extent, each can offset the disadvantages of another. The drawback is the increased complexity of system design and maintenance. Examples here might be CoalSORT (MONARCH & CARBONELL), in which browsable frames store information about each term in a semantic network, and the expert system of DEBROWER & JONES called Gift Assistant for collection management, which was built using a shell called Intelligent Developer. This shell allowed both production rules and frames to be used and also provided links to HyperCard for building graphical user interfaces.

USER MODELING

An expert system can also hold knowledge about its users, as well as its domain. This is user modeling. A good introduction is given by BROOKS ET AL. (1985) of user modeling in the LIS domain. It was not known whether 52% of the projects in the database of papers read for this chapter used user modeling. Of the remainder, 21% of projects did, as against 27% that did not.

A useful overview is provided by BRAJNIK ET AL. They describe their system, IR-NLI, as it discovers the users' educational level, their knowledge of the search topic, and the sources they have consulted. The model of the user is preserved over time to avoid repetitive questioning, and it can be extended with information about later searches by that user. Other systems that invoke user modeling are described by RICH, VICKERY & BROOKS, and ARDIS. The value of user modeling is limited if client groups are diverse and inquiries require detailed subject knowledge.

EXPERT SYSTEM TOOLS

An archetypal expert system consists of a knowledge base and an inference engine that uses the knowledge base to arrive at judgments. However, beyond the essential split between these two, there is little standardization of the system's components (PATTERSON).

The inference engine is completely independent of the content of the knowledge base. However, its design and operation are influenced by the knowledge representation used, the size of the knowledge base, and the uncertainty of knowledge items (HAYES-ROTH ET AL.). The knowledge engineer has a choice of readymade inference engines (expert system shells), the gamut of programming languages, some of which excel at inference engine building, and of knowledge engineering environments to build inference engines (SAVORY).

Other types of software can be pressed into service as expert systems—e.g., the Monographic Acquisitions Consultant (MAC) uses the spreadsheet Lotus 1-2-3. ZAGER & SMADI exploited the macro capabilities of Lotus 1-2-3 to allow it to act like an inference engine. However, this is a unique example of use of a software tool not intended for expert system construction.

For comparative reasons researchers sometimes use two or more development tools while they are building and testing different prototypes of a system. For example BLACK ET AL. used ES/P and SAGE to build two versions of HEADS, after they abandoned an attempt to write an original shell in LISP. ES/P and SAGE were both commercial shells offering good run-time facilities to help the user, although ES/P had memory limitations with an extensive knowledge base. Three prototypes of Reference Expert were developed; one using KnowledgePro, another using VP-Expert, and the third using PDC PROLOG (BAILEY). The first two allowed for quick and easy replicas of the system, while the third using PROLOG, which was more difficult to learn, gave much better performance and control over the finished product than the shells. Thus, PROLOG was chosen for the working model. Although the PROLOG version was much faster than the shells, the size of the knowledge base (over 230,000 bytes) slowed the system to unacceptable levels until a method of reducing the system load was devised.

Kiwinet is an experimental prototype for advising on selection of databases on the Kiwinet online service. It is a very small system built to permit comparison of the commercial shells EXSYS and ESIE. A. SMITH (1991) chose these because both had been used for previous LIS applications. EXSYS was more flexible in that it allowed multiple recommendations of reference sources ranked by a probability value, whereas ESIE could return only one reference source recommendation. In providing explanations to the user, EXSYS displayed the current rule under consideration and the facts collated to date, while ESIE simply used a trace mechanism to show the thinking to date. Both provided for backward chaining through the knowledge base.

Table 3, based on information in papers read for this chapter, shows that a marginal preference exists for AI languages as a development tool, but shells and conventional programming languages are not far behind. A more detailed analysis of the papers in the database reveals

Table 3
Percentages (%) of the Projects Using Expert System Tools

	Used	Not Used	Not Known
AI language	37	29	34
Expert system shells	26	40	34
Programming languages	22	44	34

that PROLOG was used by 17% of projects (e.g., FOX) vs. 14% for LISP (e.g., CHIARAMELLA & DEFUDE; TAN ET AL.); 6% of the projects used some other AI programming language (e.g., GURU, OPS5). PASCAL was used by 9% of projects, either C or C++ by 5% of projects, while the remaining 8% that used programming languages used various languages like BASIC or MODULA-2. There was no preference for any particular expert system shell.

Expert System Shells

Expert system shells (e.g., VP-Expert, Leonardo, ES/P Advisor, and Crystal) provide a complete software toolset for constructing and delivering expert systems. Shells have facilities for knowledge representation (typically production rules; see below) and can help in the creation and validation of knowledge bases. Their chief advantages lie in the development time they save and their ease of use over AI programming languages (see below). Outside of LIS, expert system shells are the most widely used method for constructing expert systems (O'NEILL & MORRIS, 1989b). They have the main disadvantage shared by all software construction sets—viz., they are restricted in the range of systems they can produce (ZAHIR & CHANG).

In comparing AI languages and shells for expert system construction, HARLEY & KNOBLOCH state:

> Expert system shells offer some of both the programming flexibility of AI languages and the programming simplicity of applications for specific knowledge domains. These shells are midway on a programming continuum, ranging from nearly unlimited design flexibility to completely predetermined functionality. If a shell is the tool used to develop an expert system, the developer will not be required to program the inference control mechanism. (p. 19)

Shells are appealing to LIS developers because they obviate the need for original programming, they offer good "Help" facilities for users, and they are comparatively low in cost. The availability of run-time or run-only packages to allow for multiple copies of the developed system is another advantage. DRENTH & MORRIS chose a shell for their proposed expert system CIDA (Company Information Database Advisor) to select online sources for business inquiries. They report that in addition to the many desirable development features of shells, they are cost effective, their developers offer good support, and future clients are likely to have the hardware requirements to run a shell-based system. DEBROWER & JONES chose Intelligent Developer for these reasons and because they could afford it and it would run on their Apple hardware.

The literature includes several discussions on the selection of a suitable shell. This choice is crucial for appropriate knowledge representation. DRENTH & MORRIS list their criteria for assessing the software and the needs of the specific application and consider the relative merits of the four shells examined in relation to these criteria. They alert readers to important factors in shell selection with their comments on the forms of knowledge representation available in the shells they evaluated. In their case, a shell was an obvious choice because expense ruled out the expert system environment and the application did not need all the features of an expert system environment. Time constraints and the availability of cheaper alternatives ruled out programming languages.

HARLEY & KNOBLOCH built Government Documents Reference Aid (GDRA) to investigate the value of an expert system to enhance user access to these publications at Stanford University Library. The second and third phases of their project involved an investigation and evaluation of the available expert system shells. They, too, list their evaluation criteria and provide a yes–no table comparing five shells against the criteria. They chose the expert system shell Level 5, and although they discuss some of the features, a more detailed discussion of the knowledge representation would have been valuable.

VEDDER ET AL. wanted to explore the strengths and weaknesses of a new range of PC-based shells and to identify appropriate tools for library prototype expert systems. They defined their evaluation criteria and assigned a shell to five different groups of postgraduate students to build a prototype for business reference questions. In considering the merits of each tool, they discuss the experiences of the development teams in learning and using the shells. Their paper provides another evaluative methodology and gives some relevant insights for the knowledge engineer. Specific information about the shells discussed in each of the above papers is now dated, but the vendors, advertisements, reviews, and announcements of upgrades in recent journals are valuable sources of current information (HARLEY & KNOBLOCH).

For the knowledge engineers the more interesting information about expert system shell evaluation comes when the knowledge engineer tests the prototype. Although DRENTH & MORRIS conducted a careful evaluative before choosing a shell for their online business information system, in a later paper (MORRIS ET AL., 1993) they discuss the knowledge engineering problems resulting from slow execution speed and severe memory difficulties encountered when testing CIDA. To overcome these problems, they needed to edit the knowledge base severely, reorganize the knowledge representation, and rewrite several external files.

Programming Languages

ALBERICO (1988) has compared shells and programming languages, looking at VP-Expert and PROLOG in detail. He determined that each has advantages, but languages give more control, although they are harder to learn. PROLOG and LISP both have substantial followings and combine a means of operation and an expressiveness geared for expert systems with the flexibility of traditional programming languages.

The literature reports on several developers who built a prototype with a shell but later chose a programming language for the final system because of the language's flexibility. This path was reported by BAILEY, for example, whose development team chose the version PDC PROLOG for its frame-based knowledge representation of sources in Reference Expert after prototyping in shells and a language. PROLOG was a good tool for developing the inference engine, which needed to sort through an extensive knowledge base to make recommendations. This was loaded into memory from ASCII files stored on disk; although PROLOG was a little slow, it ran much faster than the shells. JOHNSTON & WECKERT (1990) also chose PROLOG for Selection Advisor because it was more flexible than a shell.

Standard programming languages have been widely used because of their portability. In the 1980s the most popular language was PASCAL because of the availability of good, cheap compilers and programming expertise. Its use has waned due to the current popularity of C and its object-oriented superset, C++ (e.g., BASSANO ET AL.).

A. VICKERY notes that in 1983 when her PLEXUS expert system was planned, the range of tools was limited. There were no specialized knowledge representation languages. The available shells lacked the variety of knowledge representation forms required and the natural-language processing and interface features the developers needed. PLEXUS (VICKERY & BROOKS, p. 116) was written in TURBO PASCAL and PROLOG, although the former was chosen for the final prototype because: (1) at the time the programs were being written, no PROLOG compiler was available for microPROLOG, so run-times were very slow; (2) loading the PROLOG databases was very slow; and (3) interfacing of microPROLOG and PASCAL needed a significant amount of specialized work that was too costly. The problems were exacerbated by the growth from an original projection of a rule base of approximately 250 rules to over 1,000 rules, including a number of rule sets.

Environments

A knowledge engineering environment consists of an AI programming language, typically LISP, integrated into a set of object-oriented extensions designed for expert system construction. It thus combines the flexibility of a programming language with a dedicated construction set. The chief disadvantage is a daunting learning curve. Examples are KEE and Knowledge Craft. Significantly, only one of the projects in the database reported the use of a knowledge engineering environment. TAN ET AL. used the power of fifth-generation machines and languages to analyze the contents of documents and represent the concepts in a conceptual semantic network that allows users to browse without using keywords or relying on choosing the same indexing term as the indexer to retrieve a document. This approach closely resembles the search strategies invoked when users are not aware of documents that may be useful. An experimental prototype was developed using LOOPS. It holds 30 documents in its knowledge base and represents 120 concepts and 20 relationships. The researchers saw this approach as promising but recognized that the huge investment in traditional retrieval methods will hinder the adoption of such a radical change. They suggest that a front end using this approach would eliminate the need for users to be concerned about retrieval languages or explaining their needs to intermediaries.

USER INTERFACE

The expert system is intended to assist or advise non-expert users, but it will be consulted only if it helps users to perform that task more easily. Thus, expert systems must meet all of the requirements for good interface design (SMITH & WILSON). The problem with many expert system interfaces is that they are inflexible or boring in their style of interaction. The 20-questions syndrome is common, and Smith and Wilson note that users have little control over the dialog. While hypertext interfaces are more attractive, they have their own navigational problems that may not be appropriate in an expert system, where users need to know what information has been taken into account in reaching a decision. KnowledgePro is an expert system development tool that allows for embedded hypertext links and is favored by some developers. Smith and Wilson consider its virtues but conclude that its use of production rules and backward chaining leaves no control for the users over their choice of paths through the hypertext. They examine three combinations of expert system and hypertext: (1) expert systems with hypertext interfaces, (2) hypertext systems with expert interfaces, and (3) intelligent hypertext, which they define as an expert system within a hypertext environment where the nodes correspond to the knowledge base and the links provide the inference mechanisms. They conclude that carefully constructed combinations may be a mutually beneficial path for expert systems and hypertext to follow.

Unlike conventional computer programs, HARMON describes the expert system as being query/response oriented. Since an expert system needs input from a user on the current problem state, it needs a user interface to prompt for this information at appropriate points. The expert system is also responsible for explaining its judgments (BUCHANAN), a vital feature for user acceptance. The user interface also aids the knowledge engineer in debugging. Different types of dialog are appropriate for different users in different circumstances. It is the user interface that links the user and the knowledge base by providing menus and short answer responses, sometimes allowing the user to interrogate the system through natural-language input. CHIGNELL & PETERSON indicate that the interface is not well understood, but a poor interface will result in poor system performance.

Additionally, as KIDD & COOPER have noted, the questions that expert systems pose may not be comprehensible to non-expert clients. This would be especially true for an information retrieval system with a wide clientele. Further, explanation facilities are likely to be insufficient for information retrieval, where something wider than a justification is necessary for a wide, diverse client population with varying needs for explanation. This factor typically implies some sort of natural-language interface. CODER (FOX & FRANCE), IOTA (CHIARAMELLA & DEFUDE) and IR-NLI (GUIDA & TASSO, 1983) are notable examples. In addition to natural language, other types of interfaces are menus, limited input vocabulary, and graphical interfaces. In the database of papers read for this chapter, some 40% of projects reported some form of menu-based interface, while 25% had some form of dialog interaction.

Some systems attempt to provide a natural-language interface for commercial database systems—e.g., CITE (DOSZKOCS), EURISKO (BARTHES & GLIZE), and Tome Searcher (HAYNES). In a European context, users searching online databases may not understand the language of the database interface. Dealing with natural-language input is a significant enough challenge to the knowledge engineer without the additional burden of language translation. B.C. VICKERY briefly reports on two interfaces that offer users a language choice. INSERM is for searching MEDLINE on Telesystemes-Questel via MINITEL. The user is prompted to select keywords in either English or French, English textwords, and either author or journal as a search criterion. The system returns keywords in the chosen language, from which further selections may be entered. EURISKO allows for natural-language entry of subject queries in English or French once the user chooses the subject from a menu.

B.C. Vickery reports on a new and even more challenging venture, in which a consortium, contracted by the European Commission, is developing IMIS, a multilingual interface to online systems. Part of the interface design will be based on a variation of Tome Selector. This ambitious undertaking will accept natural-language input in English,

German, French, and Spanish. If necessary, the system will clarify the search query, then automatically construct a Boolean search statement and translate it into the language of the relevant database. Vickery gives the knowledge engineer a list of some of the inherent problems in natural-language processing, which are compounded with the use of multiple languages. Vickery concludes that further analysis and research are necessary, especially if these systems are to have a sufficiently broad base to be commercially successful.

Typically, expert systems have two interfaces; one for the developer and another for the user. LIS knowledge engineers responsible for a number of the systems discussed in this chapter have commented on the difficulties or limitations of their user interfaces. HARLEY & KNOBLOCH judge that the Level 5 developer interface is much better than the user interface, presumably because the shell is more likely to be used by a small number of individuals who are comfortable with developer interfaces. They recommend that the user interface add graphics and provide for differentiated access, tailored to varied experience in the knowledge domain, before they would use Level 5 to develop their system beyond a prototype. SOWELL also notes limitations of the user interface. For example, VP-Expert can explain the rules used by a system to make decisions, but users also need answers for "how" and "why" questions. A broader issue is that of adjusting explanations to the different needs and aspects for which users seek explanations. Obviously one area for further research is the user interface. This issue is heightened by the attractiveness of the graphical interfaces now available in the hypertext environment and used by KnowledgePro for expert system development.

DEVELOPMENT

Most expert system development in LIS has been done by prototyping, in which systems progress by incremental refinement. This is the accepted and dominant methodology because the knowledge engineering requires a high level of experimentation to achieve the degree of expertise demanded of an expert system (HAYES-ROTH ET AL.).

BAILEY & GUNNING refer to prototypes as rough drafts that are progressively modified toward the desired outcome. Expert systems seldom remain as originally conceived for long. Knowledge engineers constantly evaluate, correct, adjust, and refine the knowledge base (GASCHNIG ET AL.). In LIS, particularly with in-house systems, it may be difficult to determine when a system ceases to be a prototype, as researchers generally report future developments and modifications for their systems even when such systems are working satisfactorily (ARDIS; BAILEY). However BADER ET AL. note that development to date has been unstructured and sympathetically called incremental development or prototyping.

While flexibility may be necessary, it ought to be confined within well-defined boundaries. Documentation ought to be available that includes records of experimentation to ensure that this research is available to others and to allow for extension and maintenance of the system at a later date (MORRIS, 1992a). The unstructured development is a result of the immaturity of this field and the corresponding uncertainty of researchers in understanding how to deal with the broad base of the LIS profession.

A structured design methodology includes the following elements: (1) a feasibility study, (2) early prototype development, (3) full prototype development, (4) installation of the system, and finally (5) operation and maintenance of the system to ensure that the aims are kept in view and that the needs of all users are considered (MORRIS, 1992a). Within this cycle, FENLY points out that feasibility considerations incorporate an important management decision: can and should an expert system be applied to a particular LIS function? This question requires an examination of the potential benefits vis-a-vis other solutions and judgments about the technical suitability of the domain and the organizational support for the system, including its funding and maintenance. The most significant element according to Fenly is the cost-benefit analysis about which there is little information in the LIS literature.

Some reported systems have not proceeded beyond the concept stage (BLACKADDER; BRANCHE BROWN). Others have floundered because of the difficulties of maintaining the currency of the knowledge base. For example, DABKE ET AL. could not justify the annual expense of maintaining the currency of student reading lists and the related subject information in the expert system EELIAS. In the database storing details of the projects gleaned from papers read for this chapter, only 6% of projects reached commercial application vs. 51% of projects ending up as working prototypes; 28% reported some "other" development status while details of the development status of 15% were not provided.

Prototyping

Many researchers (BAILEY ET AL.; DABKE ET AL.; DRENTH & MORRIS; MAIN & WECKERT) comment on the positive value of developing prototypes—viz., they are relatively inexpensive and provide a flexible method of determining the best way to encode and validate the knowledge engineering. Prototypes also allow for quick development of an experimental or demonstration system to test the feasibility of a larger project or to attract funding. Lack of funds to commence full-scale development, doubts or skepticism about the acceptability or efficiency of an expert system to solve a specific problem, and the time required to develop an appropriate knowledge base also contribute to the emphasis on prototyping.

Prototyping is a legitimate contribution to the advancement of knowledge engineering skills as it contributes both to our understanding of what is feasible and to work in untried or difficult domains. Many LIS expert systems have been developed with this element at the forefront (MARCUS; VALKONEN & NYKANEN).

Some expert systems may not get beyond prototyping because once the researchers achieve their desired outcomes, the systems are not required to perform an ongoing function (WATERMAN). Nevertheless, these systems add to an ever-widening pool of knowledge. Sometimes the problem may be so difficult that extensive further research is necessary before a system could be implemented successfully. This is the case, for example, with researchers who are exploring the relationships between expert systems and natural-language processing, improved user modeling, and new approaches to document retrieval (PARROTT, 1992; TAN ET AL.; WARNER).

CARANDE wished to demonstrate to other library staff that a series of subject-specific expert systems could extend the expertise of reference librarians well beyond their specific bibliographic knowledge. He developed INDEXES using the demonstration version of EXSYS that allowed a maximum of 25 production rules but did not govern the number of sources that could be recommended. This limited prototype assigned probability weightings to possible sources based on their suitability.

Working Systems

Despite extensive activity in developing systems in the LIS field, only a few systems are reported to be operating. These are considered to be sufficiently robust and helpful to users to be integrated into the library setting for which they were developed. There is evidence that some of them have a significant impact on the environment in which they operate.

GUNNING, for example, reports that library users consulted Reference Expert 229 times within the first month of its installation at the University of Houston (June 1991). This grew to 1,749 uses at the end of three months. The system contains a CD-ROM LAN (local-area network) and became so popular that most library users avoided print sources for reference purposes. This integrated service has had such a marked influence in directing users to an increasingly wide range of resources that the library has had to extend its user instruction program and augment the service from 50 hours per week in fall 1989 to 83 hours per week by January 1992, including double staffing for 58 of these hours.

Where expert systems are integrated into the library system, management issues, such as access to electronic sources, collection policies, and organizational structures, may also need review. Although not a commercial system, copies of the Reference Expert disks are available to other libraries at no charge, and more than 400 copies had been ordered by July 1992 (GUNNING).

The U.S. National Agricultural Library wanted feedback on its expert system, AquaRef, which was designed to give assistance with a limited range of frequently asked reference questions about aquaculture. It offered to copy the system to floppy disk on request. There were over 600 requests for this system within the first nine months of its release (HANFMAN).

The Patent Information Assistant (ARDIS) was developed jointly by two programmers and two patent reference librarians, who used an iterative approach. Over the two years in which it has been in use for 83 hours a week, the team has identified interface screens that need rewriting, and the developers wish to add a module, as indicated earlier, to explain the differences between trademarks and patents. Ardis also comments that the system never tires, is never irritated, can often give users customized information in a more individual way than the staff has time to provide, which suits the confidential nature of many of the inquiries. The acceptance of these working systems provides good evidence of the interest in expert system applications in libraries.

Gift Assistant, which determines whether the library should accept a particular donation, is another expert system that is well received by the professional staff in a division of the Johns Hopkins University Library (DEBROWER & JONES). It conserves staff time and ensures that valuable gifts are processed more quickly. Its application has also provided worthwhile experience on using expert systems within the library.

Commercially Available Systems

As of 1988 few research systems had progressed to commercial availability (A. VICKERY). This is still true in 1994. Those that have, have not been successful in the market. In part this is due to the appearance of competing "advances" (e.g., graphical user interfaces, hypertext, statistically based information retrieval) and to the deep conceptual problems facing the knowledge engineer in the LIS domain. The lack of natural-language interfaces together with the difficulties of representing the common-sense and heuristic knowledge of experts in the knowledge base combine to limit the performance expected of expert systems in LIS.

Tome Searcher, an intelligent front end for searching online databases on mainframe hosts in the fields of electrical/electronic engineering, computer science, and information technology, was launched commercially in 1988 (A. VICKERY). This isolated example did not prove to be viable commercially. In addition, Tome Associates has developed and marketed interfaces to other databases on European Space Agency (ESA), STN International, ORBIT, and DIALOG. These are examples of commercial products within the same family of products that failed and have been withdrawn from the market (TSENG).

EVALUATION

Until recently, evaluation has been patchy (see Table 4) and is one of the most neglected aspects of expert system R&D (ADELMAN; LIEBOWITZ; O'KEEFE ET AL.). It is critical, however, because evaluation contributes to a better understanding of how to improve performance. Further, recognition of satisfactory performance helps to gain users' and experts' acceptance of the system's recommendations (GASCHNIG ET AL.). It is important to assess whether systems meet their design goals, particularly when a system is developed to solve a problem within a specific situation. When evaluation has been done, it is difficult to compare the evaluations of different systems because standards are lacking.

GASCHNIG ET AL. identify the following elements as being important for evaluating expert systems: (1) quality of the system's decisions and advice; (2) correctness of the reasoning techniques used; (3) quality of the human-computer interaction (content and mechanical issues); and (4) efficiency (cost-effectiveness). While there are few tools and techniques available to assist the developer with evaluation (GASCHNIG ET AL.; SHARMA & CONRATH), the greatest difficulty is determining what to evaluate in an expert system.

Table 4
Percentages (%) of the Projects Evaluated

	Done	Not Done	Not Known
Knowledge base	37	9	54
Interface	28	14	58

ADELMAN (p. 151) makes the following observation as he discusses the knowledge engineer's reliance on experts to advise on the content of the knowledge base.

> Conceptually, knowledge engineering is a measurement problem. Most of the problems for which we develop expert systems do not have objective, quantitative knowledge (e.g., ground truth in the form of laws) that we can, so to speak, take off the shelf and put into a system to solve a problem.

He notes that experts may have different or conflicting opinions on appropriate problem-solving strategies within a knowledge domain, which contributes to the difficulties of effective evaluation.

Adding a further dimension, he argues that three groups need to be satisfied with the system's performance: the sponsors, the developers, and the users, each of whom may have different criteria. Thus, a multifaceted approach is needed, one that should include technical evaluation of the rule base, empirical evaluation of the accuracy of the knowledge base relative to some objective measure or expert judgments, and subjective or user evaluation. Each of these, in turn, suggests a range of variables that will change with the nature and subject matter of the system. Finally, Adelman observes that user satisfaction is important but is not the only criterion.

By definition, an expert system should emulate the performance of a human expert within its knowledge domain, but there are no objective measures for this. Further, we do not know whether to assess the actual or the ideal performance of an expert (GASCHNIG ET AL.; O'KEEFE ET AL.). Some researchers solve this problem by declaring that the expert system's decisions must match those of the local experts. Irrespective of whether this is an appropriate measure, that level of performance is considered by many knowledge engineers to be acceptable.

BRANCHE BROWN reports that in a series of test cases where the system's decisions failed to match those of the staff, errors were found in the knowledge base. When these were corrected, the system operated as expected. DEBROWER & JONES defined 96–97% consistency with staff decisions as reasonable performance for Gift Assistant. One significant aspect of the ChemRef evaluation was the consistency of the system in suggesting the same sources as the reference librarians who specialized in that domain (SARANGAPANI).

Researchers also do not know the minimal level of performance that is acceptable to maintain the label "expert." A further complication is that there are multiple solutions to some problems. O'KEEFE ET AL. note that evaluation generally is ad hoc, informal, and of doubtful value. Their discussion of major evaluation problems includes the difficulty of knowing when a system is right or wrong.

Types of Evaluation

Evaluation can be formal, with rigorously applied criteria for measuring the performance of the decision-making expertise of the system, including randomized case selection (GASCHNIG ET AL.), assessing its acceptability to users and capacity to meet their identified needs, or it can be informal, which sometimes implies that it is largely subjective. Often the major emphasis within LIS is on informal evaluation, whether formative or summative. The formative evaluation contributes to the final shape and content of the system, with the summative evaluation taking the form of a survey of user response or a series of tasks that are put to the system. The knowledge engineers then simply count the system's successes and failures and make recommendations for modifications.

Some researchers report their work during an early prototype stage and project the nature of intended future evaluation. MICCO & SMITH have done this in their proposed extension of a project to build an expert system that is integrated with an OPAC (online public access catalog) in order to give users better keyword and subject access to books.

Knowledge engineers should be able to state evaluation criteria before they begin development and then assess whether systems meet the purposes for which they were intended, particularly when the system is developed to solve an identified problem within an organization. For example, A. VICKERY lists the system functions required in the PLEXUS prototype. These included natural-language keyboard input from users, an analysis of this input to relate the user's terms to those in the database but expressed by the system in Boolean form, and modification of the search strategy to improve user recall. This in turn led to specifications for the knowledge base content and representation. The knowledge engineers then had clear guidelines for selecting an appropriate development tool to build PLEXUS, and, importantly, they could evaluate their progress.

It has been the exception to find extended discussions of formal evaluation processes in the expert system literature within LIS although there is a growing literature in other expert system fields (ADELMAN; GUPTA). Typically, if LIS authors discuss evaluation, they include a brief section near the end indicating that they tested user response to the system or compared the system output with the performance of acknowledged experts in the domain (e.g., BUTKOVICH ET AL.; FADELL & MYERS; HANFMAN; HARLEY & KNOBLOCH).

ADELMAN advocates evaluation throughout the development process. This contributes to a better understanding of user response and more effective handling of the problem, and it allows the programming to be scrutinized before it becomes too difficult to make adjustments.

Despite claims that evaluation is minimal, GASCHNIG ET AL. (p. 242) are clear that every adjustment made during development contributes to informal and sometimes unconscious evaluation. They list the following questions as part of this process:

- Is the knowledge representation scheme adequate, or does it need to be extended or modified?
- Is the system coming up with the right answers and for the right reasons?
- Is the embedded knowledge consistent with the experts?
- Is it easy for users to interact with the system?
- What facilities and capabilities do users need?

This is a significant level of evaluation that could be reported more completely. RIDLEY discusses some of these developmental issues in relation to the evolution of QUALCAT and suggests methods to overcome some of the difficulties encountered. This paper contributes to the reader's understanding of the problems inherent in developing an automated system to apply quality control in bibliographic databases by eliminating duplicate records that would not be apparent in a report that deals only with the outcomes.

In earlier LIS papers researchers generally reported on testing target-group users to ascertain system efficiency over traditional approaches and the effectiveness of the system in giving advice. POLLITT (1987), for example, discusses the skill of doctors who used his CANSEARCH system to retrieve cancer information using a series of questions similar to those of the expert intermediaries. ZAHIR & CHANG quickly checked the overall functional validity of Online-Expert, a prototype for the selection of online databases, by asking researchers in four universities to use the system to answer eight sample test queries. Their results compared favorably with those of experts using traditional searching, considering that the system contained only 60 of a possible 150 databases available to the experts. These researchers recognized the limitations of their own evaluation and recommended a further evaluation comparing the results of other expert systems that perform similar functions. They caution that the experts may not be perfect and that user evaluation must consider not only the quality of the advice but other factors such as the time necessary for the search and the ease of learning and using the system. Readers of LIS publications, however, do not gain insight into the methodology, the variables, or analysis of the results in these papers. SARANGAPANI found that such evaluation as had been done was informal and subjective. The ChemRef system was evaluated formatively and summatively. For the former, domain experts commented on the judgments made by the ChemRef prototype. The knowledge engineers refined the knowledge base until 96% of the evaluators were satisfied with its performance. For the latter, the answers to a set of questions given by ChemRef and by domain experts were compared and statistically analyzed with favorable results for ChemRef. Additionally, a user satisfaction survey of the system was conducted. WADE ET AL. compared PLEXUS with the experimental information retrieval system INSTRUCT and found that the best results came from using terms suggested by PLEXUS to search INSTRUCT.

Fuller discussion and analysis of formal evaluation are more evident in recent studies. GAUCH & SMITH tested an expert system to reformulate Boolean queries to extract data from a large full-text database. They wished to demonstrate that the system could reformulate queries to improve the search performance of novice users who worked in a free-text retrieval environment. The evaluation tested three hypotheses: (1) that the expert system improves the search effectiveness of a novice searcher; (2) that the expert system improves search efficiency of a novice searcher; and (3) the expert system can rank the retrieved passages in decreasing order of relevance. The researchers used precision and recall to measure effective output, and efficiency was checked by the number of Boolean queries entered and the time needed for higher-level searches. The searchers worked under carefully controlled conditions with each of five sets of questions using three different interfaces, including the expert system. The outcomes were statistically analyzed to calculate differences among the systems. Gauch and Smith describe and discuss their methodology, analysis, and results in detail. They conclude that the expert system did not improve search effectiveness, but it did marginally improve recall, precision, search efficiency, and ranking. They also distributed a questionnaire to assess subjective responses.

ERCEGOVAC (1992) discusses an exacting process used to select and post-test experimental and control groups to check three hypotheses relating to the effectiveness of Mapper as an aid to cataloging. The groups were composed of graduate students who had completed a ten-week introductory cataloging course. One group cataloged selected maps using Mapper; the other did not have this expert assistance. Catalogers who used Mapper attained higher mean scores on all cataloging tasks, which is attributed to the personal knowledge included in Mapper's knowledge base.

These studies are examples of more rigorous and comprehensive evaluation strategies now reported in the LIS literature. These researchers are approaching evaluation and validation of their systems as serious elements in the development process. They offer more detailed models to evaluate systems than those generally reported and contribute to development of strategies that may enhance the reliability of the systems and work toward better public acceptance and confidence in the systems.

LIS PROFESSIONALS AS KNOWLEDGE ENGINEERS OUTSIDE LIS

In the mid-1980s expert systems were being advocated as the technology of the future and were regarded as one of the most successful achievements of AI research. Enthusiastic reporters claimed that the application of this new technology could improve efficiency, reduce cost, save manpower, increase flexibility, improve job satisfaction, and relieve pressures on experts. Not surprisingly, these expectations led to a flurry of projects devoted to the experimentation of expert system technology in real-size applications of concrete interest in business and industry (GUIDA & TASSO, 1989).

At about the same time, LIS academics and professionals were looking critically at the direction of the profession in the light of new technologies (BRITTAIN; MOORE). Of particular interest was the concept of the "emerging markets" and the new job opportunities they might afford to graduates. Several ideas were put forward, including the potential of LIS professionals to become knowledge engineers involved in the development of expert systems.

To investigate this idea, several research projects were undertaken at Loughborough University, U.K. The first was a pilot in which 15 leading expert systems researchers working in universities and the former polytechnics in the U.K. were asked abut possible roles for LIS professionals in expert systems development (MORRIS & O'NEILL, 1988).

Expanding on the theme of the pilot, a much larger, three-stage study was undertaken (O'NEILL & MORRIS, 1989a; 1989b). Stage one involved a questionnaire survey directed to the software houses in the U.K. thought to be specializing in expert systems work, of which there were 52. This was done mainly to identify the major players in the field and to get a feel for the type and number of expert systems projects being done. Stage two was concerned with in-depth interviews of 50 expert systems developers from universities, industry, and commerce. It was designed to obtain information about the number, nature, and scope of expert systems in Britain, the methodologies used in their development, and the background, experience, skills, and attributes of those working in the area. The objective was to determine whether there were any potential openings for LIS graduates in the expert systems field. Visits to all U.K. LIS schools to determine the extent of expert systems teaching and research being done—and thus current knowledge of graduates in this area—formed the final stage.

Another study was designed to assess the expert systems job market by examining the availability of jobs in this field, the type of employees sought, and whether the demand was being met (MORRIS & WALTON). The study took the form of the identification and analysis of all national advertisements for expert systems posts over six months and follow-up surveys involving the employers and ad agencies.

Several studies have also been done to assess whether information professionals were being provided with the necessary skills to meet the needs of expert systems employers. These include four surveys that investigated expert systems teaching and research in LIS schools in the U.K. and in North America (MORRIS, 1992b, 1993; MORRIS & HUTTON; O'NEILL & MORRIS, 1989c).

Basically all the research outlined above aimed to answer two fundamental questions: (1) are there realistic roles for information professionals in expert systems development, and (2) if there are, what skills and knowledge do information professionals need to fill these roles? A number of potential openings and opportunities for LIS professionals were highlighted during the research (MORRIS, 1991b; MORRIS & O'NEILL, 1990). However, the most promising role appeared to be as a knowledge engineer for building LIS applications; there were also the more traditional roles of specialist in information sources, information manager, and information intermediary. Developing expert systems for LIS applications is probably the most creative and the most exciting role as discussed elsewhere in this chapter.

The role of specialist in information sources involves providing knowledge engineers with the information they need for a broad assessment of the relevant literature before starting projects. Information professionals already provide this service and have the relevant skills, but it is rarely used by expert systems developers. Many of those interviewed didn't know that this traditional service existed in nontraditional settings. Obviously there is a need to promote LIS services more widely.

The role of information manager involves coordinating and managing information among the members of expert systems development teams. When the original research was conducted in 1988, there were several large project teams. Most were in disarray because of the lack of information coordination. It was believed that information officers appointed to the project teams would greatly increase the chance of a successful outcome. The situation has now changed; much of the large-scale expert systems work disappeared when funding dried up. Consequently, the demand for this type of role, although still needed where large project teams are involved, is now much reduced.

The role of information intermediary involves acting between the knowledge engineer and the information supplied to that person. Obvious examples are the sifting of irrelevant information and the assimilation of information from multiple sources. This role could be part of the job specification of an information manager in an expert systems team, where one exists.

Before this research was undertaken, it was generally believed that LIS professionals could make a useful bid for work as knowledge engineers, particularly in knowledge acquisition. The initial research, where expert system developers were interviewed, supported this, and indeed some LIS graduates have found work in this field both in the U.K. and in North America (MORRIS & HUTTON). Nevertheless, the difficulties of gaining credibility in the field should not be underestimated. The research—investigating job vacancies for knowledge engineering personnel—indicated that software firms and systems designers were looking for people with wide general computing experience and technical skills that would enable them to judge when expert systems technology would be appropriate and how to incorporate it into existing systems. They also wanted staff who could work on other projects and pick up skills in emerging areas of technology. Few current LIS professionals have these skills or the relevant computing experience. The situation does, however, appear to be changing. Many universities now operate modular programs that should give students greater opportunity to select computing modules. In addition, new degree programs are being offered by some LIS departments that place greater emphasis on information and technology (e.g., "Information and Computing" offered by Loughborough University of Technology). Students who take this program must spend up to half their time taking computer studies modules. Many programs also now include an optional "sandwich" year, which could be used by students to gain experience in the expert systems field. Despite these developments, one should be careful not to be overly optimistic; the number of expert systems being developed in the U.K. remains fairly low, and the trend is more toward integrated rather than stand-alone expert systems.

The best opportunities for LIS professionals seem to lie in the development of expert systems applications in their own field. Provision of traditional information services—information collection, collation, organization, representation and coordination—to expert systems teams may also provide some opportunities. However, it may be difficult to persuade funders that these tasks are essential to good systems development and that LIS personnel are the right people to undertake them. Ultimately the extent of LIS involvement in expert systems development outside LIS will depend not only on the credibility of the profession as a whole but also on the enthusiasm and commitment of individuals and their ability to impress their personality and skills on potential employers.

CONCLUSION

LIS professionals are trained to organize knowledge; this skill is a keystone of all LIS curricula. LIS professionals thus have taken to organizing their own knowledge when developing expert systems, as advocated by ARDIS and HANFMAN. However, experts tend to perceive a task as working the way they would like it to rather than the way it does. ALBERICO & MICCO note that serving as one's own knowledge engineer is analogous in many ways to acting as one's own lawyer and probably about as advisable.

The expertise of LIS professionals, which had seemed well codified and commonly accepted, has appeared less so when needed for knowledge bases that inference engines could handle. The overall effect has been a renewed and vigorous investigation of the conceptual basis of LIS skills. The interest in the nature of expertise in many vital domains of LIS is especially notable and has been fully covered under "Knowledge Acquisition" above.

The amount of activity and research in the LIS expert system field is surprising. The systems reported here typify much of the knowledge engineering work being done in LIS. When the information is collated, it is apparent that some areas, such as reference and online intermediaries, are more appealing to researchers than others, although the range of recent systems is more diverse. This suggests that LIS personnel are extending their ideas about suitable expert system domains. The increasing power of the PC and the sophistication of the software are contributing factors, but there is also a much deeper understanding of some of the problems of knowledge acquisition and representation and of how to deal with them. This is supported by more analytical rather than descriptive reporting of development issues.

The problems of user modeling and brittleness need further exploration, but again the consistent and continued research of some individuals in these areas has contributed to further understanding of the functions of these elements within the systems. One area that has become increasingly more sophisticated is the evaluation of expert systems, although knowledge engineers must either work out how to measure the performance of experts and hence expert systems or develop formal statements of measurable goals. Authors reporting on systems also need to evaluate reasons for failures as well as successes.

One interesting development is that some systems are now being embedded into much broader information systems that exploit the capacity of the expert system to give advice in a broader context. Examples such as the Reference Expert system at the University of Houston suggest further possibilities to explore. The work on user interfaces and natural-language processing in the query and dialog modes also offers potential benefits to extending the application of expert systems in the LIS field. Most important of all is the willingness of LIS staff to venture into challenging knowledge engineering problems and to use their expertise in their field, together with their own domain experts, to solve real world problems and increase their efficiency in their own working areas.

BIBLIOGRAPHY

ADELMAN, LEONARD. 1992. Evaluating Decision Support and Expert Systems. New York, NY: John Wiley & Sons, Inc.; 1992. 232p. ISBN: 0-471-54801-4.

ALBERICO, RALPH. 1988. Software for Expert Systems—Languages Versus Shells. Small Computers in Libraries. 1988; 8(7): 4-12. ISSN: 0275-6722.

ALBERICO, RALPH. 1992. The Future of Expert Systems and Artificial Intelligence in Libraries and Information Centres. In: Morris, Anne, ed. The Application of Expert Systems in Libraries and Information Centres. London, England: Bowker-Saur; 1992. 194-228. ISBN: 0-86291-276-8.

ALBERICO, RALPH; MICCO, MARY. 1990. Expert Systems for Reference and Information Retrieval. London, England: Meckler; 1990. 395p. ISBN: 0-88736-232-X.

ARDIS, SUSAN B. 1990. Online Patent Searching: Guided by an Expert System. Online. 1990 March; 14(2): 56-62. ISSN: 0146-5422.

BADER, JON; EDWARDS, JOHN; HARRIS-JONES, CHRIS; HANNAFORD, DAVID. 1988. Practical Engineering of Knowledge-Based Systems. Information and Software Technology. 1988 June; 30(5): 266-277. ISSN: 0950-5849.

BAILEY, CHARLES W. 1992. The Intelligent Reference Information Project: A Merger of CD-ROM LAN and Expert System Technologies. Information Technology and Libraries. 1992 September; 11(3): 237-244. ISSN: 0730-9295.

BAILEY, CHARLES W.; FADELL, JEFF; MYERS, JUDY E.; WILSON, THOMAS C. 1989. The Index Expert System: A Knowledge-Based System to Assist Users in Index Selection. Reference Services Review. 1989 Winter; 17(4): 19-28. ISSN: 0090-7324.

BAILEY, CHARLES W.; GUNNING, KATHLEEN. 1990. The Intelligent Reference Information System. CD-ROM Librarian. 1990 September; 5(8): 10-19. ISSN: 0893-9934.

BARR, AVRON; FEIGENBAUM, EDWARD A., eds. 1981. Handbook of Artificial Intelligence: Volume 1. Los Altos, CA: William Kaufmann; 1981. 409p. ISBN: 0-86576-005-5.

BARTHES, C.; GLIZE, P. 1988. A Case Study of Planning in Information Retrieval. Expert Systems for Information Management. 1988; 1(1): 50-65. ISSN: 0953-5551.

BASSANO, J.C.; BRAUNWORTH, M.; MEKAOUCHE, W. 1992. DIALECT 2: A Multi-Expert System for Information Retrieval. Expert Systems for Information Management. 1992; 5(1): 43-61. ISSN: 0953-5551.

BLACK, WILLIAM J.; HARGREAVES, P.; MAYES, P.B. 1985. HEADS: A Cataloguing Advisory System. In: Informatics 8: Advances in Intelligent

Retrieval: Proceedings of a Conference Jointly Sponsored by Aslib, the Aslib Informatics Group, and the Information Retrieval Specialist Group of the British Computer Society; 1985 April 16-17; Wadham College, Oxford, England. London, England: Aslib; 1985. 227-239. ISBN: 0-85142-195-4.

BLACKADDER, ALISTAIR. 1991. An Expert Selector of Online Public Access Catalogues. In: Computers in Libraries International 91: Proceedings of the 5th Annual Conference on Computers in Libraries; 1991 February 26-28; London, England. Westport, CT: Meckler; 1991. 202-205. ISBN: 0-88736-754-2.

BRAJNIK, GUIDO; GUIDA, GIOVANNI; TASSO, CARLO. 1987. User Modelling in Intelligent Information Retrieval. Information Processing and Management. 1987; 25(3): 305-320. ISSN: 0306-4573.

BRANCHE BROWN, L.C. 1993. An Expert System for Predicting Approval Plan Receipts. Library Acquisitions: Practice & Theory. 1993; 17(2): 155-164. ISSN: 0364-6408.

BRITTAIN, J. MICHAEL. 1990. Implications of Education and Training. In: Brittain, J. Michael, ed. Curriculum Development in Information Science to Meet the Needs of the Information Industries in the 1990's. London, England: The British Library; 1990. 153-205. ISBN: 0-7123-3170-0.

BROOKS, HELEN M. 1987. Expert Systems and Intelligent Information Retrieval. Information Processing and Management. 1987; 23(4): 367-382. ISSN: 0306-4573.

BROOKS, HELEN M.; DANIELS, P.J.; BELKIN, NICHOLAS J. 1985. Problem Description and User Models: Developing an Intelligent Interface for Document Retrieval Systems. In: Informatics 8: Advances in Intelligent Retrieval: Proceedings of a Conference Jointly Sponsored by Aslib, the Aslib Informatics Group, and the Information Retrieval Specialist Group of the British Computer Society; 1985 April 16-17; Wadham College, Oxford, England. London, England: Aslib; 1985. 191-214. ISBN: 0-85142-195-4.

BROOKS, HELEN M.; DANIELS, P.J.; BELKIN, NICHOLAS J. 1986. Research on Information Interaction and Intelligent Information Provision Mechanisms. Journal of Information Science. 1986; 12(1-2): 37-44. ISSN: 0165-5515.

BRUANDET, MARIE-FRANCE. 1989. Outline of a Knowledge-Based Model for an Intelligent Information Retrieval System. Information Processing and Management. 1989; 25(1): 89-115. ISSN: 0306-4573.

BUCHANAN, BRUCE G. 1982. New Research on Expert Systems. In: Hayes, J.H.; Michie, D.; Pao, Y., eds. Machine Intelligence: Volume 10. New York, NY: Wiley; 1982. 269-300. ISBN: 0-85312-431-0.

BUCHANAN, BRUCE G.; SHORTLIFFE, EDWARD H. 1984. Rule-Based Expert Systems: The MYCIN Experiments of the Stanford Programming Project. Reading, MA: Addison-Wesley; 1984. 214p. ISBN: 0-201-10172-6.

BUTKOVICH, NANCY J.; TAYLOR, KATHRYN L.; DENT, SHARON H.; MOORE, ANN S. 1989. An Expert System at the Reference Desk: Impressions from Users. Reference Librarian. 1989; 23: 61-74. ISSN: 0276-3877.

CARANDE, R. 1988. INDEXES: A Micro-Based Expert System. Small Computers in Libraries. 1988 December; 8(11): 26-27. ISSN: 0275-6722.

CHIARAMELLA, YVES; DEFUDE, B. 1987. A Prototype of an Intelligent System for Information Retrieval: IOTA. Information Processing and Management. 1987; 23(4): 285-303. ISSN: 0306-4573.

CHIGNELL, MARK H.; PETERSON, JAMES G. 1988. Strategic Issues in Knowledge Engineering. Human Factors. 1988 August; 30(4): 381-394. ISSN: 0018-7208.

CIMINO, JAMES J.; BARNETT, G.O. 1993. Automatic Knowledge Acquisition from MEDLINE. Methods of Information in Medicine. 1993; 32(2): 120-130. ISSN: 0026-1270.

COHEN, PAUL R.; KJELDSEN, RICK. 1987. Information Retrieval by Constrained Spreading Activation in Semantic Networks. Information Processing and Management. 1987; 23(4): 255-268. ISSN: 0306-4573.

COSGROVE, S.J.; WEIMANN, J.M. 1992. Expert System Technology Applied to Item Classification. Library Hi Tech. 1992; 10(1-2): 33-40. ISSN: 0737-8831.

DABKE, K.P.; THOMAS, K.M. 1992. Expert System Guidance for Library Users. Library Hi Tech. 1992; 10(1-2): 53-60. ISSN: 0737-8831.

DABKE, K.P.; THOMAS, K.M.; SHAMS, V. 1992. EELIAS: A Prototype Library Expert System. Australian Academic and Research Libraries. 1992; 22(2): 88-95. ISSN: 0004-8623.

DAVIES, ROY. 1987. Outlines of the Emerging Paradigm in Cataloguing. Information Processing and Management. 1987; 23: 89-98. ISSN: 0306-4573.

DEBROWER, AMY; JONES, DEANNA T. 1991. Application of an Expert System to Collection Development: Donation Processing in a Special Library. Library Software Review. 1991; 10(6): 384-389. ISSN: 0742-5759.

DOS SANTOS, BRIAN L.; MOOKERJEE, VIJAY S.; SALVENDY, GAVRIEL. 1991. A Conceptual Model for Optimising the Cost of Knowledge Acquisition. Information Services and Use. 1991; 11(1-2): 9-21. ISSN: 0167-5265.

DOSZKOCS, T.E. 1983. From Research to Application: The CITE Natural Language Information Retrieval System. In: Salton, G.; Schneider, H.J., eds. Research and Development in Information Retrieval. New York, NY: Springer Verlag; 1983. 38-50. ISBN: 0-387-11978-7.

DRENTH, HILARY; MORRIS, ANNE. 1992. Prototyping Expert Solutions: An Evaluation of Crystal, Leonardo, GURU and ART-IM. Expert Systems. 1992 February; 9(1): 35-45. ISSN: 0266-4720.

DRENTH, HILARY; MORRIS, ANNE; TSENG, GWYNETH. 1991. Expert Systems as Information Intermediaries. In: Williams, Martha E., ed. Annual Review of Information Science and Technology: Volume 26. Medford, NJ: Learned Information, Inc. for the American Society for Information Science; 1991. 113-154. ISSN: 0066-4200; ISBN: 0-938734-55-5.

ERCEGOVAC, ZORANA. 1986. Artificial Intelligence and Cataloging Reasoning: Promises and Pitfalls. In: Williams, Martha E.; Hogan, Thomas H., comps. Proceedings of the 7th National Online Meeting; 1986 May 6-8; New York, NY. Medford, NJ: Learned Information, Inc.; 1986. 109-117. ISBN: 0-938734-12-1.

ERCEGOVAC, ZORANA. 1990. Research on Knowledge-Based Descriptive Cataloging of Cartographic Publications: An Experimental Advice-Giving System—Mapper. Los Angeles, CA: UCLA; 1990. 295p. (Ph.D. dissertation). Available from: University Microfilms, Ann Arbor, MI. (UMI order no. 9033933).

ERCEGOVAC, ZORANA. 1992. A Multiple Observation Approach in Knowledge Acquisition for Expert Systems: A Case Study. Journal of the American Society for Information Science. 1992; 43(7): 506-517. ISSN: 0002-8231.

ERNST, G.W.; NEWELL, ALLEN. 1969. GPS: A Case Study in Generality and Problem Solving. New York, NY: Academic Press; 1969. 287p. LC: 69-12276.

FADELL, JEFF; MYERS, JUDY E. 1989. The Information Machine: A Microcomputer-Based Reference Service. Reference Librarian. 1989; 23: 75-112. ISSN: 0276-3877.

FEIGENBAUM, EDWARD A. 1979. Themes and Case Studies of Knowledge Engineering. In: Michie, D., ed. Expert Systems in the Micro-Electronic Age. Edinburgh, Scotland: Edinburgh University Press; 1979. 3-25. ISBN: 0-85224-381-2.

FENLY, CHARLES. 1992. Technical Services Processes as Models for Assessing Expert System Suitability and Benefits. In: Lancaster, F.W.; Smith, Linda C., eds. Artificial Intelligence and Expert Systems: Will They Change the Library? Papers Presented at the Clinic on Library Applications of Data Processing; 1990 March 25-27; Graduate School of Library and Information Science, University of Illinois at Urbana-Champaign. Urbana-Champaign, IL: Graduate School of Library and Information Science, University of Illinois at Urbana-Champaign; 1992. 194-214. ISSN: 0069-4789; ISBN: 0-87845-084-X.

FOX, EDWARD A. 1987. Development of the CODER System: A Testbed for Artificial Intelligence Methods in Information Retrieval. Information Processing and Management. 1987; 23(4): 341-366. ISSN: 0306-4573.

FOX, EDWARD A.; FRANCE, R.K. 1987. Architecture of an Expert System for Composite Document Analysis, Representation and Retrieval. International Journal of Approximate Reasoning. 1987; 1(2): 151-175. ISSN: 0888-613X.

FRIIS, TORBEN. 1992. Assisted Indexing (CAIN). IAALD [International Association of Agricultural Information Specialists] Quarterly Bulletin. 1992; 37 (1-2): 35-37. ISSN: 0020-5966.

GASCHNIG, JOHN. 1982. Application of the PROSPECTOR System to Geological Exploration Problems. In: Hayes, J.H.; Michie, D.; Pao, Y., eds. Machine Intelligence: Volume 10. New York, NY: Wiley; 1982. 301-323. ISBN: 0-85312-431-0.

GASCHNIG, JOHN; KLAHR, PHILIP; POPLE, HARRY; SHORTLIFFE, EDWARD H.; TERRY, ALLAN. 1983. Evaluation of Expert Systems: Issues and Case Studies. In: Hayes-Roth, Frederick; Waterman, Donald A.; Lenat, Douglas B., eds. Building Expert Systems. Reading, MA: Addison-Wesley; 1983. 241-282. ISBN: 0-201-10686-8.

GAUCH, SUSAN. 1992. Intelligent Information Retrieval: An Introduction. Journal of the American Society for Information Science. 1992 March; 43(2): 175-182. ISSN: 0002-8231.

GAUCH, SUSAN; SMITH, JOHN B. 1993. An Expert System for Automatic Query Reformation. Journal of the American Society for Information Science. 1993; 44(3): 124-136. ISSN: 0002-8231.

GERBER, BRIAN. 1992. ORFEO: An Expert Reference Advisor for Opera. Library Software Review. 1992; 11(3): 8-11. ISSN: 0742-5759.

GUIDA, GIOVANNI; TASSO, CARLO. 1983. An Expert Intermediary System for Interactive Document Retrieval. Automatica. 1983; 19(6): 759-766. ISSN: 0005-1098.

GUIDA, GIOVANNI; TASSO, CARLO. 1989. Building Expert Systems: From Life Cycle to Development Methodology. In: Guida, Giovanni; Tasso, Carlo, eds. Topics in Expert System Design. Amsterdam, The Netherlands: North-Holland; 1989. 3-24. ISBN: 0-444-87231-X.

GUNNING, KATHLEEN. 1992. The Intelligent Reference Information System: The Effect on Public Services of Implementing a CD-ROM LAN and Expert System. Library Administration and Management. 1992 Summer; 6(3): 146-153. ISSN: 0888-4463.

GUPTA, UMA G., ed. 1991. Validating and Verifying Knowledge-Based Systems. Los Alamitos, CA: IEEE Computer Society Press; 1991. 409p. ISBN: 0-8186-8995-1.

HALL, GARRY. 1992. Knowledge Engineering for Library Expert Systems: A Case Study. In: Weckert, John; McDonald, Craig, eds. Intelligent Library Systems: Papers from the Intelligent Library Systems Conference Organized by the Centre for Information Studies; 1992 September 25-27; Wagga Wagga, New South Wales, Australia. Riverina, Australia: Centre for Information Studies, Charles Sturt University; 1992. 95-106. ISBN: 0-949060-18-6.

HANFMAN, DEBORAH. 1989. AquaRef: An Expert Advisory System for Reference Support. Reference Librarian. 1989; 23: 113-133. ISSN: 0276-3877.

HARLEY, BRUCE L.; KNOBLOCH, PATRICIA J. 1991. Government Documents Reference Aid: An Expert System Development Project. Government Publications Review. 1991; 18: 15-33. ISSN: 0277-9390.

HARMON, KENNETH R. 1990. Software for Expert Systems. In: Aluri, Rao; Riggs, Donald E., eds. Expert Systems for Libraries. Norwood, NJ: Ablex Publishing Corp.; 1990. 12-23. ISBN: 0-89391-589-0.

HAYES-ROTH, FREDERICK; WATERMAN, DONALD A.; LENAT, DOUGLAS B. 1983. An Overview of Expert Systems. In: Hayes-Roth, Frederick; Waterman, Donald A.; Lenat, Douglas B., eds. Building Expert Systems. Reading, MA: Addison-Wesley; 1983. 3-29. ISBN: 0-201-10686-8.

HAYES-ROTH, FREDERICK; WECKERT, JOHN. 1992. Knowledge Systems: An Introduction. Library Hi Tech. 1992; 10(1-2): 15-32. ISSN: 0737-8831.

HAYNES, D. 1988. Tome Searcher: Intelligent Interface for Searching and Retrieving Information. Computers and Libraries. 1988; 2(1): 2-3. ISSN: 0950-8392.

HUMPHREY, SUSANNE M. 1989. MedIndEx System: Medical Indexing Expert System. Information Processing and Management. 1989; 25(1): 73-88. ISSN: 0306-4573.

HUMPHREY, SUSANNE M. 1992. Interactive Knowledge-Based Systems for Improved Subject Analysis and Retrieval. In: Lancaster, F.W.; Smith, Linda C., eds. Artificial Intelligence and Expert Systems: Will They Change the Library? Papers Presented at the Clinic on Library Applications of

Data Processing; 1990 March 25-27; Graduate School of Library and Information Science, University of Illinois at Urbana-Champaign. Urbana-Champaign, IL: Graduate School of Library and Information Science, University of Illinois at Urbana-Champaign; 1992. 81-117. ISSN: 0069-4789; ISBN: 0-87845-084-X.

JOHNSTON, MARK; WECKERT, JOHN. 1990. Selection Advisor: An Expert System for Collection Development. Information Technology and Libraries. 1990 September; 9(3): 219-225. ISSN: 0730-9295.

JOHNSTON, MARK; WECKERT, JOHN. 1991. Machine Learning for Library Monograph Selection. Expert Systems for Information Management. 1991; 4(2): 77-91. ISSN: 0953-5551.

KIDD, ALISON; COOPER, MARTIN. 1985. Man-Machine Interface Issues in the Construction and Use of an Expert System. International Journal of Man-Machine Studies. 1985; 22: 91-102. ISSN: 0020-7373.

KONIG, ECKEHARD. 1992. Application of an Expert System to Assist Retrieval from Agricultural Databases (AGRIRES). IAALD [International Association of Agricultural Information Specialists] Quarterly Bulletin. 1992; 37(1-2): 31-34. ISSN: 0020-5966.

LEVESQUE, H.J.; BRACHMAN, R.J., eds. 1985. Readings in Knowledge Representation. Los Altos, CA: Morgan-Kaufmann; 1985. 198p. ISBN: 0-93461-301-X.

LIEBOWITZ, J. 1991. Useful Approaches for Evaluating Expert Systems. In: Gupta, Uma G., ed. Validating and Verifying Knowledge-Based Systems. Los Alamitos, CA: IEEE Computer Society Press; 1991. 249-259. ISBN: 0-8186-8995-1.

LINDSAY, ROBERT K.; BUCHANAN, BRUCE G.; FEIGENBAUM, EDWARD A.; LEDERBERG, JOSHUA. 1980. Applications of Artificial Intelligence for Organic Chemistry: The DENDRAL Project. New York, NY: McGraw-Hill; 1980. 259p. ISBN: 0-07-037895-9.

LUCARELLA, D.; MORARA, R. 1991. FIRST: Fuzzy Information Retrieval SysTem. Journal of Information Science. 1991; 17(2): 81-91. ISSN: 0165-5515.

MAIN, ANDREW; WECKERT, JOHN. 1993. In Defence of Simple Expert Systems: A Case Study with Some Observations. LASIE. 1993; 23(4&5): 62-70. ISSN: 0047-3774.

MARCACCIO, KATHLEEN YOUNG, ed. 1994. Gale Directory of Databases. Detroit, MI: Gale Research Inc.; 1994 July. 2 volumes. ISSN: 1066-8934; ISBN: 0-8103-5747-X.

MARCUS, RICHARD S. 1985. Development and Testing of Expert Systems for Retrieval Assistance. In: Parkhurst, Carol A., ed. Proceedings of the American Society for Information Science (ASIS) 48th Annual Meeting: Volume 22; 1985 October 20-24; Las Vegas, NV. White Plains, NY: Knowledge Industry Publications, Inc. for ASIS; 1985. 289-292. ISBN: 0-86729-176-1.

METZGER, PAUL. 1993. Anything Goes! An Expert System for Information Sources in American Musical Theater. Library Software Review. 1993 Summer; 12(2): 23-31. ISSN: 0742-5759.

MICCO, MARY; SMITH, IRMA. 1989. Designing a Workstation for Information Seekers. Reference Librarian. 1989; 23: 135-152. ISSN: 0276-3877.

MONARCH, IRA; CARBONELL, JAIME. 1987. CoalSORT: A Knowledge-Based Interface. IEEE Expert. 1987 Spring; 2(1): 39-53. ISSN: 0885-9000.

MOORE, NICK. 1987. The Emerging Markets for Library and Information Workers. London, England: The British Library; 1987. 153p. (LIR [Library and Information Research] Report 56). ISSN: 0263-1709; ISBN: 0-7123-3090-9.

MORRIS, ANNE. 1991a. Expert Systems for Library and Information Services: A Review. Information Processing and Management. 1991; 27(6): 713-724. ISSN: 0306-4573.

MORRIS, ANNE. 1991b. Information Professionals: Roles in Expert Systems Development? In: McDonald, Craig; Weckert, John, eds. Libraries and Expert Systems. London, England: Taylor Graham; 1991. 221-232. ISBN: 0-947568-85-1.

MORRIS, ANNE, ed. 1992a. The Application of Expert Systems in Libraries and Information Centres. London, England: Bowker-Saur; 1992. 241p. ISBN: 0-86291-276-8.

MORRIS, ANNE. 1992b. Expert Systems Teaching: The Needs of Information Professionals. Library Hi Tech. 1992; 10(1-2): 127-137. ISSN: 0737-8831.

MORRIS, ANNE. 1993. The Teaching of Information Technology in Departments of Information and Library Studies in the UK. Journal of Information Science. 1993; 19: 211-224. ISSN: 0165-5515.

MORRIS, ANNE; DRENTH, HILARY; TSENG, GWYNETH. 1993. The Development of an Expert System for Online Company Database Selection. Expert Systems. 1993; 10(2): 47-60. ISSN: 0266-4720.

MORRIS, ANNE; HUTTON, S. 1991. Expert Systems Teaching and Research in North American LIS Schools. Education for Information. 1991; 9(2): 107-120. ISSN: 0167-8329.

MORRIS, ANNE; O'NEILL, MARGARET. 1988. Information Professionals: Roles in the Design and Development of Expert Systems? Information Processing and Management. 1988; 24(2): 173-181. ISSN: 0306-4573.

MORRIS, ANNE; O'NEILL, MARGARET. 1990. Library and Information Science Professionals and Knowledge Engineering. Expert Systems for Information Management. 1990; 3(2): 115-128. ISSN: 0953-5551.

MORRIS, ANNE; TSENG, GWYNETH; NEWHAM, G. 1988. The Selection of Online Databases and Hosts: An Expert System Approach. In: Online Information 88: Proceedings of the 12th International Online Information Meeting: Volume 1; 1988 December 6-8; London, England. Oxford, England: Learned Information; 1988. 139-148. ISBN: 0-904933-68-7.

MORRIS, ANNE; TSENG, GWYNETH M.; WALTON, K.P. 1989. Moss: A Prototype Expert System for Modifying Online Search Strategies. In: Online Information 89: Proceedings of the 13th International Online Information Meeting; 1989 December 12-14; London, England. Oxford, England: Learned Information; 1989. 415-434. ISBN: 0-904933-72-5.

MORRIS, ANNE; WALTON, K. P. 1989. Shortage of Expert System Personnel in the UK: Hype or Reality? Expert Systems. 1989; 6(4): 218-226. ISSN: 0266-4720.

NEWELL, ALLEN; SIMON, HERBERT A. 1972. Human Problem Solving. Englewood Cliffs, NJ: Prentice-Hall; 1972. 920p. ISBN: 0-13-445403-0.

O'KEEFE, ROBERT M.; BALCI, OSMAN; SMITH, ERIC P. 1987. Validating Expert System Performance. IEEE Expert. 1987 Winter; 2(4): 81-89. ISSN: 0885-9000.

O'NEILL, MARGARET; MORRIS, ANNE. 1989a. The Contribution of Library and Information Science to Expert Systems Development. The Electronic Library. 1989; 7(5): 295-300. ISSN: 0264-0473.

O'NEILL, MARGARET; MORRIS, ANNE. 1989b. Expert Systems in the United Kingdom: An Evaluation of Development Methodologies. Expert Systems. 1989; 6(2): 90-99. ISSN: 0266-4720.

O'NEILL, MARGARET; MORRIS, ANNE. 1989c. Expert Systems: The United Kingdom's Educational Approach. Computers in Libraries. 1989; 9(10): 14-18. ISSN: 1041-7915.

PAICE, CHRIS. 1986. Expert Systems for Information Retrieval? Aslib Proceedings. 1986 October; 38(10): 343-353. ISSN: 0001-253X.

PARROTT, JAMES R. 1989. Simulation of the Reference Process, Part II: REFSIM, an Implementation with Expert System and ICAI Modes. Reference Librarian. 1989; 23: 153-176. ISSN: 0276-3877.

PARROTT, JAMES R. 1992. Reference Expert Systems: Foundations in Reference Theory. In: Lancaster, F.W.; Smith, Linda C., eds. Artificial Intelligence and Expert Systems: Will They Change the Library? Papers Presented at the Clinic on Library Applications of Data Processing; 1990 March 25-27; Graduate School of Library and Information Science, University of Illinois at Urbana-Champaign. Urbana-Champaign, IL: Graduate School of Library and Information Science, University of Illinois at Urbana-Champaign; 1992. 118-160. ISSN: 0069-4789; ISBN: 0-87845-084-X.

PATTERSON, D.W. 1990. Introduction to Artificial Intelligence and Expert Systems. Englewood Cliffs, NJ: Prentice-Hall; 1990. 440p. ISBN: 0-13-477100-1.

POLLITT, A. STEVEN. 1986. A Rule-Based System as an Intermediary for Searching Cancer Therapy Literature on MEDLINE. In: Davies, Roy, ed. Intelligent Information Systems: Progress and Prospects. Chichester, England: Ellis Horwood; 1986. 82-126. ISBN: 0-85312-896-0.

POLLITT, A. STEVEN. 1987. CANSEARCH: An Expert Systems Approach to Document Retrieval. Information Processing and Management. 1987; 23(2): 119-138. ISSN: 0306-4573.

POLLITT, A. STEVEN. 1988. A Common Query Interface Using MenUSE: Menu-Based User Search Engine. In: Online Information 88: Proceedings of the 12th International Online Information Meeting; 1988 December 6-8; London, England. Oxford, England: Learned Information Ltd.; 1988. 445-457. ISBN: 0-904933-68-7.

QUINLAN, J. ROSS. 1979. Discovering Rules by Induction from Large Collections of Examples. In: Michie, Donald, ed. Expert Systems in the Electronic Age. Edinburgh, Scotland: Edinburgh University Press; 1979. 33-46. ISBN: 0-85224-831-2.

RICH, ELAINE. 1986. Users Are Individuals: Individualizing User Models. In: Davies, Roy, ed. Intelligent Information Systems: Progress and Prospects. Chichester, England: Ellis Horwood; 1986. 184-201. ISBN: 0-85312-896-0.

RIDLEY, M.J. 1992. An Expert System for Quality Control and Duplicate Detection in Bibliographic Databases. Program. 1992; 26(1): 1-18. ISSN: 0033-0337.

SARANGAPANI, CHET. 1990. Development and Evaluation of a Reference Expert System in Chemistry. In: Williams, M.E., ed. Proceedings of the 11th National Online Meeting; 1990 May 1-3; New York, NY. Medford, NJ: Learned Information, Inc.; 1990. 355-362. ISBN: 0-938734-44-X.

SAVORY, STUART E. 1990. Expert Systems for the Professional. Englewood Cliffs, NJ: Prentice-Hall; 1990. 188p. ISBN: 0-13-296583-6.

SHARMA, RAVI S.; CONRATH, DAVIS W. 1992. Evaluating Expert Systems: The Socio-technical Dimensions of Quality. Expert Systems. 1992 August; 9(3): 125-137. ISSN: 0266-4720.

SHORTLIFFE, EDWARD H. 1976. Computer-Based Medical Consultation: MYCIN. New York, NY: Elsevier; 1976. 264p. ISBN: 0-444-00179-4.

SHOVAL, PERETZ. 1985. Principles, Procedures and Rules in an Expert System for Information Retrieval. Information Processing and Management. 1985; 21(6): 475-487. ISSN: 0306-4573.

SMITH, ALASTAIR. 1991. Kiwinet Advisor: A Knowledge Base for the Selection of Online Databases. LASIE. 1991 July/August; 22(1): 4-17. ISSN: 0047-3774.

SMITH, ALASTAIR. 1992. NZRef: A Rule Based Reference Advisory System. In: Weckert, John; McDonald, Craig, eds. Intelligent Library Systems: Papers from the Intelligent Library Systems Conference Organized by the Centre for Information Studies; 1992 September 25-27; Wagga Wagga, New South Wales, Australia. Riverina, Australia: Centre for Information Studies, Charles Sturt University; 1992. 39-51. ISBN: 0-949060-18-6.

SMITH, DANA E. 1989. Reference Expert Systems: Humanizing Depersonalized Service. Reference Librarian. 1989; 23: 177-190. ISSN: 0276-3877.

SMITH, DAVID; EVANS, DAVID; POULTER, ALAN; SHAW, MALCOLM. 1993. Using the New AACR2: An Expert System Approach to Choice of Access Points. London, England: Library Association Publishing; 1993. 97p. ISBN: 1-85604-086-0.

SMITH, KAREN F. 1989. POINTER vs. Using Government Publications: Where's the Advantage? Reference Librarian. 1989; 23: 191-205. ISSN: 0276-3877.

SMITH, LINDA C. 1980. Artificial Intelligence Applications in Information Systems. In: Williams, Martha E., ed. Annual Review of Information Science and Technology: Volume 15. White Plains, NY: Knowledge Industry Publications, Inc. for the American Society for Information Science; 1980. 67-105. ISSN: 0066-4200; ISBN: 0-914236-05-2.

SMITH, LINDA C. 1987. Artificial Intelligence and Information Retrieval. In: Williams, Martha E., ed. Annual Review of Information Science and Technology: Volume 22. Amsterdam, The Netherlands: Elsevier Science Publishers for the American Society for Information Science; 1987. 41-77. ISSN: 0066-4200; ISBN: 0-444-70302-0.

SMITH, PAULINE; WILSON, JOHN R. 1993. Hypertext and Expert Systems: The Possibilities for Integration. Interacting with Computers. 1993; 5(4): 371-384. ISSN: 0953-5438.

SMITH, PHILIP J.; SHUTE, STEVEN J.; GALDES, DEB; CHIGNELL, MARK. 1989. Knowledge-Based Search Tactics for an Intelligent Intermediary System. ACM Transactions on Information Systems. 1989 July; 7(3): 246-270. ISSN: 1046-8188.

SORMUNEN, E.; ALKULA, R. 1988. A Prototype for a Knowledge-Based Intermediary System. In: Online Information 88: Proceedings of the 12th International Online Information Meeting; 1988 December 6-8; London, England. Oxford, England: Learned Information Ltd.; 1988. 291-300. ISBN: 0-904933-68-7.

SOWA, J.F. 1984. Conceptual Structures: Information Processing in Mind and Machine. Reading, MA: Addison-Wesley; 1984. 460p. ISBN: 0-201-14472-7.

SOWELL, STEVEN L. 1989. Expanding Horizons in Collection Development with Expert Systems: Development and Testing of a Demonstration Prototype. Special Libraries. 1989 Winter; 80(1): 45-50. ISSN: 0038-6723.

SOWIZRAL, HENRY A. 1985. Expert Systems. In: Williams, Martha E., ed. Annual Review of Information Science and Technology: Volume 20. White Plains, NY: Knowledge Industry Publications, Inc. for the American Society for Information Science; 1985. 179-199. ISSN: 0066-4200; ISBN: 0-86729-175-3.

SPARCK JONES, KAREN. 1987. Information Retrieval. In: Shapiro, Stuart C., ed. Encyclopedia of Artificial Intelligence: Volume 1. New York, NY: John Wiley & Sons; 1987. 419-421. ISBN: 0-471-80748-6.

TAN, T.C.; SMITH, P.; PEGMAN, M. 1989. RADA: An Intelligent Research and Development Advisor. Expert Systems for Information Management. 1989; 2(2): 81-104. ISSN: 0953-5551.

TRAUTMAN, RODES; VON FLITTNER, SARA. 1989. An Expert System for Microcomputers to Aid Selection of Online Databases. Reference Librarian. 1989; 23: 207-238. ISSN: 0276-3877.

TRAVIS, IRENE L. 1992. Knowledge Representation in Artificial Intelligence. In: Lancaster, F.W.; Smith, Linda C., eds. Artificial Intelligence and Expert Systems: Will They Change the Library? Papers Presented at the Clinic on Library Applications of Data Processing; 1990 March 25-27; Graduate School of Library and Information Science, University of Illinois at Urbana-Champaign. Urbana-Champaign, IL: Graduate School of Library and Information Science, University of Illinois at Urbana-Champaign; 1992. 194-214. ISSN: 0069-4789; ISBN: 0-87845-084-X.

TSENG, GWYNETH. 1992. Expert Systems and Online Information Retrieval. In: Morris, Anne, ed. The Application of Expert Systems in Libraries and Information Centres. London, England: Bowker-Saur; 1992. 167-193. ISBN: 0-86291-276-8.

VALKONEN, PEKKA; NYKANEN, OLLI. 1991. An Expert System for Patent Classification. World Patent Information. 1991; 13(3): 143-148. ISSN: 0172-2190.

VEDDER, RICHARD D.; FORTIN, MAURICE G.; LEMMERMANN, SCOTT A.; JOHNSON, RALPH N. 1989. Five PC-Based Expert Systems for Business Reference: An Evaluation. Information Technology and Libraries. 1989 March; 8(1): 42-54. ISSN: 0730-9295.

VICKERY, ALINA. 1988. The Experience of Building Expert Systems: Menu-Based User Search Engine. In: Online Information 88: Proceedings of the 12th International Online Information Meeting; 1988 December 6-8; London, England. Oxford, England: Learned Information Ltd.; 1988. 445-457. ISBN: 0-904933-68-7.

VICKERY, ALINA; BROOKS, HELEN M. 1987. PLEXUS: The Expert System for Referral. Information Processing and Management. 1987; 23(2): 99-117. ISSN: 0306-4573.

VICKERY, BRIAN C. 1992. Intelligent Interfaces to Online Databases. In: Artificial Intelligence and Expert Systems: Will They Change the Library? Papers Presented at the Annual Clinic on Library Applications of Data Processing; 1990 March 25-27; Graduate School of Library and Information Science, University of Illinois at Urbana-Champaign. Urbana-Champaign, IL: Graduate School of Library and Information Science, University of Illinois at Urbana-Champaign; 1992. 239-253. ISBN: 0-87845-084-X.

WADE, STEPHEN; WILLETT, PETER; ROBINSON, BRUCE; VICKERY, BRIAN C.; VICKERY, ALINA. 1988. A Comparison of Knowledge-Based and Statistically-Based Techniques for Reference Retrieval. Online Review. 1988 April; 12(2): 91-108. ISSN: 0309-314X.

WARNER, AMY. 1992. Natural Language Processing: Current Status for Libraries. In: Lancaster, F.W.; Smith, Linda C., eds. Artificial Intelligence and Expert Systems: Will They Change the Library? Papers Presented at the Clinic on Library Applications of Data Processing; 1990 March 25-27; Graduate School of Library and Information Science, University of Illinois at Urbana-Champaign. Urbana-Champaign, IL: Graduate School of Library and Information Science, University of Illinois at Urbana-Champaign; 1992. 194-214. ISSN: 0069-4789; ISBN: 0-87845-084-X.

WATERMAN, DONALD A. 1986. A Guide to Expert Systems. Reading, MA: Addison-Wesley; 1986. 419p. ISBN: 0-201-08313-2.

WECKERT, JOHN; COOPER, CLARE. 1990. Artificial Intelligence, Expert Systems and Librarianship: A Review of the Literature. Australian Library Review. 1990; 7(4): 281-299. ISSN: 1034-8042.

WELBANK, M. 1983. A Review of Knowledge Acquisition Techniques for Expert Systems. Martlesham Heath, England: Martlesham Consultancy Services; 1983. 48p.

WHITE, MARILYN DOMAS. 1983. The Reference Encounter Model. Drexel Library Quarterly. 1983 Spring; 19(2): 38-55. ISSN: 0012-6160.

ZAGER, PAM; SMADI, OMAR. 1992. A Knowledge-Based Expert Systems Application in Library Acquisitions: Monographs. Library Acquisitions: Practice and Theory. 1992; 16(2): 145-154. ISSN: 0364-6408.

ZAHIR, S.; CHANG, C.L. 1992. Online-Expert: An Expert System for Online Database Selection. Journal of the American Society for Information Science. 1992; 43(5): 340-357. ISSN: 0002-8231.

Introduction to the Index

Index entries have been made for names of individuals, corporate bodies, subjects, geographic locations, and author names included in the text pages and for author and conference names from the bibliography pages. The page numbers referring to the bibliography pages are set in italics, and are listed after the page numbers relating to the text pages. This format allows one to distinguish references to bibliographic materials from references to text.

Acronyms are listed either under the acronym or under the fully spelled-out form, depending on which form is more commonly used and known. In either case a cross reference from the alternate form is provided. Postings associated with PRECIS, for example, would be listed under PRECIS as readers are generally less familiar with the full name "Preserved Context Index System." In a few cases, such as names of programs, systems, and programming languages, there is no spelled-out form either because there is none or because the meaning has been changed or is no longer used.

The index is arranged on a word-by-word basis. The sort sequence places special characters first, followed by alpha characters, then numbers. Thus, O'Neill would precede Oakman and 3M Company would file after the Zs. Government organizations are generally listed under country name, with *see* references provided from names of departments, agencies, and other subdivisions. While index entries do correspond precisely in spelling and format, they do not follow the typographical conventions used in the text. Author names, which are all upper case in the text, and both programming languages and software packages (such as expert system shells), which are in small caps in the text, are in upper and lower case or normal upper case in the index.

Subject indexing is by concepts rather than by words. When authors have used different words or different forms of the same word to express the same or overlapping concepts, the terminology has been standardized. An effort has been made to use the form of index entries for concepts that appear in previous *ARIST* indexes and in the 1994 *ASIS Thesaurus of Information Science and Librarianship.** *See also* references are used for overlapping or related (but not synonymous) con-

---

* Milstead, Jessica L., ed. 1994. *ASIS Thesaurus of Information Science and Librarianship.* 1994. Medford, NJ: Learned Information, Inc., for the American Society for Information Science; 1994. 139p. ISBN: 0-938734-80-6.

cepts; *see* references are used to send the reader to the accepted form of a term used in the index.

The index was prepared by Debora Shaw, using the MACREX Plus Indexing Program, version 5.10 developed by Hilary and Drusilla Calvert and distributed in the United States by Bayside Indexing. The overall direction and coordination of the index were provided by Martha E. Williams. Comments and suggestions should be addressed to the Editor.

Index*

*Italicized page numbers refer to Bibliography pages.

Introduction to the Keyword and Author Index

The following section is an author and keyword index to *ARIST* chapters for Volumes 1 through 29. It has been produced to assist users in locating specific topics, chapters, and author names for all *ARIST* volumes to date. The index terms are sorted alphabetically as single word terms and include all author names and content words from titles (a stop-word list of articles, conjunctions, and other non-content words was used). When searching for multiword terms such as "information science," the user should search the index under the less frequently occurring term. Over the years some terms have evolved from two-word terms (data base) to one-word terms (database), so it is necessary to search under both forms. Multiple forms (e.g., adjective, verb, and noun forms) of the same word have been combined. The sort word is followed by the author(s) name(s) and the *ARIST* citation.

Keyword and Author Index of *ARIST* Titles for Volumes 1-29

About the Editor. . .

Professor Martha E. Williams assumed the Editorship of the *ANNUAL REVIEW OF INFORMATION SCIENCE AND TECHNOLOGY* with Volume 11 and has produced a series of books that provide unparalleled insights into, and overviews of, the multifaceted discipline of information science.

Professor Williams holds the positions of Director of the Information Retrieval Research Laboratory and Professor of Information Science in the Coordinated Science Laboratory (CSL) as well as Professor of Information Science in the Graduate School of Library and Information Science and affiliate of the Computer Science Department at the University of Illinois, Urbana-Champaign, Illinois. As a chemist and information scientist Professor Williams has brought to the Editorship a breadth of knowledge and experience in information science and technology.

She has served as a Director and Chairman of the Board of Engineering Information, Inc.; she was founding editor of *Computer-Readable Databases: A Directory and Data Sourcebook*; is editor of *Online & CDROM Review* (Learned Information, Ltd., Oxford, England); and is Program Chairman for the National Online Meetings, which are sponsored by *Online & CDROM Review*. She was appointed by the Secretary of Health, Education and Welfare, Joseph Califano, to be a member of the Board of Regents of the National Library of Medicine (NLM) in 1978 and has served as Chairman of the Board. She has been a member of the Numerical Data Advisory Board of the National Research Council (NRC), National Academy of Sciences (NAS). She was a member of the Science Information Activities task force of the National Science Foundation (NSF), was chairman of the Large Database subcommittee of the NAS/NRC Committee on Chemical Information, and was chairman of the Gordon Research Conference on Scientific Information Problems in Research in 1980.

Professor Williams is a Fellow of the American Association for the Advancement of Science, Honorary Fellow of the Institute of Information Scientists in England, and recipient of the 1984 Award of Merit of the American Society for Information Science. She is a member of, has held offices in, and/or is actively involved in various committees of the American Association for the Advancement of Science (AAAS), the American Chemical Society (ACS), the Association for Computing Machinery (ACM), and the American Society for Information Science (ASIS). She has published numerous books and papers and serves on the editorial boards of several journals. She is the founder and President of Information Market Indicators, Inc., and consults for many governmental and commercial organizations.

ASIS and Its Members

For over 50 years the leading professional society for information professionals, the American Society for Information Science is an association whose diverse membership continues to reflect the frontiers and horizons of the dynamic field of information science and technology. ASIS owes its stature to the cumulative contributions of its members, past and present.

ASIS counts among its membership some 4,000 information specialists from such fields as computer science, management, engineering, librarianship, chemistry, linguistics, and education. As was true when the Society was founded, ASIS membership continues to lead the information profession in the search for new and better theories, techniques, and technologies to improve access to information through storage and retrieval advances. And now, as then, ASIS and its members are called upon to help determine new directions and standards for the development of information polices and practices.